KU-559-615

ORGANIZED LABOUR IN FOUR CONTINENTS

By H. A. Marquand

THE DYNAMICS OF INDUSTRIAL COMBINATION

12s. 6d. net.

ORGANIZED LABOUR IN FOUR CONTINENTS

BY

H. A. MARQUAND

and others

LONGMANS, GREEN AND CO.
LONDON · NEW YORK · TORONTO

LONGMANS, GREEN AND CO. LTD.
39 PATERNOSTER ROW, LONDON, E.C.4
17 CHITTARANJAN AVENUE, CALCUTTA
NICOL ROAD, BOMBAY
36A MOUNT ROAD, MADRAS

LONGMANS, GREEN AND CO.
114 FIFTH AVENUE, NEW YORK
221 EAST 20TH STREET, CHICAGO
88 TREMONT STREET, BOSTON

LONGMANS, GREEN AND CO.
215 VICTORIA STREET, TORONTO

First Published 1939

Printed in Great Britain by the Kemp Hall Press Ltd.
in the City of Oxford

PREFACE

THE years that have elapsed between the signing of the Peace Treaties of 1919 and the destruction of trade unionism in Germany, Austria, Czecho-Slovakia and Spain clearly constitute a distinct period in the history of labour organization. This book is designed to help its readers to an understanding of the chief developments of the period, not by attempting an impossible synthesis, but by surveying events and trends in thirteen typical countries in Europe, America, Australasia and Asia.

When the various sections of the book were written nine of the authors were actually resident in the countries with which they deal. Professor Roll and Mr. Dobb, though living in England, were already authors of scholarly works dealing with economic and political developments in Germany and the Soviet Union respectively. Each author has treated his topic in the manner best suited, in his judgment, to bring out the salient developments during the period in the particular country concerned. Each has had complete freedom in expressing his opinions and each is solely responsible for his own judgments upon matters of controversy.

The editor wishes to record his gratitude to all his collaborators for assisting him in his task and for the patience with which they have submitted to inevitable delays in the production of the book.

Madison, Wisconsin.
February 1939.

H. A. MARQUAND.

CONTENTS

INTRODUCTION

By H. A. Marquand

In 1919 and 1920 organized labour, in every country in which modern industry prevails, was powerful and militant. Its importance in society was recognized in the Treaty of Versailles, especially by the establishment of the International Labour Organization. Union membership everywhere had reached unprecedented heights and seemed destined to mount still higher. In the European countries there was a growing demand for " direct action," independent of political parties, to secure " workers' control " in leading industries.

For the most part, the older leaders of the unions resisted these demands. They reconstituted the International Federation of Trade Unions, at Amsterdam in 1919, as a body independent of the Labour and Socialist International. But they rejected all proposals for co-operation or amalgamation with the Red Trade Union International (founded about the same time) on the grounds that it was dominated by the Communist International, which was committed to a theory of the dictatorship of the proletariat and to a policy of world revolution through violence with which they could not agree. They committed their organizations to active participation in the activities of the newly-established I.L.O., and set them upon the road to eventual, but far distant, Socialism by way of legislative reform and gradual improvement of working conditions.

Only in Italy did direct action go to the length of occupying factories. But confusion of political counsel in the environment of a peasant economy produced, instead of a victory for Socialism, the triumph of a personal dictatorship and the destruction of trade unionism. The story Dr. van Aartsen has to tell in the present volume, unlike those of the other authors who deal with Western Countries, is therefore not one of the fluctuating membership and changing policies of democratically governed unions, but of government decrees concerning organization and conditions. Writing as a resident in Italy, he has striven to give an objective account of institutions and conditions as he has seen them, without passing judgment upon the political philosophy of Fascism. In his opinion those visitors to Italy who have written that the highest social ideals have been achieved have done no good service to Italy ; for the effect of their extravagant praise has been to make suspect any favourable statement about conditions. He is convinced that considerable progress has undoubtedly been made in many directions. At the same time, however, he considers that some of this progress is due to an economic and social *risorgimento* which, though it may have been accelerated by Fascism, began as early as the opening of the present century. He has not attempted to discuss how much weight should be attached to the inspiring influence of the dictator and the patriotic organizations he has created, nor how far expenditure upon military forces and monumental buildings may have been made at the expense of the workers' standard of living. On such questions the reader must make his own judgment—which he may be aided in forming by other chapters in the book.

In the other Western Countries the World Depression of 1920-1922 soon rendered direct action impossible. But it still retained its attractiveness for some. To them the Communists appealed to join the Red Trade Union International, later renamed the Red International of Labour Unions. In Britain with its long tradition of trade union loyalty and its notorious lack of delight in theories (or, if you prefer, principles) comparatively few union branches were won over and the reformist leaders had little difficulty in maintaining their hold. In the struggle, however, they were led to increase their control over the Labour Party. In the unfavourable atmosphere of the Coolidge era, revolutionary doctrines made even less headway in America. But in Europe a definite split in the union ranks developed in many countries. In France its effect was to hamstring the labour movement for many years. In Germany, if it did not actually cause, it certainly encouraged the rise of National Socialism, which has since destroyed trade unionism in every one of its chief strongholds in Central Europe. This conflict between Communist and Social Democrat is one of the chief features of the history of unionism in the period 1920-1937.

It is still a matter of controversy about which historical judgment is not yet possible. In the chapters on France and Germany in this book Professor Philip attributes the greatest errors to the Communists, Professor Roll to the Social Democrats. The reader must form his own opinion.

The other outstanding feature of the period is partly a consequence and partly a cause of the unions' growing concern with politics. They became increasingly dependent upon legislation as a means of improving conditions, and more and more preoccupied with the devising of plans of economic reorganization in order to secure a rising standard of living. In the U.S.A., where organized labour in the past has encountered more hostility from the law and the State than in any other country maintaining a democratic form of government, federal legislation has been the chief cause of a rapid expansion of unionism, and the traditional indifference or hostility of the unions to ameliorative reforms such as unemployment insurance has been swept aside. In France also, where the name of trade unionism (*syndicalisme*) had been synonymous with a rejection of political action and a complete reliance upon industrial strength to the exclusion of social reform, the law has encouraged a wide extension of collective bargaining and provided a definite improvement in working conditions by means of shortened work periods and paid holidays. In Britain and the Scandinavian countries legal enactment has been no less important. Participation in the work of the I.L.O. has widened the range of interest of the unions and has facilitated the exchange between the leaders of views and information upon practical questions. In the industrial countries of Europe—notably Belgium, France, Britain, Holland, Czecho-Slovakia, Switzerland, and Luxemburg—the formulation of ambitious Economic Plans for a half-way house between Capitalism and Socialism became one of the chief activities of the union centres after the World Depression, and occupied much of the attention of the International Federation of Trade Unions.*

Where a complete system of Socialist economic planning is

* There has been no space in this book to deal adequately with the work of the I.L.O. and the I.F.T.U. They require a volume in themselves. But the reader will find references to them throughout the various chapters.

in operation—in the U.S.S.R.—union membership reaches a level unknown in any other country. But here its functions are markedly different from those with which we commonly associate it. Clearly, classic trade unionism was a product of the private ownership of industry and the existence of masses of propertyless wage-earners. Where there is no private ownership of industry, and investment and production are determined by means of a central plan, there is little scope, if anarchy is to be avoided, for the struggles of organized producers for shares of the product. But there still is room for consultation and even bargaining between workers and management over conditions and methods of work and the correct relation between needs and efficiency as a determinant of earnings. The experience of unions in the U.S.S.R. perhaps throws little light upon the contemporary problems of unions elsewhere ; but it is of the utmost importance in forming conclusions upon the compatibility of Socialism with democracy.

In the totalitarian countries—Japan, Italy, and Germany—though a form of private ownership of industry still exists, trade unionism has no power, if it is not completely suppressed. Standards of living are secondary considerations, for guns are preferred to butter. The necessary adjustments of labour conditions to changing techniques—the solution of problems of fatigue, output, contentment, efficiency, and so on—are made by authoritarian decree. The extent to which these are paternal or brutal, or include any provisions for ascertaining the opinions or reactions of labour, may vary with the character of the régime. But they all have in common a denial of the right of free organization and equal collective bargaining. The extension of this system by military action has removed from the European scene the once vigorous trade unionism of Austria and Czecho-Slovakia, and, before these words appear in print, may have done the same in Spain.

In the remaining nations, on the other hand, trade unionism has recently made considerable gains in numerical strength. At its formation in 1919 the International Federation of Trade Unions—including powerful centres in countries in which unionism has since been destroyed—represented 18 million workers. To-day it represents 20 million. The renewal of relations with organized labour in the U.S.A.—fortified by the active participation of that country in the I.L.O.—constitutes an accretion of force of great potential significance. A new ideological unity pervades the ranks, symbolized by the unanimous support of a boycott of German products. Though at the 1938 meeting it was decided not to continue negotiations with the trade unions of the U.S.S.R., these relations are not so bitter as they have been in the past. Nevertheless, the optimism which seemed not unreasonable in 1919 is not warranted to-day. Marked improvement in standards of living have been secured in many countries during recent years; but chronic unemployment has robbed many sections of the workers of the benefit of this improvement and has spread more widely a general feeling of insecurity. In every democratic nation trade unionism is operating in an industrial system more and more interpenetrated with State power, and it is everywhere lending its aid to preparations for war. No man can say whether war can be prevented or whether, if it occurs, trade unionism and other civilized institutions will survive.

FRANCE

BY

ANDRÉ PHILIP

Translated by H. A. and R. E. Marquand

FRANCE

At the end of the fifteen years from 1920 to 1935 the French trade union movement passed through a complete transformation. After a long period of dissension, of quarrels within the ranks and of general weakness it has, since the formation of the Popular Front, expanded considerably. One might say that it has at last reached its full strength. After recalling the principal features of French Trade Unionism and the main course of its evolution up to the split of 1921, I shall examine in succession the period of weakness and disruption during the years 1922 to 1935, and the period of advance and new found unity which characterizes these last three years.

Section 1. *Organization and Structure down to* 1921.

In order fully to appreciate the new direction which French Trade Unionism has taken during recent years, and to make clear the permanent characteristics of this reorientation, it is first of all necessary to remember the conditions which gave birth to the labour movement in France, and also the principal stages in its development.

(i) In the first place the labour movement started later in France than in other countries, notably England. It was not until the middle of the nineteenth century that modern industrialism began in France. Until the war of 1914 there had been little in the way of industrial concentration and it was still essentially a country of small or medium-scale industry.

There followed many consequences. Firstly, industrial relations were of that personal type which exists between a workman and an employer who is always near, who works at his side quite frequently, who has a similar standard of living and the same social customs, and whose political opinions are nearly akin to his own. More important, there is always before the worker the chance of rising in the social scale, of reaching economic independence—the dream of every Frenchman, who sees in it both the symbol and the guarantee of his political liberty. Up to 1914 the one desire of the average workman was to escape from the ranks of the wage-earners, to save enough money to be able to establish himself independently, either individually or in a group of co-operative producers. This explains the late growth of any class consciousness in the French proletariat, in spite of much misery and a very low standard of living. Until the end of the nineteenth century all efforts at labour organization—whether the *résistances* of 1830 to 1840, or the *Chambres Syndicales* at the end of the Second Empire—were greatly impeded by this deep-rooted individualism of the French working man.

It is this individualism as well as the predominance in this country of small and medium-scale industries—by their nature decentralized—which explains the structure of the labour movement up to the War. The basic unit of organization is the local *syndicat*.[1] This groups together in any one town all the workmen in a certain craft or industry. In point of fact, since 1906 it is the industrial *syndicats* alone which are admitted into the General Confederation of Labour as new organizations. There only remain a few craft *syndicats* and their number is steadily diminishing.

The purely local *syndicats* are part of a National Industrial Federation, but this Federation plays only a very secondary rôle in the labour movement. Its administration is extremely decentralized. The federal committee, comprising one delegate from each local *syndicat*, irrespective of the number of members in the *syndicat*, in fact confines itself to the task of recording and co-ordinating the activities of the local groups.

Much more important are the *Bourses du Travail*, which will develop later into departmental Unions, grouping all the *syndicats* of a department around a principal town. It is they who are in reality the centre of labour activity. It is they who organize meetings, establish libraries, study groups and means of mutual assistance. Finally, it is they who, faced with the problems of a decentralized industry, are more able to supply effective help in case of strikes than would be a National Federation of Industry.

It is worth noticing what the conditions were which gave rise to strikes before the War. Low wages made it impossible for the *syndicats* to fix high rates of contribution. They had

[1] The English term " trade-union " does not exactly describe this French institution, which has some of the characteristics of the trade clubs of the early days of industrialism in England.

therefore no reserve fund and could not financially support a long conflict. The only hope of success in such circumstances lay in calling a strike at the very moment when the employer had large orders in hand and when he would be most injuriously affected by the cessation of production. Strikes were therefore suddenly declared by the local *syndicats* without any previous approach for a settlement, without even any consultations with the National Industrial Federation. They were supported financially by the *Bourse du Travail* which appealed to the generosity of the public, made workshop collections, and finally decided, if it were necessary, upon a sympathetic strike, thus bringing into the conflict all the industries in the particular locality. Finally if no agreement could be reached within a short time, the *syndicat* would agree to conciliation or to arbitration, or would simply resume work, ready to strike again as soon as circumstances allowed. Such conditions of struggle, being the result of the wide geographical dispersion of the majority of industries, made the *Bourses du Travail* the organ which really directed all labour disputes.

As for the *Confédération Générale du Travail*, founded at the Congress of Montpellier in 1902, it resembled rather a League of Nations of Labour than a unitary organization. It was a piece of machinery common to a number of different *Syndicats*, performing the functions of co-ordinating and discussing, but never allowed to act upon its own initiative. The directing authority of the C.G.T.—the Executive Committee[1]—consisted simply of the Committee of the Federation of *Bourses du Travail* plus the Committee of the Federation of Industrial Federations. Sovereign power rested with the Congress, which was an annual meeting of the affiliated *syndicats*. The separate local *syndicats* were the effective constituents of the Congress, for the Industrial Federations and the *Bourses du Travail* were permitted representation merely as advisors. Each local *syndicat*, in accordance with principles of federalism, was on an exact equality with every other. Each had one vote only, irrespective of its membership. As a result the small organizations, without great responsibilities and therefore prone to favour extremist policies, could command a majority.

. . . . .

[1] *Comité Confédéral.*

In order to understand the ideology of the C.G.T. in the years before the War, it must be remembered that the evolution of the trade union movement, which was just appearing at the time of the war of 1870, was retarded for twenty years thereafter by the attempts of various political parties to capture its allegiance.

While the first labour congress in 1876 devoted itself exclusively to the defence of trade interests and seemed prepared to follow the classic trade union line of development, the Congress of Marseilles (1879) under the influence of Jules Guesde, who introduced Marxism into France, abandoned the purely trade union struggle in order to found a labour party. For a period of twenty years from that date the Federation of *Syndicats* was to undergo numerous changes as a result of frequent splits among various newly grown socialist sects. On the other hand middle-class democrats tried to attract the workers into their ranks; and both Waldeck Rousseau in 1884, by means of the law legalizing trade unions, and Millerand in 1889 attempted to attach the working-class bodies to their own political leadership.

It was to counteract such political influences that the Federation of the *Bourses du Travail* was established. Under the influence of the anarchist, Fernand Pelloutier, a first-rate organizer, it was soon to become the leading labour organization, from which was to come the guiding influence of the newly-formed C.G.T. in 1902.

The latter in consequence took care, from its earliest years, to preserve its independence, and reacted against every attempt by state or political party to tame it. This explains its preference for Proudhonist federalism rather than Marxian centralization, its anti-State attitude, the part played within it by anarchist elements, and above all the great importance it attached to the two ideas of direct action and the general strike.

Direct action was defined as follows by Griffuelhes, one of the chief pre-War leaders of the C.G.T.: " By direct action the worker himself accomplishes his aim; he acts personally against his rulers to secure the demand he has put foward; the worker originates his struggle himself; it is he who carries it on, firmly determined not to be beholden to others for having freed him."

Jouhaux, who was to be Secretary-General of the C.G.T. from 1912 onwards, also defined direct action as "the fact that the workers themselves decided to manage their own affairs with the aid of their own strength; it is opposed to the indirect action of Parliamentary democracy and political parties."

For the C.G.T., then, direct action is simply the violent expression of a desire for independence rather similar to that which one finds in the American labour movement; as in America it does not exclude efforts to obtain favourable legislation; but such an effort takes the form of outside pressure upon the State, the concerting of demonstrations in order to arouse public opinion, and not political penetration from within. It was by such methods that the C.G.T. secured public regulation of private employment agencies and the law of 1908 concerning weekly holidays.

This same anxiety to maintain independence expresses itself in revolutionary programme-making in the form of the myth of the General Strike. In contrast to the Socialist Party, which envisaged the transformation to a new social order either by the achievement of a majority in Parliament or by the forceful seizure of power, the pre-War C.G.T. postulated the destruction of political institutions by means of a general stoppage of production.

After that had been done, trade unionism would cease to be a defensive grouping and would become the central organ of the economic life of society. The workers, united in their industrial federations, would exchange among themselves the products of their labour without needing the intermediary activity of any state or any political organization. In the General Strike syndicalism embodied the ideal inherited from Proudhon, who had said: "The workshop will take the place of government." It also expressed the unconscious ideal of the average Frenchman, for whom the State is an enemy, and who sees as the main task of democracy the protection of his liberty as an individual against all forms of collective tyranny.

. . . . .

This attitude of the C.G.T. was to be entirely changed by the experience of the War and of the years which followed. When mobilization took place, the majority of workers were drafted to the front, and later to the factories commandeered by the army; the local *syndicats* lost their members and with them their power of action. The C.G.T., on the other hand, and certain large Industrial Federations, such as those of the railways and the metal trades, were recognized officially by the government and collaborated with it in the organization of the nation on a war-time footing. In this way the C.G.T. took responsibility for the securing of employment for refugees from the invaded districts, relief measures in general, the release from the forces of skilled workers necessary for the production of munitions, and for the defence of the interests of conscripted workers in the munition works.

In the general atmosphere of *Union Sacrée* aroused by the invasion of French soil, the labour movement thus awoke to a new sense of its responsibility towards the rest of the nation. At the same time its structure was noticeably modified. As strikes were impossible, the local *syndicats* and the departmental unions remained almost inactive, while the C.G.T. and the Industrial Federations, which maintained contact with the public authorities, more and more took charge of negotiations, initiated movements, and took the chief place in working-class organization.

This change in the facts of the situation was embodied in standing orders adopted by the Congress held in Paris in July 1918. Henceforward the *Bourses* became merely organs of administration and ceased to be represented at meetings of the C.G.T. The key body of the latter became the national Executive Committee, meeting once a quarter, and composed of militant delegates from the Industrial Federations and the departmental unions. This Committee henceforward appointed the Administrative Commission, which administered the affairs of the C.G.T. in the intervals between the quarterly meetings of the Committee. The importance of this change is clear: instead of being formed automatically by joining together the governing bodies of the Industrial Federations and the departmental unions, the Administrative Commission was to be elected by the national Executive Committee, representative of all the constituent bodies. The C.G.T. thus becomes a unitary organization, capable of taking initiatives and of giving direction to the whole trade union movement.

As soon as the War was over, the C.G.T., moved thereto by

its Secretary-General, Leon Jouhaux, began an attempt to exercise its new responsibility and to turn the working-class movement in a new direction. Trade unionism emerged from the War considerably strengthened. In 1918 and 1919 thousands of new members entered its ranks. The numbers of organized railwaymen, which stood at 73,000 at the end of 1917 were increased to 82,000 in 1918. The Federation of Metal Trades increased its membership from 75,000 at the end of 1916 to 205,000 at the end of 1918. The lumber-men, market-gardeners and vineyard workers of the Marne, together with farm workers of the Midi formed a united Federation of agricultural workers. Among civil servants and non-manual workers, the Postal Federation (76,000 members), the *syndicat* of teachers (575,000), the Federation of workers in commerce and finance joined the C.G.T. In 1920 the latter united 1,800,000 members. Taking into account certain non-affiliated groups, either autonomous or members of the small Federation of Catholic Workers, it is calculated that immediately after the War the grand total of organized French workers was more than 2,000,000, the corresponding figure for 1914 having been 600,000.

At the same time widespread discontent and the expectation of a new social order marked by greater justice and harmony, as a result of sufferings endured in common during the War, caused public opinion to be favourable to a change in the character of social relations, in effecting which the C.G.T. could play an important part.

For these reasons the French labour movement, abandoning its purely critical and negative pre-War attitude, but remaining faithful to its desire to be independent of the State, while taking part in the re-organization of the economic system, began to put forward a general social and economic programme which is the first manifestation of what was afterwards to be called *reconstructive syndicalism*.[1] The C.G.T. welcomed the introduction of Labour clauses into the Peace Treaty and the establishment of the International Labour Organization. It pronounced against the reconstruction of the devastated areas by private contractors, who were amassing scandalous fortunes out of the distress of their fellow citizens; and it suggested that

[1] Syndicalisme réconstructeur.

all the work of reconstruction should be carried out by co-operative bodies in which Germany could become a partner, thus handing over in kind at least a portion of reparations.

The programme proceeds to define the syndicalist conception of economic reorganization in quite novel terms, which deserve to be quoted in full:

"The C.G.T. demands for organized labour in the future the place which is its due in the management and administration of national production. Economic reorganization must be based upon the full and uninterrupted use of industrial equipment and the spreading without restriction of general and technical education. It must aim to secure the best use of human capacity, the employment of all natural resources, the application of all inventions and discoveries, and to prevent every deliberate restriction of output and every form of excessive speeding up of the producers, the effects of which are harmful to the nation itself. . . . The nation cannot, without infringing the collective rights with the guardianship of which it is entrusted, abandon its social duty, created by the labour of past generations, maintained by the collaborative efforts of economic organizations, developed by the sacrifices which each one agrees to make. In order to ensure the successive transformations of these organizations, in accordance with the forecasts of science and the needs of progress, the nation must be alert to secure the continual performance of this social duty by means of a strict and rigorous control over all those branches of production which in their commencement and development derive profit from the protection and support of the State or from making use of organs created and maintained by it. The nation must keep under even stricter control those enterprises which, in addition to this general advantage, profit from outright delegation of power or direct and repeated intervention by the State. Though it may be possible for the time being to allow this duty to be performed only in departments of activity which are socialized at the moment, there can be no toleration of the abandonments of collective property which have been agreed to by the public authorities. Though it is not desirable that State control be extended into every sphere without the active and convinced agreement of all persons concerned, it is no less essential that no necessities of life, whether of the individual, the family or the nation, shall be handed over to private enterprise unless public control obliges these interests to direct their activities in the manner most advantageous to the public well-being. This control exercised in the name of the State will not only intervene in the passive and retrospective manner now customary, it must be powerful enough to maintain constant authority over the management of production and the conditions of labour, as well as over the distribution of profits in excess of sums sufficient to cover normal interest, limited dividends and insurance against loss. Established in this manner, this control will ensure the functioning of a régime of partnership between industry and the State in businesses whose dispersion still permits of the free play of economic forces and freedom of enterprise; but whenever capitalist concentration or agreements shall be able to secure such control of a raw material or an essential commodity as to raise its price unfairly, then State monopoly must be imposed as a means of restoring equilibrium and the proper rate of production. . . . Economic reorganization will not be able to produce its full valuable effects unless the nation now takes up and establishes its due social authority over collective wealth and the means of producing and exchanging it, and unless it increasingly hands over managerial autonomy—subject to control—to the Departments, to co-operative communes, and above all to new collective bodies, having the legal privileges of incorporation, and administered by qualified representatives of producers and consumers."

To put this programme into practice the C.G.T. demanded the establishment of a Grand Council of Production, attached to the office of the Prime Minister. Composed of workers and employers, of technicians and officials, this Council should be charged with the duty of making a Survey of the country's resources and needs. When the government rejected this proposal, the C.G.T. itself set up an Economic Council of Labour, composed of representatives of the C.G.T., of the Federation of civil servants, of Ustica (*Union des techniciens de l'industrie du commerce et de l'agriculture*) and of the Federation of consumers' co-operatives.

After several weeks of deliberation the Economic Council, at its meeting in January 1920, published a series of reports which laid down in detail the Labour attitude towards the principal problems of the day. It demanded the nationalization of natural monopolies, in particular the mines, transport, and the production and distribution of electricity. In the case of each of these industries it called for the purchase of undertakings by the State, the compensation paid to the owners to be calculated on the basis of the going concern value of the undertakings and paid in the form of bonds, amortisable in forty or fifty years. The administration of these concerns should be entrusted to autonomous co-operative authorities governed by an administrative Council of eighteen members—six workers and technicians nominated by their respective unions, six consumers (three representing industrial and three domestic consumers), and six officials nominated by the State to represent the interests of the community.

Besides nationalized industries, the Economic Council provided for industries which were to be simply centralized and brought under control. These would be invited to group themselves into cartels, which would purchase raw materials, allocate to each manufacturing unit a quota of output, close down according to need certain works, concentrate production in the better equipped plants and make provision for the standardization of products. A General Council of Cartels was to co-ordinate the various industrial groupings. A Council of Agriculture would encourage agricultural co-operatives and control the marketing of foodstuffs. There should also be established a Council of Transport and a Council of Banking, while co-ordination between the cartellized and the nationalized industries would be effected by a supreme National Economic Council, organized also upon the basis of tripartite representation of producers, consumers and the State.

These proposals represented a complete change from the pre-War policy of the C.G.T. Even the concept of the working-class had been notably enlarged so as to include technicians, office workers and consumers. Syndicalism was extended to the point of wishing to represent no longer merely the interests of the proletariat alone, but the generality of national collective interests. Instead of clinging to the old programme of the nationalization of all the means of production and exchange, it merely asked for the nationalization of natural monopolies, and for the rest advocated the sort of measures which are nowadays grouped under the name of planned economy. In short, it elaborated the theory later known as that of the Mixed Enterprise, midway between State Socialism and the old revolutionary syndicalism, with its demand of "the factories for the factory-workers, the mines for the miners." Part of this programme, particularly certain details, such as a Ministry of National Economy and a Supreme

Economic Council, has in fact already been adopted in France by means of legislation.

By these propositions, however, the C.G.T. did not wholly abandon its pre-War revolutionary position. It still believes with Proudhon that in the final outcome all the large industries will be organized in industrial orders and that "the workshop will take the place of the government." It believes that its own Economic Council will gradually take over the majority of State functions and that in so far as it concerns itself increasingly with the interests of the community as a whole it is forming itself into the outline of a new State. But these doctrines have lost their former violent and purely negative character and have become an effort to secure economic reconstruction inspired by a sense of public duty.

. . . . .

This effort to build up a constructive theory was unfortunately doomed to have no result. Failure was due to a rapid loss of strength by the trade union movement during 1920 and 1921, following disputes over theory and—before long—schism.

The majority of the workers had not followed their leaders in their attempt to be constructive. The former militants remained faithful to pre-War syndicalism and protested bitterly against the relations established between the C.G.T. and the government. As for the newly-enrolled members, their attitude was more complex. The majority had come in mainly as the result of victories, had no trade union experience and no sense of the discipline necessary. They thought that there were no limits to trade union power and were far more interested in immediate tangible advantages, such as high wages and the shortening of the working day, than in a plan of reorganization elaborated by intellectuals. Yet on the other hand, because they were dissatisfied with the disappointing results of the War, they turned their eyes towards the Russian Revolution, which held out to them the great hope of a social transformation, violent but complete, which would place the proletariat in supreme power. The newly-formed Communist Party proceeded to stir up these discontents, to make itself the echo of all the protests, even the most contradictory of them; and, practising again the tactics of Jules Guesde, tried with great success to set the militants against the reformist leaders, in the hope of capturing the trade union movement and using it for its own political ends.

The seriousness of the situation began to appear as early as the spring of 1919. A strike of nearly 100,000 workers broke out in the metal trades of Paris, directed less against the employers than at the Federation of Metal Workers itself, which had just signed a collective agreement regarded as insufficiently favourable. The strike ended in complete defeat, which the Communists did not fail to attribute to the " treachery " of the responsible leaders. In 1920 again a general strike broke out on the railways, without the authorization of the Railwaymen's Federation, which, however, succeeded in settling the dispute on advantageous terms. But a month later (in March 1920) the Communists gained a majority in the National Federation of Railwaymen, and on April 28 the latter, without having consulted the C.G.T., without even having drawn up a list of demands, gave the order for a general strike and was followed by almost every other industry. The result was a veritable collapse of the Labour movement. On May 28 work had to be resumed unconditionally and 35,000 railwaymen were dismissed. The membership of the Railwaymen's Federation fell from 320,000 to 57,000, that of the Union of *Syndicats* of the Seine from 360,000 to 120,000 and that of the C.G.T. as a whole from 2,000,000 to 600,000. Worst of all it was the most serious elements, disgusted by ceaseless internal quarelling, which gave up their membership, thus bringing about a progressive enfeebling of the majority in the Confederation and a proportionate increase in the strength of the extremist elements, which remained in the C.G.T. in the hope of capturing it.

The latter formed themselves for this purpose into " revolutionary syndicalist committees " thus creating in fact within each Industrial Federation a new organization with its own machinery for discussion and decision. The Federations defended themselves by threatening with expulsion members affiliated to these committees. On February 9, 1921, the Executive Committee of the C.G.T. decided that organizations joining the revolutionary syndicalist committees thereby placed themselves outside the C.G.T. This was approved by the Lille Congress by 1,556 to 1,348 votes. For a time the minority seemed to be willing to give way and in December held a separate Congress which declared itself ready to dissolve the committees, but at the same time decided to suspend payment of affiliation fees to the Confederation and increased the number of attacks, violent and full of hatred, upon the leaders of the majority, whom it continually accused of treachery.

Trade union unity survived only until 1922. By then the supporters of the minority movement had been expelled by most of the Federations, and a new central body had been created by the Communists, bearing the somewhat ironical name of United Confederation of Labour (*Confédération Générale du Travail Unitaire*—or C.G.T.U.). Whereas in 1920 the C.G.T. had attained a membership of nearly 2,000,000, these two new organizations enrolled in all barely 800,000, of whom 300,000 belonged to the old C.G.T. and 500,000 to the C.G.T.U.

. . . . .

Section 2. *From the Split to the Restoration of Trade Union Unity,* 1922–1936.

The split of 1922 greatly weakened the trade union movement and for fourteen years it was to play merely a secondary rôle in the social evolution of France. The aspirations of the workers were to be turned, after the creation of the *Bloc des Gauches*[1] in 1924, towards political action. The chief trade union demand was to be the passing of the Social Insurance Law, which was eventually to be achieved in 1930. In the realm of industrial action, the C.G.T.U. proceeded to multiply opportunities for agitation, stirring up numerous strikes for the sake of propaganda and "revolutionary gymnastics." These were almost all failures even during favourable periods of trade activity. As for the C.G.T., it undertook internal reorganization, tuned up its strength, and created new trade union bodies without engaging in serious conflicts. Between 1922 and 1936 working-class conditions varied with the general business situation and were not noticeably influenced by trade union action.

1. In order to trace the movements in working-class standards of living between 1922 and 1936, it is necessary to recount

[1] Association of Left Political Parties.

briefly the main lines of economic development during the period, distinguishing the artificial prosperity of 1922–26, the real prosperity of 1926–30 and the world crisis of 1930–36.

In 1922 the post-War world depression, which had been accompanied in almost every country by heavy unemployment and a general decline in the strength of trade unionism, came to an end. Prices reached their lowest point in January 1922 in the U.S.A., in September in Great Britain and in February in France. At the same time, however, under the pressure of an unbalanced budget, the depreciation of the franc was accentuated. This tendency continued, in alternations of sharp falls and temporary stabilizations, for four years, reaching catastrophic proportions in 1926, when the £1 rose from 128·79 in January to 149·6 in April, to 178 on June 19, to 199 at the beginning of July and to 236 on July 16.

This fall brought in its train a general rise of wholesale prices. The inclusive index of the *Statistique générale de la France*, which stood at 320 in January 1922, reached 395 in January 1923, in January 1924 stood at 505, and at 525 in January 1925, mounting to 647 in January and to 754 in June 1926. This rise was the direct result of the monetary depreciation and sprang above all from the influence of the price of imported goods, the index of which, at the above-mentioned points, stood at 396; 531; 558; 791; and 883, while the index of home-produced goods rose only to 344; 395; 490; 507; 594; and 682. Moreover the rise in price of industrial goods (343; 427; 560; 587; 748; 846) was more than that of foodstuffs (295; 359; 441; 455; 531; 646). On the whole the rise of wholesale prices was substantially less than the monetary depreciation and the gap between the French and British price level increased from 3 per cent. in 1922 to 9 per cent. in 1923, to 13 per cent. in 1924, to 16 per cent. in 1925, to 20 per cent. in January 1926 and to 35 per cent. at the end of 1926.

The forces thus released produced important results: a bounty on exports stimulating an increased output in industries producing for foreign markets; a spread of prosperity to producers for the home market; a multiplication of nominal profits followed by an expansion of all industries (the metal trades, for example, worked at 98 per cent. of capacity) and stimulating an abundant demand for works of craftsmanship.

Then, little by little, as the falling currency found its level, it began to be perceived that even the expansion of exports, paid for at falling gold prices, resulted in losses and that the nominal profits of industry were turning into real deficits. There then began a flight of capital abroad, a rush within the country to get back to "real" values and a scarcity of investment, especially in long-term securities.

At the same time retail prices followed the general movement, but with a big time-lag. At the dates already given, the index of retail prices of thirteen articles in Paris moved from 319 in 1922, to 309; 376; and 408, reaching 480 in January and 544 in June 1926; that of the same thirteen articles in the provinces moved as follows: 324; 332; 401; 442; 503; 523. Finally the Cost of Living Index for Paris, taking into account not merely foodstuffs, but various other elements entering into a working-class budget, rose from 291 in 1922 to 324; 365; 451; and 539. As for wages, in general they followed the movements of the cost of living; the index of the weekly earnings of mineworkers rose from 319 in 1922 to 370 in 1923, to 423 in 1924, to 439 in 1925, to 469 in the first quarter of 1926, to 495 in the second, to 545 in the third, and to 593 in the last quarter. In the metal trades of Paris average wages rose from 2.68 francs per hour in 1922 (3.22 for skilled, 2.55 for semi-skilled workers and 1.99 for labourers) to 2.90 in 1923, to 3.21 in 1924, to 3.43 in 1925 and to 3.86 in 1926.

But the best information about wages is given in the replies to the questionnaires concerning wages paid in their localities which are addressed to the Joint Legal Councils for Industry.[1] These returns, published at first only once in four years, have been made annually since 1924. They furnish the following figures. The index of daily wages of males in Paris, with the base 1914=100 (corresponding to earnings then of 8·12 francs per day) rose from 350 in 1921 to 385 in 1924, to 411 in 1925, and to 510 in 1926. For the same dates, the daily wage of males in the provinces (4·51 francs in 1914) rose from 410 to 477; 504; and 584. Finally the wage of females in the

[1] *Conseils de prudhommes.* These are special courts, whose members are elected half by employers half by workmen, and judge on first instance all the juridical dissensions between employers and employees (payment of wages, apprenticeship, dismissal compensation). They have existed for half a century and their decisions are subject to appeal before the ordinary courts.

provinces (2·29 francs in 1914) rose from 412 to 496; 535; and 668.

A comparison of these wage movements with those of retail prices reveals that in 1926 in Paris wages lagged slightly behind the cost of living (510 to 545); in the provinces the difference was negligible for men (584 to 599) while female wages (668) were considerably higher. On the whole the higher grades of wages lagged somewhat behind prices while, in contrast, those of women and unskilled workers kept in step with movements in the cost of living and sometimes even went ahead of them.

The fact is that, despite the weakness of the trade union movement, the working-class was in an excellent strategic position throughout this period. The general prosperity, even if artificial, and the reconstruction of the devastated areas stimulated a considerable need for labour. Unemployment did not exist. On the contrary, the scarcity of labour made it necessary to import a large number of foreign workers—about a million during the period under consideration, totalling 262,000, in 1923; 265,000 in 1924; 176,000 in 1925, and 162,000 in 1926.

II. The period 1926–30 is that which follows the restoration of financial order and the new stabilization of the franc, a stabilization *de facto* from the end of 1926 and *de jure* from June 1928, when the new French monetary régime was introduced.

Thereafter, the rate of foreign exchange, after a rapid fall (the £1 fell from 236 at the end of July to 122·84 in December) became definitely stable, and in consequence the movements in wholesale prices which had been induced during its decline disappeared. The general index, after having reached a maximum of 754 in June 1926, fell to 640 in December, to 636 in June 1937, and 617 in December of the latter year, thereafter rising gradually up to a new maximum of 644 in January 1929. The index of prices of imports fell sharply from 883 in June 1926, to 628 in December, fluctuating thereafter between 660 (December 1927) and 651 (January 1929). The index for home-produced goods fell to a smaller extent—from 682 in June 1926, to 593 in December 1927—and rose later to 639 in January 1929. Here again the movements were more pronounced in the prices of industrial than in those of agricultural products.

The rise in the value of the franc caused for some months a stabilization crisis and a falling off of production, as a result of the restoration of parity between the French and the foreign price level. From the beginning of 1927, however, these difficulties were overcome, thanks to the easy monetary situation and the fall in rates of interest which resulted from the large-scale repatriation of capital. The general index of production, which had fallen slightly below 100 (base year 1913) rose again to 103 in April 1928, to 110 in October and to 138 in March 1929. It was not until the second quarter of 1929 that a new slackening of activity in the exporting industries gave warning of the approaching crisis, while industries producing for the home market, still well provided with orders, actually experienced the height of prosperity. Retail prices once more followed the various movements of wholesale prices, always with a certain lag and without sharp changes. They continued to rise during the second quarter of 1926, the index of the Paris price of thirteen articles moving from 544 in June to 599 in December, that of provincial prices from 523 to 647, and the Paris cost of living from 539 to 545. There then followed a fall until January 1928 (to 530; 522; and 507) and a new rise up until December 1929, at which date maxima of 614; 593; and 565 were reached.

During this period working-class conditions underwent a marked improvement. It is true that some unemployment appeared during the stabilization crisis. In October 1926 there were 17,000 unemployed in receipt of relief, 56,000 in January 1927, and in March of the latter year 70,000; but the total fell to 17,000 in January and to 1,000 in July 1928; a prohibition of the import of foreign labour was sufficient to reabsorb the workless. During 1927 only 64,000 foreign workers were brought into France, while 90,000 were repatriaated. In 1928 the total of repatriation fell to 54,000, while 98,000 new workers came in (36,000 for industry and 62,000 for agriculture). Finally in 1929 repatriations fell to 40,000 and new entries rose to 180,000, the majority this time being for industry, which took 110,000 compared with 68,000 for agriculture.

In the same period the index of mining wages, after having fallen from 610 in the first quarter of 1927 to 568 in the fourth (a result of the general depression prevailing in this particular industry in all countries), rose again at the beginning of 1928 to 583, to 635 at the beginning of 1929 and to 679 at the end of 1929.

In the Paris metal trades hourly wages moved from 3·86 francs in 1926 (4·41 for skilled, 3·70 for semi-skilled workers and 2·74 for labourers) to 4·48 in 1927, to 4·57 in 1928, to 5·06 in 1929 and to 5·71 (i.e. 6·85; 5·30; 4·22 respectively) in 1930. The index of average wages derived from the inquiries of the Joint Legal Councils shows for Paris 510 in 1926; 513 in 1927; 526 in 1928; 608 in 1929 and 671 in 1930. Corresponding figures for the cost of living in Paris are: 545; 498; 531; 565; and 597.

For other towns the returns are as follows:

	Wages of Males	*Wages of Females*	*Provincial Cost of Living*
1926	584	668	599
1927	593	648	522
1928	619	701	551
1929	680	799	582
1930	732	864	621

The general improvement in the standard of living at this time was remarkable.

III. With the year 1930, however, France entered the world economic crisis which, as far as she was concerned, continued to grow worse until 1936. The signal for decline was given in January 1928, by the index of prices of imports which, from a maximum of 669, fell to 651 in January 1931, to 300 in January 1932, remaining stable thereafter at about that level until January 1936, when it stood at 306. The fall of prices abroad injured French export trade and the depression in industries producing for the foreign market spread gradually throughout the country's industries. The index of wholesale prices fell from 644 in January 1929, to 390 in December 1932; after a slight rise to 396 in June 1933, it fell again to 344 at the end of 1934 and began a slight rise to 364 at the beginning of 1936.

Lastly, the index of prices of home-produced goods, attaining its maximum (639) in January 1929, fell comparatively slowly down to January 1935 (366), rising again until the beginning of 1936 (396). It is important to note that, though at the beginning of the depression the fall of the prices of industrial goods was more marked (638 January 1929 to 362 January 1932), they later became almost stabilized (366 January 1934), falling again slightly in 1935 and down to June 1936 (352). Agricultural prices on the other hand were stickier at the beginning (539 January 1929 to 480 June 1932), afterwards sinking to a low point (333) in June 1935, and then beginning to rise again at the beginning of 1936 (370).

Throughout this period the French economic system was working under severe strain; retail prices, though they followed the general tendency to fall, did so to a less extent than, and with a lag behind others. They reached their highest point in 1930 (649 for the thirteen articles in Paris, 646 for the other towns and 590 for the cost of living in Paris), falling evenly until June 1933 (when they reached 476; 463; 516 respectively), rising again in December and reaching their lowest (441; 403; 486) in January 1936. Wages followed the general movement even more slowly. The index of mining wages fell by about 12 per cent. between 1930 and 1932 and thereafter remained stable. In the Paris metal trades between 1931 and 1935 skilled workers suffered reductions in daily wages amounting to 6·2 per cent., semi-skilled 7 per cent. and labourers 7·3 per cent.

Lastly, the general wages index for Paris fell from 671 in 1930 (cost of living 597) to 613 (cost of living 478) in 1935. In the provinces, while the wage index for male workers in 1930 stood at 732, that for female workers at 864 and the cost of living at 621, by 1935 these figures had fallen to 666; 792; and 460 respectively. Wages, that is to say, displayed a marked resistance to the prevailing movement during the period and there was a rise in the daily real wages of the workers.

But movements of daily wages do not tell the whole of the story; for from 1930 to 1936 the number of days' work obtained, both by workers in general and even by each individual worker, was considerably reduced by the wide and rapid spread of unemployment. The latter cannot be measured statistically with accuracy because of the notorious inadequacy of the information we possess about this subject. The most complete information is provided by the quinquennial censuses, but the returns are published so late that they cannot easily be used. From these returns we know to-day that during the course of the depression of 1921 there were in France 537,140 unemployed, amounting to 4·96 per cent. of the wage earners (7 53 per cent. in industry, 3·83 per cent. in commerce, 6 per cent. in the professions) and that in the prosperous year 1926 there were 243,420 unemployed—that is, 1·98 per cent. (2·69 per cent in industry, 2·26 per cent. in commerce, 4·02 per cent. in the professions). The results of the census of 1931, however, are not yet available.

The number of unemployed receiving relief is used to measure unemployment at any given time. This is the easiest figure to use, but there should be no illusion about the information it gives. Unlike Great Britain, France possesses no general system of unemployment insurance. There is simply a collection of relief funds, created on the initiative of the municipalities and subsidized by the State. The institution of such funds is not compulsory and at the present moment a very large number of rural communities do not possess them. On the other hand the worker is averse from accepting relief and, out of regard for his dignity, has recourse to it only at the limit of his means when all his resources are exhausted. The totals thus obtained therefore understate the facts. Moreover, their movements are not always a reliable guide. The longer a depression is prolonged, the more the workers resort to public relief and the more the number of funds is increased (it rose from 378 in 1931 to 1,350 in 1934). Yet this does not necessarily imply a corresponding increase in the actual number of unemployed.

These qualifications having been made, we can say that the number of unemployed receiving relief increased as follows:

Unemployed Receiving Relief

March 1930	...	1,000	January 1933	...	250,000
December 1930	...	13,000	May 1933	...	317,000
January 1931	...	28,000	December 1933	...	277,000
March 1931	...	50,000	February 1934	...	350,000
December 1931	...	161,000	December 1934	...	419,000
			June 1936	...	418,000

Complementary information is afforded by the inquiries of the inspectors of Labour concerning the average number of hours worked in the establishments under their jurisdiction. This provides a measure of partial unemployment. The number of factories not working 48 hours per week was 3 per cent. in 1930 rising to 16·7 per cent. at the beginning and 30 per cent. at the end of 1931 and to 42 per cent. in 1935. The average number of hours of work was 47·8 in 1930 and 43 hours in 1935. Taking into account both total and partial unemployment, the inspectors calculate the reduction of employment between 1930 and 1936 to be about 20 per cent.

Similar results are obtained from attempts to calculate from returns of the apprenticeship tax (assessed upon the total payroll of each undertaking liable to tax) the total sum received by workmen as wages. The latter falls from 77 million francs in 1930 for wages in industry and commerce, to 50,400,000 francs in 1935. Those of railway employees fell from Fr. 8,500,000 to Fr. 7,000,000 and of other groups similarly, making a total fall for all wages of Fr. 122 millions in 1930 to Fr. 87 millions in 1935, a reduction of 30 per cent., corresponding closely to the fall of money wages by about 10 per cent. and the reduction of employment by about 20 per cent. at which we have arrived by means of other calculations.

If, instead of daily real wages, we consider the total earnings of the working class, we find that these have suffered a serious reduction during the depression. Their fall is undoubtedly less severe than that of other incomes, labour's share of the national income being 52·2 per. cent in 1934 as compared with 43·3 per cent. in 1914 and 47·1 per cent. in 1929, while that of capital was only 19·8 per cent. (19·6 in 1914 and 16·4 in 1929), that derived from pensions 7·9 per cent. (1·4 in 1914 and 4·7 in 1929), and the mixed incomes of independent business men 20·1 per cent. (35·7 in 1914 and 31·8 in 1929).

This relative improvement in its position, however, did not prevent the working class from complaining of undergoing a reduction in its standard of living, from deploring the split which reduced the trade union movement to impotence, nor from generating by degrees a protest movement and a will to struggle which led at the beginning to 1936 to the restoration of unity and the birth of the *Front Populaire.*

IV. The years from 1932 to 1936 were marked at first by a stagnation, later by a general reawakening of the French Labour movement, culminating in February 1936, in the restoration of trade union unity. We shall examine in turn the evolution of the C.G.T. and that of the C.G.T.U., and finally the restoration of unity.

(*a*) The C.G.T. was severely injured by the split in the working-class ranks, but soon undertook a determined effort at reorganization, which enabled it steadily to regain the influence over the working masses which it had lost.

Whereas in 1922 its affiliated *syndicats* numbered 3,996, they numbered no more than 1,296 at the Congress of 1923. In 1925 there were affiliated 1,728 local *syndicats*, 36 Industrial Federations, 85 departmental unions, giving a total of 500,000 affiliated members. In 1927 there were 2,216 *syndicats*; 2,359 in 1931, with 884,000 members; in 1933 the membership exceeded 900,000. At the latter date the chief C.G.T. unions were the *Syndicat* of Railwaymen with 89,000 members, the Miners' Federation with 82,000, and Federations of metal workers (42,000), transport workers (33,000), workers in textiles (39,000), electricity (30,000), printing (18,000), leather and hides (16,000), building (21,000), of clerks (20,000), and, more important, of teachers (91,000), postal workers (58,000), health services (10,000), in other public industrial services (52,000) and the Civil Servants' Federation (106,000).

Some explanations concerning the last-named organizations are necessary. The C.G.T., of all the labour organizations of the world, was the one in which civil servants held relatively the most important place. These workers commenced to organize themselves before the War and there were established in turn unions of postal workers and teachers, and then of other public servants. After the split, these bodies at first remained independent of the two confederations, joining together in the powerful Federation of Civil Servants which, in 1927, included 91 *syndicats*, and 220,000 members divided into various sections corresponding to the various departments of the government: central administration, air, war, marine, navy, *économie nationale*, finance, public utilities, teaching. The three most important sections were those of teaching, the Teachers' union having 80,000 members—half of the State teachers; public utilities, the postal union having 60,000 members; and lastly that of finance, with a union of workers in registry offices, custom and excise, etc.

It was in 1929 that the Civil Servants' Federation, after long negotiations, joined the C.G.T. Strictly, the latter, which organizes workers by industry and not according to the employer for whom they work, ought to have required the dissolution of the Federation and the separate affiliation of each section as an Industrial Federation. That would have been to destroy a type of organization which had proved its strength. A compromise was therefore reached: only the Federations of the postal, teaching and health services were affiliated directly to the C.G.T., the other sections provisionally holding membership through the Civil Servants' Federation until it should be possible to constitute them as Industrial Federations.

The affiliation of the Civil Servants—who constituted in 1929 about a quarter of the C.G.T. membership—was bound to modify considerably the whole make-up and tactics of the Labour movement. Such a modification had also been encouraged by the change achieved in 1925 in the system of voting for the election of members of the Executive Committee. Henceforward each *syndicat*, instead of having equal rights irrespective of membership, has the right to one vote for the first 50 members, two for 51 to 100 members, 3 for 100 to 250 members, 4 for 250 to 500 members, 5 for 500 to 1,000, and an additional vote for every additional 1,000 members.

At the same time as the structure of the C.G.T. was being modified, its methods of action were entirely transformed. The Confederation had been too greatly weakened by the split to be able for some time to engage in big struggles such as those of 1919 and 1920. Moreover, the departure of the youngest and most active elements ensured the predominance in union meetings of the older leaders, who were more experienced and much more inclined to temporise and compromise. In fact in all conflicts, while the C.G.T.U. organizations seemed to fan the flames and often to outbid the others, making excessive promises for the sake of political aims, the C.G.T. always played the part of a moderator, making overtures to secure agreement, often asking public authorities to intervene as mediators and to arbitrate upon points of dispute.

At the same time, the C.G.T., formerly so strongly hostile to the State, became remarkably friendly towards it. Unquestionably, it remained faithful to the principle of direct action and sought to bring pressure from outside upon the government without itself entering into political struggles. Nevertheless in 1924 it drew up a minimum programme which it submitted to candidates at the elections. In the international field it took part in various institutions such as the I.L.O. and the League of Nations, through which it came into daily contact with the government delegates. Moreover, at home the chief feature of its policy was to secure the application of laws recently enacted and to ensure the passing of other legislation favourable to the workers.

The C.G.T. concerned itself first of all with defending from all attacks by employers the social legislation passed at the end of the War, especially the Eight Hour Law. It was also concerned with the problems raised by the immigration of foreigners. Rejecting any form of labour nationalism, it recognized the principle of complete freedom of immigration, subject only to medical control and the requirement of certain professional qualifications. For the rest, it remained faithful to its pre-War watchword of "equal pay for equal work," demanded the organization by the State of employment agencies, and the distribution of labour, and made efforts to organize the foreign workers by allotting to them special propagandists speaking their own language.

At the same time as it strove to secure the application of existing legislation, the C.G.T. also attempted to obtain new laws favourable to the working class in particular, holidays for workers, the recognition of shop stewards, and above all laws of social insurance. For some time previously the trade unions themselves had made substantial achievements in this respect. The Federations of workers in printing and publishing, in metals and in clothing and the employees of the tramways of Lyons had established for their members health insurance funds. The Union of the *Syndicats* of the Seine had opened several clinics, rest houses and convalescent houses. Others—including again the street car workers of Lyons—had superannuation funds providing pensions for their members. The printing and publishing workers added death benefits to the latter insurance, while the railwaymen had established an orphanage.

Despite the interest on the investments thus made by the unions, it was very clear that they were completely insufficient in face of the needs of the workers. Union subscriptions were generally too small to permit the development of benefit services to the same extent as is possible in English or American unions. For this reason the C.G.T. organized a campaign in favour of the introduction into France of a general system of social insurance. This was done in 1930. For five years thereafter the principal activity of the C.G.T. consisted in establishing in all parts of the country insurance funds known as *Le Travail*, operating within the framework of the law, but administered entirely and autonomously by union organizations.

Since 1931, the C.G.T. has organized a beginning of working-class education. This functions in two stages: a number of different Labour Colleges in the principal industrial towns and a Workers' Institute of Higher Education in Paris, directed by Professor Lefranc. The courses of study at the Colleges comprise French Grammar and Literature, Handwriting, Mathematics, Economics, Economic and Social History, Economic Geography, Esperanto, Industrial Law, and the History of the Working Class Movement. These courses, taught by members of the Teachers' Union, can also be pursued by means of correspondence and are published in pamphlet form, thus allowing all workers to take part in the study. The Institute of Higher Education is concerned with more advanced studies in which the actual presence of the student is necessary. There are courses in Literature, Working Class History, Child Education, Economics and Law.

Finally, the C.G.T. has concerned itself with the question of the organization of leisure time. Since 1931 it has taken part in creating a National Committee on Leisure, initiated by the Consumers' Co-operatives. It has also taken part in the organization which maintains non-denominational Youth Hostels; it has established a Labour Sports Federation and has taken part in movements for developing people's musical and dramatic activities.

On the whole it seems true to say that the C.G.T. has gone beyond and developed its minimum programme drawn up in

1919–20. Its policy has been both more prudent and more broadly conceived. More prudent, in that it has not put its trust in local strikes hastily launched, and that it has been more and more ready to accept conciliation and arbitration. Broader, in that it has advanced beyond questions of wages and hours of work to concern itself with the problems of education and leisure.

These new characteristics appeared even more definitely when, in 1934, in view of the prolongation and deepening of the depression, the C.G.T. worked out a general plan of economic reorganization and entered, side by side with political parties, into the *Front Populaire* in order to carry the plan through. The plan followed the main lines of the constructive programme of 1919, while adapting the latter to the problems of the moment. The 1919 plan was mainly concerned with methods of increasing production so as to repair the ravages of the War: that of 1934 was above all an effort to struggle against the depression and its two consequences, unemployment and the fascist menace.

Viewing the depression as the result of an insufficiency of purchasing power among the masses, the programme pronounced against any policy of deflation and proclaimed the need for a planned economy. It insisted that it was necessary to modify the political constitution in order to secure the latter. Side by side with Parliament—which would decide the general direction of policy, but would have no expert competence in economic affairs—it proposed to establish a Supreme Economic Council, which would be constituted by means of a modification of the existing National Economic Council. This Council would have the duty of making a preliminary expert study of every proposed piece of legislation. Its report would be brought before a joint committee of both Houses of Parliament for debate. When the principle of the legislation was approved, it would also be its duty to draw up regulations for its enforcement.

A planned economy under the direction of a Supreme Economic Council requires as an essential condition the control of the banking system. This part of the programme, which had been barely mentioned in 1919, became later one of the principal items of the programme. The C.G.T.

distinguished three types of saving: temporary surpluses; saving for security; and saving for gain, corresponding to the three types of Bank: deposit banks, saving banks and industrial banks. It pointed out the evils of the present banking system, which in fact confused different types of risk, furnished no security to savers and provided a means of political domination. It insisted upon the need for establishing henceforward a public credit system, comprising a government Deposit Bank, the Co-operative Banks, and the Post Office Savings Bank. It called for the public control of banking institutions, beginning with the most urgent task, the nationalization of the Bank of France.

As in 1919, the programme went on to demand the nationalization of key industries, namely: insurance, electricity and heavy metals. It also called for the unification under public control of industries in which private ownership was still allowed to prevail.

By thus putting forward a programme of general economic reorganization, the C.G.T. was definitely entering the field of politics. Its desire to be independent, though it still existed, no longer expressed itself in the negative pre-War form. Since 1934 collaboration on a basis of equality seemed to be possible between the various political parties of the *Front Populaire* and the C.G.T. Moreover the latter was more ready than in 1902 for the establishment of a united trade unionism of the British type.

(*b*) The C.G.T.U., established, immediately after their expulsion, by unions under communist influence, had undergone a development radically different from that of the C.G.T. While the latter became more prudent, the C.G.T.U. on the other hand became, despite the unfavourable circumstances, more and more aggressive, calling strikes in which the C.G.T. unions joined only when they were in full swing. While the latter would soon try to negotiate a compromise, the C.G.T.U. unions declared for a fight to a finish, sometimes accompanied by violence, and attacked with extreme bitterness the C.G.T. leaders, whom they accused of treachery. While the C.G.T. passed further and further beyond the bounds of purely economic activity and posed as the protagonist of the general public welfare, the C.G.T.U. entirely neglected its proper functions and submitted to the close control of a political party.

These tactics, which had caused the original split, were to produce sharp antagonism within the new organization. As early, in fact, as the first Congress, at St. Etienne, three trends of opinion showed themselves: the orthodox communists, such as Frossard (to-day a Radical minister), the revolutionary Syndicalists faithful to the anarchist attitude of pre-War years, and a group favouring conciliation, who wished to preserve a relative trade union independence while still keeping in collaborative contact with the Communist International. The last group for a time obtained the majority and it was with a number of reservations that the C.G.T.U. joined the Red International of Labour Unions. But in fact these reservations were soon forgotten and trade union independence of politics was never respected by the leaders of the Communist Party, the members of Parliament being often at the same time at the head of the Unions. From then onwards there was always disagreement within the C.G.T.U. It underwent the experience common to all disciples of the Communist Party—the expulsion in turn of all the various opposition groups. This soon produced a revolt of the regular trade unionists. There followed the secession of the building workers of Lyons and then the birth of a third organization—the *Confédération du Travail syndicaliste révolutionnaire*,[1] which tried in vain to revive the pure pre-War traditions of complete independence. In the very midst of the C.G.T.U. an organized opposition appeared after 1929, which engaged in a vigorous struggle against communist domination. Here again expulsions were frequent, and the members of the minority finally rejoined the C.G.T. From 1932 onwards a decline in strength could not be arrested. The membership of the C.G.T.U. fell from more than 500,000 at the time of the split to less than 250,000. Strikes called irresponsibly were almost all failures. The workers, disheartened by internal quarrels within the organization, withdrew from the C.G.T.U. and rejoined the C.G.T., or, more often, simply gave up their union membership.

(*c*) The division of the working-class forces thus enfeebled the trade union movement, while the more the industrial

[1] Revolutionary Syndicalist Confederation of Labour.

depression deepened the more futile did these internal struggles appear to the mass of the people. From 1930 onwards a strong movement in favour of the restoration of trade union unity grew up among the rank and file. For six years, however, the two central organizations competed with ruse and artifice to secure the greatest possible influence within the re-established single organization, while each declared itself in favour of unity.

After the fascist threat of 1934 the movement to secure unity became better defined. The C.G.T.U. proposed an agreement for a United Front for action. The C.G.T. replied by proposing the re-establishment of a single organization. Joint committees were appointed within which two conflicting conceptions of procedure were discussed. The C.G.T.U. wished to begin by an alliance between the two bodies on a footing of absolute equality (though the C.G.T. had 900,000 members and the C.G.T.U. barely 250,000) and the appointment of a committee containing equal numbers from each. The latter would organize amalgamations of the different Federations and would prepare for the first Congress. The C.G.T. refused to accept such a committee. It wished to commence by amalgamations of the local *syndicats*, then of the departmental unions, then of the Federations, finally completing the work with the holding of a federal Congress.

After two years of discussion, the latter procedure was eventually adopted. During the autumn of 1935 the fusion of the *syndicats* was carried out, and in February 1936 the extraordinary Congress of Unification was held at Toulouse. It approved provisionally the line of policy of the C.G.T. The comparatively decentralized structure of the trade union movement was maintained, though the communists pronounced in favour of "democratic centralization" with complete control by the executive of the C.G.T. over the departmental unions and the Federations. In international affairs, the C.G.T. remained affiliated to the Amsterdam International while, however, undertaking to work within it for a fusion with the Moscow International. At the same time the Congress approved the policy of participation at Geneva, which had formerly been so violently attacked by the C.G.T.U.

The new Executive of the reorganized C.G.T. was constituted

by the addition to the four former secretaries of the C.G.T. of the two principal leaders of the C.G.T.U., Racamond and Frachon. Finally, the Congress affirmed the necessity of trade union independence *vis à vis* all political parties, and formally forbade the combination of a political post with that of Secretary of the C.G.T. (though not that of secretary of an Industrial Federation, each one remaining free to decide this matter for itself). Trade union independence, however, was not given the same interpretation as before the War. It did not exclude a certain collaboration with political parties for the attainment of a definite programme. Thus the reunited union movement solemnly renewed its adherence to the *Front Populaire*, and the Toulouse Congress called for the rallying of the working class and democratic forces behind the programme which is still known as " le plan " of the C.G.T.

Section 3. *The* Front Populaire *and the Growth of the Labour Movement after June* 1936.

After 1936 the situation of the working class underwent a new transformation and the C.G.T., as the result of a great mass upheaval, entered a period of unprecedented expansion. The restoration of trade union unity, opening up new possibilities of direct industrial action, was almost completed when the electoral triumph of the *Front Populaire* and the subsequent announcement of the formation of a government under Socialist direction came to give the workers the certainty that the coercive power of the State would cease thenceforward to be used during social conflicts solely to the advantage of the employers.

Immediately there broke out all over the country a wave of strikes, accompanied by the occupation of factories, which reached its crest at the end of June 1936 with 12,000 strikes, involving 1,831,000 strikers. This movement provoked keen controversy. Some saw in it the result of activity on the part of Communists, seeking from the beginning to create difficulties for the Socialist government. Others laid the blame at the door of extremist plotters, Trotskyists in particular. The truth seems to be simpler. For five years the workers had suffered from unemployment, low wages, and continuous lowering of their standard of living. Now for the first time they had an opportunity to take their revenge and to improve their conditions. For these reasons the inspiration to strike came from the depths of working-class consciousness, escaping at the beginning from all control by the unions and, even more, from the authority of any political party whatever.

The C.G.T. immediately sought to co-ordinate and take charge of the movement. That was not easy at the beginning. From one day to the next its membership rose from a million to five million. It did not possess a sufficient administrative machine to cope with this avalanche of newcomers. For a month the Secretaries of *syndicats*, overwhelmed with work, had to be content with a general supervision of negotiations, leaving to worker-delegates, elected in each factory, the task of conducting the struggle under their own control. As for the government, it was obliged to devote its time, during its first weeks of office, to the work of conciliation, arbitration and social legislation. In principle condemning as illegal the new form of stay-in strike, but convinced in fact that it was a guarantee that the course of events would be peaceful, and that when one is confronted by nearly two million strikers it is better to have them " sitting down " rather than " marching on," and refusing in any case to use the forces of the State against the working class, it arranged a meeting on the 7th and 8th June at the Hotel Matignon (the office of the Prime Minister) of representatives of the C.G.T. and of the most important organization of employers, the *Confédération Générale du Patronat Français*. These two groups soon came to an agreement to accept the establishment of collective agreements in every French industry, as well as the appointment of shop-stewards whose function would be to complete trade union action by presenting to the employers the *individual* grievances of those whom they represented. They also agreed upon an immediate rise in wages of from 7 to 15 per cent., which was later to be completed by an additional increase in abnormally low wages.

At the same time the government secured the passage by Parliament of a mass of social legislation changing from top to bottom the condition of working-class life in France. First there were laws concerning shop stewards and collective labour agreements, defining and making compulsory the terms of the

Matignon agreement. There followed the Forty Hour Law and the legalisation of holidays with pay (15 days holiday for one year's work, 8 days for six months). Almost at the same time there were passed into law the most important measures demanded by the *Front Populaire*—the nationalization of armament manufacture and of the Bank of France, and the establishment of a Wheat Office which was the thin end of a wedge designed to secure the organization of the market for agricultural produce.

These various actions in time bore fruit, and before long industrial strife died down. By July there were only 1,751 strikes in progress with 181,000 strikers, in August 542 with 56,000, and in December 269 with 15,000. Later legislation, providing procedure for conciliation and arbitration, made possible by means of further rises in wages the progressive adaptation of the wages of labour to movements in the cost of living and the gradual consolidation of the gains made in June 1936.

It is too soon yet to judge with accuracy the exact effect of all these changes upon the conditions of life of the workers. We shall attempt, however, with the aid of the data available in July 1938, to trace the course of the movements of the standard of living of wage earners during these two years. We must draw attention above all to the legal changes which have occurred and to their effect upon the present position of the French labour movement.

I. The social reforms of June 1936, and the laws which followed have profoundly changed the legal conditions governing labour action in France and have created whole new pieces of juridical machinery in which the C.G.T., recognized officially as representing the interests of the workers, occupies a place of the first importance. In order to appreciate the significance of these changes, it is necessary to study in turn the legal position of the labour movement before 1936, the law concerning collective agreements, and lastly the text of the various regulations establishing procedure for conciliation and arbitration.

Before 1936 the statute relating to the legal status of *syndicats*, without being as favourable to the unions as the British Act, had already been improved on several occasions.

In regard to criminal acts, the law of May 25, 1864, had

repealed the prohibition of combination and replaced it by forbidding infringements of the freedom to work. That of 1884 had recognized the legality of *syndicats* and repealed articles 415 and 416 of the Penal Code which prohibited union organization. Article 414, however, still exists. This punishes with from six days' to three months' imprisonment, whoever " with the aid of violence, assault, threats or fraudulent actions shall have brought about or maintained a concerted cessation of work." This article seriously limits the right of picketing by reason of the interpretation given by the courts to the term " threats " (*menaces*). They have defined this as " every act of intimidation of such a kind that a man of average strength may be led to act against his will." Because of this definition the entry of workers into a workplace to compel blacklegs (*jaunes*) to cease work is contrary to the law. Similarly, the blacklisting of ships to persuade sailors to join a strike is punishable,[1] also an order given to musicians in an orchestra to cease work because of the presence of a non-unionist,[2] or, more generally, the pressure brought to bear upon an employer, by the threat of a stoppage of work, to compel him to dismiss a non-unionist. On the other hand, the Court of Lyons on July 8, 1931, upheld by the Court of Cassation on November 25, 1932, decided that a circular warning notifying the members of an organization of a projected action in common was not punishable, if it was merely a matter of agreement not accompanied by " displays, demonstrations or physical acts likely to cause a breach of the peace ".

But another question arises: may not actions which are permissible from the point of view of criminal law be capable of involving their authors in civil liability? The question arises with regard to strikes and to blacklisting. To take strikes first, do they constitute a breach or merely a suspension of the labour contract? While, for the majority of those who take part, the strike is not intended to break, but rather to modify, the labour contract, is not an abandonment but a temporary refusal to fulfil the contract, not necessarily either involving damage to the employer's ability to make profits or giving just

[1] Court of Cassation, December 17, 1926.

[2] There are three courts in France: ordinary courts, courts of appeal, and one court of cassation, which may be called " high court."

cause for the dismissal of the workers, nevertheless the Court of Cassation has hitherto ruled that the strike is a breach of the labour contract. If it has not been preceded by the tendering of notices, the strikers could be obliged to pay damages for vexatious breach of contract. In fact, for a long time past, the latter liability has not had results of any significance. As the workers have no money, damages can never be recovered; and up to 1936 the funds of the *syndicats* were equally negligible.

The other problem of liability, which, as we have already seen, also arises in criminal law, is that of the blacklisting of non-unionists. Here it is recognized in principle that normal exercise of the right of combination should not entail even civil liability; but it is all the more necessary to determine, according to the so-called theory of abuse of rights, what is a normal exercise. In this matter the practice of the courts is to analyse the motive which seems to have inspired the act complained of; and they find against workers or employers if their actions seem to have been inspired less by the motive of defending their occupational interests than by a desire to harm someone else.

Thus, according to a decision of the Court of Cassation of May 27, 1910, an employer abuses his rights by dismissing a workman solely on the grounds of his membership of a union. On the other hand, however, on March 9, 1915, the same court judged valid the clause of a contract of employment by which the worker agreed not to join a union while he remained in his present employment. The court found that in this instance the employer was safeguarding his trade interests rather than attacking the union. In the same way, workers can agree together to blacklist a firm which does not pay the union rate of wages, the latter fact proving that the blacklisting is inspired by a desire to preserve the union wage and not by a wish to injure the particular undertaking. In short, the same legal theory which condemns the workers when they strike to obtain the dismissal of a non-unionist recognizes as legal the same strike if an undertaking to observe the closed shop has been entered into by the employer as part of a collective labour agreement. In 1920 the Court of Cassation ruled that "if the employer undertakes to recruit his workers from the union and thus renounces his right to choose his employees freely, this purely temporary renunciation, not having as its prime motive an intention to injure other workers, is not contrary to the law of 1884."

So far we have described a system of jurisprudence which was on the whole much less favourable to the labour movement than that of Great Britain. In one respect, however, even before 1936, French legislation was particularly progressive, namely, in respect to the defence and representation of trade interests. It was a cassation judgment of 1913 which, after prolonged hesitation, recognized the action of a trade union as being distinct from the actions of the individual members " provided that," ran the decision, " the civil act of the union is not intended to further the individual interest of one or more of its members, but definitely to secure the protection of the collective advantage of the occupational group considered as a body and represented by the union."

This doctrine was embodied in legislation for the first time in the law of July 10, 1915, concerning minimum wages for persons working at home, which allowed a *syndicat* composed of factory workers engaged in the same industry to sue employers who violated the law. Later, the law of March 21, 1920, provided that " the *syndicats* may, before all courts, exercise all the rights of a party to a civil suit in relation to actions which operate to the disadvantage, direct or indirect, of the collective interests of the occupational class which they represent."

Gradually therefore the tendency grew to see in the *syndicat* not merely a grouping of the rights of individuals, but a representative of occupational interests. In consequence, the law of March 1919, which introduced the eight-hour day into France, simply laid down the principle to be observed, leaving to agreements between workers and employers, confirmed by the Minister of Labour, the determination of methods of application. Similarly, the law of December 29, 1923, concerning the weekly holiday, foresaw that there must be diverse methods of instituting the latter and proclaimed as follows: "When an agreement shall have been arrived at between the *syndicats* of employers and of workers in a defined region concerning the conditions upon which a weekly holiday shall be given to employees, the prefect may by decree, upon request of the *syndicats* concerned, order the closing to the public of the establishments of the given trade within the region for the day of the holiday." Thus there began to appear a method of action concerning social conditions which is peculiar to France: the regulation of labour on the basis of agreement. More and more the collective agreement tended to be considered as the law of the trade concerned, the *syndicat* thus receiving regulatory power delegated by the State.

Collective agreements, however, were neither very numerous nor much encouraged in France. They increased in number soon after the War, reaching the total of 557 in 1919, but later fell to 343 in 1920, to 159 in 1922, to 58 in 1927, to 29 in 1935. Moreover, in contradiction to the spirit of all the preceding legislation which emphasized the function of the *syndicat* as an organ of the law, the statute of March 25, 1919, which gave legal status to collective labour agreements, preserved the conceptions of private law. The agreements were not binding upon third parties. Nobody was bound without manifesting either tacitly or explicitly his willingness to adhere to the contract; whence arose a complex system of adherences and non-adherences. The agreement was binding upon the signatories, whether individuals or groups, provided that a member of the groups did not contract out within eight days following the agreement. The fulfilment of the agreement was guaranteed merely by the rules of private law, in particular by suit for damages, to be brought by the *syndicat* in the name of the interests of its trade group.

The Law of June 24, 1936, considerably modified the juridical position of the *syndicats* and gave rise to a new type of collective agreement in private law having the force of public regulation.

At first sight the existing law concerning collective agreements does not appear to be entirely upset; the new law in fact comes as a complement to the old, an addition to and not a substitute for the hitherto prevailing Labour Code. It defines a collective agreement as " a contract relating to conditions of labour." Such an agreement has still to be drawn up by the parties concerned and to be enforced in the same manner as envisaged in the law of 1919. Important modifications, however, were introduced.

In the first place, though the law leaves the task of drawing up the agreement to the parties concerned, it lays down certain provisions which must compulsorily be included in such an agreement. These include minimum wages according to class of worker and region (the latter being extensible to include the whole nation); the period allowed for holidays; the organization of apprenticeship; rules governing differences in interpretation of the provisions of the agreement and the procedure for revising it; rules concerning freedom of trade union action and freedom of opinion for the workers; and the recognition of shop stewards. The latter must exist in all establishments employing more than ten workers. They are elected by the general body of the workers and have the right to present to the management the individual demands of their electors, the collective demands being the affair of the *syndicats*. The shop stewards may in addition obtain the assistance on any occasion of a representative of their *syndicats* when putting forward their demands. The law finally lays it down that collective agreements must not include provisions contrary to law, though they may contain clauses more favourable to the workers than the existing legislation.

If one of the parties refuses to conclude a collective agreement, nobody can compel it to do so; but the Minister of Labour may make arrangements for the meeting of a mixed commission to discuss this agreement. The function of the Minister is thus exclusively one of mediation. In the event of a repeated refusal by one of the parties, he may not himself dictate the terms of an agreement; but each side is obliged to assist in such mediation and to make a reasonable effort to arrive at an understanding.

To whom shall be addressed the summons to establish the mediation commission provided for in the law? The law lays it down that it shall be sent to " the most representative organizations of the branch of industry or commerce concerned." Thus: " an employer could not in fact refuse systematically and without reason to conclude a collective agreement with the most representative group of his workers. Such a refusal would constitute an abuse of power on his part and an injury to the workers' right of combination which may entail suit for damages against him."[1]

The law applies to both industry and commerce. Agriculture and the professions, on the other hand, remain for the

[1] Lefas judgment, April 14, 1938.

time being outside. It speaks of the "branch of industry." Thus it is Industrial Unionism which is officially recognized, in conformity with the general structure of the French labour movement.

Finally, the law recognizes the most representative organizations, just as they were defined by Article 389, Part XII, of the Treaty of Versailles establishing the International Labour Organization, and interpreted by the decision of the Hague Court on July 31, 1922. In principle, in a given industry or region, the most representative body is the one which has the largest number of members; it matters little that this majority be not maintained in any particular establishment or occupational category. Thus the award of the arbitrator, Blondel, on October 12, 1937, refused to recognize the representative character of the French Union of Professional *Syndicats*.[1] The reason, among others, was that the technicians and employees whom it claimed to represent had a majority only in certain establishments and not in the region and the industry as a whole. However, the size of the membership is not sufficient by itself; beyond that, it is necessary to find out whether, taking into account the age of the organization, its activity, the size and regularity of payment of members' contributions, and the importance of its reserve funds, the group under consideration possesses sufficient solidity and independence. Thus the Blondel award already cited invoked as another reason for refusing recognition to the French Union of Professional *Syndicats* (a *Croix de Feu* organization) the recent date of its establishment and the insufficiency of its contributions to cover normal expenses.

On the other hand, in instances where the workers may be divided among numerous organizations approximately equal in importance, the Minister may call upon them all to appoint on the commission a proportional delegation incontestably representative of the occupation.

But undoubtedly the chief innovation arises from the procedure provided by the law for extension. It is possible for the Minister of Labour, under certain conditions, to transform the private agreement into a veritable obligatory code for the whole of the industry in a defined region.

[1] *l'Union des Syndicats professionnels français.*

This procedure has very rapidly been used. Indeed it corresponded to a necessity which was quickly perceived by all those affected. In the large towns strongly organized *syndicats* were obtaining good conditions of labour. Elsewhere, wages remained lower and social legislation was not always respected. Firms operating in the country or in small towns thus created difficulties for those in the big towns, which were obliged to meet heavier social burdens. The result might have been a migration of firms to the country and a growth of unemployment in the towns. It was therefore to the interest of both parties to impose observance of the agreement upon those who had refused to sign it and to make it obligatory, at least over a whole region.

In order that a collective agreement may be extended, it is necessary that the request for extension be made jointly by the organizations concerned, which must both be, for their respective sides, the most representative groups in the industry and the region under consideration.

The agreement must contain the provisions required by the law and no others. As far as the first requirement is concerned, the legal procedure is very strict. If an agreement does not include all the obligatory provisions, the Minister cannot modify it and must refuse to permit its extension. He may, however, order the extension of the agreement with the exclusion of particular clauses, which seem to him illegal, but which do not affect the essential principles of the agreement.

An important discussion arose about clauses establishing the closed shop. We have seen that in the past the Court of Cassation had recognized the legality of such a restriction of the right of hiring labour provided that it had been established by agreement and not as the result of pressure. A judgment of the Court of Lyons on January 18, 1938, however, had declared invalid a "closed shop" clause on the ground that it was contrary to trade union liberty. This clause, according to the Court, always had the objective, not of protecting the interest of the occupational group, but of suppressing a minority union. This opinion of the Court of Lyons seems to be disputable. It is to be hoped that the Court of Cassation, remaining faithful to its previous attitude, will remember that the closed shop clause need not be invalid in itself, but only when it has been proved that it was inserted with the sole aim of injuring another organization, and this admitted restriction upon liberty of choice of trade union is not justified by the necessity to protect the interests of the occupational group. On the other hand it is beyond doubt that such a clause, which may be valid in a private agreement, cannot be included in the extension of an agreement without impairing liberty of choice of union.

If the agreement complies with the required conditions, the Minister orders an inquiry among the workers and employers in the industry and the region concerned. He must also ask, without being obliged to follow it, the advice of the appropriate section of the National Economic Council. He may then proceed to make his order for extension, which is immediately applicable. It is hoped to make the application of extension of agreements retrospective to the moment when the request for extension was first made; this in order to prevent employers from refusing to sign an agreement, so as to profit from the delay of its execution during the interval which elapses before its compulsory extension. Legislation, however, is necessary before this can be secured.

The decree of extension makes the agreement obligatory within the given region and industry. Any person infringing the agreement is liable to a fine of from 5 to 50 francs—for each payment made in violation of the terms of the agreement. (The fine in the majority of cases is five francs for each illegal weekly payment per worker paid.)

The decree does not run for a definite period. It remains valid until the agreement thus extended ceases to have effect, whether on account of notice to terminate being given, or because of revision by the parties concerned, or because (on account of the withdrawal of some parties) the groups tied by the agreement are no longer the most representative. In such a case there arises a curious judicial situation: an act of public law (the decree of the Minister) has ceased to have effect on account of an agreement of private persons acting voluntarily.

The law of June 24, 1936, provided that as part of the obligatory clauses of collective agreements, there must be included "procedure by means of which disagreements concerning its application shall be settled and whereby the agreement may be revised and modified." In the space of a few weeks more than 3,000 agreements covered French industry, for the most part containing provision for conciliation, and more rarely for arbitration. Concluded mostly for six months or one year, they involved the risk that they might expire more or less simultaneously. The government might therefore again find itself faced by two million strikers, as in June 1936.

It was in order to avoid this danger that the government on two occasions took it upon itself to extend the legal duration of the agreements signed in June 1936, and took mediatory steps to secure their orderly and peaceful revision.

The first action of this kind dates from the monetary law of September 1936, which effected the first devaluation. It was easy to foresee that this would entail a rise in prices, stimulating new demands by the workers and strikes. The Chamber of Deputies had wished to establish by law the sliding scale, by which every change in the cost of living would be accompanied by a corresponding variation in wages. In face of the opposition of the Senate it fell back upon the following formula: " In the event of a notable increase in the cost of living (as compared with the index for October 1) occurring before December 31, 1936, the government may, upon the advice of the National Economic Council, establish machinery for conciliation and arbitration, effective for a period of six months, in order to regulate differences produced by this rise and affecting the drawing up, execution and revision of clauses in collective agreements relating to wages."

These powers were much too limited, since they concerned only differences *relating to wages*. The government eventually, after long negotiations with the organizations of employers and workers, preferred to put forward a new proposal, submitting to arbitration *all collective disagreements*. Here again there occurred a conflict between Chamber and Senate over the questions of the application of arbitration to agriculture (refused by the Senate), of trade union representation on the national conciliation committees (the Chamber wanting representation by the most representative body, the Senate proportional representation) and of the choice of arbitrators (whether by the government or by the courts). Finally, on December 31, 1936, the following formula was adopted:

> "Where a collective agreement determining rules for conciliation and arbitration does not exist, the government is authorized until the end of the ordinary Parliamentary session of 1937, and for all collective labour disputes, to establish methods of procedure for securing conciliation and arbitration by means of orders in council."

An order of January 12, 1937, laid down fundamental rules of arbitration, to be followed thenceforward. In case of dispute, a mixed departmental Commission, composed of employers and workers, divided into sections according to occupational group, should invite the parties involved to conciliate. If conciliation were not achieved within four days, the question came before a national mixed commission of the industry, which also had four days to effect a conciliation. In the event of a deadlock, each party was asked to nominate an arbitrator. If either refused, the arbitrator was chosen by the Minister from a list previously drawn up from among various civil servants of the Chief Offices of State. If the two arbitrators did not agree within four days upon a joint decision, they must choose a further arbitrator from the above list. This procedure began to work at once. In the first quarter of 1937, out of 3,500 disputes 2,929 were settled at the first stage of conciliation, 182 at the national stage, 165 by agreement between the two arbitrators, and 224 by further arbitration. Fifty-one disputes arising before the law was enacted were brought directly to arbitration. Of the last group of 275 arbitrations, 55 were still under consideration, while 220 decisions had been handed down, affecting 1,800,000 workers. Only 12 of the latter encountered difficulty in application, 6 from the side of the employers, 6 from that of the workers.

The procedure, that is to say, worked well. Nevertheless certain gaps revealed themselves. On the one hand, the excessive number of stages of consideration notably retarded the settlement of the disputes; the figures quoted above show that in fact a single conciliation and a single arbitration would have been sufficient. On the other hand, the arbitrators of last resort, chosen individually, at first rendered varying decisions, often contradictory. It was necessary to create a co-ordinating body able to initiate the esablishment of a veritable system of law on these matters.

An important reform was accomplished by the law of March 4, 1938, completed by the decree of April 3, 1938. This, in the first place, refers to the obligation resting upon the parties to provide in collective agreements procedure for conciliation and arbitration. This was to have become the regular practice. When such provision is not part of an agreement, or is only partially contained in it, the law provides henceforth for a single conciliation, either locally at the hands of a committee of both employers and workers presided over by the prefect, or, if the dispute's repercussions are serious, by means of a national committee presided over by the Minister of Labour or his nominee. Both committees are composed of an equal number of workers and employers, representing the organizations involved according to their respective importance, local or national. They are divided, according to industries, into occupational groups.

If conciliation is not successful, the parties are invited to choose an arbitrator. If they do not reach agreement upon this choice within two days (as is very frequently the case), the arbitrator is selected by the prefect, if conciliation has been local, from a panel of ten persons drawn up by the First President of the Court of Appeal. If conciliation was national, the Minister chooses the arbitrator from a panel of sixty drawn up by the National Economic Council.

Appeal against the decision of the arbitrator may be made, on grounds of incompetence, of judgment *ultra vires*, or of violation of the law, before a Superior Court of Arbitration. The latter consists of three members of the Council of State (one of whom presides), two high Civil Servants, either in office or retired, two representatives of workers and two of employers, chosen by the most representative organization[1] and an equal number of substitutes. It functions in fact as a special section of the Council of State and in its meetings adopts the procedure of the latter. It does not act as a further tribunal of arbitration, but merely gives decisions for or against the demand for annulment of an arbitral award. When it quashes the first decision, it sends the parties before another arbitrator. It may not make

[1] In the case of workers, this is the C.G.T.

a judgment on facts, the arbitrator having supreme power to size up a given situation and to judge of the intentions of the parties. The Court takes cognizance only of questions of principle concerning the competence of the arbitrators and their interpretation of the law, this being necessary in order to elaborate by degrees a unified code of practice.

The Court was established at the beginning of May 1938, and up to the vacation of that year had already rendered a certain number of decisions relating to the application of the procedure of arbitration and to the powers of the arbitrators. One question, indeed, had to be settled at the outset: what exactly is the field within which arbitration may be applied? Unlike the majority of foreign systems of legislation, French law makes no distinction between the interpretation of an existing law or collective agreement and the elaboration of a new agreement. All such matters are submitted to arbitration, provided that a disagreement of a collective character has arisen thereon between employers and workers.

But how is this " collective character " to be defined? Here two difficulties were encountered. The employers, in the first place, claimed that arbitration should not apply to any case where a strike had been declared—a circumstance which frequently prevailed. The law of December 31, 1936, included in Article 1 the statement that " all collective labour disagreements must be submitted to processes of conciliation and arbitration BEFORE any strike or lock-out." By striking beforehand, said the employers, the workers are infringing the very law which they are trying to invoke; moreover, according to the decisions of the Court of Cassation before 1936, they are breaking their labour contract. Therefore the employer has for the time being no employees: therefore he had no disagreement with anyone.

The arbitrators have always refused to accept this reasoning and the Superior Court, in one of its decisions—that of May 16, 1938—found that the act of declaring a strike without previously resorting to arbitration no doubt constitutes an abuse of the right to strike, which may entail the award of damages against the *syndicat* by a court of common law, but that this could not absolve the parties from their legal obligation to find a peaceful solution of the dispute. By making this declaration, the Court of Arbitration is taking up a position opposite to the traditional attitude of the Court of Cassation; it holds that there is a collective disagreement in these circumstances, that the striking workers are still in the service of their employer, and that in consequence the strike does not break the labour contract, but merely suspends its application.

In a large number of other cases, employers have contested the competence of the arbitrators and have held that the issue was one not of collective disagreements but of the disagreements of individuals which could be settled only by Courts of Common Law. In this type of case the arbitrators have gradually evolved a jurisprudence which the first decisions of the Court of Cassation seem to confirm.

In order that collective disagreement may exist, it is first of all necessary that a demand may have been made upon or on behalf of a wage-earning group, either organized in a *syndicat* or expressing its views only through elected representatives. It is further necessary that this demand be presented in relation to a rule or a principle contained in a collective agreement or in a labour law, thus involving the collectivity of workers and not merely certain of its members.

The question becomes acute when it is one of the dismissal of workers—a matter which the employers have always refused to submit to arbitration. At present it seems to be agreed that dismissals of individuals, even when simultaneous, do not involve a collective interest provided that they are effected for strictly individual reasons, such as incompetence or indiscipline at work, or general dismissals necessitated by the economic situation. On the other hand, collective disagreements, falling within the province of the arbitrator, arise from every dismissal of an elected representative of the workers on the grounds, not of his ability as a worker, but of his activity as a delegate. More generally, all dismissals for acts connected with the exercise of trade union rights are in violation of the clauses of the collective labour agreement.

The collective character of the dispute therefore depends upon the real motives which have inspired the employer's action. In order to evaluate these, the arbitrator must make a careful inquiry. If the workers are able to adduce only presumptions against plausible and serious reasons advanced by the employer, the arbitrator declares that no case arises. If he decides, on the other hand, that the unconvincing character of the motives put forward by the employer and the nature of the acts alleged allows him to presume that there may have been wrongful dismissal, then he takes up the case. Thus the Vassal judgment of April 25, 1938, lays it down that "the lack of verisimilitude or the inaccuracy of the reasons adduced by the employer must lead the arbitrator to think that the dismissals were effected from unavowed and arbitrary motives." Similarly, the Bourrel judgment of April 11, 1938, declared that "the dismissal of workers who were delegates for the reason that it was necessary to engage in their place workers acquainted with the operation of new machines is unlawful if it cannot be proved that the employer ascertained whether the dimissed workers did or did not possess the knowledge which he required from their successors." On these various points the Superior Court has not yet pronounced; it has merely confirmed—by its decision of May 18, 1938—a ruling that the dismissal of a union delegate on the ground of his union activities constitutes a collective interest.

The competence of arbitrators being thus defined, what are their powers? The Court has already given certain directions upon this matter. In the event of disagreement concerning the conclusion or the revision of a collective agreement, the arbitrator may not, as part of his award, compel one of the parties, against its will, to sign an agreement, but he may impose an equitable settlement of the dispute, which is binding upon the parties until such time as a collective agreement shall be signed by them, and this settlement may contain all or some of the clauses of the agreement under discussion.

In his decision the arbitrator may cover all matters concerning which there is collective disagreement. Principal among these are obviously questions of wages. During the eighteen months that the law of December 31 has been in operation, many varied decisions on this subject have been made by arbitrators. In the determination of wages they have taken account of minimum standards of living, variations in the cost of living, comparable rates of wages in other industries in the region, possibilities of making profits, and general economic conditions.

The law of March 6, 1938, gave the arbitrators general

directions upon this subject. A change in wage rates is possible only if there has been either a change in living costs of at least five per cent. during the last six months or of at least ten per cent. within a shorter period. Arbitrators are in these cases asked to raise wages in proportion to the rise in the cost of living, unless the employers prove that the rise is incompatible with the economic conditions, either local, regional or national, of the branch of economic activity for which the demand for alteration has been made. This requirement has been quickly applied by the arbitrators. As a decision upon it has not yet been made by the Superior Court, we may refer, in order to explain it, to the judgment given on May 16, 1938, for the textile industry of Belfort, by M. Capitant, Professor in the Faculty of Law at Strasbourg, which has been generally followed by his colleagues:

"Whereas it follows from Parliamentary debates that it is necessary to distinguish two components in wages, one varying in proportion to the cost of living, the other remaining fixed; whereas the variable portion is that which, as it is indispensable for assuring subsistence to the worker, ought to be guaranteed to him in real value as a minimum independent of variations in the value of money . . . whereas the employers' side refuses any rise in wages, declaring such to be incompatible with the economic and financial situation of their businesses: but whereas the proof which the law demands from them could be supplied only by establishing on the one hand the facts of the economic situation of the industry concerned and on the other the relative importance of wage changes among the various factors capable of influencing that situation, in order that the arbitrators may be placed in a position to measure the effect of a rise in wages upon the fortunes of the businesses, taking into account the means by which the extra charge attributable to each one may be met; considering moreover that the arbitrators have a duty to be especially strict in their requirements concerning the nature and quality of the documents produced when it is a question of the adjustment not of total wages, but of living wages, the revision of which is rendered necessary by the rise in the cost of living."

Consequently, as he considered that the documents submitted did not prove the incompatibility of the revision of wages asked for with the economic situation of the industry concerned, the arbitrator raised, in proportion to the cost of living, both the family allowances and the minimum wages paid in the establishments. The worst paid workers thus saw their wages following the cost of living, while the others benefited only by a smaller increase. The law thus appeared to create a tendency towards a sliding-scale confined to the minimum necessary for existence, slow in its application (six months' delay except when the rise exceeded 10 per cent.), and adjusted by taking into consideration some of the difficulties of an industry, on condition that it abandon the tradition of absolute secrecy concerning its business and furnish the arbitrator with exact information about its position.

In addition to questions of wages the arbitrators, as we have seen, have had to take under consideration a large number of disputes about dismissals. When they have found themselves able to do so, they have often awarded payment of compensation to wrongfully dismissed workers, have ordered their re-employment, and have even gone so far as to impose upon the employers a fine for each day of delay in carrying out their decision.

There is, however, considerable diversity regarding these matters in the decisions of the arbitrators, and the need for some supplementary legislation begins to be felt. A Bill was introduced into Parliament in the summer of 1938 to establish legal regulation of engagement and dismissal. It provides in particular that businesses will have to recruit the great majority of their personnel through the public Employment Exchanges, governed by a commission representative in equal proportions of employers and workers. It provides, in case of large-scale dismissals, for a rotation, taking into account family expenses and seniority in employment, giving a right of first preference in new engagements of labour up to six months. Finally, it requires that rules of discipline shall be incorporated in collective agreements, the arbitrators to have full authority concerning their interpretation.

A final question remains to be answered: what sanctions may the arbitrator impose to enforce his decision? The law declares recourse to the arbitrator and acceptance of his decision to be compulsory, but at the same time it preserves the right to strike and to lock out. In other words, there could be no penal sanction in these matters, except in the case of a decision interpreting the clauses of a collective agreement extended by decree of the Minister. In all other cases, sanctions are limited to the moral pressure of public opinion and to the possibility of securing a judgment for damages in the ordinary courts against a party committing a breach of the award, on the grounds of an abusive exercise of property rights or of the right to strike. This sanction is in fact more effective against the employer than against the worker.

The Labour movement as a whole has declared in favour of the new legislation. The C.G.T. indeed received therefrom official recognition. In 1938 it unites nearly five million members, while neither of the rival groups—the Christian Labour Confederation[1] (Catholic), a genuine trade union organization, but under Church influence, and the Confederation of Professional Unions,[2] a "yellow" organization benefiting from employer support—has a membership exceeding 500,000. For the country as a whole, the C.G.T. is therefore the most representative organization. On most occasions its Federations and Departmental Unions are also the most representative in given industries or regions—with the sole exception of Alsace and of organizations of clerks, in which the Catholic groups are sometimes more numerous. It is therefore almost always the C.G.T. *syndicats* which sign the collective agreements, which nominate arbitrators on behalf of the workers, and which represent labour on all the Boards having equal representation. The C.G.T. in fact is officially recognized as the authentic expression of the French world of labour.

Moreover, the multiplication of collective agreements, which rose sharply in number from twenty to several thousands and the institution of shop-stewards, who are in fact representatives of the trade union within the factory, have notably increased the freedom of workers at the place of work and have raised their status. No doubt there is still much to be done in order to check arbitrary actions and unfair dismissals on the part of employers. For this reason the C.G.T. is demanding insistently the passage of the law concerning recruitment and dismissal. It must be recognized, however, that within the last two years a profound change in the atmosphere of the

[1] *Confédération des Travailleurs Chrétiens.*
[2] *Confédération des Syndicats Professionnels.*

workshops has been produced, and that a breath of democratic air has entered them.

After some hesitation, even arbitration has been accepted by the workers because, despite its name, it is not in fact compulsory. There does not exist, as in the totalitarian countries, a special magistracy for labour, whose orders are imposed by the power of the State. In France the State is simply placing at the disposal of employers and employed new machinery for regulating disputes in conditions in which, in regard to issues which are not fundamental, it is more advantageous to both sides to accept the decision of an arbitrator than to run the risk of affronting public opinion and engaging in ruinous strife. It is therefore to be hoped—and the first signs suggest that there is ground for doing so—that the practice of resort to arbitration will help the labour movement to discipline itself and to put a stop to wild strikes, hurriedly called and spreading, by way of sympathetic action, without notice being given even to the union officials.

Though arbitration may favour such a reorientation of trade unionism, yet, since no sanctions are attached, it does not impede the exercise of the right to strike. A strike may be useful in drawing public attention to acute grievances of the workers, and may also influence the decision of the arbitrator, since the state of mind of the workers ought to be an element in helping him to make his decision. It is also an indispensable means of compelling an employer to accept the arbitral award. In exceptional cases, when a question of prime importance is at issue, it may be preferable to violate an unfavourable arbitral award and engage in a struggle, while still trying to arrive at an agreement by other means. The practice of arbitration is still too novel to enable one to foretell its future. So far it has worked well, without restricting the right to strike, and has made it possible to secure the peaceful settlement of the great majority of disputes.

It is difficult too to give an opinion upon the probable fortunes in the near future of a Labour movement which is now in the midst of a period of transformation. Conflicting doctrines struggle within it. In spite of unification, the dispute between communists and socialists—or more generally the supporters of union independence of politics—continues. At one moment it seemed that a disguised attempt by communists to capture the C.G.T. would succeed. Such an attempt was successful in Paris and district; but during recent months there has been a vigorous reaction against this new attempt at colonization by a political party and the communists have lost much ground.

This struggle also has effects on questions of trade union action. It vitally affects problems of home and still more of foreign politics (e.g. the Spanish question), although fairly general agreement seems to prevail concerning the social laws and arbitration. The militants are adapting themselves to the new legal machinery, acquiring habits of discussion and friendly negotiation, and a new sense of their responsibilities. As one of the secretaries of the C.G.T., Belin, has recently written: " French trade unionism is no longer in opposition; it is no longer an outlaw; it accepts the idea of a system of labour law; social reforms no longer seem unclean to it; it submits to arbitration; it seeks to make collective agreements; it places itself under the power of the law, which demands subjection, but gives protection."[1]

The C.G.T. seems therefore to have entered upon a path which brings it nearly into line with classic Trade Unionism. One difference, however, persists. There could be for it no thought of confining itself to the defence of working-class interests within the capitalist system. Recent experience has shown it clearly how limited remain the possibilities of material improvement within contemporary capitalism. It ceaselessly demands modifications of the system which appear to it to be indispensable in order to consolidate the reforms which have been won and to make possible the achievement of further gains. In other words, this C.G.T., born of reaction against parties and political activity, is to-day, curiously enough, compelled to become preoccupied with politics and to bargain with political parties in order to defend at long range the interests of its members. We must now test the success or failure of this policy by examining the evolution of the conditions of living of wage earners during these last two years.

II. The social reforms of June 1936 have profoundly changed

[1] *Le Peuple*, January 1938.

the relations existing between wages and prices. In previous years change originated almost always with movements in prices. Wages adjusted themselves thereto only after an interval—more in consequence of the favourable strategic position of French labour than as a result of trade union action. In recent times, on the contrary, it was wages which first experienced a sensational rise. This, together with the effect of other social laws, produced in turn a rise in prices to which wages were later adjusted by new upward movements. Let us begin by examining the level of wages at different periods, and then compare with it the corresponding level of prices.

The Matignon agreement, as we have seen, provided for a raising of wages by from 7 to 15 per cent., together with a supplementary rise in abnormally low wages. But when collective agreements were signed, this last category was found to be much more important than even the employers' organizations had estimated. In the provinces, especially in women's occupations, daily wages of 8 and 10 francs were fairly frequent. Wholesale increases took place, and in fact, when the Matignon agreement was applied, it resulted in an increase of wages of from 15 to 25 per cent. In the autumn the application of the forty-hour week law resulted in a new rise of 20 per cent. in hourly wage rates. Finally, arbitral awards gave new wage increases, after the devaluation of the franc and the subsequent continuous rise in the cost of living, bringing the increases up to 50 per cent. of daily earnings by the end of 1937.

To take some examples, miners' wages rose from Fr. 32·33 (index 599) in the first quarter of 1936 to Fr. 46·95 (869) in the first quarter of 1937, and by the first quarter of 1938 had reached Fr. 60·13. From June 1936 to October 1937 daily wages had risen by from 66 to 68 per cent. in the case of underground workers and by 70 per cent. in the case of surface workers. These percentages correspond almost exactly with the increases of wages as a whole. In fact, on account of short-time working, there were not more than five work days per week before 1936; and the forty-hour week—made easy of application by numerous provisions for flexible adjustment—did not notably change the actual duration of work, which indeed was later to be slightly increased.

In the metal trades of the Paris neighbourhood, average

hourly wages rose steadily from Fr. 5·20[1] in the first quarter of 1936 to Fr. 10·36 in the first quarter of 1938.[2] From the end of 1935 to the end of 1937 the increase of hourly wages amounted to 79 per cent. for skilled workers, 94 per cent. for semi-skilled, and 100 per cent. for unskilled—an average increase of 85 per cent. As the forty-hour week was strictly applied in these trades, these figures represent a rise in weekly earnings of 49 per cent. for skilled workers and 66 per cent. for the remainder.

New information is provided by the Association of Electrical Trades Employers concerning the wages paid to workers by its members in all parts of France. In this instance, the average rise was one of 80 per cent. from October 1935 to October 1937, constituting a weekly rise of 50 per cent.

More complete information, provided by the inquiries of the "conseils des prudhommes," shows that hourly wages of male labour in the provinces rose from Fr. 3·80 in October 1935 to Fr. 5·60 in October 1937—the index at the latter date reaching 1217. Similar figures for female labour show a rise from Fr. 2·26 to Fr. 3·08 (index 1339) in the same period. For Parisian wages the figures are Fr. 6·23 and Fr. 10·06 at these dates (index 1150 in October 1937). Compared with 1935 there has been a provincial increase of 47 per cent. for males and 36 per cent. for females, and a 60 per cent. increase in Paris. It is difficult to calculate for these groups the average weekly increase, since the information provided covers mainly small and medium-sized trades in which the forty-hour week has been applied unevenly and in diverse ways, ranging from five days of eight hours in four establishments to six days of six hours and forty minutes in smaller businesses, with in some cases days of unequal length. It must also be noted that it was this type of small-scale industry which suffered most from the depression and resorted most frequently to short-time working before 1936. One may roughly estimate the rise in weekly earnings from the end of 1935 to the end of 1936 to have been 35 per cent. for men and 30 per cent. for women in the provinces, and 45 per cent. in Paris.

To interpret correctly the movements of working-class earnings as a whole account must be taken of fluctuations in

[1] Fr. 6·38 for skilled, Fr. 5·05 for semi-skilled, Fr. 4·09 for unskilled workers.
[2] Skilled: Fr. 11·31; semi-skilled: Fr. 9·80; unskilled: Fr. 8.

unemployment, whether complete or partial. Here two main movements must be noted. Between March 1936 and September 1937 a marked improvement occurred, the number of workers unemployed falling from 465,000 to 307,000. Since then, however, the total rose again to 412,000 in February 1938. Since the latter date a purely seasonal improvement brought the figure down to 362,000 in June 1938. Partial unemployment, having entirely disappeared during 1937, returned again during 1938. The average weekly duration of work, which was 45·8 hours in 1936, was 40·4 hours in 1937 (about the maximum permitted by law) and fell to 38·7 hours in the spring of 1938.

Let us now, in order to compare them with the figures for wages, consider the fluctuations in other indices, especially those of prices and of productive activity.

The years 1936 and 1937, unlike that of 1935, saw an exceptional rise in the index of wholesale prices, under the triple influence of the Social Laws (rise in wages, holidays with pay, forty-hour week), the rise of world price levels and the successive currency devaluations. The general index for 45 articles rose from 347 in 1935 to 405 in 1936, to 563 in 1937 and 653 in June 1938—a total rise of 87 per cent. A weighted index based upon 126 articles shows an even higher rise, moving from 338 in 1935 to 660 in June 1938—a total increase of 95 per cent. On the same base as the general index the rise is almost the same for home-produced (374 to 688) as for imported goods (299 to 591). For agricultural the rise is higher (344 to 659) than for industrial products (351 to 648).

Retail prices underwent less marked fluctuations. For Paris the index of the price of 13 articles rose steadily from a minimum of 446 in July 1936 to 698 in July 1938. A new, more exact, weighted index for 34 articles shows a rise in the same period from 461 to 698. According to the index taken, the rise in Paris is therefore one of 57 or 52 per cent. For the provinces, the index for 13 articles stood at 408 in May 1936 and 648 in May 1938—showing a rise of 54 per cent. in November 1937, and a total rise of 60 per cent. by the summer of 1938. The index for 34 articles indicates a rise of 44 per cent. up to November 1937 and 51 per cent. up to June 1938.

The cost of living index has been modified so as to make

easier comparison of the information returned by the various regional commissions. The returns are compiled in a budget, comprising 60 per cent. for foodstuffs, 10 per cent. for housing, 5 per cent. for heating and lighting, 15 per cent. for clothing, 10 per cent. for miscellaneous expenditure. With 1930 as the base year (100) this index has moved as follows:

May 1936	80·3	November 1937 ...	110
November 1937 ...	91·1	May 1938 ...	115.3
May 1937	94·4		

This represents an increase of 36 per cent. up to November 1937, and a total increase of 44 per cent. up to May 1938. The older index, applied to Paris, shows a total rise of 42·5 per cent. between mid-1935 and the first quarter of 1938.

To sum up, since the spring of 1936 there has been a rise in wholesale prices of from 90 to 95 per cent., in retail prices of from 55 to 60 per cent., in the cost of living of from 42 to 44 per cent. Since wages were raised by the end of 1937 by 68 per cent. for miners, 50 per cent. for skilled and 66 per cent. for unskilled metal workers in Paris, 50 per cent. for electrical workers, 35 to 40 per cent. for the average of all wages, we may conclude that so far the French working class has rather benefited considerably from what has been done.

Undeniably, it has not preserved the whole of the advantages gained in 1936 by the Matignon agreement. The greater part of the wage increases then introduced were later swept away by the rise in the cost of living. For some this has been a bitter disappointment. Nevertheless, in comparison with the situation in May 1936, the rise in wages has on the whole remained greater than the rise in living costs. For unskilled workers this has been notably true, for the increase in their real wages has almost equalled the percentage agreed upon at Matignon. It has been far less true for skilled workers and still less for the middle industrial groups—minor executives, technicians, foremen, and especially clerks and civil servants, whose discontent is one of the major difficulties of the present time. Nevertheless, on the whole the balance of loss and gain for the last two years shows a small gain in average real weekly wages, to which must be added the forty-hour week and paid holidays.

Though the working class has seen its situation improved,

France nevertheless remains in a difficult economic and financial situation. The general index of production, which stood at 94 in 1935 and reached its lowest point (93) in August 1936, rose after the first devaluation to 105 in April 1937, fell again to 91 in August 1937, picked up to 102 in December, and fell back to 91 in April 1938. The last-named average is due to indices of 101 and 108 for manufacturing and extractive industries benefiting from increase of armaments. Peacetime industries remained at a lower level of output: the index for textiles, for example, stood at 58, that for building at 50. As for foreign trade, the index of volume of imports, on the base of 1928 as 100, was 89 in 1935 and rose to 104 in 1937, but fell again to 98 in May 1938. That of exports moved from 55 in 1935 to 52 in 1936, to 57 in 1937 and to 58·5 in May 1938. There has, therefore, been for some months an improvement in the French Balance of Trade; but from all points of view the economic situation remains very serious.

This is not the place to study the causes of these economic difficulties. Let us point out merely that the French Budget, which to-day absorbs nearly 40 per cent. of the national income, is overwhelmed by the burdens of past debts and of the increasing cost of national defence. Moreover industry in France is too often backward, fiercely individualist, attached to absurd principles—such as business secrecy—which prevent competitors from communicating to one another such information about the general state of markets and production as is essential if a healthy co-ordination of effort is to be secured. Above all the flight of capital abroad has reduced investible funds to the minimum. The rate of interest is excessively high. The State finds it difficult to borrow and more and more has to have recourse to advances from the Bank of France. Private savings are dried up. The curious situation exists, that while the government is compelled to resort to monetary inflation, the French economic system is suffering from a drastic deflation of credit.

It seems as if the time has come when, if the gains of 1936 and the standard of living of the worker are to be preserved, substantial modifications must be made in the French economy. The banking system must be reorganized and, with the aid of a managed currency, credit must be expanded so as to revive an economy which is healthy in itself, but rendered anaemic at present by a universal deficiency of means of payment. Production must be increased, if need be by adding some hours to working time, but on condition that that shall have been preceded by a regrouping of businesses and a co-ordination of productive activity. The latter will require collective agreements concerning output and prices, integrated by means of the nationalization of certain basic industries so as to prevent the emergence of a group of trusts in control of markets and able to exact monopoly prices.

The C.G.T. has perceived the need for such an attempt to set up a planned economy. It declares itself ready to take its share in responsibility and to give the consent of the working class to certain sacrifices, on condition, first that the financial interests be rendered powerless to take advantage of this. In agreement with the Socialist Party, it calls insistently for a modification of the original programme of the *Front Populaire*, so as to include in it the necessary measures. If in the near future a government be formed which intends to make a sincere attempt to secure reorganization and a planned economy, it will be able to count upon the firm support, perhaps upon the official participation, of the workers' organization.

French trade unionism is moving in a new direction. No longer does it adopt the purely negative anti-State attitude of pre-War days. Yet there is no question of forming a Labour Party, dominated by the unions. The predominantly rural character of France would suffice to make that impossible. Still less is there desire for the neo-Guesdist tactic of the communists—the assertion of party control over the unions. On the contrary, it may be prophesied that for a long time to come we shall continue to see on the French political scene, though under a variety of names, formations resembling the present *Front Populaire*, uniting the principal political parties of the Left with the C.G.T., on a footing of complete equality and aiming at carrying out a programme drawn up in collaboration and worked out in detail.

GERMANY

BY

ERICH ROLL

GERMANY

No study of contemporary Germany, least of all one concerned with labour problems, can fail to draw an obvious line of division. Up to 1933, German development can be discussed in similar terms to those appropriate to other highly industrialized, capitalist countries. But with the coming into power of the national-socialist party, a fundamental change has occurred. Not that Germany has ceased to be a capitalist country: in spite of superficial indications to the contrary, it can be shown that the significant features of a capitalist economic structure are fully preserved in present-day Germany. It is the political structure of the country which has undergone a radical transformation. Democratic forms of government have disappeared; Germany has become a fascist, totalitarian state. And there are sufficiently great differences, particularly in relation to the status of labour, between a democratic capitalist country and one under a fascist dictatorship to necessitate a sharp chronological demarcation. The present chapter is thus divided into two parts: the Weimar Republic and Nazi Germany.

The Weimar Republic

(1) The Background

The clue to much that has happened in post-war Germany is to be sought in the conditions in which modern industrial capitalism first developed there. During the seventeenth century, Germany had ceased to be a factor of any consequence in the commercial development of the world, and for nearly 250 years she remained outside the main stream of capitalist expansion. In 1848, she was still without national union; there existed thirty-six independent states, including five kingdoms, each possessing its own laws, customs duties, currency and system of weights and measures. The customs union of 1834 had only imperfectly overcome these barriers in the way of a large national market. Economically, Germany was a predominantly agricultural country; before the 1848 revolution, only a quarter of the population lived in towns and over two-thirds were engaged in agriculture. In marked contrast to France (which was also still largely agricultural) Germany was, with the exception of certain parts in the south and west, a country of large estates. In the second half of the nineteenth century, when measures of agrarian reform had already been adopted, between 64 and 80 per cent. of the land in the eastern provinces was in the hands of large landowners. Until the war peasant proprietorship made little progress in any but the western areas.

Industry developed very slowly and in the middle of last century handicraft production was still predominant. A modern working class was only beginning to exist. But factory production made rapid strides during the second half of the century and by 1914 Germany had caught up with her older rivals. All the relevant figures show the increasing rapidity of this development. Between 1845 and 1880 the length of railways increased from 2,131 km. to 33,865 km. In about the same period the output of coal increased from 6·5 million to 59 million tons, that of pig-iron from 400,000 to 2·7 million tons and that of steel from 1·3 million to over ten million tons. Germany's foreign trade rose in the same period from a total value of 2,000 million marks to nearly 6,000 million. The increase, though not always at a similar rate, continued during the subsequent decades, and during the twenty years preceding the war Germany's production grew much faster than that of England, as the following approximate figures show:

Per cent. Increase 1895–1913

	Coal	*Iron Ore*	*Pig Iron*	*Steel*
Germany	167	192	249	252
England	52	27	33	131

Other facts also illustrate Germany's entry into the field of highly developed industrial nations. Concentration in industry made rapid strides. Between 1882 and 1907, the number of people employed in small workshops rose by 25 per cent., in large factories by over 200 per cent. and in the largest undertakings by 350 per cent. Similarly, there was an increase in the number of combines and other monopolistic arrangements. In 1890 there were in Germany 137 cartels, in 1913 there were over 600. The intimate connection between the banks and industry, the very great and very rapid increase in foreign investments (German capital invested abroad rose by 250 per cent. between 1902 and 1914 to a total of 44,000 million marks) and the increasing interest in colonial development showed that, economically, Germany was in no way behind those who had started earlier.

The social and political structure of the state also underwent big changes. By the end of the nineteenth century, Germany had a large industrial working class. In 1895, workers accounted for 50 per cent. of the population; and by 1907, when the last pre-war occupational census was taken, the figure had risen to 76 per cent. There was a similar rise in the proportion occupied by the middle classes. From 25 per cent. in 1895, their share in the total population rose to 34 per cent. in 1907. The large landowners and the upper industrial and commercial classes formed, before the war, only a little over 1 per cent. of the German people.

Simultaneously with the growth of capitalism, there took place some progress towards the establishment of democratic parliamentary government. Many of the outward forms of popular representative government were present in pre-war Germany. But although many of the elementary civil liberties and social reforms had been wrung out of the absolute monarchy and although the franchise had been gradually extended, parliament in pre-war Germany was not fully representative of the real class struggle. Not only did parliament reflect imperfectly the growing strength of the working-class movement, it did not even show the industrial and commercial bourgeoisie to be in possession of full political power. As late as 1914 the battle against feudal survivals had not been decisively fought. A large part of political power was still in the hands of the Emperor, the Junkers and the upper ranks of the army and bureaucracy. The social struggle in pre-war Germany was thus of a twofold character: it aimed at the completion of the liberal revolution which had been a part of the objective of the fight for national union; and it was also a struggle against capitalism by a proletariat, more or less clearly inspired by socialist ideas.

The German working-class movement, like that of other countries, derives from two sources: the spontaneous struggle against the evils of the early factory system, and the revolutionary interpretation of the liberal ideas of the eighteenth and nineteenth centuries. In both its economic and political aspects, the German labour movement, like the capitalist system which gave it birth, appeared late on the scene. But it was precisely because of this lateness that many of the fundamental problems of labour have found their clearest expression in Germany. Working men's associations, often developed out of craft guilds and gradually taking on to themselves the attributes of trade unions, can be found in Germany in the first half of the nineteenth century. In 1848, the first attempt was made to unite many of these scattered associations in a central organization. The *Deutsche Arbeiterverbrüderung* which resulted from this early attempt was mainly inspired by the ideals of the friendly society. But it gave a great impetus to the formation of individual unions which had wider aims, such as the establishment of minimum wages and maximum hours and the introduction of a general system of social insurance. And it is significant that Simon Buttermilch (known as Stefan Born), one of the founders of the *Arbeiterverbrüderung*, was a member of the Communist League and a friend of Marx and Engels.

For the next few decades, progress in working-class organization proceeded on political rather than on economic lines. A large number of educational societies (Bildungsvereine) for working men was formed under the guidance of the liberal *Fortschrittspartei*. In 1863, a number of these societies formed themselves into a separate party, the *Allgemeiner Deutscher Arbeiterverein*. This was under the leadership of Lassalle, and was the first independent political working-class organization. It later became one of the foundation stones of the German social-democratic party. Both Lassalle and the later leader of the *Arbeiterverein*, Schweitzer, were strongly opposed to the formation of trade unions, but Schweitzer had eventually to make some attempt to cater for the growing demand. Meanwhile, the individual trade unions, embodying a considerable Marxian influence, developed, and some of the liberal associations whose theory was one of harmony also continued to exist. Many of the unions in Schweitzer's party, together with other unions which had come under the influence of August Bebel and Wilhelm Liebknecht and which had joined the Marxist First International, formed themselves in 1869 into the *Sozialdemokratische Arbeiterpartei*. Until 1875, this party (generally referred to as the *Eisenacher*, after the place at which its constituent congress was held) and the *Arbeiterverein* continued to exist side by side. There were serious differences of opinion between them, not only in relation to socialist theory but also in relation to questions of organization, trade unions and, above all, the problems of national union. With the achievement of this union, many of the immediate tactical differences disappeared and in 1875, at Gotha, the two parties amalgamated.

Trade unions acquired a more socialist character from that time onwards and already in 1887 there were at least twenty-five central organizations of unions of this kind, comprising about 50,000 members. From 1878 to 1890 the working-class movement came under the ban of Bismarck's anti-socialist laws. Not only the party but all individual trade unions were dissolved, including the non-socialist ones. Under the camouflage of friendly societies or skittle clubs, many working men's associations managed to survive and, when the anti-socialist laws were repealed in 1890, the re-establishment of the political and economic branches of the working-class movement was comparatively rapid. In that year, there were formed the *Sozialdemokratische Partei Deutschlands* and the *Generalkommission der Gewerkschaften Deutschlands*, which remained the chief organizations of the German working-class movement until the war. They both grew in strength and in 1914 the social democratic party polled nearly four and a half million votes, or one-third of the total electorate. In the same year the so-called free trade unions, organized in the *Generalkommission*, had a membership of over two million, an annual income of seventy-one million marks, and an annual outlay in benefits to its members of forty-eight million marks.

While the social-democratic party was the only political working-class organization, there were a number of non-socialist trade unions, though these were considerably less important than the free trade unions. The Christian trade unions, organized in the *Gesamtverband der christlichen Gewerkschaften*, had, in 1914, 283,000 members, an annual income of

5·8 million marks and a total expenditure on benefits of 2·4 million. The liberal *Deutsche Gewerkvereine* (*Hirsch-Duncker*) had in the same year only 78,000 members, an annual income of 2·5 million marks, and annual benefit payments of 1·6 million marks.

By 1914, a certain amount of social legislation had been passed; but Germany was still behind England in the extent to which the state had been forced to concede the workers' claim for better conditions. At the beginning of the present century, the eleven-hour day was still the legal norm for adult female workers. The employment of women in occupations now considered unsuitable was common. Factory legislation was in its infancy; and measures for the prevention of accidents and for the provision of ventilation and proper washing facilities were wholly inadequate. Payment of wages in kind, arbitrary fines, and greatly restricted rights of association and assembly also proclaimed the backwardness of social policy.

In the field of social insurance, greater progress had been achieved. A beginning had already been made in the last two decades of the nineteenth century. In 1883 the first health insurance scheme (which was of very limited scope) was adopted. It was not until 1911 that a general compulsory system of health insurance was established. Similar progress was made with accident insurance, the first attempt dating from 1884, and with old-age pensions, which were first introduced in 1889. In 1911, the existing laws relating to all three branches of insurance were extended and consolidated; but unemployment insurance was still a notable omission. Nor had any progress been made with the recognition of collective bargaining and the establishment of standard rates of wages. A number of highly skilled craft unions, particularly the printers, had propagated the idea of the standard "tariff" in the second half of the nineteenth century; but the trade union movement in general did not adopt it as an integral part of its programme until the beginning of the present century. Employers, however, remained hostile; and the attitude of the state was negative.

With the stress of the war, this and other branches of social legislation received a considerable impetus. In 1916, as part of the Auxiliary Service Act, compulsory works committees were set up and a state system of conciliation begun; and in 1918, the eight-hour day was introduced. In the same year, the state recognized collective bargaining between organizations of employers and employed.

This brief sketch may serve as a background to the account of Germany's post-war development which is to follow. It shows that by 1914 German capitalism had made astonishing advances from its small and late beginnings, and that labour, too, had grown in power and had succeeded in obtaining many concessions. And it is important to remember the consequences of Germany's late start. The hothouse development of its economy in the fifty years preceding the war left many characteristic features and problems. It accounts for the intimate connection between the state, industry, and finance which has always marked German capitalism. It accounts also for the policy of protectionism and for the earlier and more rapid growth of combines and monopolies. It explains also the unresolved conflict between the bourgeoisie and the remnants of feudalism which showed itself in political struggles over representation, recruitment for the public service and civil liberties, and in the economic conflict over agrarian and fiscal policy.

The German working-class movement has also undergone a characteristic development. From the very beginning, the choice between the "reformist" and the revolutionary aims has urgently faced German labour. In spite of the union of 1875, a deep division remained between those who were prepared to collaborate with the capitalist state and those who wished to extend the daily struggle of the workers into a fight for the overthrow of capitalism. For a time this division could remain below the surface; but the issues of the war and the post-war period brought it again to the fore.

(2) Post-War Economic Development

The economic history of the Weimar Republic may be conveniently divided into three phases: inflation, lasting until the end of 1923; recovery, from 1924 to 1929; and the subsequent depression which culminated in the coming into power of the national-socialist party. As a result of the war,

German capitalism, hitherto one of the most powerful competitors in world economy, found itself forced back into very narrow confines. The loss of colonies, though perhaps not of as great importance as other losses, deprived German capital of highly desirable sources of monopolistic profits. It cost Germany her substantial foreign investments and it robbed her of economic and strategic bases for further imperial expansion.

The loss of German territory in Europe was possibly even more serious. With Alsace-Lorraine, Upper Silesia, and other areas, Germany lost a considerable portion of her mineral resources, heavy industries, and markets. It is estimated that 43 per cent. of the capacity of her blast furnaces and 37 per cent. of that of her steel mills were situated in these territories. Through the destruction of Austria-Hungary and the establishment of a series of independent states, which endeavoured to buttress their new-found independence with measures of economic nationalism, Germany also lost a large pseudo-colonial area. This was a territory which on account of its economic backwardness and its political and military dependence was ideally suited to be the vassal of the more advanced capitalist system of its neighbours.

Crippling reparations burdens, measured at first in astronomical figures, added to the problems created by war finance and war-time distortion of the productive system. A national debt thirty times as great as in 1913, a note-issue which had grown from 6,000 million marks in 1913 to 22,000 million marks in 1918, a reparations obligation, fixed in 1921 at 132,000 million marks, and the destruction of much of her foreign trade through customs barriers combined to bring about a violent inflation which finally reduced the German currency to one million-millionth part of its pre-war value.

We shall see later what were the social and political consequences of this development. At this stage it may be noted that industry remained seriously disorganized during the inflation period. Its main lack was working capital. The decline in the purchasing power of wage earners and the need for an export surplus to meet the reparations payments forced industry to concentrate on export markets which were becoming less and less accessible. Production during this period never recovered to its pre-war level, as the following indices show:

1913	1919	1920	1921	1922	1923
100	53	62	78	89	56

Technical efficiency diminished during this period. The depreciated currency prevented imports of manufactured goods, monopolistic arrangements were increasing under the stimulus of inflationary speculation, and working capital was lacking. All these factors removed the incentive to improve plant and machinery.

Superficially, industry seemed to be very active, particularly in 1922. The rapid depression of the currency lightened and sometimes completely wiped out the real burden of any loans which firms had raised. Other costs, such as wages, lagged behind the rising prices and also widened the profit margins. The large, highly-integrated concerns especially were able to make full use of this situation and become wealthy through borrowing. But these financial advantages were more than offset by substantial disadvantages in production. Technique, as has been pointed out, did not improve as rapidly as it did elsewhere (the low cost of labour also made mechanization less attractive); and the "flight into goods," which caused the investment of large amounts of borrowed money in plant and buildings, caused a marked increase in productive capacity which subsequent developments made it difficult to employ. It drained the country still further of working capital which was already seriously deficient.

The inflation also altered the structure of industry. It led to a considerable increase in the number of individual firms. At one time, this is said to have been four or five times as large as in 1913 and, although many of these new enterprises afterwards disappeared, the number remained swollen to twice the pre-war figure until the depression. At the same time, concentration of control through cartels and combines proceeded apace, stimulated by the inflationary conditions and by the disruption of established connections, particularly in the coal and iron and steel industries, caused by the territorial changes. Most characteristic of the period was less the extension of the cartel type, or even of the horizontal combine, than the great increase in vertical or multilateral combination—the megalomaniac

Konzernbildung of which Stinnes will always remain the symbol. Many of these concerns collapsed during the post-inflation crisis. But combines, horizontal and vertical, remained in larger number in the coal, iron and steel, potash, copper and similar industries. In the manufacturing industries, the combines which survived were generally of the horizontal type and more limited in scope, but the chemical industry was already beginning to be subject to the series of combinations which were ultimately to result in the gigantic trust—the *I. G. Farben.*

The inflationary period came to an end in 1924 after the settlement of the reparations problem by the Dawes Plan and the loans associated with it, the stabilization of the mark, and the deflation with which it was accompanied. But the real cause of the recovery movement between 1924 and 1929 was the great influx of foreign capital into Germany. In spite of the scaling down of the reparations payments and the Dawes loan, Germany's need of a large export surplus to meet her foreign obligations remained very pressing. Not only would such an export surplus have been difficult to achieve in the nationalistic post-war world, the attempt to create it would have involved a deflationary movement of such severity that the German social structure, already weakened by the inflation, would have collapsed under the strain. Foreign loans were the remedy. It is estimated that between 1924 and 1929 Germany borrowed 25,000 million marks from abroad. The amount of Germany's foreign investments which were resumed during that period is estimated at less than 10,000 million marks, leaving a net addition to Germany's foreign debt of 15,000 million marks.

The U.S.A., Great Britain, Holland, Switzerland and, to a less extent, France and Sweden, were the sources of these funds. Their distribution over different types of German borrowers shows that nearly one-third went to private enterprises, and nearly one-fifth to public and semi-public enterprises of states, provinces and municipalities. The rest is fairly evenly divided among the federal government and its enterprises, and among states, provinces and municipalities. These loans enabled Germany to rebuild and expand her productive machine, to avoid the immediate deterioration of the standard of living which would have followed a deflation, and to meet her foreign commitments, in spite of the fact that 1926 was the only year throughout the period in question when exports exceeded imports.

During the period Germany's foreign trade expanded greatly. Imports rose from 77·4 per cent. of their 1913 value in 1925 to 90 per cent. in 1928, the comparable figures for exports being 58·3 per cent. and 77·2 per cent. Production also recovered: taking 1925 as the base year, the index of production stood at 95 per cent. in 1926, but rose to 120 per cent. in each of the subsequent two years and to 122 per cent. in 1929. Between 1926 and 1928, the number of firms increased by 11·1 per cent. (after having declined from its very high inflation level), and the numbers of workers employed by 20 per cent. There was a more than proportionate increase in the size of the larger undertakings, as measured by the number of workers employed, percentage of real assets held, or amount of machine power used. Another index of industrial expansion is the growth of new investment in capital goods (about 30,000 million marks), the increase in stocks, and the much larger amount written off for depreciation in this period of intensive rationalization.

The spread of combines, retarded by the liquidation during the immediate post-stabilization crisis of many of the speculative growths of the inflation, began again in 1926. This time the horizontal combine predominated, because it was in a more favourable position to borrow money abroad. The cartel movement was greatly intensified and so was the linking-up of the banks and industry. Efficiency also increased and in many branches of industry Germany soon surpassed other countries. The rationalization movement, as it came to be called, included a variety of aims, such as standardization and simplification of products, the adoption of methods of scientific management, vocational training, and the avoidance of waste through co-operation between industries. Sometimes it was defined so as definitely to cover industrial combination. But even where it did not deliberately have this aim, it generally encouraged still further the formation of combines.

The recovery of production, while all-embracing, was not uniform. The following figures show the movement in the principal industries:

	1913 (allowing for territorial changes)	1924 million tons	1928
Coal	140·8	118·8	150·9
Raw iron and blast furnaces	10·9	7·8	11·8
Raw steel	11·8	9·7	14·5
	(not allowing for territorial changes)	(million marks)	
Cotton	2,350	3,720	4,490
Wool	1,720	2,390	2,570
Chemicals	2,400	3,000	4,000

In general, though the basic heavy industries expanded very considerably during the period, the most striking advance, particularly from the point of view of competitive strength in world markets, was that of the newer trades, such as the chemical and the electro-technical industries. The total number of employed persons increased by 1·5 million between December 1925 and December 1929. But as we shall see again later, Germany also suffered substantial unemployment throughout the recovery period. But this, together with other indications of weakness in the economic position, did not create any misgivings. Most observers at the time summed up Germany's economic development as one of unexampled recovery.

This is not the place to discuss the causes of the depression upon which Germany, together with the rest of the world, entered in 1929. Whatever other causes different theories of crises may enumerate, it is certain that Germany's post-war economic relations with the rest of the world were highly abnormal. For the first time the economic and financial methods of imperial expansion—capital exports—were applied to a country whose own economic structure made it an inevitable rival in that very expansion. The capitalist system in Germany was sufficiently far advanced to make it impossible to treat her for any length of time as a colony. Germany's economic structure was too much akin to that of her lenders. She was herself a powerful competitor for world markets of industrial goods, for sources of raw materials and for profitable opportunities of capital investment. She had, moreover, a powerfully organized working class, used to a fairly high standard of living, which could not easily be prevented from struggling against the attempts to provide, in addition to the profits for German capital, a foreign " tribute " as well.

So long as the large net influx of foreign funds continued, the danger inherent in the situation was not obvious. But the capital which found its way into Germany was, originally, short-term money, a part of the international short-loan fund which in the disturbed post-war conditions was highly " nervous " and volatile. It was always liable to be withdrawn, and such withdrawals would face German industry with the necessity of finding precisely that which it had not got: liquid capital. In 1929, as the result, first, of the boom in Wall Street, which attracted all available funds into speculation and, later, of the slump which was so severe as to cause a general scramble for liquidity, the influx of foreign capital into Germany diminished, ceased and, finally, turned into a panic withdrawal. By July 1931, 3,000 million marks out of a total of 11,000 million marks short-term debt had been withdrawn and the financial crisis had broken.

From that time onwards, the depression continued to run its course in Germany and the rest of the world. The following indices illustrate the extent of the decline; they also show that in some respects the depression was more severe in Germany than in the world as a whole:

Industrial Production: 1928 = 100

	1930	1931	1932
Germany	87·1	68·5	54
World	96	87	77

International trade : Per cent. fall in values 1928–1932

	Imports	*Exports*
Germany	68	50
World	60	62

The fall in the German production figures was largely accounted for by a fall in the output of capital goods, as the following figures show:

Output of capital goods (Germany) 1928 = 100

1930	1931	1932
84	54·2	35·4

The number of insured persons in employment also fell very rapidly:

	'000
July 1929	18,539
July 1930	16,843
July 1931	15,020
July 1932	12,756

Among the changes in the industrial structure consequent upon the depression, a fresh impetus to combination may be noted, as also a further strengthening of the bonds between state and industry. The threatened collapse caused the state to intervene first in banking and later in many industries, notably in iron and steel and shipping. Fresh funds were put at the disposal of the firms concerned and the government acquired, nominally at any rate, a certain measure of control.

Though freed by the Lausanne agreement of 1932 from the reparations burden, the depression faced Germany once again with the task of adjusting herself to the economic results of the war. The deflationary way of doing this—difficult, if not impossible, to achieve—had been obviated for a time by the capital imports from abroad. Now the government attempted to institute a deflation of appropriate magnitude, in spite of the serious risk of social upheaval which this entailed. This was the policy of the emergency decrees of the so-called "presidial cabinets" which preceded Hitler. Drastic cutting of costs, by reduction of wages and social services, together with an effort to mitigate the effects of this reduction by price control, was the technique adopted. It did not lead out of the depression, but only intensified the political struggle. Eventually, in 1932, this policy was supplemented by inflationary measures, such as tax-remission for firms increasing the number of workers employed, and the creation of fresh credit facilities for industry.

It is impossible to say how successful as a palliative this policy would have been, since it was not tried for long enough. It is nevertheless a fact that a number of indices seem to show that, by December 1932, Germany, together with the rest of the world, was beginning to recover slightly. Production, which had reached its lowest level in August 1932, rose by December of that year by 10 per cent.; in the comparable period of 1931 it had fallen by 20 per cent. The index of sensitive commodity prices, at its lowest in June 1932, had risen by over 10 per cent. in December. And the index of share prices rose in the same period by over 20 per cent. As we shall see, the figures which indicate the position of the worker did not develop in a similar way. But on the basis of the figures mentioned, it is possible to say that the depression passed its lowest point in the second half of 1932.

(3) The Position of Labour

In the brief account given above of Germany's economic development between 1920 and 1932, nothing has been said about the fate of the working class. The question we now have to examine is: how did the German worker fare in this up and down of post-war business fluctuations? The following problems are relevant to this question: employment and unemployment, wage rates, earnings and hours, cost of living and the social services. A survey of the indices under these headings makes some general appraisal of the development of the standard of living possible.

Before the war, unemployment was slight: in 1913, it accounted for only 2·9 per cent. of the trade union membership. Although the unemployment problem became very serious only after the stabilization, it is not true to say that the decline in the standard of living caused by the inflation was compensated for by increased and steadier employment during the period of currency depreciation. Throughout the first post-war phase, unemployment remained substantially above the pre-war level. Between January and October 1923, the figure was 5·5 per cent. of the trade union membership; during the next two months it jumped to 16·2 per cent.; and nearly 1·5 million people were then in receipt of relief.

There can be no doubt about the very serious decline in the earnings of the German workers during the inflation period. The time-lag in the adjustment of money-wages to rising prices is notorious; and Germany was no exception. Frequent attempts were made to raise wages in order to keep pace with the rising cost of living (which at the beginning of 1921 was 11·8 times, and at the end of 1923 1,247,000 million times the pre-war figure); but until the latter part of 1923, wages were based on the price-index of the preceding month. The result was a large and rapid decline in real wages. It is estimated that the average real wage (taking 1913 as the base year) was seventy-five in 1922 and sixty-five in 1923. This average conceals moreover a fairly wide range; and very many classes of labourers were so badly off that they could barely maintain half a reasonable standard of subsistence. Rent-control, bread subsidies, and, in some instances, increased employment, were quite inadequate as off-setting factors. And it has been suggested that if the average decline in real earnings of the salary and wage-earning classes is put at 500 marks per annum (a not unreasonable estimate) the "contribution" of the salariat and workers to the "forced saving" of the inflation was between twenty-four and twenty-eight million marks.

The recovery period which followed the inflation raised the condition of the German worker above the unbearably low level which it had reached in 1923. But it would be a mistake to suppose that the standard of living of pre-war days was substantially exceeded. Employment increased during the years of relative prosperity; but unemployment, though fluctuating, became a permanent and disturbing feature of the German economy. Already in the first quarter of 1924, as an immediate accompaniment of the currency stabilization, unemployment reached 22·7 of the trade union membership—the highest pre-depression figure.

In the subsequent two years, it fell again, as production grew under the stimulus of the influx of foreign capital. But the recession of 1925–6 sent unemployment figures up again. From 1927 to the end of 1928, the figures fell once more; but there was a sharp rise in December 1928, due to a temporary depression caused largely by the political difficulties over reparations negotiations. A further fall occurred in 1929, but the cessation of foreign loans and other factors heralded the coming depression and the year ended with a very heavy unemployment figure. These movements are shown in the following table:

Per cent of Trade Union members unemployed			*Total Unemployed*
	Wholly	*Partially*	
June 1925	3·5	5·2	401,000
Dec. 1925	19·4	19·8	1,712,000
June 1926	18·1	17·2	2,081,000
Dec. 1926	16·7	7·3	2,127,000
June 1927	6·3	2·7	1,061,000
Dec. 1927	12·9	3·1	1,714,000
June 1928	6·2	5·9	1,075,000
Dec. 1928	16·7	7·5	2,265,000
June 1929	8·5	6·7	1,260,000
Dec. 1929	20·1	8·5	2,851,000

Thus it will be seen that, in spite of the recovery, unemployment, though fluctuating, remained fairly high during the five years concerned. On an average it was over 11 per cent. of the trade union membership, i.e., between four and five times the pre-war figure. One of the causes of this high level of unemployment is to be found in the changes in the population and its age composition. In 1923, the population of Germany was about sixty-three million, or 6 per cent. less than in 1913; at the same time, Germany had lost 13 per cent. of her territory, much of which was particularly highly industrialized. In addition, the older age groups, those classed officially as forming the labour supply, had increased their share of the total from 48 per cent. in 1907 to 57 per cent. in 1925.

Much more important was the appearance of technological unemployment and the simultaneous "proletarianization" of large sections of the middle classes. Deprived, as the result of the inflation, of their capital, many small independent entrepreneurs had to join the army of wage-earners; and they were joined by those members of middle-class families whose savings and fixed incomes had dwindled and who had, therefore, to re-enter the process of production. But the rationalization movement, with its formation of combines and increased pace of mechanization, led to a relative decline in the demand for labour; and a large industrial reserve army became an integral part of Germany's post-war economy.

Nor was the rise in wages between 1924 and 1929 large

enough to compensate for the much more precarious conditions of employment. The average weekly tariff rates which were 28·65 marks in 1913, were still only 25·75 at the beginning of 1925; by the end of 1928 they had risen to 46·35 marks. In order to ascertain the significance of this rise as far as the standard of living is concerned, we have, of course, to take into account the changes in the cost of living. Taking 1913–4 as the base year, the index stood at 127·6 in 1924, 139·8 in 1925, 141·2 in 1926, 147·6 in 1927 and 151·7 in 1928. On the basis of these figures, real wages are estimated to have moved as follows:

1913 = 100

1924	1925	1926	1927	1928
81	97	96	98	104

According to this estimate, real wages appear to have reached and just exceeded the pre-war level by 1928. Actually, this calculation ignores a number of factors which off-set much of the apparent increase. Since the estimate is based on average wage rates, it ignores not only the spread between rates for different industries and different classes of skill, but also the difference between wage-rates and earnings. This difference becomes particularly important when considering a period in which unemployment and short time were heavy. When losses caused by these two factors are added to the increased deductions on account of the special wages tax introduced in 1925, social insurance, trade unions and illness, the rise in real wages becomes much less marked. We must, moreover, remember that computations of real wages are based on cost of living indices which are notoriously inadequate. The German index appears to be particularly subject to the usual defects, which arise from the fact that the original weighting of the budget on which the calculation is based becomes irrelevant with the passing of time. Rent, for example, which was originally given a weight of 20·35 per cent., rose much less than other items, owing to rent control; while transport costs, which stood in June 1928 at 191·8 per cent. of the pre-war level, were lumped together with all miscellaneous expenditure which was given a total weight of only 9·28 per cent.

The impression, then, of very high real wages during the recovery period needs serious revision. We can sum up by saying that real wages undoubtedly rose from the very low levels of the inflation, but that they only just reached pre-war figures when the depression set in. This impression is confirmed when we look at the German national income. According to Professor Angell's estimate, the national income rose by over 55 per cent. between 1913 and 1928, but if changes in prices are allowed for, this increase is reduced to barely more than 12 per cent. There is no evidence to show that the share going to the working class increased during that period. The proportion of the total income paid in wages and in salaries was practically the same in 1928 as it was in 1924. If we take into account the larger proportion of people in both the wage-earning and the salary-earning group, our conclusion concerning the position of the working class is strengthened. Professor Angell is of the opinion that the distribution of the national income in Germany was particularly unfavourable, i.e., that an extremely large number of people were in receipt of incomes well below the *per capita* average.

Whatever the extent of the advance which the working class enjoyed during the recovery there is no doubt that it was lost during the depression. The following are the figures for unemployment :

Per cent. of Trade Union members unemployed			*Total in January*
	wholly	*on short time*	000's
1930	24·4	16·2	3,218
1931	37	2·7	4,887
1932	48	24·2	6,042

Earnings declined continuously after 1928, showing a particularly sharp fall from 1929 onwards. Taking 1928 as the base year, hourly tariff rates in January of each year were as follows:

1929	1930	1931	1932
103·1	107·1	106·7	89·6

But in addition to this reduction in standard rates, piece and overtime rates were cut down. The working of short time became more general, and the gigantic increase in unemployment still further diminished earnings. Already at the end of 1931, the reduction in the earnings of industrial workers is estimated to have amounted to 40 per cent. as compared with 1929, while the official cost of living figure had only fallen by 13 per cent. Thus real earnings had been severely reduced even before the compulsory cutting-down by means of emergency decrees had exerted its full force. In 1932 the fourth emergency decree cut all wages (regardless of the existence of collective agreements) by between 10 and 15 per cent. ; and the Papen programme, which contained a mixture of deflationary and inflationary measures, allowed a further reduction of as much as 12·5 per cent. off tariff rates in return for the employment of more workers.

It is necessary to supplement this account of employment and earnings with some mention of the social services in the post-war era, before the picture of the standard of living is complete. The progress of social legislation in the Weimar Republic will be discussed in detail in the next section, which deals with the working-class movement. Here, a few indications of the extent to which living standards were affected by social services may be given. The revolution of November 1918 gave a great stimulus to the workers' demands for improved conditions guaranteed by the state. Foremost among these was social insurance. With the addition, in 1927, of a compulsory general unemployment insurance scheme, all the four branches of insurance, sickness, accident, old age and employment, were covered. The scope of the unemployment scheme was, however, much less wide than that of the British scheme (although clerical workers earning not more than 6,000 marks per annum were included), the percentage of the total working population to which it applied being 57·2 as against 67·4 in Great Britain.

There can be little doubt that the extension of social insurance was substantial and that it benefited the worker in the pre-depression period. In 1913, the cost of social insurance was 1,248 million marks, in 1924, 1,855 million marks, and in 1928, well over 5,000 million marks. The cost of unemployment benefits alone was 220 million marks in 1913, 439 million marks in 1926 and 850 million marks in 1928. During the depression, however, a considerable reduction in benefits took place. This reduction was particularly striking in unemployment insurance. The increase of unemployment during the depression placed, of course, a heavy financial burden on the insurance fund as the following figures show:

000,000 *marks*

Financial year April 1 to March 31	*Expenditure*	*Own Income*	*Deficit (−) Surplus (+)*
1928–9	1,192	843	−349
1929–30	1,338	890	−448
1930–31	1,807	1,194	−613
1931–32	1,266	1,289	+23

Thus it will be seen that until 1931 there was a steadily increasing deficit, an experience which was shared by the unemployment insurance fund of Great Britain. Direct and indirect steps were taken to remove this burden. In October, 1931, the period during which standard benefit was payable was reduced from twenty-six to twenty weeks. In 1932 a number of decrees effected substantial reductions in the scale of benefits. A complicated system was introduced by which benefits were made dependent on the size of the locality in which the applicant lived (there were three categories), as well as on already existing differences which were based on wage-groups. The estimated average reduction which resulted was 23 per cent. There were similar reductions in transitional benefits (*Krisenfürsorge*), the rates under this heading being maxima which had not to exceed local poor relief scales. In addition, a means test, hitherto reserved for married women, was introduced and rigorously applied.

The net effect of these measures was a remarkable change in the proportions of the numbers in the different classes of benefit as the following table shows:

	Of all unemployed, there were in receipt of:		
	Insurance benefit %	*Transitional benefit* %	*Poor relief and no benefit at all* %
January 1929	81	5	14
January 1930	69	8	23
January 1931	52	17	31
January 1932	31·2	26·4	42·4

In addition, it should be noted that those not in receipt of any relief at all, who formed a negligible proportion in 1929, accounted for no less than 14 per cent. in 1932.

To sum up, the standard of living of the German worker, after being greatly reduced during the inflation, recovered subsequently to a considerable extent. Though real wages just before the depression were probably not higher than before the war, a number of other improvements had been introduced. The eight-hour day, the more comprehensive system of social insurance, better laws relating to hygiene, safety and the employment of women and children, and improvements in the educational system must all be put on the credit side. But the advances of the years 1924 to 1929 were shown to have been insecurely founded once they were attacked during the depression. Falling real wages and declining social services inevitably point to a decline in the standard of living, which statistics of consumption and the evidence of observers during the critical years amply illustrate.

(4) The Working-Class Movement

We must now examine the actions of labour in defence of its interests in the Weimar Republic. The development of the trade unions, the growth of labour legislation and the relation between political ideas and working-class organizations are the problems to be analysed.

The general strength of the trade union movement increased greatly after the war. The republican constitution was strongly influenced by the demands of the organized working class, and although it did not fulfil the socialist aims of the revolutionary sections of labour, it represented a great advance on the semi-feudal, absolutist conditions of 1914. Article 157 of the Weimar constitution put labour under the special protection of the state. Article 159 guaranteed the right of association for the purpose of safeguarding and improving labour conditions. And in subsequent articles a number of other fundamental rights, such as social insurance, an equal share with employers in the regulation of economic life under the aegis of the state, and guaranteed free time to employees for the exercise of public duties were added. Together with the establishment of the eight-hour day, these constitutional guarantees represented a first instalment of the fulfilment of the claims of the people's commissars in the November revolution.

Not only the state, the employers too, were forced, at any rate in the immediate post-war years, to concede many of the claims of organized labour. In November 1918 an agreement was signed between the central trade union organizations and the employers' associations which established a Central Joint Council (*Arbeitsgemeinschaft*) on the basis of certain recognized principles. These included recognition of trade unions, unfettered freedom of association, the common regulation of the condition of employment, the eight-hour day and the negotiation of collective agreements. The *Arbeitsgemeinschaft* broke down under the strain of the inflation. Many employers obstructed its working, or tried to pervert its purposes by the fostering of concealed company unions. Many trade unions were reluctant to relinquish their socialist aims through this kind of association of capital and labour. Some of the purposes of this Central Joint Council were, however, taken over by the Works Councils which had statutory backing. More will be said about these presently.

Whatever progress had been made since the war, either in direct relations between workers and employers or through legislation, had been entirely due to continual pressure by the trade unions. The effectiveness of this pressure was an indication of the growing strength of the unions. The three principal central organizations after the war were: *Allgemeiner Deutscher Gewerkschafts-Bund* (formed in 1919 as the successor to the *Generalkommission*), the *Gesamtverband der christlichen Gewerkschaften* and the *Deutsche Gewerksvereine* (*Hirsch-Duncker*). Of these, the *A.D.G.B.* was always far and away the most important; but all three showed a marked increase in membership after the war as compared with pre-war days. And there was a steady rise during the inflation.

From 1923 onwards, membership of all three classes of trade unions declined; but some of the ground won was retained, the figures for the *A.D.G.B.* remaining at between four and five million up to the depression. The following table shows the development of the three trade union associations in the post-war period up to the depression:

I is the *A.D.G.B.* II is the *Gesamtverband.* III is the *Gewerkvereine (H.—D.)*

Year	*Membership in Thousands*			*Total income in Thousand Marks*			*% of Expenditure on Benefits other than on Strikes, etc.*			*% of Expenditure on Strike Benefits*		
	I	II	III	I	II	III	I	II	III	I	II	III
1914	2,076	283	78	71,033	5,864	2,545	60·4	40·9	59·5	7·6	5·8	11·9
1919	5,479	858	190	247,307	25,615	5,511	22·1	14·2	31·9	22·7	9·1	18·3
1920	7,890	1,077	226	747,114	84,815	12,510	18·7	13·9	21·4	20·5	10·7	18·7
1921	7,568	986	225	1,249,248	145,394	23,208	18·3	14·9	16·5	28·4	2	24·3
1922	7,895	1,049	231	10,229,166	1,416,917	—	7·2	11·6	—	14·6	29·8	—
1923	7,138	983	216	—	—	—	—	—	—	—	—	—
1924	4,618	613	147	97,038	9,679	1,705	15	16·5	25·6	242	21·9	15·2
1925	4,156	588	158	147,527	14,060	2,908	26·3	22·7	40·2	23·6	26·4	14·3
1926	3,977	532	163	148,140	15,563	3,439	45·8	37	49	4·5	12·9	3·5
1927	4,150	606	168	182,252	20,815	3,906	31·6	25·3	35·8	8·8	19·6	8·2
1928	4,654	646	169	221,696	24,619	4,098	33	25·1	33·5	17	26·5	21·5
1929	4,906	673	169	251,385	27,634	3,727	41·3	34·2	39	6·3	14·2	8
1930	4,822	659	163	231,655	26,799	3,613	51·2	42·8	58	4·1	11·1	6·2

Thus it will be seen that the fluctuations were fairly uniform; they followed an obvious course: great increase during the immediate post-war years under the stimulus of the revolution, the republican constitution, and the labour disputes of the inflation; and decline after the "normalization" in 1924. From then until the end of the temporary period of business stability, the figures remain fairly constant. But throughout that period all the unions between them covered only a little more than one-third of the labouring population. Of the total, the *A.D.G.B.* accounted for about 86 per cent. in 1928.

As regards their programmes, no marked change from pre-war days had taken place in the minor unions. The *Gesamtverband* represented a federation of various central organizations of Christian trade unions; until 1918 it included all Christian unions, but after that it was confined to organizations of workers only. Clerical employees were organized in two separate unions which, together with the *Gesamtverband*, were federated in the *Deutscher Gewerkschafts-Bund*. The *Gesamtverband*, though including catholic and protestant workers, was largely influenced by catholic social philosophy. It rejected socialism and believed in a state which was conscious of its responsibilities. It had a leaning towards medieval ideas and spoke generally in terms of different social estates (*Stände*) which ought to live in co-partnership. It is not unlikely that the partial similarity of its terminology to that used by national-socialist theorists helped to undermine some of the workers' resistance. Though incomparably inferior in strength to the *A.D.G.B.*, the *Gesamtverband* had a substantial following among certain sections of workers. The following are some of its federated unions which had a large membership, both absolutely and in relation to the free unions.

	Membership 1930 (*in thousands*)	
	Gesamtverband	*A.D.G.B.*
Mining	100	193
Agriculture ...	78	162
Catering	21	31
Tobacco	22	73

In general, it may be said that with the very striking exception of the mining industry and the tobacco trades (workers in the latter had been pioneers of trade unionism in the nineteenth century), the strength of the Christian unions was in agriculture and in the less highly developed capitalist industries.

The *Gewerkvereine* (*H.-D.*) can also be discussed very summarily. Their total membership in 1930 was only one-thirtieth that of the free trade unions. They were proportionately stronger in some highly skilled crafts. The following figures give an indication of these relatively more important unions:

	Membership 1930 (*in thousands*)	
	Gewerkvereine (*H.D.*)	*A.D.G.B.*
Metal trades ...	75	951
Hotels and catering	8	31
Leather	4	35
Barbers	1	4

The programme of the *Gewerkvereine* (*H.D.*) was based on essentially liberal principles. Great emphasis was laid on the friendly society functions of the union. Strikes, though not rejected entirely, were regarded as ultimate weapons, to be employed only when the utmost effort at mediation had failed. Complete independence of political parties was insisted on; and socialist aims were definitely ruled out. On the other hand, the *Gewerkvereine* claimed to be neutral in matters of religion; and they were always very anxious to differentiate themselves from the "yellow" unions. In the course of the post-war period their programmatic statements appeared to have become increasingly nationalist. But they certainly never succeeded in getting beyond the narrow confines which were imposed upon them by their craft-union character and by their strongly reformist outlook.

The *A.D.G.B.* must be regarded as the chief representative of organized labour in the Weimar Republic. In 1930 it had thirty-one affiliated unions with nearly five million members. The following is a list of these unions arranged in order of membership numbers:

	000		000
Metal	951	Stone	63
Public enterprises and transport	683	Painting and Decorating	59
Building	476	Bookbinding	57
Factory	456	Engineers and firemen ...	51
Wood	309	Graphic trades	40
Textiles	288	Leather	35
Railway	248	Catering	31
Mining	193	Saddlery, etc.	30
Food and drink	177	Lithographers	25
Agriculture	162	Musicians	21
Carpentering	106	Hat manufacture ...	17
Printing	90	Dairying	13
Clothing	73	Tilers and slaters ...	11
Tobacco	73	Coppersmiths	7
Boots and shoes	69	Barbers	4
		Chimney sweeps ...	3

The *A.D.G.B.* claimed to base itself on socialist principles, and in 1919, when it was formed, it was one of the strongest supporters of the socialization laws which were to apply to the coal-mining, iron and steel and potash industries. It was composed of national unions; and it saw as its aim to "represent the common trade union interest of the German workers, through the collaboration of its federated national unions." Its methods were: agitation and propaganda, research, education, definition of spheres of different unions, arbitration in cases of conflict, and the furthering of relations with similar organizations in other countries. Like its counterparts, the British T.U.C. and the French *C.G.T.*, the *A.D.G.B.* was composed of national associations only. But it made substantial progress with measures of local association under its own aegis. The local branches of its affiliated unions were obliged to belong to local and district councils which were organs of the *A.D.G.B.* In 1928 and 1929 there were thirteen such district councils and 1,285 local councils comprising 12,188 affiliated union branches with a total of over four million members, i.e., about 86 per cent. of the total membership of the *A.D.G.B.*

The constitution of the *A.D.G.B.* was not unlike that of similar bodies elsewhere. A congress, held as a rule every three years, was the supreme authority. Congress was composed of delegates—one for every 15,000 members—and its method of voting was normally by majority of delegates present. At the request of 100 delegates, however, the block vote was used. Congress elected a committee of fifteen members—seven paid and eight unpaid—which was subject to the general supervision of a council composed of representatives of the executives of affiliated unions. The capitation fee of unions to the *A.D.G.B.* was a 2½ *pfennig* a week for every male adult member. Among its general activities was the issue of a weekly paper, *Gewerkschaftszeitung*, the maintenance of a publishing and bookselling business, and joint control, with clerical unions and co-operative societies, in banking and insurance firms.

In the international sphere, the *A.D.G.B.* was one of the most powerful members of the so-called "Amsterdam" International, the International Federation of Trade Unions. Until 1920 the *A.D.G.B.* had affiliated to it a number of "black-coated" unions, organized in the *Zentralverband der Angestellten.* In 1921 this body joined the *Allgemeiner freier Angestelltenbund;* but this, together with the union of clerical workers, *Allgemeiner Deutscher Beamtenbund*, maintained close contact with the *A.D.G.B.*, all three being pledged to work together. Although many "black-coated" workers' unions were naturally to be found in the camp of the liberal or Christian unions, a very considerable proportion of them—more than in other highly organized countries—were closely linked with the main body of the trade union movement.

The decline in membership after the inflation was caused by the large permanent unemployment and the inability of the *A.D.G.B.* to devise new policies in the face of this situation. But apart from this fundamental limitation, it can be said that much of the work of the *A.D.G.B.* went on as usual. Official statistics claim some achievement in reduction of hours and increase in wages:

Year	*Persons affected* (000)	*Reduction in hours per week*	*Increase in weekly wages* (*marks*)
1924	179	4·5	3·02
1925	670	1·0	2·86
1926	140	2·3	1·42
1927	2,139	3·5	2·26

Most observers are in fact agreed that the rise in money-wages between 1924 and 1929, which has already been referred to, was almost entirely due to continual trade union pressure. The most powerful instrument which the unions could use in this respect was the collective agreement, and there is no doubt that, over the whole period, the scope of collective bargaining increased greatly. In 1926 well over eleven million employees (out of a total in the health insurance scheme of 16·5 million) were covered by collective agreements. The *A.D.G.B.*, in 1927, concluded 1,600 new agreements covering 2·3 million workers and amended or supplemented 2,000 agreements concerning 5·5 million workers. Collective agreements which were recognized by the state in 1918, were legally binding, ran for a stated period of time, and could not—until the measures of the depression period—be revised in a downward direction. But, however successful in the field of wages, the early post-war achievements in regard to hours were soon lost, and this loss contributed to the subsequent weakening and disappearance of the collective agreement.

The great development of collective agreements meant that labour disputes arose generally at the expiry of an agreement when the unions agitated for better conditions. In time, fights for the preservation of existing conditions, threatened by the more subtle means of unfavourable revision of hours, became more common. After the onset of the depression, when living standards were subjected to a frontal attack, disputes assumed a different character. The problem of industrial disputes is so intimately bound up with the statutory conciliation machinery set up after the war that it is better dealt with, together with the question of workers' representation, in connection with the general question of post-war social legislation.

To complete this account of the trade union movement, it

may be said that, although the *A.D.G.B.* included many craft unions or descendants of craft unions, the problem of craft *versus* industrial unions was never so urgent in Germany as in Britain or the U.S.A. On the whole, the unions in post-war Germany were more strongly organized than in other countries and were subject to great central control. In so far as trade union policy may be likened to an attempt at monopolization (the worker in his struggle against the monopoly of capital endeavouring to form a monopoly in order to sell his commodity, labour power, as dearly as possible), the German unions were concerned more with the regulation of price than with the curtailment of supply. The collective bargain and the extensive conciliation and arbitration machinery were the media. Only indirectly through unemployment insurance was supply curtailed by pushing up the " reserve " prices of the labourers.

Before we proceed to discuss the more fundamental problems of trade union policy—which in post-war Germany always involved wider political considerations—it is necessary to look at a few aspects of post-war social legislation. We have already touched upon the consolidated insurance scheme which was established in 1927. It has also been pointed out that the eight-hour day was established as the norm. But in this respect the newly-won position of the working class was soon attacked. The legislation of 1919 provided for a maximum working period of eight hours a day and forty-eight hours a week. In addition, in each week, thirty-six hours' continuous rest (normally between Saturday and Monday) was provided for, night work was much restricted and a Saturday half-day was allowed. There were more favourable provisions covering women and juveniles, as well as dangerous trades.

The 1919 Act laid down general desiderata but was ineffective without detailed legislation establishing practical rules. The first legislation of this kind was the Act of December 1923. But between the end of the war and that date the original intentions had been very considerably undermined. For two years after the original Act a number of separate agreements were reached between employers and trade unions. Some of these were favourable to the workers—on the railways the eight-hour day was accepted, and in coal mining the shift was reduced to seven-and-a-half hours and later to seven hours—but the net result of isolated action was to create a great variety of conditions. This variety was much to the liking of those, like the Ruhr magnates, who were anxious to maintain the longer working hours in order to raise the competitive strength of German industry. In some of the newer, more highly mechanized, and internationally more competitive industries, such as the electrical trades, the employers were more ready to concede the claim for shorter hours.

In 1921 a bill was presented in the Reichstag which aimed at a consolidation of existing practices; but although it maintained the principle of the Washington convention, it introduced very many exceptions. This bill was not passed at the time, but the undermining of the eight-hour day proceeded apace. The trade union and social democratic party leaders were not only unable to stop this process, but many of them did in fact use the same arguments as their opponents (such as the reparations burden) to justify the acceptance of sweeping exceptions to the original norm. The fruit of this policy was the 1923 Act which adopted many of the principles of the 1921 proposals and made provisions even more unfavourable to the workers. Collective agreements providing for more than eight hours were allowed and made binding. Workers were obliged to make up by overtime any deficiency in daily work below eight hours. And overtime of two hours a day on thirty days of the year was allowed.

The net effect of this Act was to abolish the eight-hour day. In 1924 the *A.D.G.B.* took a census of hours worked which showed the following results. Of 2,454,000 workers employed in 46,122 works, 45·3 per cent. of all employees normally worked forty-eight hours a week or less; 8·3 per cent. worked from forty-eight to fifty-one hours; 33·4 per cent. from fifty-one to fifty-four hours; and 13 per cent. above fifty-four hours. It must moreover be remembered that the year in question was one of depression and many factories were on short time.

As the result of pressure, an order was issued in 1925 by the Minister of Labour including blast-furnaces, coke ovens and coal bye-product works in the class of dangerous trades, and insisting on the principle of the eight-hour day. But this order was ineffective and the position continued to deteriorate. In

1927, however, some progress was made. An act of that year strengthened the provisions of the law of 1923 and almost restored the position of 1918-9. The steel interests again resisted, threatening a complete lock-out. The necessary order by the Minister of Labour was, however, given, though it allowed in exceptional cases an interval of six months for the change over to the three eight-hour shifts.

The subsequent onset of the depression displaced the question of hours as an important issue in favour of the more serious problem of unemployment. The struggle between capital and labour became then concerned with the introduction of short time. The Brüning government, in 1931, made great efforts in this direction with a view to spreading employment, but these efforts met with resistance from the workers. In some instances, however, such as a number of oil mills, shortened shifts and lower wages were introduced. The Papen government set up a number of committees to enquire into the possibility of short time in various industries, and when these committees reported in January 1933, they almost invariably mentioned the workers' objection to the lower earnings which short time would involve. It was not until the first year of the national-socialist government that the practice of short time became more widespread.

The most characteristic features of German labour legislation were the works councils and the elaborate machinery for conciliation and arbitration in industrial disputes. The principle of workers' representation was laid down in the constitution itself. And in 1920 an Act established works councils in all undertakings employing not less than twenty persons. Two types of councils, one for salaried employees and one for wage-earners were set up. Their method of election differed for small and large firms: in the former, at least one shop steward was allowed; in the latter, representation varied according to the size of the labour force employed. In addition, district economic councils were formed; and workers, employers, consumers and independent experts were invited on a national scale into the Federal Economic Council (*Reichswirtschaftsrat*).

The function of the works councils was defined in general terms as the protection of the interests of the workers. But largely owing to the fear of the trade unions that the councils might usurp some of their powers, the works councils were not given the right to deal directly with collective agreements on hours or wages. They were limited to advisory function in these matters; and it was made quite clear that they were subordinate to the trade unions. They were, therefore, more concerned with shop conditions and acted in minor disputes concerning these. They were also given the power to nominate one of the directors who, in theory, had exactly the same right as other members of the board. In practice, however, these workers' directors were easily made ineffective by being prevented from acquiring any knowledge of the facts bearing on the policy of the company and by being kept off the more important administrative posts.

The trade unions were extremely suspicious of the 1920 Act. They feared that the new councils would seriously rival their own organization and that they might become either company unions and thus instruments of the employers, or (and this was probably more important) revolutionary weapons of the working-class struggle on the lines of the workers' and soldiers' councils of the immediate post-war period. The struggle over the control of the works councils which developed after 1920 was largely determined by the alignment of different political sections in the labour movement. The main conflict was between the radical section of the working class—led by the communist party and, in the early post-war days, by some syndicalist unions—and the *A.D.G.B.* The former were on the offensive; they wished to capture the councils in order to use them as a counterweight to the reformist and bureaucratic unions. The latter were anxious to preserve their centralized control.

The *A.D.G.B.*, and the clerical unions allied with it, used to the full their organizational superiority. Having failed to get the works councils officially incorporated in the trade union machinery, they proceeded to aim at indirect control; and this they obtained in time. They created special machinery for co-ordinating the work of their members who were on works councils with that of the district committees of the unions. But with the passing of an anti-revolutionary resolution at the first—and only—official works councils congress summoned by the free unions of 1920, their chief aim became to prevent the works councils from developing into potentially revolutionary elements. Over the country as a whole their fight against communist influence in the councils—being a part of the general attack by the unions and the social democratic party no less than by the right-wing parties—was successful. Though in some districts, notably the Ruhr mining area, communist influence persisted for a long time, as the following figures show:

Ruhr Mining District

Per cent. of total works councils members

Union	1921	1922	1924	1925
A.D.G.B.	45·67	41·7	33·85	43·3
Communists and Syndicalists	31·74	32·87	42·72	30·32
Others	22·59	25·43	23·43	26·38
	100	100	100	100

The German machinery for state conciliation and arbitration of industrial disputes was almost complete in spite of its youth. After the preliminary attempts during, and immediately after the war, a decree was issued in October 1923 which, supplemented by an administrative order of the same year, formed the basis of the law until the end of the Weimar Republic. The country was divided into a number of districts, in each of which conciliation and arbitration boards were established. Each district was also given one permanent arbitrator. The boards were concerned with collective disputes, i.e., those arising out of collective agreements or affecting a number of firms or whole industries at a time. Individual disputes were excluded, and remained to be dealt with by works councils or, after 1926, by labour courts. Political and sympathetic strikes were equally excluded from this particular conciliation machinery.

The chief characteristic of the new machinery was that it was, in the last resort, compulsory. Although parties were free not to submit disputes to this machinery, once they had done so awards could be declared to be binding. Considerable power was thus given to the state in determining the relations between employers and workers and much of the conditions of the working class were made dependent upon general political forces. Much of the opposition to the conciliation machinery, which came from the communists and the more radical sections of the trade unions, was inspired by a deep-rooted suspicion of any measure which helped to tie working-class organization to the apparatus of the capitalist state. There is certainly evidence that the existence of this machinery considerably reduced the number of industrial disputes. But these continued to fluctuate with the general course of economic development, as the following table shows:

Industrial Disputes in Germany (Political Disputes excluded)

Year	*Number of Disputes*	*Undertakings*	*Number of workers affected*	*Number of working days lost*
1921	4,788	57,758	1,540,351	26,316,390
1922	5,201	52,783	1,969,263	28,894,434
1924	2,012	29,218	1,634,317	36,023,143
1925	1,766	25,214	758,071	16,855,856
1926	383	2,949	99,227	1,271,884
1927	871	10,480	493,680	5,936,006
1928	763	8,082	723,415	19,481,258
1929	441	8,606	223,878	4,372,907
1930	366	3,507	213,931	3,816,971
1931	497	4,994	177,643	1,990,000

(Figures for 1923 are not given, as they are vitiated by the French occupation of the Ruhr district.)

The depression led to a strengthening of the compulsory character of the machinery. In 1931 a presidial decree made it possible to pronounce binding awards against the will of the parties if this was considered "in the public interest." This decree was later renewed and made still more stringent by a clause which allowed the Minister of Labour arbitrarily to alter the period of validity of an award. And under the emergency decrees of 1931 and 1932, by which wages were substantially reduced, the scope of compulsory arbitral awards was widened still more.

Much of the difference of opinion concerning works councils and compulsory arbitration was the outcome of deep-seated conflicts within the labour movement over problems of political aims and strategy. We must devote the concluding pages of this section to a consideration of these conflicts.

The tragedy of the German working-class movement is that it failed to achieve unity. There is no single factor in its post-war history which stands out so much as its division. Reference has been made to the historical roots of the German working-class movement. The disunity between *Lassaleaner* and *Eisenacher* which weakened early German socialism persisted during the post-war period. It would, of course, be erroneous to make a mechanical comparison between the grounds of division in the latter half of last century and those which caused impotence in the face of fascist attack in the nineteen-thirties. Then, it was a question of the correct tactics vis-à-vis the problem of national union, vis-à-vis the creation of trade unions, vis-à-vis Bismarck's Prussianism; the socialist revolution was as yet a distant aim, though Marx and Engels and, to a large extent, the *Eisenacher* whom they influenced, regarded correct immediate tactics as of vital importance for the attainment even of that ultimate goal. But after the war the question of the proletariat's seizure of power was itself on the agenda. Striking analogies remain. The followers of Lassalle (though ultra-" left " in the matter of trade unions owing to their acceptance of the iron law of wages) were in favour of collaboration with Prussian autocracy. The *Eisenacher*, though by no means fully imbued with Marxism, realized to a much greater extent the need for independent working-class organization, both political and economic, and of continual action to safeguard to the maximum possible extent labour's interests. This they regarded as the only way to prevent the ultimate aims which were embodied in their theory from being jeopardized.

The Gotha Union put a stop to the dissension for the time being and made possible the growth of a numerically powerful movement. In theory the party and the free trade unions claimed to accept Marxism though both Marx and Engels severely criticized their programmes; but since the few decades between the Gotha Union and the war saw an enormous development of German capitalism and its entry into the imperialist phase, the practical policy became increasingly reformist. The capitalist system was accepted; and the task of the working-class movement was regarded as one of squeezing concessions out of employers and state. There were, of course, differences of opinion based on different interpretations of Marxism; but until the war these differences had not led to an organizational split. There were three wings: the revisionists, led by Eduard Bernstein, who were prepared openly to jettison Marxian socialism; the "left," led by Franz Mehring, Rosa Luxemburg and Karl Liebknecht, who though not entirely correct in their interpretation, were nearest to Marxism; and the centre, led by Kautsky, who claimed to preserve Marxism intact, but whose practice supported reformism.

The severest test of the movement came with the war; and the movement failed lamentably. In spite of repeated denunciations in past congresses of imperialist wars, 1914 found all the leaders prepared to support the Kaiser and the military in the name of patriotism. The movement had grown so bureaucratic and so intimately linked with the existing machinery of the state that it was incapable of resisting the powerful military propaganda.

It was not until the reverses on the field and the hardships at home had broken through the hold of the leadership that the working masses were able to return to their principles. The November revolution was the outcome of a spontaneous rising of the masses, and it was precisely because it remained spontaneous and because it had to be carried out in defiance of the party and trade union leadership that it did not result in the establishment of a socialist republic. The 1918 revolution was not a liberal, bourgeois revolution, as it has sometimes been described. It is true that much remained to be done to make of Germany a modern capitalist democracy, and that the Weimar constitution completed a half-century long process of liberalization. But in the advanced conditions of modern Germany, at a time when capitalism was being called in question everywhere, and, above all, when one socialist state, the Soviet Union, was already in existence, no revolutionary movement could fail to have a socialist content.

The revolution was, however, beaten not only by the forces of reaction, but by the collaboration with them of many of the workers' leaders themselves. And with the murder of Liebknecht and Luxemburg, with the suppression of the workers' and soldiers' councils, with the rapid neutralization of much of the social legislation which had been passed owing to the pressure of the revolutionary fervour of the masses, the counter-revolution began to consolidate its position for the launching of the counter-offensive. The revolution had failed because there had been no revolutionary party in existence which would have assumed the leadership. The hurriedly improvised Spartacus League was not powerful enough with the aid of the left wing of the Independent Socialists to supply the deficiency. But from that time the German working-class movement remained split into two sections: the communist party (*K.P.D.*) and the old social-democratic party (*S.P.D.*).

After the period of revolutionary struggles and extensive and radical labour disputes which accompanied the inflation, the *S.P.D.*—though still clinging to some version of Marxist theory—became more openly reformist than it had been in pre-war days. Its leaders and the leaders of the *A.D.G.B.*, with which the party was more closely linked than was the case with trade unions in other capitalist countries, succumbed completely to the apparent prosperity of the years 1924–1929. They accepted the growth of monopoly as a step forward in the direction of socialism. They developed the theory of "organized capitalism" as a substitute for their previous analysis of the economic system. Capitalism, they said, had changed its character. It had ceased to be competitive; and the increase of monopoly made it easier for the state to lay down rules for the conduct of private enterprise which considerably diminished the possibilities of oppression and exploitation. At the same time it would be easier in future to take over these monopolies and transform them into socialized undertakings. But since "organized capitalism" appeared to these social democratic theorists much more resilient and less subject to economic crises, the prospect of socialization seemed a very distant one.

Although, as we have seen, the signs of recovery were deceptive, German economy revived sufficiently during the period in question to make it possible for concessions to be granted. Unemployment was heavy, the rise in real wages was much less spectacular than was sometimes believed; nevertheless the rise of the standard of living from its deplorable inflation levels was sufficiently marked to make it possible for *S.P.D.* and *A.D.G.B.* to maintain their strength. But it was in that period of collaboration, of the emasculation of works councils, and of the acceptance of compulsory arbitration, that the bonds between the labour leaders and the state grew more intimate than ever. Trade union machinery became increasingly ossified and bureaucratic; and there was enough evidence of jobbery and corruption to make subsequent communist (and national-socialist) criticism of boss rule (*Bonzentum*) find much more support among the rank and file.

The depression shattered the pleasant dreams of a gradual *hineinwachsen* into socialism. The attack upon the workers' standards was launched with great ferocity, and the existing trade union machinery, which had hitherto put complete faith in the state, found itself incapable of resisting. For a time official theorists were still explaining the crisis as a temporary phenomenon which would disappear sooner or later. More rationalization, a return to free trade, credit inflation, were the measures which the right wing of the labour movement propagated and which it opposed to the growing demands for the use of the strike weapon. Even the collapse of the "Weimar coalition," and the beginning of the series of autocratic presidial cabinets did not shake the faith of these leaders in the coming return of prosperity. The theory then put forward was that of "toleration"; the lesser evil of the Brüning and Papen regimes had to be supported against the threat of national-socialism.

The result of this policy was to compromise those responsible in the eyes of the masses. The leaders became identified with the most reactionary governments which post-war Germany had had; and although the voting strength of the *S.P.D.* did not, for some time, seriously diminish, it became more and more difficult for the party to assume active leadership. The trade union leaders, in particular, who had taken a leading part in propagating the idea of toleration, were met with increasing hostility. Trade union membership showed a significant decline: by the middle of 1932 it amounted to only a little over three million, the lowest figure since the war. Taking into account the very high proportion of unemployed among trade union members (including those on short time;

the percentage stood in the middle of 1932 at 68), it will be seen that the effective membership, especially from the point of view of finance, was extremely small.

The communist party opposed this policy throughout the post-war period. It has been asserted in the past that communist policy underwent many violent changes. In retrospect, however, it appears that although there were changes, these were necessitated by the changing economic conditions, the changing possibilities of transforming social-democratic policy itself and the struggles within the communist party for the establishment of an internal unity and the adoption of a single line. That line appears to have been consistently pursued. In the first post-war phase, at the height of the revolutionary wave, the chances of pushing the November Revolution to a socialist conclusion appeared bright and tactics were designed to use all the new means, e.g. works councils and the republican parliament, for revolutionary ends. The rôle of the social democratic and trade union leaders made it inevitable that the main attack of the communists was directed against them; and so it remained consistently until 1933.

But changing conditions caused variations in the details of that attack. During the period of stabilization, while not abandoning their criticism of social democratic policy, the communists endeavoured to work through the free trade unions (the chief independent communist union at that time was the *Union der Hand-und Kopfarbeiter* which had 160,000 members) and to radicalize the rank and file whenever they could. These united front tactics, with the emphasis on the daily activities of the labour movement, caused violent discussions inside the communist party—parallel, of course, with the similar discussions against left and right "deviations" which were then going on in Russia and in the Communist International —and caused the formation of a number of small splinter groups, the largest of which was under the influence of Trotskyist doctrine.

The party came out of these discussions much strengthened and was able to take advantage of the conditions created by the depression to increase its influence among the masses. The social democratic party's theory of "organized capitalism" and economic democracy, its increasing dependence on the state machine, and its toleration of the autocratic presidial cabinets, caused the communists to intensify their campaign against the trade union and social democratic leaders. The theory of social fascism—a development of Lenin's theory of social-chauvinism which he used in his analysis of the rôle of social democracy before and during the war—was evolved. It stigmatized social democracy as the agent of reaction and counter-revolution within the working-class movement and as the force responsible for preparing the ground for fascism. Work within the trade unions was not abandoned, but a Revolutionary Trade Union Opposition (*R.G.O.*) was formed. The efforts for the establishment of a united front were intensified. Emphasis was laid on the need to make such unity arise "from below," i.e., through collaboration of the rank and file in their local organizations, but not to let it interfere with the continued attacks on the leaders.

But this unity was not achieved. Communist policy was represented as out to "smash" the trade unions; moreover, many of the older members of the social democratic rank and file regarded the attacks on their leaders as disloyal, in spite of the fact that they increasingly distrusted their leaders' policy. The result was that the two working-class parties continued to exist side by side, commanding even during the two years of fiercest attack a combined strength of one-third of the members of parliament, but disunited and offering no common resistance to the growing forces of fascism.

Nazi Germany

The national-socialist party is not, of course, a part of the working-class movement but, on the contrary, bitterly hostile to it. But its true function remained concealed prior to its coming into power. We may, therefore, begin by saying a few words on German fascism prior to 1933. The *Nazional-sozialisische Deutsche Arbeiterpartei* arose in Bavaria at the time of the inflation. After being formed of a nucleus of isolated *déclassé* individuals with a large variety of extravagant social theories, it began to attract adherents from among the petty-bourgeoisie, who as the result of the inflation had for the first time been drawn into the political struggle. Clerks, small shopkeepers and rentiers and peasants, together with a number of adventurers with no social roots, were attracted by its variegated programme. Denunciations of liberalism, of the socialist movement, of the parliamentary " system " were combined with anti-semitism, extreme chauvinism, and vaguely anti-capitalist romanticism into a hotch-potch which was ideal for demagogic purposes. But the party had to wait for a long time before it became of any political significance. Although it grew to some size in the chaotic days of the inflation, when the Ruhr occupation put a premium on nationalist propaganda and when the counter-revolution was ready to utilize any weapon to attack the working-class movement, it soon declined again. Even as late as 1928 it had only thirteen deputies. But by 1930 its representation had risen to 107 and its vote to 6,400,000. Two years later, at the peak of its parliamentary career, it had 13·7 million votes (37 per cent. of the total) and 230 members in the Reichstag. How is this enormous growth to be explained?

It can be said at once that if the national-socialist party had been a party representative of the middle strata of society—a theory which is sometimes put forward—it would never have reached these figures. But it did not remain an obscure grouping attracting only elements of the petty-bourgeoisie: it became a mass party, rivalling the parties of the working class, and including, certainly in its later stages, many working-class adherents. Two factors were responsible for this growth: the adoption of the national-socialist party by the reactionary forces—Ruhr magnates, Junkers, the military—as their chief weapon against the labour movement; and the disunity and weakness of the labour movement in the crisis.

The *N.S.D.A.P.* was, from the very beginning, in receipt of substantial subsidies from certain sections of heavy industry and finance and from the large landowners. This gave them the means for their elaborate organization, extensive propaganda and the development of mercenary semi-military formations. With the growing intensity of the crisis the need for some mass basis for the increasingly reactionary and autocratic presidial cabinets became more urgent. This gave the national-socialists their chance; they were called into the cabinet when the social-democrats had been heavily compromised and were beginning to lose support, and when they themselves, owing partly to the slight improvement in business conditions and partly to the widespread knowledge that they, the opponents of the system, were negotiating with Papen and were not opposing his emergency decrees, were also beginning to lose some of their hold. Both for them and for those who brought them into the government it was very much a case of now or never.

The weakness of the disunited labour movement has already been indicated. It enabled national-socialist propaganda to attract large masses of the juvenile unemployed and even to make some inroads into their more solidly organized and skilled factory workers. Their propaganda was admirably designed for this purpose, and it was powerfully backed by their terrorist technique. Attacks on parliament and on the bosses of the trade unions, and promotion of disorder so as to bring democratic institutions into disrepute prepared the ground. Denunciations of the rapacious (*raffender*) as distinct from the creative (*schaffender*) capitalist, promises that the " slavery of interest " would be broken and a general declaration in favour of the common interest (*Gemeinnutz vor Eigennutz*) followed.

The party was always extremely careful to combine its attacks on " Jewish Marxism " with protestations of its opposition to the reaction. Its attitude to the trade unions was typical in this respect. The national-socialists rejected the socialist aims and the Marxist theory of the trade unions; but they claimed to recognize trade unions as necessary institutions, so long as business was run by liberal entrepreneurs with no social conscience. In the regenerate third realm it was claimed that the state would protect all interests and that self-defence would be unnecessary. The party's industrial branch, the *N.S.B.O.* (national socialist factory cell organization) was, therefore, often forced to take part in labour disputes (such as the 1932 Berlin transport strike); and in the latter stages of the depression its rank and file members had become very radical.

The way in which the Nazis actually obtained power need not be discussed at any length here. One or two points may, however, be mentioned because they illustrate still further the weakness of social democratic leadership. Hitler became

Chancellor in January, 1933, as the result of an intrigue between Papen and a small clique behind him, at a time when the party had nothing like a majority in parliament (at the elections in November, 1932, it had lost two million votes), and when the government was not based on any democratic suffrage. Between January and March 5, 1933, when the new elections were held, a regime of terror was instituted which, together with the Reichstag fire, enabled the party to elect 288 deputies, which was still less than a majority. After that the terror became more open and included the suppression of the communist party. But the social-democrats did not resist; they were still hoping to tolerate and to collaborate. The *Gewerkschaftszeitung* of April 29 published an article welcoming the national-socialist May Day as a day of victory for the working-class movement. And on May 17, the social democratic deputies voted for the government's resolution in the Reichstag. But none of these acts of submission was enough. On May 2 all trade union buildings were occupied and all leaders arrested; and on May 13, all trade union property was confiscated. On June 23 the social democratic party was prohibited and its few remaining extreme right wing leaders were arrested. The next month the formation of all new parties was forbidden and the way to the consolidation of the totalitarian régime was open. From that time, too, the German labour movement ceased to exist, at any rate, legally. Germany no longer has any working-class organization in the accepted meaning of the term.

It is nevertheless necessary to look at some of the institutions which the new régime has set up as ostensible substitutes for trade unions. At first it was thought that the national-socialists would maintain the structure of existing institutions and adapt them to their end; but the exigencies of the régime made this impossible. Indeed, the fact that the otherwise amazingly easy progress by which existing institutions were *gleichgeschaltet* to national-socialism was found impracticable in the sphere of working-class organization is significant. It lends support to the theory which regards the fundamental function of the present régime as the breaking of existing labour organizations as a prerequisite for a warlike economic and foreign policy.

The prime consideration of German policy since 1933 has been the creation of the conditions which would enable Germany to resume her struggle for a larger share of strategic advantages, outlets for investment, markets and sources of raw materials. It is not suggested that this struggle was the same as the inter-imperialist rivalries which brought about the Great War: the world of the ninteen-thirties was in many fundamental respects different from that before 1914. But it is not possible to examine within the scope of this survey either this problem or the details of policy by which it was sought to achieve the aim here referred to. A few general remarks must, however, precede an examination of national-socialist labour policy.

The main task of the present rulers of Germany in the first year of their power was to reduce unemployment as rapidly as possible. The reasons for this were manifold. In the first place, it was essential to take the unemployed "off the streets." They were a serious source of political instability; and a reduction of unemployment from the six million level at which it stood at the beginning of 1933—by whatever means it was obtained—would be a most spectacular political achievement. Moreover, measures by which unemployment was in fact reduced involved the institution of just those social controls which were indispensable for the more distant aims. The first year of national-socialist policy saw, therefore, not only the open political terror, the abolition of the most elementary rights of defence of the working class, and the use of all the paraphernalia of extreme economic nationalism (defaults on foreign debts, exchange control, export subsidies, etc.), but also a large-scale public works policy.

The chief characteristic of this policy was the creation of maximum employment. Rearmament, which was to become the guiding force of subsequent development, was as yet in the background: foreign-political considerations necessitated a certain degree of gradualness; and at home, too, the new institutions had to be perfected and the financial machinery adequately prepared. However, even in the first year, the ultimate aim of rearmament was not lost sight of: barracks, strategic roads and fortifications were built for their political significance, no less than in order to create work. But the main desideratum of the works then undertaken was that they should involve a low proportion of costs other than labour costs. In this way, every mark laid out created the maximum demand for labour; the state's expenditure on relief was reduced to the utmost; and the call on the small foreign exchange resources to provide expensive raw materials was reduced to a minimum. It is estimated that 3,000 million marks were spent in the first year.

To the creation of employment which this meant, must be added the institution of labour camps and other forms of compulsory labour service, the wholesale arrests for racial or political reasons, and the purging of unemployment registers for similar reasons, as means for reducing the unemployment figures. From a statistical point of view this policy was a great success. The monthly average of unemployment in 1933 was 4·8 million; in 1934 it was only 2·7 million. In the following four years the work-creation aspect of economic policy gradually sank into the background as employment increased; and further reduction of unemployment became incidental to rearmament. In this period it is estimated (since official figures are absent) that the German government spent well over 40,000 million marks, the vast bulk of which was raised by means of short-term borrowing. The unemployment registers certainly show the effects of this policy. The following table gives the unemployment figures since the present régime came into power.

Figures in 000's

	Employment	*Unemployment*
October 1933	14,063	3,745
1934	15,636	2,268
1935	16,508	1,829
1936	17,785	1,076
1937	19,128	502

In the winter of 1937–38, unemployment rose, reaching nearly one million; but it has again declined since and has kept below the half-million level.

The figures of production show the same trend:

Industrial Production 1928 = 100

Monthly Averages	*Total Index*	*Capital Goods*	*Consumption Goods of elastic demand*
1933	61·5	44·9	80·1
1934	80·9	74·8	89·6
1935	95·3	102·4	85·6
1936	107·8	116·6	95·6
1937	119·2	128·8	101·7

This table shows also—as would be expected from the policy by which industry has been made more active again—that the capital goods trades have increased much more than the consumption goods trades. This means not only the possibility of a less than proportionate rise in living standards (something more will be said about these in a moment) but also lopsided development of the industrial structure which, combined with the enormously increased floating debt, creates serious problems for the future.

Since 1937 the carrying out of Germany's present economic policy has become more difficult, owing to the rise in world prices and the shortage of foreign exchange needed for the purchase of raw materials. The rigours of the economic régime had, therefore, to be intensified; and this was done by the introduction of the four-year plan (more properly the second four-year plan) which had to adjust economic policy to the raw materials shortage and to the transformation of a state of unemployment into a definite scarcity of labour. The second four-year plan is designed to increase the use of domestic raw materials (timber, low grade iron ores), to stimulate the production of substitutes—particularly synthetic plastics in the place of metals—and to increase still further the regimentation of labour.

The institutions by which labour has been brought under the yoke of the war economy of the totalitarian régime are based on a law of January 20, 1934 (*Gesetz zur Ordnung der nationalen Arbeit*), which came into force on May 1, 1934, though some of its principles were already embodied in the early decrees which followed the suppression of the trade unions. Fifteen executive orders were given out in the first two years after the passing of the act for putting it into effect. The " philosophy " of nationalist-socialist labour legislation states as three fundamental principles the unity of entrepreneur and workman, in sharp contrast to the class struggle basis of previous working-class policy; the leadership principle, " full authority downwards, full responsibility upwards "; and rigid state control over industrial relations. National socialist labour legislation starts from the principle that the interests of employers and workers are naturally harmonious, since they are dependent upon the general interests of the " folk community." The *Betriebsgemeinschaft*, or factory community, is divided functionally and not on the basis of class interest. It consists of the leader, or employer, and the following (*Gefolgschaft*), or employees. The leader is " master in his own house "—a principle which the entrepreneurs have welcomed enthusiastically. He has power to decide on all matters affecting his business, including wages, hours and other working conditions. Collective agreements are no longer in existence. The only rule to which the employer must conform is embodied in one section of the Act. It lays down that the employer must issue in writing works rules and wage schedules (*Betriebsordnung* and *Tarifordnung*) stating details of hours, wages and salaries, piece-work schedules, fines, grounds for dismissal and other minor matters. All new contracts must be concluded on the basis of these regulations.

The employer alone decides on the form and content of the regulations. But in order to diminish the appearance of absolute power, the Act sets up three new institutions which are claimed to exercise control in the interest of the workers and of the community. These are the Mutual Trust Councils (*Vertrauensräte*), the labour Trustees (*Treuhänder der Arbeit*), and the Social Honour Courts (*Soziale Ehrengerichte*). The Mutual Trust Councils exist for enterprises employing more than twenty persons; they are composed of the employer and from two to ten employees. The employer, in conjunction with the head of the national-socialist cell organization in his firm, draws up a list of members which is voted on *in toto* by the workers. If it is rejected by them or if no agreed list can be drawn up by the employer and the chief of the party cell, the Labour Trustee may himself appoint the members. The council has only advisory functions. It is supposed to discuss measures for improving efficiency and the works regulations prior to their publication. It is also supposed to exert its influence for the prevention or settlement of minor disputes. These councils presented the most hopeful means for the re-creation of some kind of independent working-class organization; and, largely under communist influence, the "underground" working-class movement appeared to have decided to use them in this way. But the authorities were aware of the danger to themselves of allowing even so limited a scope to workers' representation; and the elections for the Trust Councils have been postponed both in 1936 and in 1937.

The Labour Trustee is a Reich official with considerable power. He issues wage schedules; he lays down general rules for the drawing up of works regulations; he supervises the Mutual Trust Councils; he has to approve of dismissals affecting more than 10 per cent. of a firm's employees, and he makes binding awards in all cases of dispute which are not settled within the firm. The Labour Trustees are really officials of the Ministry of Labour. There is one in each administrative district of which there are fourteen in the country.

The Social Honour Courts have to deal with all alleged infringements of social honour either by workers or employers. These consist of "malicious exploitation" of the workers or insults to their honour, "incitement to the class struggle," or "disturbance of the *ésprit de corps* of the business," repeated and frivolous complaints about the employer, etc. There is one court in each of the fourteen industrial districts. They are composed of one professional judge and two assessors, whose names are submitted by the Labour Front. The penalties which they may impose range from warnings to fines up to 10,000 marks, and dismissal in the case of workmen or "denial of the qualification to be a leader" to an employer. In the latter case it is important to notice that disqualification applies only for purposes of the labour law; it does not mean that the entrepreneur in question ceases to be an employer.

Other parts of the new labour law consist almost all of

measures of regimentation. Practically every salary and wage earner in receipt of less than 1000 marks a month has now to possess an employment book; emigration of skilled workmen is normally prohibited; " closed zones " into which labour may not migrate have been instituted; and the allotment of labour over different branches of industry is rigidly controlled. This aspect of labour legislation is most obviously in harmony with the general totalitarian character of national-socialist policy. It was crowned in July 1938 by a complete Labour Conscription Law which enables the authorities arbitrarily to move workers according to the needs of state policy. This was supplemented at the end of 1938 by a law conscripting women.

Of all the substitutes for pre-1933 labour legislation which the law of 1924 introduced, the Labour Front is the most interesting. It was constituted on May 10, 1933, and given legal form in 1934. It was designed to become the successor of the suppressed trade unions whose funds it took over. Since March 1935, however, it has become more closely based on national-socialist ideology and it now includes employers as well as workers. Membership is theoretically voluntary, but in practice the pressure to join is so great that it amounts to compulsion. Although employers are not legally bound to employ only those workers who are members of the Labour Front, in practice there is every reason why they should. Contracts by the state, municipalities and other public bodies generally carry with them a condition excluding non-members; and it must be remembered that a very large part of Germany's economy is entirely dependent on public orders. Political pressure to join the one national-socialist mass organization is naturally very great also. The Labour Front, consequently, has a membership which is very much larger than that ever achieved by the trade unions. The number of members is estimated to be in the neighbourhood of twenty-six million. Contributions vary according to income, which is graded into twenty classes. The annual income was 310 million marks in 1935; and the capital fund stood in the same year at 250 million. But it is interesting to note that administrative expenses at that time amounted to approximately eighty-two million marks per annum, which was 27 per cent. of the total income, as compared with an average annual administrative expenditure of the *A.D.G.B.* in the years 1924 to 1930 of a little over eight million marks, or 6·9 per cent. of income.

The structure of the Labour Front is very complicated. Apart from staff, legal and treasury departments, its central administration has two main bureaux: the organization office and the "strength through joy" (*Kraft durch Freude*). The former was originally and still is, to some extent, the backbone of the Labour Front. It has fourteen sections, concerned with such matters as press, propaganda, political education, vocational training; but it also contains eighteen trade divisions which corresponded to some of the divisions of the old trade union structure. There are also territorial divisions which reproduce for each area the central structure. Although the Labour Front has been given certain functions of conciliation and arbitration which partly overlap those given to the other institutions created by the new labour legislation, there is little evidence that its power to regulate industrial relations has markedly increased. It is mainly used as a method of keeping together the masses under some central control, and as a convenient instrument of co-ordination in so far as changes in national economic policy involve certain changes in labour structure.

The more significant activities of the Labour Front now fall under the "strength through joy." This movement, which is akin to the Italian "*dopo lavoro*" is designed to provide social amenities in the workers' leisure time. It organizes sports meetings, dances, theatrical and musical events for its members. And it provides cheap holiday facilities. It is difficult to assess the precise value of the work which "strength through joy" has accomplished. On paper, it looks imposing enough. But it must be remembered that it has replaced the very numerous activities of trade unions, political and social working men's clubs, which were a very marked feature of republican Germany. It is doubtful whether, taking into account the loss of these activities and the extremely expensive administrative machinery, the achievement is really substantial, even when the fact that all organizations like "strength through joy" are used as instruments of national socialist propaganda at home and abroad is left out of consideration.

Two other branches of German labour policy may be mentioned. They were originally introduced in connection with the "*Arbeitschlacht*," the fight for the reduction of unemployment; but they have remained as integral parts of the present economic structure, since they have been found very useful both in facilitating the regimentation of labour and as a means of political propaganda. They are the Land Help (*Landeshilfe*) and the Labour Service (*Arbeitsdienst*). The Land Help was set up quite early in the new regime for the purpose of settling juvenile unemployed on the land. Between 160,000 and 180,000 young men and women were transferred in this way, though the figures have been falling lately owing to the shortage of labour in industry. The Land Help gives the farmers who engage these workers a monthly financial grant out of its saving on unemployment benefit. The transferred workers are given board and lodging and a small cash allowance. The complaints which have been made against the system seem to suggest that its main use is to reduce unemployment benefit, provide some landowners and farmers with cheap labour and strengthen the machinery of compulsion over the individual.

The Labour Service, though instituted as part of the reforms of unemployment relief before the advent of national-socialism, has become a permanent feature of the state only since 1933. It is compulsory: every young German must serve in it for six months prior to his military service; and a similar corps, though on a much smaller scale, exists for women. The work of the service is generally concerned with land reclamation, soil improvement and forestry; but the political importance of the service is probably as great as that of any actual work. The young men are subject to rigorous military discipline; and they are given only 25 pfennig a day pocket money.

The social legislation of the third Reich has kept practically unchanged the existing law relating to insurance, has centralized the different welfare organizations which existed before 1933 and brought them under the control of the party, and has added one new institution, the Winter Relief (*Winterhilfe*). Every year between October and April a campaign is conducted to collect contributions in money and in kind both from individuals and from institutions. On the first Sunday in each winter month every German is expected to have a one-dish meal and to hand over to the collectors a sum of money representing the saving thus achieved. Every means of propaganda is employed to obtain contributions, and it is fair to regard the system as being in effect compulsory.

It is not easy to make an estimate of the effects of national socialism on the standard of living. Hourly wage rates have remained remarkably stable according to official statistics and this nominal wage-level is about 17 per cent. below that of 1928. In order to arrive at a first estimate of real wages, we have to take into account various deductions and the cost of living. The deductions for the virtually compulsory membership of different national-socialist organizations are very considerable and amount to between 12½ and 25 per cent. The official cost of living index has shown also very great stability in recent years, and it is on these grounds alone that one may infer that real wages have not been maintained. If we take into account the inadequacy of the official cost of living figure which, according to a recent report of the British Commercial Counsellor at Berlin, assumes very meagre requirements for a German family of five, this impression is further strengthened. In addition, we must bear in mind the recurring shortage of certain food stuffs (eggs, butter, edible fats, etc.) and other goods, and the widespread deterioration in the quality of manufactured consumption goods. It would seem then that real wages have perceptibly declined, though it is difficult to make an estimate of any accuracy. A decline of 20 per cent. would probably be the lowest that one may assume.

We may sum up the effects of the national-socialist régime on the position and status of labour in the following terms. Among the destruction of all democratic institutions and civil liberties, the abolition of labour's freedom to organize and defend its interests is the most striking and fundamental. The state claims to be an impartial arbiter, who looks after the interests of the whole community including those of labour. In effect, however, the new institutions, such as the Labour Front, are mere sham: their practical effects as organizations of workers are nil. The decline in the standard of living, the introduction of a great variety of wages and hours, the dilution and regimentation of labour, show that the socialist part, at any rate, of national socialism, was nothing but demagogy. The revival of a genuine working-class movement involves the disappearance of the totalitarian régime.

GREAT BRITAIN

BY

H. A. MARQUAND

GREAT BRITAIN

THE end of the war in 1918 was followed by a brief boom, the result partly of an urgent need to satisfy demands postponed during war-time and partly of continued inflation. In Great Britain this was a period of industrial dislocation, caused by a rapid shift from war-time to peace-time demand and by the return to civil life of a demobilized army. Acute social tension was relieved, but not removed, by the payment of out of work donations to ex-soldiers and munition makers. The threat of a strike to secure national ownership of the mines was bought off by the appointment of a Royal Commission, with the implied promise of far-reaching reforms. The lightning railway strike of 1919, which was completely successful, was only one of 1,350 stoppages during the year in which thirty-five million working days were lost in disputes involving nearly 2,600,000 workers. This was the year in which, for the first time since war began, wages caught up with rising retail prices, and in which six million wage earners secured substantial reductions in their hours of work. Labour was scarce, and still in a mood of exhilaration following armistice and victory. Organized employers hastily agreed to participate in a National Industrial Conference, which drew up plans for a universal eight-hour day and a statutory minimum wage.

This brief period of soaring prices and rapid social change belongs logically to the era of the war, of which it was the direct outcome. It came to an abrupt end with the breaking of the boom in the summer of 1920. Wholesale prices ceased to rise in March and fell rapidly throughout 1921, falling less sharply during 1922 and finally reaching stability, or even beginning to mount again, towards the end of the latter year. Retail prices and the cost of living, however, did not fall so soon or so fast as wholesale prices, and wages lagged behind them both. As a result of the Industrial Courts Act of 1919, existing wage rates were preserved as a minimum until September 1920, while 7,600,000 workers gained wage advances during the latter year. The worker in full employment in 1920 was therefore notably better off than he had been before or during the war. But unemployment was mounting. In December 1920 there were 858,000 workers in receipt of unemployment benefit, which had just been extended to cover the bulk of wage earners outside agriculture, domestic service, the railways, insurance and banking. By January 1922 the number had reached 1,948,000.[1]

Falling prices and mounting unemployment led inevitably to wage reductions. The working of sliding scale agreements (based on the cost of living or on the selling price of products) resulted in weekly decreases totalling about £3,700,000 in 1921, and £1,700,000 in 1922. The total net weekly decreases of those years amounted to about £6,061,000 and £4,210,000 respectively. By the beginning of 1923 wage rates as a whole bore the same relation to the cost of living as they did in 1914. The only substantial gain that labour retained from the period of post-war advance was a notable reduction in hours of work. During 1919 and 1920 nearly seven million workers had secured reductions amounting to nearly forty-three million hours per week. In the months of slump immediately following, there were even, on balance, some small additions to these figures.

The brief but sharp depression of 1920–1922 was felt in other countries and had effects similar to those in Britain. But in most other countries—notably the U.S.A.—it gave way to a period of industrial expansion and mounting prosperity. In Britain, however, it was an uneasy introduction to an era in which conditions were radically different from those to which the nation had been accustomed before 1914. The war had made important changes in three directions—the international location of industry, the relative economic situation of the leading industrial countries, and the foreign exchange values of currencies—which involved profound effects upon the economic structure of a country so largely dependent as Great Britain upon international trade.

It so happened that many of the chief exports of Great Britain—coal, ships, iron and steel and machinery, for example—were goods which were of prime importance in time of war. While war was in progress the industries making these products were working beyond normal capacity, while in many instances reductions in hours of labour produced an increase in numbers

[1] Totals for Great Britain, excluding Northern Ireland.

employed.[1] Yet at the same time other countries were also rapidly expanding the same heavy industries within their own frontiers, in order to obtain munitions. As soon as the coal mines, shipyards and workshops of Europe were fully at work again after the end of the war, there was inevitably a contraction in the demand for the labour of British coalminers, engineers and shipbuilders. Other nations were not prepared to revert to the pre-war conditions of international trade, for the war had shown the military advantages of self-sufficiency, while the peace treaties had increased the number of sovereign states having power to raise tariff barriers. Moreover, countries such as India and Japan were seeking to become industrialized and to satisfy by their own production their need for textiles and other basic necessities. Some contraction from the war-time scale of production in the heavy industries of Britain was inevitable. That problem of readjustment was intensified by the growth of economic nationalism.

The war left Germany a heavy debtor to the Allies and converted the U.S.A. from a debtor to a creditor country. As far as Great Britain was concerned, this situation, while the principles of the Balfour note were observed, need in itself have created no difficulty. But the high tariff policy adhered to by the U.S.A., regardless of the change in her debtor-creditor position, caused a steady drain of gold from Europe to America. Unfortunately, the monetary policy adopted by Great Britain immediately after the war entailed the maximum disadvantage in these circumstances.

The restoration of the Gold Standard at the pre-war parity with the United States dollar was a major aim of British financial policy from 1919 onward. This necessitated an approximation of the British to the American price level. As any very large rise in the latter was not to be expected, a fall in the former had to be achieved by means of deflation. It is probably true that deflation was not the cause of the break in the boom of 1920. Nevertheless, once the slump began, advantage was taken of the opportunity thus afforded. A high Bank Rate was maintained, while State expenditure—especi-

[1] There were actually 120,000 more persons employed at coal mines in 1920 than in 1913.

ally upon education—was drastically curtailed. By 1922, the value of the £1 had been raised to $4.25 from the $3.80 at which it had stood at the beginning of 1920.

Yet in the uneasy world situation of 1921–1924 any further progress in this policy was impossible. The failure of France to secure the expected reparations from Germany produced a mounting budget deficit and extreme fluctuations in the value of the franc. The difficulties of post-war liquidation in the smaller countries of Middle Europe and the Near East added to the confusion of the currencies, while the French occupation of the Ruhr in 1923 was followed in Germany by the most spectacular inflation and monetary collapse in history. Not until the adoption of the Dawes Plan in 1924 did the world trade situation once again become favourable to the attempt to make the pound look the dollar in the face.

While 1921 and 1922 were years of wage reduction and heavy unemployment in Britain, 1923 and 1924 saw an upward tendency in business activity. In the former year the coal industry had a brief period of prosperity, and output in the exporting districts reached record levels, owing to the stoppage of the Ruhr coalfield. Unemployment began to decline and the fall in wages was arrested. In 1924, the year of the first Labour Government, there were numerous strikes and a pronounced upward movement of wages, together with a slight increase in trade union membership.

During the Dawes Plan period from 1924 to 1929 an apparently stable equilibrium was reached in most of the countries of the world. Output and employment increased rapidly. From the U.S.A. came tales of fabulous prosperity. The damage done to French industry by the war had been repaired; so far from suffering unemployment France actually had to encourage immigration to satisfy her demand for labour; while she soon began to acquire gold at a rapid rate. Even in Germany, though the wiping out of savings by inflation had created grave problems for the future, re-equipment of industry, rapid expansion of public works and active participation in the New Economic Policy in Russia caused a substantial increase in employment, though during the phase of most active rationalization unemployment was also considerable. In Europe as a whole the aggregate production of crude products increased by nearly 4.5 per cent. per annum between 1925 and 1929.

It is now known, of course, that the achievement of this world prosperity was largely due to foreign lending by America —totalling $6,069,000,000 in the five years 1924 to 1928— greatly in excess of her receipts as a creditor during the same period. By this means the disharmony between the existing economic structures of the nations and their changed financial relationship was temporarily concealed. At the time the dangers in the situation were not clearly perceived. In the United States public opinion was inclined to believe that prosperity had been secured because, rather than in spite of, the tariff. In Europe the signing of the Locarno Pact and the entry of Germany into the League of Nations diverted attention from the fundamental contradictions which underlay the boom.

Great Britain, however, was not permitted to participate to the full in the prosperity of the rest of the world. The upward movement of trade and employment in 1924 had been accompanied by a rise in prices and a consequent relapse in the dollar value of the £1. But the monetary authorities were not prepared to purchase internal equilibrium at a sacrifice of external prestige. The restoration of London as the world's financial centre and participation in the profitable business of foreign lending appeared to demand the re-establishment of the pre-war parity of dollar and pound. As soon, therefore, as rising prices in the U.S.A. brought this objective within range towards the end of 1924, preparations for the change were begun. The Bank Rate was raised, and in April 1925 the restoration of free convertibility of the £1 into gold at the pre-war rate was announced.

This decision involved an immediate rise of 10 per cent. in the external value of British currency. It was anticipated that a continuance of the rise of American prices would make it possible to retain the rate of $4·86 to the £1 without the drastic reduction in British costs and prices which would otherwise be necessary if a satisfactory volume of exports were to be maintained. Instead the American price level began to fall almost from the moment the decision was taken, and continued to fall thereafter. The £1 had been over-valued. To complicate the situation still further, when France restored the Gold Standard in 1926 the franc was under-valued. There was in consequence a chronic tendency for gold to leave London, which necessitated the maintenance of a high bank rate and consequent restrictions of credit throughout the years from 1925 to 1928. If and when a decline in the volume of America's foreign lending should once again give her a large favourable balance of payments, the struggle to maintain the new exchange rate would have to be abandoned.

The chief exporting industries of the country had already had to face the difficult task of contraction from the war-time volume of production and employment. To some extent they had prepared for this process by means of wage reductions and writing-down of capital; but even in 1924 they were still by no means adjusted to the conditions of that year. Re-organization into more efficient business units had made little progress, and there were still attached to these industries large numbers of surplus workers. Moreover, these were old-established heavy industries in which new methods of production and consumption began to make rapid changes as soon as the war was over. The introduction of mechanical methods in getting and hauling coal, the use of substitutes such as hydro-electric power and oil and, above all, economy in the use of coal in industry and for domestic heating, caused a high rate of technological unemployment among miners. Similarly in the cotton industry mechanical methods and the use of substitute textiles caused displacement. In shipbuilding and the manufacture of iron and steel the substitution of machinery for labour was revolutionary. After 1925 these industries were subjected to the severe additional strain of a 10 per cent. rise in the foreign price of their exports. For the coal industry, in particular, this was rendered even more burdensome by a fall in the external purchasing power of the French franc, the currency of one of its principal markets.

Throughout the whole period of world prosperity from 1925 to 1929, therefore, the old established industries of Britain, upon which her great world trade had been established, were chronically depressed. There was a constant effort to reduce costs so as to compete in foreign markets. There was constant pressure to secure greater productivity from the worker at a lower rate of wages. There was chronic unemployment in these industries at a far higher level than in the rest of the trades of the country. Their workers, wrote Mr. J. M. Keynes in 1925, "represent in the flesh the 'fundamental adjustments' engineered by the Treasury and the Bank of England to satisfy the impatience of the City Fathers and to bridge the 'moderate gap' between $4·40 and $4·86. They . . . are the 'moderate sacrifice' still necessary to ensure the stability of the gold standard."

These staple exporting industries of Great Britain are largely concentrated in coalfield areas, such as the West of Scotland, Cumberland, Durham and the Tyneside, Lancashire and South Wales. At least one-fifth of the unemployment which persisted during the Dawes Plan period consisted of workers completely surplus to the requirements of the exporting industries. The districts where they lived became the depressed areas, the plight of which has been the gravest social problem of Great Britain from the end of 1926 to the present time.

The persistence of a high rate of unemployment in Britain during a period of world prosperity was not properly understood within the country itself. It was customary for leaders of public opinion to refer, even in 1928 when an active boom was in progress, to "the present depression." The budget of the Unemployment Insurance Fund continually failed to balance because it was framed upon the expectation of a general rate of unemployment at first of five and one-third per cent. and later of 7 per cent., whereas the percentage scarcely fell below 10 during the whole period that the restored Gold Standard was in operation. But the unemployment was not due, as some foreign observers alleged, to faulty budgeting or over-generous "doles." It was the product in part of the inexorable advance of industrial technique and in part of policy deliberately undertaken in spite of protests and warnings.

While the old staple industries were suffering, trades manufacturing mainly for the home market were expanding. Between 1924 and 1929 the numbers in employment in coal mining had fallen by 25 per cent., in pig iron manufacture by 19 per cent., in steel making and in shipbuilding by 10 per cent. In the same short period numbers in employment in the rayon industry had increased by 40 per cent., in the manufacture of electrical apparatus and of furniture by 30 per cent., in motor vehicle and aircraft manufacture by 21 per cent. The numbers in employment in wholesale and retail trade had increased by 26 per cent., and in entertainments and sport by 17 per cent. The difficulties of the export trades and high rates of interest were not sufficient to cut Britain off completely from the prosperity of the rest of the world. As technical advances and reduced costs enabled consumers to economize upon their purchases of the products of the older industries, they increased their demand for the goods and services of the expanding trades. Unemployment in the latter varied from about 4 to 8 per cent. during the period, while the older industries had averages varying between 12 and 28 per cent.

These newer industries, catering largely for the final consumer, were naturally attracted to manufacturing sites well situated for distribution of their products in the large centres of population. The development of new sources of power and economy in the older forms of fuel made it unnecessary for them to be located near the coalfields. London, the South-East, Birmingham and the Midlands became the chief centres of the new automobile, clothing, electrical, food, furnishing, and light engineering factories. From the industrial North and from South Wales came a steady stream of migrants to these developing areas. But the new industries by no means absorbed the whole of the surplus labour of the coalfields. It was not easy to transform miners or shipbuilders into machine-minders, or even into waiters or hairdressers. Nor were older workers with family responsibilities and ties easily able to move into new districts. Much of the labour required for the new factories and services came from the rural areas of Southern England. Much of it consisted of the daughters of local workers already residing in the neighbourhood of the new developments. Between 1921 and 1931 the net increase of population by migration was 615,000 for South-East England. There were corresponding heavy decreases in the older industrial regions.

If the policy of 1925 was to be successful, it was essential that internal costs and prices in Great Britain be forced down to correspond with the new rate of exchange between British and foreign currency. This would involve a large increase in the real burden of all fixed-interest bearing debt, whether government stock or the bonds of local authorities and private enterprises. For the former, the appropriate policy of a capital levy was rejected by the electorate. For the latter, what Lord Bradbury called " the painful but salutary process of ordinary liquidation " was the only remedy. But this too proved far more difficult to attain than may have been expected. The most attractive solution of the problem, especially in industries where the proportion of labour to capital costs was high, was to reduce wages. This, however, met with a strong resistance from organized labour, culminating in the General Strike of 1926.

After the defeat of the miners, following the failure of the General Strike, there were considerable wage reductions, affecting in three years some five and a half million workers and amounting to a decrease of weekly wages of £643,000. But these reductions scarcely compare in size with those of 1921 and 1922, and there were actually increases in the same period amounting to £65,000 per week and affecting some 600,000 workers. The decreases were substantial in the coal-mining, shipbuilding and textile industries and in transport, building and public works contracting. But they were comparatively insignificant or non-existent in the lighter industries, in printing and paper-making, and in public utility and administrative services. The resistance of the institutional frame-work of society to pressure on its cost and wages structure was thus remarkably effective. The £1 remained over-valued, the unemployment of readjustment persisted, and during both 1928 and 1929 there was a net loss of gold from the Bank of England. As soon as a real business depression arrived the pre-1914 Gold Standard had once again to be abandoned.

When the Great Depression was ushered in with the collapse of the American bull market in the autumn of 1929, a Labour government was in office and approximately 11 per cent. of the insured workers were unemployed. For a time an attempt was made to check any increase by means of a policy of expenditure upon public works. But the numbers unemployed mounted steadily month by month and the Unemployment Insurance Fund—based, as we have seen, upon assumptions totally incompatible with the monetary policy of the time—

was forced to borrow ever-increasing amounts. Soon gold began to leave the country at a rapid rate. The Chancellor of the Exchequer, who had himself moved in the House of Commons in 1925 a motion stating that "a return to the Gold Standard with undue precipitancy may aggravate the existing grave condition of employment and trade depreciation," saw no remedy for the situation but drastic "economy" of the type against which he and his party had protested bitterly in 1921 and 1922. Every effort was made to preserve the stability of the £1. The Labour government itself was destroyed in the process, when the majority of its members refused to agree to a reduction of unemployment benefit by one-tenth. A Coalition government was formed which duly reduced unemployment pay and cut down State expenditure by £70,000,000. Loans were obtained from France and America, and for a few weeks the value of the £1 was maintained. But within a month of the new government's formation the Gold Standard had been abandoned. Within four months the £1 had fallen to $3.40, a rate rather lower than that which had prevailed in 1920.

The suspension of the Gold Standard arrested the fall in prices which had continued since 1925. But the change was not yet sufficient to induce recovery. The world situation for a time was dominated by the deepening depression in the U.S.A. Moreover, the British government persisted for some time in a deflationary budget policy, drastically restricting all forms of public works, carrying through increases of taxation and contributions to unemployment insurance, and continuing reductions in the salaries of public servants as well as in the rates of unemployment pay. A means test was imposed upon recipients of public relief who had exhausted their right to unemployment benefit. Protective tariffs were imposed which increased the regressive character of the tax system and furthered the accumulation of gold which the fall in the value of the £1 had stimulated. Unemployment remained at a high level, and even tended to increase, during 1932.

During the three years of acute depression from 1930 to 1932 wage reductions affected seven million workers, though the total weekly loss of wages was less than £1,000,000. As this was a period of steadily falling prices, those workers who were in full employment during the period were able substantially to improve their standard of living, despite wage cuts. So heavy was the incidence of unemployment, however, that this advantage was not widespread, while the condition of the chronically unemployed in the depressed areas grew steadily worse as their savings dwindled away and their physique deteriorated. A high level of unemployment, coupled with widespread disillusionment at the ignominious failure of the second Labour government, resulted in a continued fall of trade union membership. In these circumstances wage reductions met with weakened resistance and the great majority of disputes were settled on terms favourable to the employers.

A complete system of revenue and protective tariffs had been established at a moment in which circumstances offered peculiarly favourable chances of success. The outstanding characteristic of the Great Depression was the widening gap between the prices of manufactured goods and those of raw materials and farm produce. Great Britain was in the main an importer of the latter and an exporter of the former. Consequently, during the years of the depression, the terms of international trade were changing in her favour: so great was the fall in the prices of her imports that she was able to continue to purchase with greatly reduced exports a scarcely diminished quantity of essential agricultural products from abroad. In these circumstances, tariffs restored a favourable trade balance without raising the price of the people's food,[1] while a stimulus was given to further expansion in industries producing for the home market. By the end of 1932 wage reductions were decreasing in number, and during 1933 they began to give way to increases.

After the abandonment of the effort to maintain the pre-war Gold Standard, exchange stability was secured by the establishment of an Exchange Equalization Fund. This was used, after the devaluation of the American dollar, rather to prevent than to encourage a rise in the value of the £1. The freedom of currency management thus attained made possible successive reductions in the Bank Rate, large conversions of short-term public debt into long-dated securities, and the maintenance

[1] The price, of course, might have fallen if there had been no tariff.

from mid-year 1932 onwards of extremely low rates of interest in the money market. These low rates before long affected the demand for mortgages for house-building, and stimulated a boom in that industry which soon spread to other industries. Great Britain led the way in the moderate world recovery of 1933–1937.

During these last five years unemployment in Great Britain[1] fell from a total of 2,877,000 in January 1933 to 1,294,000 in August 1937. From the latter date onwards the numbers unemployed began to increase again, and other indices of business activity showed a downward trend which suggested the onset of a new depression. After 1933 the favourable trend in terms of trade began to be reversed. The period as a whole was one in which the average annual percentages of unemployment were considerably above the level of 1924–1929, which had once been regarded as years of depression. Nevertheless, this was undoubtedly considered by public opinion to be a period of comparative prosperity. During 1930–1933 the public had seen what a depression could be like and it had learned to regard an unemployment figure of 1,500,000 as fairly satisfactory. It understood better than it had done in the past that something approaching half of the total numbers unemployed at any given moment were only temporarily out of work or had been unemployed at most for only a few months. It believed that the general economic situation of Great Britain was better than that of the U.S.A., whereas in 1925–1929 it had appeared that the reverse was true. The international political situation grew steadily more dangerous and to some extent distracted attention from home discontents. But above all during this period there was no severe internal strain such as had been caused by the financial policy of 1925–1929. As usual during a period of rising prices, trade union membership and the number of industrial disputes increased; but in no other five-year period since the beginning of the twentieth century have there been fewer working days lost through industrial disputes. The rise of retail prices was very gradual and the upward movement of wages was more than sufficient to offset it. For the first time since 1926 there were substantial increases in wages in mining,

[1] Excluding Northern Ireland.

shipbuilding, textiles and other older industries as well as in the more favoured trades and services.

The years from the collapse of the boom of 1920 to the beginning of the depression of 1938 can thus be divided roughly into five periods. The first is that of the post-war slump down to about the end of 1922. Then follow two years of unrest and uncertainty before the adoption of the Dawes Plan. The third period from 1925 to 1929 is the period of strain caused by currency over-valuation. Then come the three years of the Great Depression. The last period consists of five years of Moderate Recovery. In the whole eighteen years the industrial machine has moved in a series of jerks, sometimes in short sharp rushes, sometimes almost standing still and showing such signs of strain that a complete breakdown seemed likely. But on the whole the machine has moved forward. The mass of the population, whatever the future may hold, was at the end of 1937 definitely wealthier than in 1914.

Measurement of such changes is difficult. British official statistics are sadly inadequate in many respects, especially for the measurement of that none-too-easily defined concept the cost of living. Any attempt to estimate movements in real wages is hedged about with difficulties. The differing fortunes of railway locomotive drivers, shipyard engineers, process workers in aircraft factories, coal miners, agricultural labourers, waiters, or shop assistants cannot be easily compounded in an average. How shall we measure the welfare of a clerk in regular employment at a dog-racing track whose only home is a single room in a Glasgow tenement, or compare it with that of a dock-worker living on a municipal housing estate and unemployed three days a week? How much importance in our balance shall we attach to the persistence, in one of the richest countries of the world, of dreary days of unemployment without end in the slowly decaying townships of the depressed areas? What weight shall be given to improvements in housing, the extension of old-age pensions, a marked increase in preventive medical services?

It is not part of the purpose of this book to examine carefully such questions as these. We are concerned rather to describe the behaviour and growth of labour organizations in the changing circumstances of these years. But some summary sentences are appropriate here. Firstly, the substantial reduction in hours of work gained during and just after the war has on the whole been retained by labour. In the mining industry there has been a net increase of half-an-hour per shift; there has also been a substantial increase in the textile industry, and minor increases in some other trades. But to offset these changes Labour has made big gains in road transport and in distributive services, and has also secured reductions of hours of work in the building trades and elsewhere. Secondly, the Census of Production of 1930 estimated that since 1934 there had been an average increase of 10 per cent. in the quantity of output per person employed in manufacturing industry; it is reasonable to believe that the increase of productivity continued during the years of Moderate Recovery. Thirdly, average real wages, which fell from 1921 to 1923, increased substantially during the Dawes Plan period of 1924–1929, increased still more during the years of the Great Depression, and have probably moved up slightly since. Fourthly, this improvement has been shared unevenly between industries and occupations. Light industries, public utilities, and the printing trades have gained most; railways, docks, municipal services, furniture, pottery making, and certain other semi-light industries have done fairly well; coal mining, textiles, shipping and iron and steel making have done badly. Fifthly, semi-skilled workers and labourers have considerably improved their wages and conditions as compared with those of skilled workers. Sixthly, throughout the period it remained legal for children to work for wages at the age of fourteen. Lastly, even when allowance has been made for the lack of comparable statistics for the period before 1920, the rate of unemployment has been on the whole considerably higher than before 1914. This must be recollected when considering the improvement in average real wages. The unemployment insurance system has been widely extended at various times during the period, and has become so important a guarantee of security not only to the worker but to the whole economic system that it is accepted by all classes and parties.

. . . . .

Organized labour in Britain was stronger in 1920 than ever before or since. During the war which had just ended, scarcity of labour, rapidly rising prices and the urgent need for more and more production at all costs had combined to increase the membership and power of the unions. Their most prominent leaders had become Cabinet Ministers. The ability of the unions to win improved conditions for their members had caused millions to flock into their ranks in 1918 and 1919. Politicians had promised a great reconstruction of national life and an immense improvement in the lot of the common people, when the war was won. In an atmosphere of optimism, trade union membership rose in 1920 to more than eight million. Amalgamations in the engineering, woodworking, building and other trades as well as among general labourers increased the strength of the unions almost as much as a growth in numbers.

Progress was also made in political organization. In 1918, an election, fought before the army was demobilized and before war-time hysteria had died down, was held at a very unpropitious time for the Labour Party. Many of its gifted orators had earned popular hatred by opposing entry into war or by advocating a negotiated peace. Inevitably they lost their seats. Yet the Party polled two and a quarter million votes and returned fifty-seven members to Parliament. It was stronger than ever before. Moreover, it adopted a new programme, for the first time committing itself definitely to Socialism, and for the first time providing for the direct recruiting (instead of through affiliated Societies) of individual members in each Parliamentary constituency. By 1920 it was rapidly gaining adherents, and the propaganda of Socialism was being heard as never before, at local elections, at street-corner meetings, at huge Sunday gatherings arranged by the affiliated Independent Labour Party and held in public parks or theatres. The Party was no longer a mere Parliamentary group interested only in matters affecting the direct interests of the trade unions. It was rapidly becoming the only alternative to the government of the day. In the industrial regions of the country it soon gained power in many local authorities. The formation in 1920 of the Communist Party of Great Britain, composed of dissident socialists who wished to adhere to the newly established Third International, added excitement to the debates of the theoreticians of socialism, but scarcely affected the mass of the membership of the unions and the Labour Party.

Though 1920 saw the beginning of the post-war slump, the atmosphere in the trade union world throughout the year was that of the militancy which had characterized 1919. The year opened with a big dispute in the iron foundries, and numerous others followed, mainly as the result of demands for wage increases. In March a special meeting of the Trades Union Congress was called to consider the situation in the coal-mining industry. The Miners' Federation had in 1919 threatened to strike to secure not only increased wages and shorter hours, but the nationalization of the mines. This had been called off when the government agreed to set up a Royal Commission to study the organization of the industry, and promised to accept its findings. Though four reports emerged from this Commission, it was true to say that a majority including the Chairman (a high court judge) favoured some form of nationalization. The government, nevertheless, refused to proceed with nationalization, and the miners' leaders were justly indignant. The Trades Union Congress and the Miners' Federation therefore jointly organized during the winter of 1919–20 a campaign of public meetings which, however, failed to win popular support. At the March meeting the miners appealed for the calling of a general strike. The proposal was rejected by a large majority. Congress was not prepared to use industrial action to secure what was regarded as a political demand.

The miners therefore acted on their own, but since the trade unions as a whole had refused to back it, they abandoned the demand for nationalization. In July they put forward demands for increased wages and a reduction in the price of coal. These were refused by the government, which still controlled the mining industry, and notices, to expire in September, were tendered by the miners. In this interval the Miners' Federation approached their colleagues of the Triple Alliance to ask for support when the strike should begin. The Triple Alliance was an informal association of the Miners' Federation, the National Union of Railwaymen and the Transport Workers' Federation, established in 1914 with the object of trying to ensure that collective agreements in the three industries concerned should expire at the same time. It was thought that if this could be arranged then each union would be in a stronger position when negotiating for a new agreement with its own employers, because the possibility of a simultaneous strike of all three unions would intimidate each set of employers and, indeed, the whole capitalist class. Combined action by all three bodies was held in reserve as a weapon rather than explicitly avowed as an object. By the general public the Alliance was regarded (mistakenly) as designed simply to bring about one day a general strike of three organizations which between them might cut off the nation's supplies of food, heat and power.

The main object of the Triple Alliance had never been achieved. Nevertheless, the Miners' Federation in approaching the Alliance was fulfilling the clause in the constitution which provided that the partners should notify one another of action likely to involve the others. The existing situation in 1920 was, however, a very inauspicious time to make such an approach. The National Union of Railwaymen had gained a satisfactory new agreement in 1919, and the Shaw Award under the Industrial Courts Act had just given dock-workers a substantial wage advance with a promise of further improvement in conditions. In these circumstances it was not likely that the other unions would agree that any principle was at stake or would endanger their gains in order to help the miners to achieve higher wages.

Before the matter could be decided, the whole of organized labour, political and industrial, was caught up in a dramatic united movement which for a few days made the solidarity of the working class a reality. Since the end of the main European War in 1918 the Russian Revolution had been fighting for its life against counter-revolutionary armies financed by the Allied Powers. The newly-formed Polish Republic had taken a hand in this war in the hope of extending its territory; but in the summer of 1920 the Polish armies were heavily defeated, and Warsaw itself was in danger of attack. A speech by Mr. Lloyd George (Prime Minister) on July 21, and a note to the Bolshevik government by Lord Curzon (Foreign Secretary) on August 4, seemed to suggest that the British government was preparing to extend its indirect intervention into open war.

Though the leaders of British Labour had no sympathy with the political philosophy of the Bolsheviks, though they had often enough been denounced by them as traitors to the working class, they were determined that the Russian Revolution must not be destroyed by foreign Powers. The British working class knew that it wanted no more war. The Labour Party held demonstrations all over the country on August 8, at which the slogan " not a man, not a gun, not a sou " was repeated again and again to vast crowds, whose enthusiasm surpassed all records for Labour meetings. The next day a meeting of the representatives of the Parliamentary Labour Party, the Trades Union Congress and the Executive of the Labour Party passed a resolution in which it warned " the Government that the whole industrial power of the organized workers will be used to defeat this war," and established a Council of Action to proceed with plans for enforcing the decision.

On August 13 a Conference of the Executives of the Unions and representatives of the Labour Party was held in London. This Conference fourteen years later was described by Philip Snowden, one of the principal architects of the Labour Party, as " the most impressive I have ever attended." It unanimously gave powers to the Council of Action to call a general strike if circumstances demanded it. " The thousand delegates," wrote Snowden, " sprang to their feet and broke into a hurricane of cheering."

Trade Union leaders of many years' experience, who were on the extreme Right Wing of the movement and were Socialists only in name, supported the resolution. Mr. J. H. Thomas, the Secretary of the National Union of Railwaymen, declared that a general strike " would mean a challenge to the whole constitution of the country. The step was momentous, but it was justified in order to prevent war." Such speeches from such leaders, reflected Snowden, " could only be explained by assuming that they were acting under some emotional impulse."

There was no war with Russia, and the union leaders were not called upon to make good their " challenge to the whole constitution of the country." The establishment of the Council of Action and the great Conference in London can be regarded as the peak of the period of labour militancy that followed immediately after the war. As the Conference was sitting, prices were falling and the slump began.

The solidarity of August proved to be no help to the miners in September. The Triple Alliance received their request for aid with no enthusiasm. The notices to cease work were withdrawn, and new negotiations with the government began. This time the demand for a reduction in the price of coal—which was a gesture to the rest of the Labour movement and could not benefit the miners—was withdrawn. But the negotiations broke down and a strike took place from October 16 to November 3. A limited wage advance was granted, but the new agreement was to expire in March 1921.

The chief result of the dispute and the threatened possibility of a Triple Alliance strike was the passing of the Emergency Powers Act, under the terms of which the government may declare a state of emergency if there is a threat of action "of such a nature and on so extensive a scale as to be calculated, by interfering with the supply and distribution of food, water, fuel or light, or with the means of locomotion, to deprive the community, or any substantial proportion of the community of the essentials of life." During the state of emergency Orders in Council may be issued giving the government very wide powers of operating and maintaining essential services. This Act was later to be used with great effect during major industrial disputes.

The re-organization of the Trades Union Congress which took place during 1920 proved in the long run to be of greater importance in the world of labour than the more spectacular events of that year. The Congress had come into existence in the 'seventies of the nineteenth century in order to provide a means of influencing Members of Parliament to act in ways favourable to the interests of organized labour. Its meetings were annual, and the only continuing organ it possessed was named, very significantly, the Parliamentary Committee. The main business of the latter was to lobby Members of Parliament and to present the views of the unions as a whole to government departments, Commissions of inquiry and similar bodies. For more than a generation it pursued a non-partisan policy similar to that followed by the American Federation of Labour. In 1895, in order to resist the Socialist efforts to take a more definite attitude, it expelled from membership the local Trades Councils (corresponding to American City Centrals), which had actually been the originators of the Congress, but were rapidly coming under the influence of the new Independent Labour Party. However, after the adhesion of many trade unions to the Labour Representation Committee in 1901 and still more after the full establishment of the Labour Party between 1906 and 1911, the Parliamentary Committee became more and more partisan in character, while at the same time its function as an organized lobby became less and less necessary. A group of leaders of unions which paid the piper and called the tune of the Labour Party were in an anomalous position as members of a Parliamentary Committee of the Trades Union Congress, especially as some of them were Members of Parliament themselves.

Though the original purpose of the Parliamentary Committee had thus disappeared, the Congress was unwilling to give it extended industrial powers. The older craft unions were reluctant to be drawn into disputes originated by the more militant industrial or general unions which grew up between 1889 and 1912. They had no desire to imperil their funds, and still less to surrender craft privileges. The newer unions feared to impair their own sovereignty. Instead of developing the Parliamentary Committee into an organ of industrial co-ordination, the unions relied upon the General Federation of Trade Unions (established in 1899), which, by a system of mutual insurance, provided assistance to unions engaged in disputes without impairing their autonomy. By 1913 there were 150 unions, with a total of 884,291 members affiliated to the General Federation. In 1914, as we have already seen, three of the more militant industrial, or general unions established the Triple Alliance. The Annual Congresses of the Trades Union Congress became holiday occasions on which speeches could be made without committing the speaker's union to any action, and at which resolutions could be passed which nobody expected to be carried into effect.

During the war, when it was often convenient to the government to deal with a central body representing the whole of organized labour, the prestige of the Trades Union Congress was raised. During the railway strike of 1919 a mediation Committee composed of representatives of other unions had proved of value in effecting a settlement. Moreover, it was becoming increasingly obvious that the Triple Alliance was a failure. The suggestion was therefore made that the Trades Union Congress be given powers to co-ordinate industrial action by the unions and to mediate in disputes when requested.

The new constitution, which was approved in 1920 and came into operation in 1921, divided the affiliated unions into seventeen Trade Groups. To each Group, in rough proportion to the total membership of the unions composing it, was allotted representation upon a General Council, which now took the place of the Parliamentary Committee. Candidates for membership of the General Council were to be nominated for each group by and from among the unions within that group, but to be elected by the whole membership of the Congress, by the method of card voting in proportion to affiliated membership. With the addition of two women representatives nominated by unions having female members and elected by the whole Congress, the General Council was to consist of thirty-two members in all. The composition of the Council is illustrated in the table on page 140.

This new constitution was finally adopted by the 1921 Congress, but a suggestion made by the Parliamentary Committee that a full-time Chairman be appointed failed to secure acceptance. More significant still was the rejection of a proposal that the new Council should have power to consult with any union concerned in an important industrial dispute in order " firstly to obtain an equitable settlement of the dispute without a stoppage of work, and, secondly, failing such a settlement, that the machinery and resources of the movement generally may be co-ordinated and applied in such a way as to secure a successful issue." It was the first section of this proposal, rather than the second, which aroused hostility. The big unions would not accept any clause in the constitution which might limit their sovereignty or their right to strike without consulting anybody but themselves. They were unprepared to face the fact that other unions would be unwilling to come to the aid of one engaged in a strike unless

THE TRADES UNION CONGRESS

Trade Group	No. of Unions 1924	No. of Unions 1936	No. of Unions 1937	No. of Reps. on Gen. Council	Membership 1924	Membership 1936	Membership 1937
1. Mining and Quarrying	8	7	8	3	789,411	523,860	544,705
2. Railways	3	3	3	3	446,241	413,031	448,779
3. Transport (other than Railways)	10	9	9	3	412,867	539,033	605,893
4. Shipbuilding	4	4	4	1	132,043	73,480	77,541
5. Engineering, Founding, Vehicle Building	23	27	27	3	430,822	342,458	449,212
6. Iron and Steel, and Minor Metal Trades	19	19	19	2	151,707	109,774	119,178
7. Building, Woodworking, Furnishing	16	18	18	2	355,431	303,867	326,619
8. Printing and Paper	13	14	13	1	159,835	161,319	168,793
9. Cotton	35	48	49	2	236,649	189,857	185,385
10. Textiles (other than cotton)	17	17	14	1	153,158	108,076	104,771
11. Clothing	9	8	8	1	92,889	85,959	91,792
12. Leather and Boot and Shoe	5	6	6	1	84,101	96,363	101,995
13. Glass, Pottery, Chemicals, Food, Etc.	16	18	18	1	189,135	249,975	275,472
14. Agriculture	1	1	1	1	30,000	31,000	32,000
15. Public Employees	9	5	5	1	143,864	50,212	60,429
16. Non-Manual Workers	8	7	9	1	63,610	54,157	74,310
17. General Workers	6	3	3	3	456,472	282,130	341,773
TOTAL	203	214	214	30	4,328,235	3,614,551	4,008,647

With the addition of two representatives of Women Workers, the Council numbers 32 in all.

they were satisfied that the strike was necessary and unless they were given some share in determining the peace terms. For the moment therefore, all that could be hoped for from the creation of the Council was that the grouping system might help to settle the demarcation difficulties which existed between unions in the same trade or engaged in similar work. It was hoped by some that the establishment of the groups might one day help to bring into existence a comprehensive system of Industrial Unionism.

During the two years of deep depression which followed the collapse of the boom in 1920 organized labour was on the defensive. The total membership of trade unions fell by 33 per cent., and the female membership by 35 per cent. The temporary gains of the period of inflation had been wiped out. But the mass of the membership, especially in the basic industries, was still solid, and far from ready to accept wage reductions without a struggle.

In February 1921 the government announced a decision to restore the coal mines to private ownership at the same time as the wage agreement, made in November 1920, expired. The owners called for a resumption of the pre-war practice of making district, and not national, wage agreements, and demanded drastic wage reductions. The demands were rejected, and a lock-out began on March 31. The Miners' Federation again approached the Triple Alliance. The circumstances were more favourable to co-operation than those of the previous year, for now it was clear that all workers would have to suffer wage reduction if the miners were defeated. The Triple Alliance, having failed to secure renewed negotiations between the owners and the Miners' Federation, announced on April 8 that a strike of railway and other transport workers would take place on April 12. Immediately the government declared a state of emergency, and used its powers under the 1920 Act to enrol a special Defence Force, besides calling up Army reservists. All over the country men who had fought side by side in the Great War found themselves in opposite camps. The mood of organized labour was not bellicose, but quietly determined.

The government now took a hand in the dispute and, while it was negotiating, the Triple Alliance strike was postponed to

Friday, April 15. On the Thursday night the whole nation was tense with excitement, and Mr. George Lansbury was announcing to an enthusiastic company of dancers at a Herald League reception that "to-morrow may see the dawn of the Social Revolution." As he was speaking, Mr. Frank Hodges, Secretary of the Miners' Federation, was putting before a meeting in the House of Commons suggestions for a temporary settlement. The next morning he was repudiated by a majority vote of his Executive. But the rejection of possible terms of settlement, without the approval of the Triple Alliance, was unsatisfactory to the leaders of the railwaymen and the transport workers. They decided to withdraw the strike orders given to their members. By all the militant elements in the Labour movement the day has been known since as Black Friday. It was the end of the Triple Alliance. The lock-out of the miners continued, and by the end of June they were obliged to return to work at greatly reduced wages, which were to be adjusted in future on the basis of the proceeds of the industry in each of the thirteen districts.

Cotton workers and shipyard joiners were also involved in stoppages of work during 1921 and both had to accept some reduction in wages, while in many other industries reductions were made in accordance with the normal working of agreements. The next big dispute of the period occurred in 1922 in the engineering industry, where the Amalgamated Engineering Union refused to accept a proposed agreement permitting the working of overtime at the discretion of the employer. Eventually the dispute was extended to forty-seven other unions, and a lock-out of 250,000 workers took place. After three months the unions were obliged to sign an agreement recognizing the right of the employers "to manage their establishments" and providing machinery for making changes in working conditions "in the process of evolution." It was generally recognized that a limit had been placed to any extension of "workers' control."

Advocates of self-government in industry had received an even more severe blow in 1921, with the collapse of the Building Guild. This was an ambitious attempt by an organization of workers to build houses independently of the capitalist employer. It was greatly helped by the existence of a State subsidy to housing which provided capital while work was in progress. For a time it was apparently successful, and similar guilds were established to make clothing, pianos and furniture. But its promoters were far too sanguine. They used capital unwisely, failed to build up reserves of profits, and were planning ambitious extensions at a time when they would have been better engaged in detailed administration. Moreover, democratic election of persons who had to exercise managerial and commercial functions in many cases proved a failure. When the conditions of the housing subsidy were revised, the Guild collapsed. With it Guild Socialism disappeared.

With the gradual lifting of the depression and the artificial stimulus given to the coal mining industry in 1923, the decline in trade union membership was arrested, but a campaign to secure new recruits was a failure. The Trades Union Congress of that year was notable for the number of inter-union disputes which were ventilated in the public sessions. The bitterness of the accusations and counter-accusations provoked a protest from the veteran miners' leader, Robert Smillie. Rapidly changing conditions of labour, with the introduction of new mechanical processes and the perfection of new substances, were affecting many trades; and the substitution of machinery for labour had been accelerated during the depression. Moreover, now that the post-war wave of enthusiasm for trade unionism had subsided, the leaders of several unions which had built up a membership on the crest of the wave were struggling anxiously to maintain themselves. They were accused of "poaching" members from other unions—and the accusations were too often justified. On the other hand, some of the larger unions were said to be striving to strangle the smaller. It was clear that the trade union house must be put in order, and that the only body to do it was the General Council.

Already the Council was proceeding to tidy up the loose ends of organization and to interest itself in a wider sphere of responsibility. It withdrew from the Labour and Socialist International (which it had joined in 1917), leaving the British Labour Movement to be represented in this political body by the Labour Party, but remained a member of the International Federation of Trade Unions. It refused to accept a proposal that the National Unemployed Workers'

Committee Movement should become affiliated to Congress, but it established a Joint Advisory Council with that organization. A new full-time Secretary to the Council was appointed, with the proviso that the office could not be held by a Member of Parliament. Finally the Congress empowered the Council to continue the experiment, begun in 1922, of owning and publishing—in association with the Labour Party—the *Daily Herald*. The Council also drew up an ambitious scheme for a system of Workers' Education " embracing residential colleges in various important industrial centres, with classes, week-end and Summer Schools." This scheme, however, never aroused general enthusiasm. It remained on paper for three years, being embellished from time to time, and was finally abandoned after 1926.

In 1924 further progress was made. The Disputes Committee of the General Council had had to hold some forty meetings between September 1923 and July 1924. They were largely concerned with accusations of member-poaching. Evidently some clear principle of demarcation or organization must be found if such disputes were not to become a source of serious difficulty and weakness. Yet the structure of British trade unionism scarcely permitted the application of any principle. The craft unions organizing skilled and—in some cases—semi-skilled workers spread horizontally across industry, being concerned to maintain the skilled standards of men requiring the same training and doing the same type of work for a variety of different employers. Conflict between them and the general labour unions was infrequent, for the latter also extended horizontally across a number of different industries, organizing the less-skilled and more poorly paid workers. Cutting vertically across these two types of union, however, were the industrial or employmental unions, seeking to enrol all workers, skilled or unskilled, in the same industry or the same employment. Here there were innumerable sources of friction. The vertical unions are few—indeed, in the major industries of the country only the Miners' Federation and the National Union of Railwaymen fully represent the type—but they claim to enrol workers performing a great variety of tasks. The National Union of Railwaymen had frequent disputes with other engineering unions as well as with the

Associated Society of Locomotive Engineers and Firemen. It also quarrelled with the Transport and General Workers' Union over the organization of road transport workers employed by railway companies. The Miners' Federation of Great Britain and its district organizations had disputes with a great variety of craft societies as well as with unions organizing general labourers. Moreover, inter-union disputes were not confined to matters arising from the overlapping of unions based upon different principles of organization. The Trades Union Congress had never attempted to lay down a rule recognizing only one union as the appropriate organization for a given class of worker. In many trades, therefore, there exist a number of unions catering for the same or for very similar types of worker. This is true of labouring and semi-skilled occupations no less than of the skilled crafts. Disputes therefore arise over the transfer of members from one organization to another as well as over the allocation of work. In extreme instances bribery and even strike-breaking were resorted to in the competition for membership.

The 1924 Congress laid down four rules concerning the transfer of members from one union to another. In future every worker applying for membership of a union must state if he has been a member of any other union and " what his financial relationship to that union is." If he has been a member of another union, then the latter must be consulted before his application is accepted. No member in arrears with payments to one union should be allowed to transfer to another. No union should accept transfers from members of another union which is engaged in a trade dispute.

This solution of the problem was empirical and eminently practical. It simply recognized the existence of a large number of unions based upon diverse principles and provided a means for minimizing friction among them. The rules laid down were not always observed, but as time went on the General Council was able to secure better and better observance of them. In instances where disputes were frequent and where labour was weakened vis à vis the employer by its own dissensions, the Council adopted the practice of establishing Advisory Councils—e.g. for the coal mining industry—

composed of all the unions having members in the industry concerned. It insisted on the submission of all disputes to the Disputes Committee of the Council; and by holding in reserve the threat of suspension or disaffiliation secured observance of its decisions. The number of inter-union disputes was gradually reduced until during the years of the Great Depression they almost disappeared. During the subsequent trade recovery the number has again increased; but the procedure for dealing with them has become so well established that they are no longer a very serious source of weakness.

The 1924 Congress was not satisfied with a hum-drum solution of inter-union difficulties. It hoped that a drastic reduction of the number of unions, with a consequent increase of strength as well as elimination of friction, might be achieved by a comprehensive reorganization, and therefore instructed the Council to prepare a scheme for organization by industry. Strong opposition on the part of some of the general labour unions and the older craft unions indicated that the achievement of such a scheme would not be easy. A final decision on this matter, however, was not taken until 1927. For the next two years there were more exciting affairs to claim attention.

While the trade unions had been losing membership during the depression, the Labour Party was rapidly gaining strength. In the General Election of 1922 it increased its poll to 4,237,000 and its representation in the House of Commons to 142. For the first time it became the official Opposition. Its leader, Ramsay MacDonald, acquired a new prestige. During the war he had been execrated, and for four years he had been out of Parliament, finding a warm welcome only among the Left-wing elements of the Party, who had either been themselves opposed to the war or had been revolted by the terms of the peace treaties. As Leader of the Opposition he now seemed to stand for a complete break with the whole home and foreign policy of the post-war coalition. Only professional politicians and close students of public affairs remembered the correct parliamentarianism and cautious gradualness of his attitude in pre-war Parliaments. During the General Election of 1923 his progress through the industrial districts resembled that of a Messiah. His party scarcely increased its electoral vote of the previous year, but secured 192 seats, many of them being gained by minority votes in " three-cornered " contests. MacDonald formed a government, which held office, for rather less than a year, with grudging support from the Liberal Party.

There is no space here to recount the history of the first Labour Government. It may reasonably be claimed that its actual achievements—the conduct of negotiations leading to the Dawes Plan, the suspension of work on the Singapore naval base, the reversal of the policy of economy in education services, amendment of unemployment insurance and pensions legislation in the interests of the unemployed and the aged, the establishment of minimum wages in agriculture, and a far-reaching Housing Act—were highly creditable in the political circumstances and in the time available. But the keen political workers in the Party had been led to expect that a Labour Government would be radically different from other governments. They might have been satisfied in the circumstances by minor legislative and administrative reforms had there been a difference of temper and attitude in the ministers whom they had put into office. Instead they found that the Cabinet was anxious upon every possible occasion to emphasize that there was no break in continuity in its attitude to every traditional institution. The wearing of Court dress, zealous attendance at Society functions, the establishment of a club to impart deportment to the wives of Members of Parliament, the acceptance of knighthoods by members of the government were trumpery things in themselves. But they were correctly regarded by members of the Independent Labour Party—which had provided the fire and zeal of socialist propaganda—as a symptom of an intention to carry on the King's government with no substantial change in the social or economic system. The most significant acts of the government were negative. The Chancellor of the Exchequer buried in the papers of a Royal Commission the proposal for a levy on capital, which had been one of the chief items in the Party's election programme, and which, if it had been carried out, might have made a vital difference in the public finance of 1931. The Prime Minister, who was also Foreign Secretary, and who had declared a year before that " there will never be peace so long as the Versailles Treaty is in existence," repudiated a demand for a revision of the Treaty made by the Home Secretary at a by-election.

The Socialists were disillusioned by the behaviour of their leaders in office, but their criticisms were not so embarrassing as the actions of the trade unions. A strike of railway locomotive men was actually in progress when the government was formed. During its short lifetime there were two strikes of dock-workers, a lock-out in the shipyards and one in the building industry, a threat of a strike by coal miners, an unofficial strike on the London underground railways, and a strike of tramway and bus workers in London. Economic circumstances, as has already been explained, favoured attempts to raise wages and improve conditions. Rank and file members of the unions undoubtedly thought that it should be easy to gain advances when a Labour government was in office. To Cabinet ministers the strikes were a nuisance. In so far as they were genuinely striving to consolidate power for the transformation of the capitalist system, temporary improvements in wages were of no importance and they resented the waste of time occupied in mediation. In so far as they were determined to carry on the work of government as respectably as any of their predecessors, they felt themselves obliged to maintain essential services in the interests of the " community." The trade union world was shocked when during the London transport strike the government actually proclaimed a state of emergency, under the terms of the hated Act of 1920. The strike was settled before the emergency powers were used; but the relations between the Labour Party and the General Council of the Trades Union Congress were severely strained.

The government came to an ignominous end in the autumn of 1924. The Attorney General, who knew nothing of the history of the Labour Movement, mishandled the proposed prosecution of a Communist editor for calling upon soldiers not to fire upon strikers, and so precipitated a General Election. The Prime Minister, exhausted by the strain of his two offices and made nervous and irritable by continual criticism from both the socialist and the trade union wings of his party, made an even greater blunder in his handling of the " Zinovieff Letter." Had the time and the occasion for the election been better chosen, it cannot be doubted that the Party would have made considerable gains, for the mass of Labour voters remained loyal and the temper of the whole movement was militant. As it was, anti-Labour electors refused to vote for Liberal candidates and though the Labour vote was well maintained, most of the seats gained by Labour in "three-cornered" contests were lost. A Conservative government took office with a large majority. In a mood of irritation with the politicians the Labour movement swung towards industrial action.

The formation of the Labour government had temporarily taken away from the leadership of their unions and from the councils of the Trades Union Congress several of the older and more cautious trade union officials. In their absence younger men, more responsive to the militant mood of the rank and file, secured positions of importance, while some of the older leaders who remained were disappointed by their failure to secure political office and were far from averse from embarrassing the government. The Trades Union Congress of 1924 was presided over by A. A. Purcell, an official of the National Amalgamated Furnishing Trades Association, one of the most pronouncedly Left-wing of all the unions. It actually adopted a programme, called the Industrial Workers' Charter, which included many political objectives. Though in fact this Charter became buried in the declaration of "objects" in the Standing Orders of the Congress and has scarcely been heard of since, its adoption was symptomatic of impatience with the achievements of the Labour Party, which would normally have been regarded as the proper vehicle for the achievement of such aims. The Congress rejected a proposal to affiliate the National Unemployed Workers' Committee Movement to the Trades Union Congress, but endorsed the activities of the National Joint Advisory Committee of the two bodies which had been established in 1923. It recognized the secretaries of Trades Councils as its local correspondents and called upon the Trades Councils to conduct joint propaganda campaigns with the N.U.W.C.M. in favour of an Unemployed Workers' Charter. It endorsed the action of its representatives in the International Federation of Trade Unions in insisting upon continuing negotiations with the Russian Trade Unions for international unity, and gave an enthusiastic welcome to a fraternal delegation from the U.S.S.R. Most important of all, however, was its decision to revise standing orders so as to give greater powers of co-ordination to the General Council.

In 1923 a proposal of a similar kind had been rejected, partly because of opposition by the Miners' Federation, which feared a possible infringement of union sovereignty, partly because of an objection by the general labour unions—which have large memberships but low rates of contributions—to a clause which empowered the Council to raise levies in proportion to membership from affiliated unions. By 1924 the situation was changed. The General Council itself brought forward virtually the same resolution as that which had been rejected the year before, but dropped the suggestion of a levy. Its spokesman was Arthur J. Cook, recently elected Secretary of the Miners' Federation in succession to Mr. Frank Hodges, who had taken office in the Labour government. After only three speeches, the resolution was carried by an almost unanimous vote. It required affiliated unions to keep the Council informed of all disputes likely to involve large bodies of workers. So long as there was a prospect of an amicable settlement of such a dispute by the regular machinery of the trade the Council, unless requested to do so, should not intervene. But if there should occur a deadlock in the negotiations " of a character as to directly or indirectly involve other bodies of workpeople affiliated to the Trades Union Congress in a stoppage of work *and/or to imperil standard wages or hours and conditions of employment* " then the Council might consult the union concerned, offer advice, and if necessary report to Congress. *If the advice of the Council were accepted* by the union and still " the policy of the employers enforces a stoppage of work by strikes or lock-out, the Council shall forthwith take steps to organize on behalf of the union or unions concerned all such moral and material support as the circumstances of the dispute may appear to justify." It was not long before these new powers were used.

During 1925 the General Council continued its militant policy. It sent a delegation to Russia to further its project of a World Labour Conference which might unite the International Federation of Trade Unions and the Red International of Labour Unions. After a further rebuff for this policy from the majority of the International Federation of Trade Unions, which insisted that, while it would consider the affiliation to itself of the Russian Unions if they would accept its constitution, it would not negotiate with the Red International of Labour Unions, the General Council proceeded to establish a Joint Advisory Council with the Russian unions. It also continued its joint action with the National Unemployed Workers' Committee Movement, apparently finding no great embarrassment in association with its Communist leaders.

At the beginning of May the Gold Standard was restored to the pre-war parity. The Labour Party in the House of Commons protested that the return was made too soon, but raised no objection to the parity at which it was effected. In July the General Council called a special conference on unemployment which passed a resolution suggesting that foreign policy was responsible for the loss of export trade, but failing to make any reference whatever to the new monetary policy and the deflation which it entailed. The Labour movement had failed to perceive the significance of the decision. It proceeded to enter into the biggest struggle of its history without understanding that the effort to maintain wages could not be successful unless monetary policy were completely reversed.

During June and July the Council, in virtue of its new position as a co-ordinator of action, took a prominent part in disputes in the cotton textile and coal industries. In the former instance, after a short stoppage of work, the employers' demand for a reduction and the workers' for an increase in wages was referred to a Court of Enquiry. But the request of the coal-owners for a reduction in wages and a revision of the agreement led to far more serious developments. The Miners' Federation approached the General Council, which immediately appointed a special committee to watch the dispute and placed at the disposal of the miners the research and publicity departments which it maintained jointly with the Labour Party. The Federation placed itself "unreservedly in the hands of the General Council" and the Special Committee proceeded to discuss with all the important transport unions (except the National Sailors and Firemen's Union, which refused to participate) plans for refusing to handle coal in the event of a stoppage of the mines. It also considered plans for raising funds from other unions and established special contact with the International Transport Workers' Federation and the International

Federation of Trade Unions. Finally when negotiations with the government and the mineowners had produced few concessions and actually elicited a suggestion that working hours be increased, the General Council and the Executive of the four unions concerned issued instructions to all transport workers to stop the movement of coal from midnight on July 31. On that day the government announced that it would pay a subsidy to the industry so as to maintain existing wages until May 1, 1926, while a Royal Commission would be appointed to report on the economic condition of the industry.

At the September Congress the President referred in glowing terms to this victory, saying that he and his colleagues had "lived a glorious week—one that will ever be remembered. It was historical." The Congress, however, refused to accept a proposal to strengthen the Council further by giving it power to raise a levy from affiliated unions and to call a strike by other unions to assist "a union defending a vital trade union principle." It referred the whole question to the Council for further enquiry. The debates were marked by the return to Congress of Right-wing leaders, such as Mr. J. R. Clynes, Mr. J. H. Thomas and Miss M. Bondfield. The two latter returned to their seats on the General Council, to which Mr. Ernest Bevin was now for the first time elected.

The interval which remained before the expiration of the coal subsidy was not, however, used to much purpose, either for enquiry or for preparation, by the unions. For some time unions in the mining, engineering, railway, transport and shipbuilding industries were actually engaged in considering a scheme for a new Industrial Alliance, which was not finally abandoned until the end of 1925. The government, on the other hand, announced before the end of September the formation of an Organization for Maintaining Supplies, and followed this in November with other plans for dealing with a "national emergency."

The indefatigable A. J. Cook, in a succession of meetings up and down the country was heartening the miners for a struggle by infectious rhetoric and by the constant repetition of the hypnotic phrase—"Not a penny off the pay, not a minute on the day." On the railways and in the engineering shops workers in other unions were threatened with wage reductions, and became convinced that the miners' struggle was their struggle. The rank and file of the Labour movement were more sympathetic with the miners than ever before. A number of Labour Party successes in Parliamentary and local elections showed that public opinion tended to be on their side. The threat to strike in July 1925 had been completely successful. The unions in consequence were over-confident for the future. The General Council made no effective plans for a General Strike. Its more militant members thought that it would be easier to win than it proved to be. The more cautious hoped that there would be no strike. Meanwhile the government laid its plans in detail.

When the Royal Commission reported in March its recommendations, as might have been expected, satisfied neither side. But the government was unwilling to adopt them unless both parties agreed. By paying a subsidy the government had admitted that costs of production in the industry were too high. By pledging themselves to accept no reductions of wages or increase of hours the miners were making a substantial lowering of costs impossible. If they were to be successful something had to give way—and that something was the government's monetary policy. When the strike eventually took place the government was therefore right in claiming that it was a strike against the government. At the same time the trade union leaders were right in claiming that the miners were only the vanguard in a fight that was the fight of the whole working class. If their wages were reduced, then the wages of almost every other worker must also be reduced, so as to make the monetary policy successful.

It is impossible here to give a full account of the great strike which began on May 4, 1926. Certain salient features only can be mentioned. Strictly speaking, it was not a *general* strike, though that is a convenient term by which to refer to it. In consultation with the General Council of the Trades Union Congress the executives of their unions called out all railway men, workers in road and dock transport, iron and steel, other metals and heavy chemicals, builders (excepting housing and hospitals), and printers. Unions connected with the supply of electricity and gas were directed to "co-operate with the object of ceasing to supply power." Many other workers, of course, were rendered idle indirectly in the course of the dispute, but they were not strikers. This selection of workers was made with some show of reason, but was not carefully thought out. It was designed to prevent the movement of coal and the development and use of substitutes for it, and at the same time to check propaganda hostile to the strike. But in large numbers of instances men were called out from factories which continued to work. Printers and furnace-men employed in a soap-works, for example, would be ordered to cease work, while the manufacturing and packing workers would continue. The places of the strikers would be filled by " blacklegs," for in such factories it often happens that the majority of the workers are not trade unionists themselves and have no incentive to defend the interests of the craftsmen who do belong to unions. Even where the unskilled workers were unionists, but were not themselves called out, they were not prepared to make sacrifices for the sake of the craftsmen. When the strike was over scores of loyal craftsmen therefore lost their jobs. Yet their participation in the strike had helped nobody. It was little wonder that there was a decline in union membership in the months immediately following the strike.

The stoppage of the printing of newspapers had certain advantages, and in so far as news could be carried by word of mouth the General Council, with an army of skilled public speakers at its command, was in a strong position. But the government controlled the broadcasting service, which was used with great effect. It was also able to produce its own news-sheet, the *British Gazette*, which was little less provocative than private newspapers would have been, while it had the prestige of being official. All that the trade unions permitted their own fully equipped daily newspaper to issue was a similar news-sheet, the circulation of which was much smaller than it need have been because no efficient transport service had been provided for it.

The nine days of the strike were so remarkably free from violence that the whole world was astonished. This may partly have been due to the temperament of the British people and to the almost complete absence of weapons in private possession in Britain. But fundamentally the explanation undoubtedly was that neither the strikers nor the general public believed that they were challenging constitutional government or making an attack upon the community. Both strikers and public believed that they were engaged in an unusually big trade dispute for the sole purpose of helping the miners.

In fact, of course, once the government had proclaimed an emergency, established its Organization for the Maintenance of Supplies, appointed special constables and called out reserves, the strike could only succeed by beating the government. If it lasted long, it would defeat itself by the exhaustion of union funds and eventual starvation. Yet the only way to shorten it was to call out key men in the public utility services, cut off supplies of light and power, and paralyse communication. In that event the government would be bound to use armed forces to maintain the services.

There can be no doubt that the General Council wished to confine the strike within the bounds of a trade dispute. Some at least of its members felt that they had been forced (by the tactics of the government) into a position in which they were in charge of a movement much bigger and more dangerous than anything they had intended to start. The senior leaders of the Labour Party never concealed their hostility to the strike, and Mr. J. H. Thomas, while it was still in progress, made a public speech attacking "the principle of a General Strike" and emphasizing the purely industrial nature of the dispute. On the other side of the quarrel, there is no doubt that influential members of the government had been determined, since the success of the General Council's threat in July 1925, that an outright conflict with the unions and a definite defeat of a large-scale sympathetic strike was necessary. This section of the government appeared to control policy while the strike was in progress. While the government was determined upon victory, many of the leaders of the General Council were equally determined not to defeat the government.

During the course of the dispute Sir John Simon, who was not then a member of the government but was the best-known King's Counsel of the time and one who had taken a prominent part in the framing and interpretation of trade union legislation, reminded strikers that by leaving their employment without notice they had committed a breach of contract and were liable to suit for damages. He further stated that because notice had not been given, the strike was illegal and "every trade union leader who has advised and promoted this course of action is liable in damages to the uttermost farthing of his personal possessions." Mr. Justice Astbury, in a judgment given in a case brought by the National Sailors' and Firemen's Union (which opposed the strike) against some of its officials who attempted to order members to strike, later pronounced the strike illegal on the ground that the strikers were not engaged in a trade dispute and declared that union funds could not be legally used to support a strike which was illegal. These pronouncements may have tended to hasten the end of the conflict, but they can scarcely have had the decisive influence which some writers have attributed to them. Mr. Justice Astbury's judgment has been severely criticized by very competent legal authorities; and it may well be doubted whether many strikers were intimidated by Sir John Simon's threat of County Court proceedings. Moreover, the desire to end the strike had existed almost from the day it began.

The General Council had not prepared for a prolonged struggle with the government. An organization for the distribution of food and other necessities and for the maintenance of communications between the General Council and the men on strike had to be improvised at the last minute. The local Trades Council—or in some cases specially improvised Councils of Action—were the bodies used for these purposes. At first there was great confusion. In the localities there was overlapping between the Trades Councils and the Joint Transport Committees, charged with the duty of issuing permits for food transport. At headquarters there was failure to utilize the services of individuals and organizations who offered help, and a lack of appreciation of the need of the localities for information and guidance. But as the days passed, great improvements were made, and there was little wavering by the strikers, especially in the industrial regions. When the engineers and shipyard workers were called out on May 12 the number of strikers was probably greater than at the beginning. The strike was not broken, it was abandoned. It was an impressive display of sympathy with the miners, of loyalty to the unions and obedience to their leaders, of capacity to improvise local organization, of ability to stand firm in face of appeals to patriotism and threats of force. But the end of the strike was not at all impressive.

Just as the Triple Alliance in 1921 had had no firm understanding as to the terms on which the dispute could be settled, so the General Council in 1926, while it had authority to conduct the strike, had no power to make an agreement to end the strike of the miners. During the last four days of the dispute the Council discussed possible terms of settlement with Sir Herbert Samuel, the Chairman of the Royal Commission which had reported upon the mining industry. The latter acted unofficially and made it clear that he had no authority from the government to negotiate. There resulted from the discussions a Memorandum which in the opinion of the Council formed a satisfactory basis for a settlement of the mining dispute. It provided for a withdrawal of the lock-out notices which had been posted by the coalowners at the beginning of the dispute, and for the continuance of a government subsidy pending a final wage settlement. There should be no wage reductions " unless there are sufficient assurances that the measures of reorganization proposed by the Commission will be effectively adopted." A National Wages Board, associating owners and miners " with a neutral element and an independent chairman " should be established as the wage authority for the industry. Certain guiding rules concerning minimum wages were also laid down and a policy for the organized transference of displaced labour was suggested.

When the Memorandum was put before the miners' Executive, the latter body naturally wished to know whether there was any guarantee that the government would endorse it if it were accepted. No firm guarantee could be given, and the Executive reiterated its refusal to accept any reduction of wages. On the morning of May 13 a delegation from the General Council visited the Prime Minister and informed him that the strike would be ended forthwith.

The record of this interview makes it clear that the government made no promise to adopt the proposals of the Samuel Memorandum, nor undertook to secure reinstatement for strikers. If any members of the delegation thought that they had come to ratify an agreement between equal parties, they were quickly disillusioned by the terms in which the Prime Minister dismissed them.

In the subsequent recriminations, which lasted for many months, the leaders of the miners declared that they had been betrayed. The General Council blamed the miners' Executive for rejecting the Samuel Memorandum, asserting that had they agreed to it then the government could have been induced to implement it, that the miners should have given plenary powers to the General Council to settle the dispute, and that because this was not done the latter had no alternative but to call the strike off. Whatever views be held about these arguments, there is no doubt that the strike was a failure. The miners maintained their resistance for a further six months, and then returned to work beaten on every issue: hours of labour were increased from seven to eight per shift, wages were fixed independently in each district and were drastically reduced. The funds of the union were almost exhausted, membership fell off, and in Nottinghamshire the owners entered into an agreement with a new breakaway organization called the Miners' Industrial (non-political) Union, which also secured some membership in other coalfields.

The members of other unions were confronted, when they returned to work, with demands for a worsening of conditions and even for a repudiation of union membership. Railway workers, for example, were told that they must recommence as new employees with past service no longer counted, and on day-to-day contracts. In these conditions there was a resurgence of militancy, and on May 14 there was virtually an unofficial general strike, to insist upon the maintenance of union conditions. Finally trade union agreements were restored as far as the majority of the larger employers were concerned, but in many instances strikers were never reinstated. The railway unions signed an agreement admitting "that in calling a strike they committed a wrongful act against the Companies," and promising "not again to instruct their members to strike without previous negotiations with the Companies."

During 1927 a Trade Disputes and Trade Unions Act was passed by Parliament. It makes illegal any strike which (*i*) has an object other than the furtherance of a trade dispute *within the trade or industry in which the strikers are engaged* or (*ii*) is "designed or calculated" to coerce the government either directly or by inflicting hardship upon the community. Since these clauses of the Act have not been tested in the courts it is not possible to say how the definition of "trade or industry" or the meaning of "calculated" may stand after judicial interpretation. It is fairly clear, however, that trade unions will not be prepared, while the law stands on the statute book, to undertake purely sympathetic strikes; a concerted cessation of work could only be achieved legally by the simultaneous presentation of unacceptable demands in a number of different trades. Even then the strike, though far from "general," might be illegal if it compelled government intervention. Besides providing for the punishment of persons instigating, or encouraging others to join illegal strikes, the Act provides that the Attorney-General may apply for an injunction to restrain a union from financing an illegal strike, and prevents unions from expelling or depriving of benefits members who refuse to join an illegal strike. This latter provision was made retrospective to May 1, 1926. The Act also "renders criminal many acts by pickets which hitherto do not seem to have been statutory offences."[1] It further forbade regular employees of government departments to belong to any association or federation not consisting solely of government employees. Thus it deprived the Trades Union Congress and the Labour Party of the funds derived from certain unions of postal workers and civil servants. Finally, by substituting "contracting in" for "contracting out," it rendered more difficult the raising of political funds by the unions.

. . . . .

In 1928 the General Council made a report to the annual meeting of the Trades Union Congress which is an illuminating summary of the opinions held within the unions since the War and a guide to the understanding of the policy which has been followed since the failure of the General Strike. The arguments of the report follow closely the lines of an article published nine months before by Mr. (now Sir) Walter Citrine, who had become Secretary to the Congress towards the end of 1925.

[1] Hedges and Winterbottom, *The Legal History of Trade Unionism*, p. 130.

" Broadly speaking," says the report, " there were three possible lines of policy open to the Trade Union Movement. The first was to say, frankly, that the unions will do everything possible to bring the industrial machine to a standstill, to ensure by all possible means the breakdown of the entire system, in the hope of creating a revolutionary situation on the assumption that this might be turned to the advantage of the workers and to the abolition of capitalism. That policy the Trade Union Movement has decisively rejected as futile, certain to fail, and sure to lead to bloodshed and misery.

" The second course was one of standing aside and telling employers to get on with their own job, while the unions would pursue the policy of fighting sectionally for improvements. The objections to this course are that it is entirely inconsistent with the modern demand for a completely altered status of the workers in industry, and that it is a futile policy, a confession of failure, for unions to say that they are going to take no hand in the momentous changes that are taking place in the economic life of the nation.

" The third course is for the Trade Union Movement to say boldly that not only is it concerned with the prosperity of industry, but that it is going to have a voice as to the way industry is carried on, so that it can influence the new developments that are taking place. The ultimate policy of the movement can find more use for an efficient industry than for a derelict one, and the unions can use their power to promote and guide the scientific reorganization of industry as well as to obtain material advantages from that reorganization."

From 1920 to 1926 the trade union movement was uneasily shifting between the first and the third of these policies. Once or twice in 1919 and 1920 events seemed likely to push the movement into choosing the first. In 1926 it might have seemed to outside observers that it had been adopted, though, as has been shown above, there was no real ground for such a belief. After 1926, and continuously since, the third policy has completely dominated the movement. The second still represents the instinctive attitude of large masses of ordinary members of the unions, but—except perhaps in some of the smaller craft societies—it has little attraction for the leaders.

The trade union sometimes appears to its most zealous members to be an organ of the class struggle of the workers against the exploiters. It seems as if the working class can only gain the full fruits of its labour by expropriating the capitalist.

Such a conception leads to a policy of frequent demands for improvement of conditions and of resistance on principle to all reductions of wages, whatever the circumstances. But when the zealous member becomes an official and is responsible for the welfare of the other members of the union his attitude to policy begins to change. It is not simply that he is now living on a salary derived from an organization the funds and membership of which he must preserve if he is to continue to receive his income; it is not that he has signed collective bargains with employers and allows his antagonism to become blunted by frequent association with them. It is rather that he perceives more clearly than he did before the day-to-day needs of his members. The importance of the maintenance of employment to the father of a family, of the ability to rely upon the punctual payment of benefit to the widow, the unemployed, or the sick come to seem at least as great as that of establishing a new social order. The responsible leader therefore tends to operate his union as an institution within the capitalist system. Sometimes he will organize it like any other capitalistic monopoly, restricting entry and raising the price as high as the traffic will bear. More often—in Great Britain, at any rate—he effects a compromise between the two extremes of the purely business-like and the revolutionary attitude, and will strive to increase the actual share his union takes in the management of industry while reserving for the political organ—the Labour Party—the task of gradually changing the ultimate control. But the union itself must remain a continuing institution within the framework of the capitalist system, arising naturally out of the system of large-scale production and the employment of large bodies of men by one employer.

There are, of course, variations in the completeness with which this conception is held. All leaders might not write so complacently as Sir Arthur Pugh, Secretary of the Iron and Steel Trades Confederation, who stated in *The Times* in June 1938 that " under modern conditions of mass production, involving the employment of large bodies of workpeople by individual concerns, the workers' organizations, in conjunction with those of the employers, provide the essential means for the amicable adjustment of labour questions which are inseparable from the conduct of a great industry. This results in the satisfactory regulation of the relations between employer and employed and security against unnecessary friction and dislocation which might otherwise prevail." But even Arthur Cook, whose sincerity and courage when in 1926 he demanded "not a penny off the pay, not a minute on the day" cannot be denied, in 1931 declared to the Trades Union Congress: "There are those who blindly think that the way to destroy capitalism is to destroy the industries where the lives of our men are invested. . . . Are we to wait until capitalism has been smothered and there is no work, are we to wait until the end before we start? . . . What is the use of passing resolutions again and again against reductions when you cannot prevent them because of the economics of your industry? Do not shut your eyes to the economics of your industry." In these words he was in effect summarizing the policy first adopted in 1927.

At the Congress of 1926 the President in his introductory address had urged that though the unions had shown their determination to resist wage reductions, they favoured "the more enlightened policy of reducing costs by the most economic use of national resources; by the fullest application of science and invention and the elimination of wasteful methods of production and distribution." At the 1927 Congress his successor in the chair spoke with approval of co-operation with employers "in a common endeavour to improve the efficiency of industry and to raise the workers' standard of life." This was followed by an invitation to the unions to formulate their attitude to the changing conditions of industry which came from a group of employers headed by Sir Alfred Mond, afterwards Lord Melchett, the founder of Imperial Chemical Industries Ltd., one of the largest combinations in the world. As a result the General Council entered into a series of conversations during 1928 with this unofficial, but influential, group. There was some opposition to this move on the ground that the Mond group had no power to pledge other employers to support any decisions which might be reached, while the General Council might be committing the trade union movement to a dangerous degree. A. J. Cook in print and in public meetings as well as in the Council denounced the whole policy as class-collaboration contrary to the interest of the workers. The Amalgamated Engineering Union supported him to the extent of objecting to negotiations with an "unofficial" group of employers. This was an interesting temporary alliance between representatives of the skilled craft unionists, whose monopoly is threatened by the development of rationalization, and the Left-wing socialist who dislikes collaboration with the bourgeoisie. But the opposition was out-voted and the talks continued.

Agreed resolutions were eventually published which favoured the recognition of trade unions and the method of collective bargaining, denounced the practice of victimizing workers for union activity, approved of schemes of industrial rationalization if carried out with the co-operation of organized labour and with safeguards for displaced workers, suggested the need for a joint inquiry into monetary policy with special reference to the Gold Standard, and advocated the establishment of a National Industrial Council. The latter body should consist of the General Council of the Trades Union Congress on the one hand and of representatives of the Federation of British Industries and the National Confederation of Employers' Organizations on the other. It should meet once a quarter to discuss any question suggested by either side and should establish and direct a permanent bureau for continuous investigation into industrial problems. It should also provide machinery for establishing Conciliation Boards in any industry in which disputes occurred.

The suggestion, in effect, was that in return for collaboration in rationalization the unions should be permitted to participate in talks ranging over a wide variety of topics normally excluded from collective bargaining. By this method something like an agreed industrial opinion upon such questions as monetary and fiscal policy might be developed. When it was seen that regular machinery for discussion with fully authoritative bodies of employers was proposed, the opposition within the General Council was withdrawn. But the majority of the employers felt so strong after the defeat of the unions in 1926 that they saw no necessity for a Joint Industrial Council. When the proposal was put before the Federation of British Industries and the National Confederation of Employers' Organizations it was rejected, on the very unconvincing grounds that the latter had no authority to deal with general questions of economic policy and that the former could not deal with labour problems.

The two organizations of employers did agree, however, to a scheme of *ad hoc* consultations with the General Council. When any matter was raised by the latter, an allocation committee of the other two bodies was to decide which of them was to discuss it. Either of the two could also, of course, initiate a discussion with the General Council. Under this scheme discussions took place later between the General Council and the Federation of British Industries on the relations of finance and industry, on Commonwealth trade (resulting in a joint memorandum to the Imperial Conference), on the regulation of the film industry, and on trade with Russia. Technological unemployment has been discussed with the National Confederation of Employers' Organizations. But the full and regular examination of such questions that was hoped for by the originators of the talks has not occurred. Employers have not sought active partnership from labour in the development of industry. Mechanization and improvements in efficiency have been carried through with comparatively little opposition, and on the whole the unions have tended to acquiesce because they have not been strong enough to resist. If and when labour becomes scarce again and the unions grow militant, the employers may regret that they once refused the opportunity to establish a National Industrial Council.

While Mondism was still under discussion, the illusory ideal of Industrial Unionism was finally disposed of. An exhaustive inquiry had been made by a special committee of the General Council, whose report, presented to the 1927 Congress and printed in the official report of the proceedings, is the most penetrating analysis of the structure of British trade unionism yet published. It shows clearly that in circumstances where there prevail so great a number of unions with so wide a variety of membership, constitution and historical tradition, any previously conceived scheme of organization would come into conflict with too great a number of vested interests to be practicable. Moreover, industry itself is continually changing and even if boundaries could be satisfactorily defined they would become out-of-date almost as soon as established. But greater co-ordination of the existing unions would add strength: " the most effective way is by unions with closely related trade interests to seek amalgamation." Pending amalgamation, "unions with closely related industrial interests should enter into joint working arrangements on all industrial matters with a view to joint negotiations on questions of rates of pay and working conditions, and also the elimination of competition for members and consequent overlapping." Rather than prescribe any formal scheme of organization the committee suggested that every union should be invited to declare *in writing*—(1) whether it is prepared to participate in amalgamation negotiations with other unions, (2) the extent to which it is prepared to agree to joint working arrangements with other unions, (3) with which unions, in its opinion, is there the greatest possibility of progress being made in negotiations on either or both of the above questions.

This empirical solution of a chronic problem was not so markedly successful as that adopted in 1924 for avoiding and settling inter-union disputes, but some results did follow. It is true that the greatest amalgamations since 1920—those which made the Transport and General Workers' Union—were not effected through the agency of the General Council. But the latter has been able to assist and pilot to a successful conclusion some amalgamation negotiations of importance—notably in the garment-making industry. On several occasions, after agreed schemes have been drawn up with its aid and approved by the executives of the unions concerned, its efforts have been frustrated at the last moment by the ordinary members of the unions, who either have not taken the trouble to vote in sufficient numbers to satisfy the law or have feared to lose some special privilege adhering to the separate identity of the union. As Mr. Ernest Bevin in the debate on the report on organization said of the British trade unionist, "You can make a great speech to him on unity; but when you have finished he will say: 'what about funeral benefits?'" There is no doubt, however, that the difficulties to be overcome are better understood than they were before this report was made, and there is ground for believing that amalgamations of outstanding importance may yet be brought about, in which the principle of dual representation of the worker—by district and by trade—which has been successfully adopted by the Transport and General Workers' Union, will be applied.

After the failure of the General Strike there was a sharpening of antagonism between Left and Right in the Labour movement. Those who had been disillusioned by the conduct of the Labour Government in 1924 were disgusted by the way in which the strike had been called off in 1926. Mr. James Maxton, Chairman of the Independent Labour Party, joined A. J. Cook, while the latter was denouncing the conversations with the Mond group of employers, in issuing a manifesto criticizing the collaborationist policy of the majority leaders. Their subsequent public campaign was a failure, partly because Mr. Maxton was not prepared to launch a new Socialist party, partly because neither had any capacity for constructive organization. As a result, however, many of the more Left-wing trade unionists and members of the Independent Labour Party began to join the Communist Party, while the majority leaders determined to deal even more drastically than before with "disruptive" elements.

In its early days the Labour Party, as a loose federation of trade unions and socialist societies, having little power and therefore little responsibility, had included in its membership without much difficulty persons holding a wide variety of collectivist opinion. When, however, it remodelled its constitution to admit individual members and adopted a firm declaration of a socialist aim, the anomaly of differing conceptions of policy within the Party became more glaring. As it drew nearer to the assumption of power, its leaders increasingly felt the need for greater discipline so as to present a consistent attitude to the electorate and to ensure an obedient body of supporters in Parliament. In 1924 it was decided that no member of the Communist Party (which of course was not affiliated to the Labour Party) could be selected as a Labour Party candidate for Parliament or allowed to be an individual member of the Party. In 1925 the Party appealed to the trade unions not to send Communists as delegates to Labour Party conferences. By 1926 several local labour parties had been disaffiliated from the main Party for not expelling Communist members. In all such instances new local parties were established. Up till then the trade unions had maintained their tradition of allowing full rights to all members, whatever their political attitude or activity. From 1927 onwards, however, they began to follow a policy which resembled that of the Labour Party.

The breaking off of the close relations with the Russian trade unions which had been maintained during the lively years of 1924 and 1925 helped in the new orientation. During 1926 the British members of the Joint Advisory Committee frequently protested at the public criticism by the Russian leaders of the conduct of the British General Strike; but the meetings continued and the Committee declared that it would "unwaveringly and persistently struggle for the unity of the International Trade Union Movement." In 1927, however, the criticisms were repeated; and when the General Council refused to attend a joint meeting on the question of the British government's hostility to Russia (which it held to be outside the terms of reference of the Committee), it was roundly accused of "sabotage, opposition, procrastination and evasion." The Council reported to the Trade Union Congress that the Russians had tried to make the Committee a nucleus of a new international, and that it should be abandoned. Undoubtedly, the repeated bitter personal attacks upon union leaders by Communists, both at home and abroad, had much to do with the acceptance of this recommendation.

Complaints against these personal attacks figured prominently in the speeches in the 1927 Congress, when it was decided that Trades Councils affiliated to or associated with the National Minority Movement should be refused recognition by the General Council. The Minority Movement, which was associated with the Red International of Labour Unions, had been launched in 1924 and had secured the affiliation of a few union branches and local trades councils. It was also decided at this Conference to discontinue the association between the General Council and the National Unemployed Workers' Committee Movement, which was thought to be too much under Communist influence. In 1928 a new scheme for the establishment of Unemployed Associations in connection with the Trade Councils recognized by Congress was brought forward, and it was announced that Trades Councils disaffiliated from the Labour Party, because of refusal to expel Communists, would not be recognized by the Council. Substitute Trades Councils would be organized in association with the Labour Party. Congress also authorized a full inquiry into " disruptive elements " in the movement.

The lead of the General Council was followed by many of the larger unions, such as the National Union of General and Municipal Workers, the Transport and General Workers' Union, the National Union of Railwaymen and others. In general, members of the Minority Movement or Communist Party were prevented by these unions from holding office. Only a few delegates from certain smaller unions and from the Miners' Federation have remained since 1928 to express Communist Party opinion at the annual conferences of the Trades Union Congress. Even in the Miners' Federation, in which Communist and Left-wing membership was larger and more influential than in most other unions, the executive carried through disciplinary action, enforcing its opposition to the Minority Movement.

The report on " disruptive elements " presented to the 1929 Congress showed that ninety-two unions reported that they had had no experience of " disruption," while of the thirty-two which replied in the affirmative only in eight was the effect " reported as having been serious." Some other unions were so little interested that they did not bother to send information. Others are said not to have replied in order to give no advertisement to the Minority Movement's activities. This suggests the conclusions that in only certain branches of industry had Communist propaganda made any headway, that certain executives had been in greater danger of losing control than others, and possibly that some leaders were more interested in heresy hunting than others. It is fair to say, however, that certain leaders were singled out for attack in the Communist press and that it was hardly surprising that they replied with vigour.

In so far as the campaign against " disruption " permitted the General Council to influence affiliated unions in their attitude to the discipline and the qualifications for office of their own members, the prestige of the Council was increased. In 1928 it was further strengthened as the result of a dispute between the Miners' Federation and the National Union of Seamen (formerly the National Sailors' and Firemen's Union). The latter union, under the leadership of J. Havelock Wilson, had figured often in Congress quarrels of the past, and some of its officials had been attacked for their too close association with the ship-owning employers. It had refused to participate in the General Strike and had taken legal action against those of its officials who attempted to do so. During the subsequent lock-out of the miners it had assisted Mr. G. A. Spencer, a prominent miners' leader in Nottinghamshire, in forming the "non-political" union already referred to. Later it lent £10,000 to the latter union, and dismissed eight of its officials who sought to prevent this action. It lent organizers and motor cars and issued a journal for the "non-political" union from its offices. Refusing to desist from these activities, it was expelled from the Trades Union Congress by the 1928 Congress. A new Standing Order was also adopted giving the General Council power to summon before it for investigation any affiliated union pursuing activities "detrimental to the interests of the Trade Union Movement or contrary to the declared principles and policy of the Trades Union Congress," and to suspend it from membership, if found guilty, until the Congress itself should give a final decision.[1]

The events which led to the downfall of the Labour government which came into office in 1929 further strengthened the General Council. As in 1924, the Labour Party came into office at a time when unemployment (except in the coalfields) was comparatively small and when a fall in wages, which had been going on for some time, had been arrested. Its success in gaining 289 seats may be ascribed partly to these economic conditions, partly to the resentment felt by organized labour against the Trade Union Act of 1927, partly to mere boredom on the part of the electorate with a government which had held office for nearly five years, partly to the increase of the youthful vote by the extension of the franchise to women between twenty-one and thirty years of age, partly to the absence of any election scare or stunt and the choice of the uninspiring slogan "Safety First" by the Conservative Party,

[1] For a time the Council assisted the Transport and General Workers' Union in establishing a section for seamen. But after the death of Havelock Wilson in 1929 the situation was changed, and in 1930 the National Union of Seamen was reaffiliated, after promising never again to give support "moral, financial or otherwise" to the "non-political 'union' or any unions connected therewith."

and very largely to a recrudescence of the Liberal Party and a consequent big increase in the number of " three-cornered " contests. Though the Party was far stronger in Parliament than in 1924 there was even less indication of a desire to break with tradition than there had been when it first took office. There had been a distinct move to the Right since then. Knighthoods, which had been confined in 1924 to the Law officers in the government, were conferred upon several members of Parliament and prominent supporters in the country, and other distinctions were distributed for political services in the customary manner. Only at the Foreign Office was a welcome indication of independence given by Arthur Henderson, who promptly dismissed a highly-placed official who was unwilling to carry out his policy, and whose efforts resulted in the only big achievement of the Government —the withdrawal of troops from Germany.

The business of Parliament throughout the period of the second Labour government was dominated by unemployment. The government inherited a debt on the Unemployment Insurance Fund of £36,000,000, which had been accumulated during the period of attempted readjustment after the restoration of the Gold Standard. Before it had been in office a few weeks, the Great Depression had begun. Unemployment steadily increased throughout the period, and, despite increases in contributions, the debt mounted higher and higher. There is no need to recount here the story of the eventual collapse of the government. Suffice it to say that it never appeared for a moment to understand what was happening. Having referred repeatedly to the period 1924–1929 as one of depression, the Labour Ministers could only describe the world depression as an " economic blizzard "—a phrase which accurately indicated their ignorance as to its causation and their feeling of complete helplessness in face of it.

Despite the markedly less militant attitude of the General Council the relations between it and the government were not very much more cordial than they had been in 1924. This was mainly due to the growing aloofness and distrust of the union leaders shown by Philip Snowden and Ramsay MacDonald. It was scarcely the fault of the government that the Liberal Party insisted upon unacceptable amendments to its proposals for the modification of the Trade Union Act of 1927; but the union leaders were annoyed that these were not introduced until January 1931, and were naturally disappointed when they were abandoned. Nor was it to be blamed for being unable to reduce the working shift in the coal mines by more than half an hour; but this failure left some resentment in the minds of the leaders of the Federation. As far as the ordinary worker was concerned his experiences during the lifetime of the government were anything but happy. In the summer of 1929 a lock-out of cotton spinners resulted in a wage reduction. During 1930 a lock-out of weavers in the same industry, to enforce a demand by the employers for an increase in the number of looms per weaver, was unsuccessful; but it was notable that the employers refused to meet the General Council, which had been asked to intervene by the unions. Later in the same year a lock-out of workers in the woollen industry resulted in a disastrous defeat and wage reductions. Still later in the year and during 1931 wage reductions became general, and in a large number of instances they were accepted by the unions by negotiation.

During 1929 and 1930 the General Council had been discussing with representatives of the Federation of British Industries the relations of finance and industry and had been preparing and presenting its evidence to the Macmillan Committee appointed by the Chancellor of the Exchequer to report on that subject. Mr. Ernest Bevin, Secretary of the Transport and General Workers' Union and by now one of the two most influential persons on the General Council, was a member of the Committee. The evidence presented was a very accurate account of the development of monetary policy since the war and a penetrating discussion of the alternative policies possible in the existing situation. The relation between the wage level and employment was clearly perceived, and the Council came firmly down in favour of maintaining money wages even at the cost of perpetuating unemployment. " We are quite convinced that the right policy is to concentrate upon raising the efficiency of labour, not upon reducing the purchasing power of the wage earners, so intensifying the evil." It recognized that this policy might necessitate the devaluation of the £. When the Report of the Committee was published, the General Council issued a public statement in which it said: " The Macmillan

Committee is opposed to a revision of the gold parity of sterling. Notwithstanding the objections to such a policy the General Council reiterates their (*sic*) belief that some such measure may have to be taken."

It is not surprising that when the General Council was called into consultation on August 20, 1931, with the Economic Committee of the Cabinet and representatives of the Labour Party, they refused to agree to cuts in Civil Service wages and salaries and in unemployment benefit in order to preserve the Gold Standard. Four days later the Labour Government broke up, and it was natural that the General Council should in consequence be drawn nearer to those who now succeeded MacDonald, Snowden, and Mr. J. H. Thomas in the direction of the Labour Party's affairs. At the meeting of the Trades Union Congress in September, Arthur Henderson, the new leader, was cheered to the echo when he declared: "There is not going to be less consultation with the industrial side, but more."

The Trades Union Congress and the Labour Party had for many years possessed machinery for consultation, first in the form of a Labour Joint Board, and since 1921 as a National Joint Council. Until 1930 the General Council had five representatives out of a total of ten on this body. It had met comparatively rarely, and then often only to hear explained certain proposals involving action in Parliament which the Trades Union Congress wished to draw to the special attention of the Labour Party. Arthur Henderson suggested, however, to the 1928 meeting of the Trades Union Congress that "the National Joint Council ought in some respects to be a cabinet of the Labour Movement," for "the common understanding of policy." In 1930 it was reconstituted, this time with seven representatives of the General Council out of a total of fourteen. From the downfall of the second Labour government onwards it was increasingly used, and at monthly meetings considered the main political questions of the day, often issuing manifestos or public statements indicating the considered view of the whole organized Labour movement. Such regular discussions necessarily have a profound influence upon the policy of the Labour Party. As some of the representatives of the Party upon the Joint Council have in fact been trade union officials, the trade union view has tended to predominate. In 1935 the name of this body was changed to that of National Council of Labour, and its membership increased to sixteen, of whom eight were General Council representatives. Its pronouncements cover so wide a political field that it has definitely become the "Cabinet of Labour," of which Mr. Henderson spoke in 1928. It is no exaggeration to say that the policy of the Labour Party is now framed by it, for the annual conferences of the Party are dominated, except on rare occasions, by the block votes of the affiliated unions, and these have on many occasions been cast in accordance with the views formed by the leaders in the discussions of the National Council of Labour. Mr. Hugh Dalton, Chairman of the Labour Party, declared to the 1937 meeting of the Trades Union Congress that "we on the political side are determined that this close co-operation shall continue up to and beyond our conquest of political power in this land."

The growing political influence of the Trades Union Congress has been shown since 1931 in the increasing number of programmes on political subjects which it has sponsored. Indeed, there has been complaint in the Labour Party that the decisions of its annual Conferences in October have already been made beforehand at the Trades Union Congress meeting in September.[1] In 1932 and 1933 it was occupied in drawing up a programme for workers' participation in industry, which was largely concerned with the question of the best means of selecting the directorate of socialized industries. In the three years 1934 to 1936 it approved schemes for the socialization of the Iron and Steel, Cotton, and Coal-mining industries respectively. In 1936 also it declared its opinion on the future of the Gold Standard and monetary policy—unfortunately not so well conceived as its pronouncements upon this subject in 1930. In 1937, wisely ignoring the article in its constitution which pledges it to work for "adequate State pensions for all at the age of sixty," it adopted a scheme for State pensions for industrial workers on retirement at the age of sixty-five. Throughout the years 1933 to 1937 it made at every meeting decisions concerning Fascism, armaments and war. Almost

[1] In 1937 it was decided to hold the Labour Party Conferences in future at an earlier date.

without exception these decisions and programmes, having been discussed in the National Council of Labour, were accepted by the Labour Party after endorsement by the Trades Union Congress.

. . . . .

The years of the Great Depression were a period of great difficulty for organized labour. Total trade union membership which had stood at 5,506,000 in 1925 had fallen during the Gold Standard period to 4,858,000 in 1929. From then onwards there was a steady decline to 4,389,000 in 1933 at the bottom of the depression. The membership of the unions affiliated to the Trades Union Congress shows a similar fall over the same periods from 4,365,000 to 3,744,320 and then to 3,294,000.[1] On the whole, however, the decline in membership is less than might have been expected in view of the severity of the depression. The movement of the index of wages records a remarkable ability to resist reductions. Between June 1929, when the decline began, and November 1932, after which it ceased, the decline of the index was of the order of only 5·05 per cent. During the same forty months the decline in the official cost of living index was of the order of 10·6 per cent. The number of workers suffering reductions of wages was not half that of those so affected during 1921 and 1922, and the amount of the weekly decrease of wages was not a tenth of that effected then. Once the Gold Standard was abandoned, the special pressure on the exporting industries was relaxed. Wage reductions were more evenly spread throughout industry, and indeed were more severe in building, transport and public utilities and services than in manufacturing industry, with the possible exception of textiles.

The only industrial dispute of major importance during 1931 and 1932 occurred in the cotton industry. There were prolonged stoppages of work in both the spinning and weaving sections, resulting in every case in wage reductions. The system of more looms per weaver was introduced piecemeal by employers

[1] The Trades Union Congress figures refer to a date earlier than that at which they are published and their movements therefore always appear to lag one year behind those of the Ministry of Labour. An adjustment to allow for this has been made in the above statement and in the diagram on page 175.

The somewhat steeper fall in the Trades Union Congress figure between 1925 and 1929 is explained by the compulsory withdrawal of unions of State employees.

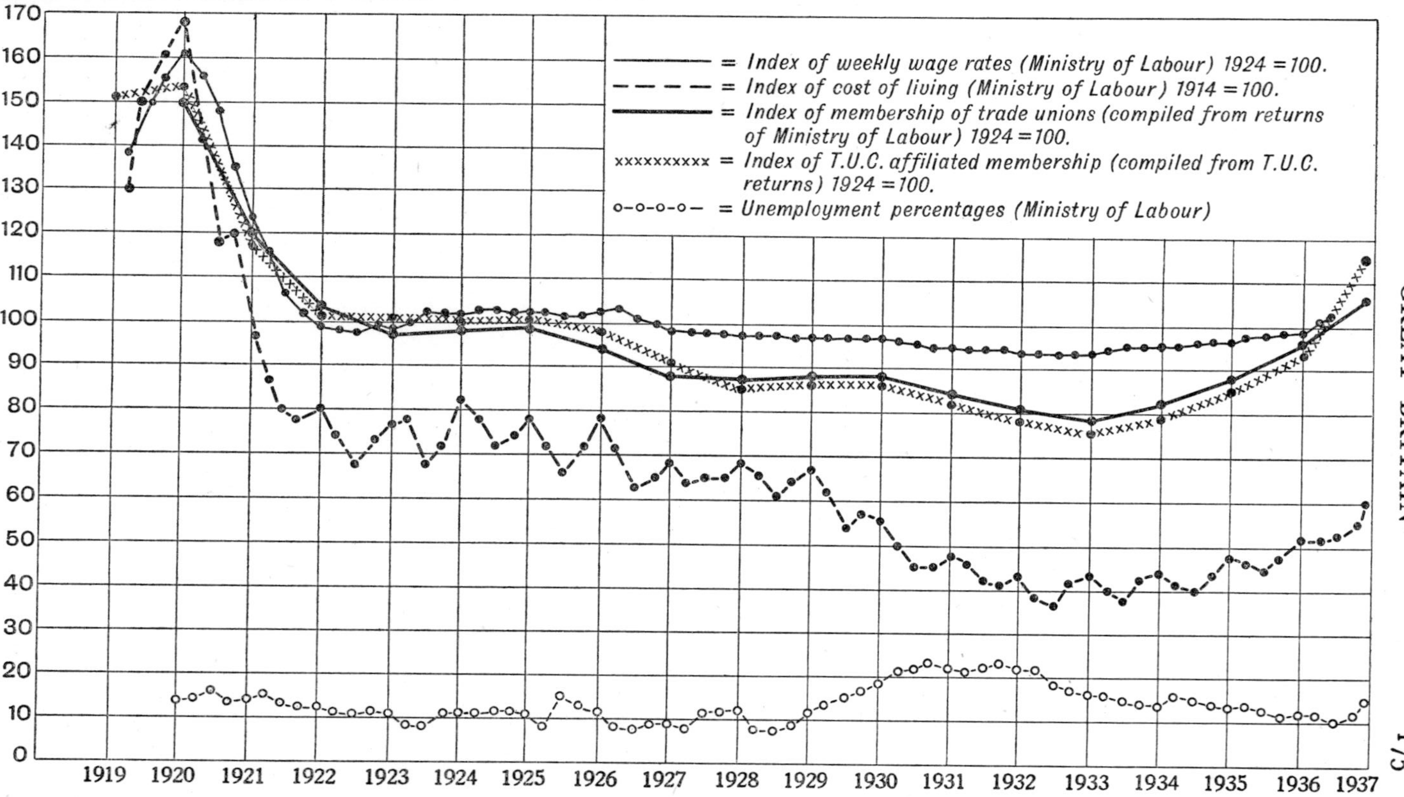

= Index of weekly wage rates (Ministry of Labour) 1924 = 100.
= Index of cost of living (Ministry of Labour) 1914 = 100.
= Index of membership of trade unions (compiled from returns of Ministry of Labour) 1924 = 100.
xxxxxxxxxx = Index of T.U.C. affiliated membership (compiled from T.U.C. returns) 1924 = 100.
o-o-o-o- = Unemployment percentages (Ministry of Labour)
170
160
150
140
130
120
110
100
90
80
70
60
50
40
30
20
10
0
1919
1920
1921
1922
1923
1924
1925
1926
1927
1928
1929
1930
1931
1932
1933
1934
1935
1936
1937

acting on their own initiative, and provoked a spontaneous resistance by the workers which took the form of mass picketing accompanied by some violence against blacklegs. The calling in of police from neighbouring areas was followed by baton charges and many prosecutions for picketing offences under the 1927 Trade Union Act. The movement almost outran the control of the union leaders. In September 1932, an agreement was reached, incorporating substantial wage cuts and the recognition of the six-loom system under certain conditions.

The number of insured workers unemployed in Great Britain and Northern Ireland continued to rise from June 1929, when it stood at 1,164,000, until January 1933, when it reached 2,955,000. During the years of deep depression the existence of this army of workless men and women dominated the whole economic and political situation. Since October 1931 the amount of standard benefit paid to claimants entitled to it had been reduced by 10 per cent. and the payments in respect of their wives from nine shillings to eight shillings per week, though there had been no change in the weekly payment of two shillings per week in respect of each dependent child. Those who had not acquired, or had exhausted,[1] rights to standard benefit received transitional payments (furnished by the State) from local authorities according to their needs as determined by a test of means. The deductions were rendered none the more palatable by proofs that the cost of living had fallen in equal or even greater proportion. For it was well understood that the cuts which had been made in the salaries of teachers, civil servants and others (including Members of Parliament and Cabinet ministers), had not imposed an equivalent sacrifice in standard of living. In the depressed areas the operation of the means test affected and embittered hundreds of thousands of families whose condemnation to continuous idleness for a decade or more was the greatest social evil of the time.

The unions were virtually helpless in the face of chronic unemployment. Some unions, such as the Miners' Federation, permitted the unemployed to retain their membership upon special reduced terms, while of course excluding them from any voice in the determination of industrial policy.

[1] Normally the right was exhausted after 156 days' payment of benefit.

Others showed no interest in men who could not afford to pay the full customary subscriptions. But union membership was of little tangible advantage to idle men. To the member of long standing there was a psychological satisfaction in not being excluded from the group. To the few who were interested in politics and administration, continued membership offered an opportunity to take a share in meetings, discussions, propaganda activity, and perhaps to become a candidate for election to a local authority. But to the younger men who had had little or no employment, or to the mass who were indifferent to social affairs except in periods of excitement, continuance of union membership had little attraction.

The Unemployed Associations, established by the Trades Councils with the aid of the General Council of the Trades Union Congress were rarely very effective or well supported. The Trades Union Congress was excessively anxious to exact a promise from all members that they would join a trade union when they obtained work. Too often there was only the scantiest possible provision for the unemployed man's desire to exercise his capacity for craftsmanship, and the members were expected to be content to organize meetings and demonstrations to agitate for abolition of the means test or other reforms. As this meant, for the majority, listening to other people's speeches, they tended to become tired of it after a time.

When the National Council of Social Service began, with the aid of government grants which, in the depressed areas at least, were very substantial, to organize Unemployed Clubs, the unions and the Labour movement generally were rightly suspicious of the motives behind this new development. The Trades Councils and the Trades Union Congress refused to co-operate. Unfortunately, however, they failed themselves to make adequate provision for the occupational needs of the unemployed. They showed a quite unnecessary fear of the power of unemployed men to compete unfairly with the employed. The unemployed ex-miner working in an Unemployed Club is as effective in competing with the skilled furniture-maker or shoe-maker in a modern factory as is a horse-cab driver in competing with taxis in New York or London. To attempt to prevent him from making furniture or clothing for his home and family or even for sale to his unemployed friends is to deprive him of natural human rights and can help nobody. The result of this policy was to encourage the growth of the Social Service activities. Finally in 1935 the General Council appointed a special committee to review the situation, which reported that the " trade union movement by itself" could not " adequately provide the need " and suggested that it would be as well if union members were to participate in the work of the Social Centres, ascertaining that safeguards against unfair competition be maintained. The General Council, however, would not go as far as this report; and, while permitting the exercise of some discretion by trade unionists according to local circumstances, reiterated the need for more Unemployed Associations of the type it had already created. On the whole, it may be said that the attitude of the unions to the unemployed and their recreational and occupational needs has been disappointingly negative, while the way in which unemployed workers have refused to undercut trade union standards has been wholly admirable, and a striking demonstration of the feeling of working-class solidarity.

In agitation against the conditions of life of the unemployed the Associations set up by the Trades Councils were not so effective as the National Unemployed Workers' Committee Movement. Gone were the days when this body co-operated with the General Council and sent delegates to address the Trades Union Congress. Led by Communists, it organized marches on London and on certain large provincial towns. In 1931 and 1932 these attracted wide support. Marches upon towns where the Trades Union Congress was in session became customary during these years—but the marchers were always refused admission. There was no co-operation between the orthodox and the political Ishmaels until 1935, and then it was short-lived.

January 7 of that year was the appointed day for the taking over by the newly established Unemployed Assistance Board, under the terms of the Unemployment Insurance Act, 1934, of all recipients of transitional payments. Part of the Board's function was to render approximately uniform throughout the country payments to the unemployed which had been determined since 1931 by local authorities. Its regulations for the determination of allowances were found, when they were applied, to involve sweeping reductions in the payments hitherto made by the local authorities. The income of the whole household of every claimant was taken into account when assessing his needs. Unemployed workers found themselves suddenly made dependent to a humiliating extent upon the earnings of employed relatives, and the scanty earnings of young people were to be devoted to the maintenance of unemployed parents, brothers or sisters. Indignation was widespread, and was especially bitter in South Wales, which had suffered more than any other Region from unemployment, and in which the Labour-controlled local authorities had been unusually generous to the unemployed. Giant demonstrations, uniting Communists and clergymen, shop-keepers and trade unionists, chapels, churches, unemployed clubs, union lodges, and party branches were held in every valley in the Region, and culminated in a passionate and united meeting in Cardiff, which recalled the days of the Council of Action in 1920 and was even more fully representative of the whole community than the gatherings of that time. In other industrial Regions a similar protest movement quickly grew, until on February 5 the hated regulations were withdrawn, and the Cabinet Minister nominally responsible was obliged to resign. The feeling thus roused may have helped to raise the Labour Party vote in the General Election of November to eight and a half million (with 154 seats). But the temporary unity thus achieved was soon shattered, and the indignation against the means test then manifested could not be roused again. New regulations were later issued by the Board and allowances were quietly and successfully brought down to a uniform level by the device of spreading the reductions over a period of eighteen months.

The period of Moderate Recovery, from 1933 to 1937, was remarkable for the prevalence of unprecedented industrial peace. The recovery was not sufficiently rapid to create an acute scarcity of labour except for highly skilled men in engineering workshops, and then only towards the end of the period. The toal of unemployment did not fall below 1,300,000 and the slow upward rise of the cost of living was far from sufficient to obliterate the gain in real wages made during the depression. Though money wages as usual lagged behind the movement of prices, the rise was substantial and was shared by all sections of industry.

The miners led the way in pressing for wage increases. In 1933 an improvement was obtained in South Wales by recourse to arbitration and in 1935 a well devised national campaign, relying to a great extent upon appeals to public sympathy, was successful in obtaining advances in all districts. For a short time miners resorted, without the sanction of their union, to the new method of the " stay-down " strike, in imitation of the example set by French and American workers. This method was used with some effect in a renewed struggle to eliminate the " non-political " union from the coalfields. Popular feeling against this organization, which was commonly believed to be subsidized by colliery owners, ran high and resulted in riots in South Wales and Nottinghamshire. It soon became apparent to the more sagacious advisers of the owners that in the changed circumstances of the industry the goodwill of the Miners' Federation might be more valuable to them than the continued existence of the " non-political " union. In South Wales adjustments were made in the machinery of collective agreements which considerably improved their working, the miners' leaders themselves exerted their influence against resort to " stay-down " strikes, and eventually the South Wales members of the " non-political " union were absorbed by the Federation. In Nottinghamshire a somewhat similar solution of difficulties was found by amalgamating the " non-political " union with the Federation. At the end of 1937 the Federation's membership and financial position were immensely stronger than in 1933.

Some share in this development must be attributed to the change in the " party line " adopted by Communists after the triumph of Hitler in Germany and the entry of the Soviet Union into the League of Nations. It is significant that the improved industrial relations in the South Wales coalfield were inaugurated after the election to the Presidency of the South Wales Miners' Federation of Mr. Arthur Horner, a prominent Communist, who had been the chief leader of " disruptive " activities a few years before. The new Communist Party policy of supporting the Labour Party and doing all in its power to strengthen the democracy which it had once denounced as a bourgeois pretence placed its members in some situations well to the Right of the Left-wing of the Labour Party.

But the main explanation of the peacefulness in industrial relations in Great Britain during these years is undoubtedly the change which had been effected in the institutional framework of the capitalist system. The Coal Mines Act, 1930, sponsored by a Labour Government, had established a new system of legalized control of output. Subsequent modifications in the system increased the powers of the colliery owners to limit production and raise prices by means of a discriminating monopoly. Wage advances and rising prices were tied together, and employers and workers had a close mutual interest in maintaining the system. Similar methods of control, with the aid of a Tariff Advisory Committee appointed in 1932, were later applied to the steel industry. Many branches of agriculture have been organized under monopolistic marketing boards and some have been subsidized heavily by the State. Competition in tramp shipping was successfully limited and freights raised by the working of an ingenious system of subsidy. The shipbuilding industry, rationalized with the aid of the Bank of England, also received some subsidy, while elimination of surplus capacity in textiles has been encouraged by legislation. The whole system of road transport has been reorganized on the basis of restriction of entry, and wages and conditions have been remarkably improved with the aid of State-appointed Commissioners. In other industries there has been a rapid extension of trade association control, always with State approval. Again and again this system of State capitalism, or capitalism-on-the-dole, has secured the approval (sometimes grudgingly) of the workers' organizations, for it has almost invariably been accompanied by some improvement in conditions.

Compulsory collective bargaining has existed in certain British industries since the passage of the first Trade Boards Act in 1909, and the decisions of the Boards so established are legally enforceable. This system, however, applied until about 1930 only to trades in which union organization was weak or non-existent. Since then, however, legislation for the Road Transport Service has obliged the Commissioners when granting licences to have regard to wages and conditions agreed upon in collective bargains. Similar provisions apply to firms in the sugar refining trade which receive State subsidies. Under procedure laid down in the Cotton Manufacturing Industry (Temporary Provisions) Act, 1934, the collective bargain arrived at by the unions and the organized employers in the industry was applied by law to all manufacturers. Such legislation had been disapproved of in principle by the Trades Union Congress on more than one occasion before 1926. The unions had feared that it might tend to reduce their membership by extending to workers in unorganized establishments advantages gained by the unions. On this occasion, however, the law received Labour approval. Now that the principle has been established in one industry, it is probable that it may be extended to others.

State action in another form has fostered trade unionism in a direction in which it might not have been expected to operate. In the distributive trades, in which union membership has always been weak, the Ministry of Labour began about 1935 deliberately to encourage collective bargaining. The larger employers, especially in the grocery, retail tailoring and drapery trades, were by no means averse from extending regulation in their industry; and during the succeeding months the Shop Assistants' Union was able to sign no less than fifty agreements, usually involving wage increases, and doubled its membership. Conditions in these trades were regulated already by Shops Acts, which are mainly concerned with limitation of the hours during which trading may take place. In the background of the movement for encouraging collective bargaining lay the threat of additional legislation, and it is probable that in future the competition of the small shopkeeper with the bigger concerns and the multiple and department stores may be further limited, and the conditions of wage earners further improved, by means of legal enforcement of collective bargaining. The Ministry has also encouraged the practice of granting holidays with pay to manual workers. In the steel, coal-mining and other organized industries agreements involving the granting of one week's paid holiday were entered into extensively during 1936 and 1937. It is expected that during 1938 and 1939 this practice will be extended into industries operating under the Trade Boards Act. If so, the institution will quickly become universal throughout industry.

The greatest internal problem affecting the trade union movement during the years since 1926 has been that of extending organization into the newer industries and the rapidly expanding services. It is a problem of several facets. The main strength of the unions is in the older and heavier industries. While these have been contracting the unions' energies have been largely occupied in maintaining membership and resisting attempts to worsen conditions. They have not been greatly concerned, and indeed have not had the time, to bother much about conditions in the new industries. The latter have grown up for the most part in areas where there is no strong union tradition and where the influence of the established unions scarcely penetrates. Moreover, they are large employers of female and juvenile labour. Women and young persons are notoriously not easy to organize—in Britain just as in other countries. In such circumstances there are only two possible methods of extension of organization—spontaneous action by the workers themselves under pressure of unsatisfactory conditions, perhaps with the aid of sympathizers, or deliberate attempts by the Trades Union Congress by means of propaganda and the provision of paid assistance.

There have been several spontaneous movements during the years of business recovery. In many of these the cause of strikes has been the instalment of the Bedaux system of work measurement and payment by results. In strikes at the Firestone tyre works and the Ford Motor Company near London, at Lucas's accessories factory in Birmingham, at the Pressed Steel works near Oxford, and in other less important instances Communist organizers played a prominent part. In many such cases strikers have joined the appropriate trade unions, and the effect of Communist leadership has been in some cases to induce employers to consider the desirability of entering into agreements with the regular union leaders, who will undertake to protect them from sudden stoppages or infractions of the agreement.

Ever since 1923 the Trades Union Congress has been concerned at the lack of organization among women workers. At almost every annual Congress since then resolutions have been passed urging trade unionists to induce their children to become union members. After 1925 more attention was devoted to the problem, and following a sharp decline immediately after the General Strike the female membership of the unions began to rise slowly while the male membership was still declining. During the depression there was a slight fall, but from 1933 onwards the trend was upwards again. A National Advisory Committee on Women's Organization has been established from among the unions most concerned, and it organizes its own annual conferences, week-end schools for officials and other activities. A national Woman Officer has been appointed. On the whole, however, the results are disappointing. Circulars and questionnaires sent out to affiliated unions about the organization of women and young persons have been ignored by the majority, and action is necessarily ineffective because insufficient funds are devoted to it.

Greater success has attended efforts to organize new industries, though here again there has been a pronounced lack of interest on the part of unions which are not directly affected. Such unions as the Transport and General Workers' Union and the National Union of General and Municipal Workers have made headway, especially in the light metal trades. In the case of the rayon industry, an interesting agreement between five unions concerned was maintained for several years, which prevented overlapping and the growth of demarcation disputes. But a concerted drive throughout the areas of expanding industry, backed by adequate finance, has never taken place. Special campaigns in such districts as Slough and Birmingham have met with some success. But when in 1936 a scheme to add to the staff of the London Trades Council a number of full-time officers to undertake recruiting work in Greater London was put forward by the General Council and a number of unions principally concerned, it was rejected by a Conference of local Trades Councils. A renewed effort at a special campaign in this area during 1937 was a comparative failure, mainly on account of similar frictions and jealousies.

Discussion of these important questions occupied less of the attention of the Trades Union Congress during the years 1933 to 1937 than the problem of destroying or preventing Communist influence within the unions. From 1930 onwards the

Labour Party had been developing a policy not only of refusing membership of the Party to Communists, but of warning, and finally forbidding, members to associate themselves with a long list of organizations—such as the League against Imperialism, the Friends of the Soviet Union, the Workers' International Relief, etc., etc.—which were said to be under Communist control. Warnings against these bodies were given by the General Secretary of the Trades Union Congress in 1933 and 1934. In 1935 Circular 16 was issued by the General Council to all Trades Councils recognized by it and Circular 17 to all unions affiliated. The former stated that " the recognition of Congress will be withdrawn from any Council which accepts delegates connected in any way with either Communist or Fascist organizations or any of their ancillary bodies." The latter asked the unions " to give consideration to the possibility of drawing up regulations or amending the rules of your organization so as to empower them to reject the nominations of members of disruptive bodies for any official position within your organization." While forty-one unions agreed to this policy, twenty-five refused to participate in it and many others showed indifference. In the subsequent debate the reference back of the letter to unions was lost by the fairly narrow margin of 1,869,000 to 1,427,000 votes, though the circular to the Trades Councils was approved by a much larger majority. The general labour unions were in favour of the whole policy; but the Miners' Federation and some of the most powerful craft unions disliked the suggestion of interference with union autonomy, and Mr. John Bromley of the Associated Society of Locomotive Engineers and Firemen, who had once been the target of bitter attacks in the Communist press after the General Strike, stoutly declared: " our experience with our Communist members has been a singularly happy one. We have always known where they would be in a strike." At the next Congress it was announced that 350 Trades Councils were " implementing national policy on this subject," while four were being reconstructed and forty had been removed from the register either for not replying or for refusing to obey. In that same year, 1936, a long manifesto denouncing the Communist policy of the " United Front " was issued by the National Council of Labour, and a motion for the affiliation of the Communist

Party was rejected by the Labour Party by 1,728,000 to 592,000 votes. The " United Front " policy had been launched in 1935 with the aid of the Independent Labour Party (disaffiliated from the Labour Party since 1932) and the Socialist League. The resolute opposition shown by the Labour Party led to the voluntary dissolution of the latter body. Later the Independent Labour Party renounced the policy in favour of a more intransigent socialism, and by 1937 it was supported by few persons outside the 5,000 members of the Communist Party and the 50,000 members of a Left Book Club founded in 1936.

The triumph of Hitler and the subsequent destruction of trade unionism in Germany led to anxious debates throughout the ensuing years in the Trades Union Congress, the Labour Party and the National Council of Labour. So short a time after, it is difficult to assess the significance of the decisions taken or to judge of the motives which may have influenced them. It seems, however, as if the triumph of Fascism abroad increased the rapidity of the move to the Right which had been noticeable in the trade union movement since 1927. Trade unionism seemed more and more to wish to establish and justify itself as an institution within the capitalist system and to have less and less sympathy with the revolutionary and internationalist policy which had tempted it sometimes in the past.

In 1933 the Labour Party Conference passed a resolution pledging itself to take no part in war and favouring resistance by means of a general strike. This resolution was not welcomed by the National Council of Labour, and in 1934 the Trades Union Congress passed a resolution in favour of an " International Police Force " and of " resistance to the aggressor," despite the protest of a delegate that " every capitalist class is an aggressor." This policy was adopted by the Labour Party a month later. From then onwards gradual but logical steps were taken until in 1937 the Congress approved of the government's programme of increasing armaments, though the General Secretary reminded the meeting that resistance might still be possible if the armaments were used " on behalf of Fascism."

In 1936 the Trades Union Congress was persuaded to approve of the policy of " non-intervention " in the Spanish War, though it added to its resolution the admission that " the utmost vigilance is necessary " to prevent the policy acting unfairly against the Spanish government. The Labour Party Conference a month later passed a similar resolution, albeit in face of strong protests from socialists who thought it was a clear duty of a socialist party to favour the free purchase of arms by a legitimate government which was following that very policy of " resistance to Fascism " so strongly advocated by the Labour supporters of British re-armament. After speeches by Spanish delegates to the Conference, a revulsion of feeling among the mass of the delegates was too strong to be resisted and the policy was changed. A few days later the National Council of Labour declared in favour of the sale of arms to the Spanish government " in view of the fact that the non-intervention agreement has proved ineffective in its operation."

Support of " non-intervention " was the furthest move to the Right that the leaders of the Labour movement had yet made. It seems to be explicable only by the strong influence, especially within the trade unions, of Catholic opinion. It was this influence which produced the only big Parliamentary revolt against the Second Labour government—on the question of public subsidies to schools maintained by religious bodies. It also played its part in the extreme hostility shown to the Communist Party in recent years, and it is significant that unions with a large Irish membership were most prominent in the exclusionist campaign. When the Spanish struggle began, at least one Catholic Labour Member of Parliament openly indicated his sympathy with General Franco. This religious influence within the movement cannot be estimated in any statistical form; but there is no doubt that it exists and that the movement cannot be understood unless that fact is known.

. . . . .

The outstanding development of these eighteen years in the history of trade unionism has been the growth in the prestige and power of the General Council of the Trades Union Congress. In 1920 it was doubtful what functions it would perform. It was thought that central power might fall to the Triple Alliance or some other body. At the beginning of 1938 it is a well founded closely-knit institution, with eight fully established departments and nine advisory Councils, continually influencing policy in the International Federation of Trade Unions and the International Labour Organization, as well as on Trade Boards and in the administration of social insurance and workmen's compensation. It has the right to determine the policy of a newspaper with a daily circulation of 2,000,000 copies. It has power to determine the demarcation between unions, and it strongly influences the local Trades Councils. Above all it possesses predominant influence over the policy of the Labour Party, which eighteen years ago seemed to have absorbed the functions of the old Parliamentary Committee. In its Councils two men are outstanding: Mr. Ernest Bevin, leader of the largest single union in the country, the Transport and General Workers' Union, which has more than 540,000 members, and Sir Walter Citrine, the General Secretary, who has been President of the International Federation of Trade Unions since 1931. They occupy the place of influence once filled by Robert Smillie, Ben Tillett, and Mr. J. H. Thomas.[1] The lucid statements and explanations of the General Secretary, logical, penetrating, compelling, and the forceful eloquence of Mr. Bevin, a man whose mind is always capable of grasping a new idea, have dominated all the discussions in recent years upon political and social policy and above all on international affairs. Their influence upon the immediate future of the movement is bound to be considerable.

In the changing economic structure of the past eight years the trade unions have tended more and more to emphasize their function as continuing institutions for the regulation of wages and conditions and the orderly marshalling of labour within the capitalist system, and have rarely thought of themselves, as in times past, as organs of class struggle. There is even a danger, in some industries at least, that a desire for a greater share in management which seemed so significant to historians in 1920, may merely eventuate in a partnership in State-supported restrictive monopolies.

The history of these years has shown that even in times of deep depression the unions, once they have been firmly established, can retain their membership, on the basis of established loyalty, of tangible benefits received, and of benefits,

[1] It is interesting to note that the speeches of Mr. Thomas in the heyday of his prestige occupy 492 lines in the Congress report of 1921, and 355 lines in that of 1923. In the report for 1936 Sir Walter Citrine's speeches account for 1,252 and in 1937 for 1,396 lines.

already partly paid for, which the member expects to receive in the future. But appeals to class solidarity, to the payments and benefits promised to regular members, to the arguments that it is unfair to take advantage of the conditions won by trade unionism without supporting it, have failed to secure any big increase in membership or any significant extension to the expanding industries. Large gains in membership have only been made in the past at times of upheaval or as the result of militant action to secure big social changes. But that is not the temper of our time in Great Britain.

ITALY

BY

J. P. VAN AARTSEN

ITALY

A. Social Conditions and Economic Development

1. Italy, like most European countries, has seen a rapid increase of its population during the last century or so. In 1901, 32,475,000 inhabitants were counted; in 1921 (the new provinces with 1,613,000 inhabitants included) 37,974,000; in 1931, 41,177,000; and in 1936, 42,445,000.

Of the population gainfully employed[1] in 1901 some 58·8 per cent. were occupied in agriculture; but in 1931, though Italy remained still in the first place an agricultural country, other occupations had obtained a greater importance than before. The following table illustrates the distribution:

Occupational Group	*Per cent. of occupied population*	
	1921	1931
Agriculture	54·3	48·7
Industry and transport	31·0	33·9
including metallurgical industry	(4·7)	(5·7)
" textile industry	(0·9)	(1·2)
Commerce	6·7	8·3
Other occupations	8·0	9·1

This same classification applied to the principal geographical regions—North Italy (including Emilia), Central Italy, South Italy,[2] Islands (Sicily and Sardinia)—shows that industry is rather concentrated in the north, while the south has remained mainly agricultural (the data refer to 1931):

Occupational Group	*North*	*Central*	*South*	*Islands*
Agriculture	43·7	49·0	56·0	56·4
Industry and transport	37·7	31·9	29·1	29·4
including:				
metallurgical industry	(8·0)	(4·5)	(3·2)	(2·3)
textile industry	(2·1)	(0·7)	(0·3)	(0·1)
Commerce	9·3	8·0	7·2	6·7
Other occupations	9·3	11·1	7·7	7·5

[1] In the first three years mentioned: 10,989,000; 13,155,000; and 13,281,000 respectively. Data for 1936 are not yet published.

[2] The southern part of the continent, including territories as far north as Abruzzi and Molise.

Agriculture in Italy is largely carried on by peasants, who rarely or never employ paid labour and, in many instances, hire themselves out as they cannot make a living on their holding, and by share-tenants. The latter group represents some 30 per cent. of agricultural "employers." In industry masters of enterprises (excluding artisans who have their own workshops) form 14·5 per cent. of the population occupied in industry, while other employers constitute only 5·3 per cent. The typical industrial enterprise is not very big.

A further impression of the importance and distribution of the main industries may be derived from the following table which gives total numbers (in 1000's) of gainfully occupied persons in industries in which this total, for the whole country, surpassed 100,000 in 1931.

	Kingdom	*North*	*Central*	*South*	*Islands*
Woodworking	551	298	93	108	52
Cereal-working	186	98	27	40	21
[1]Working of animal products	390	169	59	107	55
Metal-working, other than mining and melting	947	624	154	116	53
Building, road and waterway construction	1,028	550	128	188	108
Textile industries...	584	514	39	28	3
Production of special sorts of cloth ...	139	107	18	11	3
Dressmaking, home cleaning, personal treatment	643	357	105	135	46
Chemical industries	179	107	22	45	5
Production and distribution of motor power, gas, light, heat and water ...	111	67	19	17	8

2. Italy has shifted her economic centre of gravity during the last thirteen years. This shift, however, is much greater than can be shown from statistics. There are no index numbers for a continuous period from 1920 to 1937: data for the first part of this period are mostly lacking; and there have been so many changes in organization during recent years that a statistical comparison would have little value. Therefore only the following comparisons are given.

[1] Products other than milk, meat, eggs, fish, silkworm eggs and animal fibres.

The condition of Italian roads in the beginning of the 'twenties and even up to 1928 (when a special society under State supervision was founded for the primary roads: Azienda Autunoma delle Strade Statili) were rather poor. Nowadays there are not only a great number of very well maintained highways, secondary roads also have been greatly improved; the network has become considerably denser and many roads, even those which are mainly of local importance, are now practically free from dust. The train communications too have been considerably increased, but here—except for some important tunnels which have shortened the distance from south to north—the changes concern mainly the efficiency of the traffic. Trains, which after the World War, were rather irregular in arriving and even in leaving the principal stations, have been very punctual during the last ten years at least. Their speed has been increased, partly thanks to better maintenance of railroads and rolling material, partly as a result of the use of better and faster engines. A large number of electrical engines are in use on the main lines of communication (most of which are electrified), while motor carriages have been introduced on the lines of small importance where the slower and heavier steam traffic has been abolished for passenger transport.

In navigation, too, great progress has been made. It is irrelevant from the point of view of this study that many of the new ships of the mercantile marine may be used as light cruisers. It should be indicated only that whereas at the end of 1920 there were 495 Italian steam and motor ships with a tonnage of 835,000 net register tons, by the end of 1936 there were 1,284 ships with 1,832,000 tons. Of these some 22 per cent. were built between 1921 and 1925, some 19 per cent. between 1926 and 1930 and some 4 per cent. later.

For the development of industry we possess index numbers of production (base year 1928 = 100). Though they give an impression of the average relative movement of production during different years, they cannot take into consideration the progress in quality which has undoubtedly been made lately. These index numbers, calculated by the Office for Studies and Research of the Ministry of Corporations, are reproduced in the following table:

	1929	1931	1933	1935	1937
Textile industry	101·7	89·9	76·3	76·8	83·7
Metallurgical and mechanical industry	104·6	82·5	72·8	102·6	130·1
Paper and printing industry ...	106·8	98·7	110·5	139·7	150·0
Building industry	139·6	87·7	93·4	162·3	95·9
Industries for the production of heat, light and energy ...	106·5	109·6	119·2	135·8	154·6
[1] Extractive industry	—	—	—	98·9	127·8
[1] Chemical industry	—	—	—	99·6	133·2
Total industry	109·2	84·7	80·5	102·4	108·7

It is not necessary to give any details of the development of agriculture since the War. So much has been written about this subject, and especially about the Wheat Campaign (Battaglia del Grano), that it is sufficient to indicate here that from 1925 an attempt has been made to increase the production, first mainly of wheat, later of other products, including animal products. Aid has been given through protective measures, organization and education. On the other hand farmers and peasants have been heavily taxed, but their position is not bad in general. The index numbers of prices, calculated by the Central Institute of Statistics, show that (base year 1928–100) the prices of agricultural products sold fell rapidly, those of commodities and services purchased rather more slowly. There was some readjustment, however, during recent years and what is perhaps of more importance, the continuous progress in methods of farming enables the farmer (even with an unfavourable relation between the two series of index numbers), to obtain a favourable final result. The movement of prices is seen in the following table:

	1931	1934	1937
Agricultural products sold	69·1	55·9	83·8
Commodities and services purchased... ...	82·4	71·3	85·0

Agriculture is on a higher level in the north where in many regions there are large farms of typically capitalistic structure. Farm labour is heavy during the very hot summer months and poorly paid. Accommodation for the labourers, though much improved in recent years is here, as in the greater part of Italy, insufficient. In Central Italy holdings are often smaller and on a less capitalistic footing; they are generally given out on a

[1] These data have been calculated only since September 1935.

share-tenancy contract, that is, the proprietor furnishes the greater part of live and dead-stock, he prescribes the general lines according to which the holding is to be kept, what crops are to be grown, and how they will be sold; the share-tenant furnishes his labour and that of his family. He gets a share (generally half) in the out-turn. In the south there are small very labour-intensive horticultural holdings, which, rents being high, give the peasants a poor income. There are further large labour-extensive holdings worked by extremely backward and poor farm labourers who live in the smallish towns in the neighbourhood where hygienic conditions are poor. As the towns consist mainly of farm labourers and poor peasants, they are too poor to construct adequate hygienic facilities. By degrees, with the help of State subvention, these conditions are being changed, but much remains to be done.

3. It is necessary to give, besides these outlines of the distribution and importance of occupations and industries, some impression of other social conditions. This may well start with a survey of illiteracy. In 1901, 48·5 per cent. of the total population of six years and over could not read or write. By 1931 this percentage had been reduced to 20·9. In that year 8·2 per cent. of the indicated classes in North Italy were illiterate, 20·6 per cent. in Central Italy, 38·7 per cent. in South Italy and 39·0 per cent. on the Islands.

The North Italian is generally more advanced and more energetic than the man from the South or the Islands. He is more accurate and keeps better up to a given promise. Thanks to these characteristics and his better education he may be entrusted with work of a finer nature than that generally done by the Southerner. The skilled industrial labourers are mostly of Northern stock, the unskilled and general work being done by Southerners. The latter also form the majority among the construction and road-building labourers.

The number of births is relatively much higher in the south than in the north. Per 1,000 married women between fifteen and forty-four years of age there were born in 1920–1922 (yearly average) 245 living children in Lombardy (the main industrial centre) against 322 in Campania (Napoli and the provinces near to it). In 1935–1937 these figures were 164 and 265 respectively. The lowered birth-rate has been accompanied by a fall in the death-rate. The latter rate, which stood at 18·0 per 1,000 inhabitants in 1920–1922, was only 13·9 in 1935–37. The death-rate from tuberculosis, during this same period, has fallen sharply.

In the field of education important progress has been made; the number of pupils frequenting elementary schools has risen from 3·5 million in the beginning of the 'twenties to nearly five million during these last years.

4. In 1920 the working population lived mostly in very poor conditions. As a result of enlargement of the right to vote in 1913 and of war-time developments these workers became a factor of great political importance. They started organizing themselves on a large scale in revolutionary groups. But the number of leaders for this suddenly uprising movement was very insufficient, as was recognized by the socialists themselves.[1] Thus, large groups of labourers, not yet educated for trade union action, without sufficient leaders, mostly without any general education and—due to the miserable conditions in which they lived—rather inclined towards revolutionary action, started strikes with very far-reaching objects. The result was a favourable change in their contractual conditions, but also a disorganization of a great part of production and a consequent increase in unemployment. At the same time the lack of general education and of efficient leadership meant that many of the advantages obtained in collective labour agreements could not be brought into practice.

It is not possible to give correct information on unemployment. For the earlier years the figures are rather incomplete; for the later years the unemployed have been obliged to register with the Employment Exchanges, but may have done so at more than one local office at a time and often no notice has been given when work has been found, the result of this being that it has only been possible to make vague estimates. It may be said that during the first years after the War there were large oscillations in the number of unemployed registered, running from a maximum of 607,000 in January 1922 to a minimum of 304,000 in July 1922. During the first years of

[1] See Rinaldo Rigola (for a long time General Secretary of the socialistic trade organization): *The Reconstruction of the General Confederation of Labour in Italy*, in *International Labour Review*, September 1921.

Fascist government, registered unemployment was smaller (maximum 392,000 in January 1923, minimum 116,000 in September 1924). For the period since the application of economic sanctions during the Abyssinian war,[1] no statistics on this matter have been published. For the preceding years we know that unemployment was at its maximum in 1934 when the average total was 1,118,000.

Besides these figures of unemployment, index numbers of employment in industry are published, calculated by the Confederation of Industrialists. With 1929 as the base year, they give the average numbers of workers employed in 1933 as 79·4, in 1935 as 93·9, in 1937 as 104·5. The total number of hours worked has increased more slowly, the index number for 1933 standing at 75·1, for 1935 at 81·0, and for 1937 at 91·7. This is a clear illustration of the reduction of working hours used as a measure for the reduction of unemployment (see below). An example of this reduction is the fact that in April 1938 some 21·4 per cent. of the workers in industry worked less than forty hours per week, 50·7 per cent. worked from forty to less than forty-five hours, 20·2 per cent. from forty-five to forty-eight hours and only 7·7 per cent. more than forty-eight hours.

5. Italy is a country with relatively poor natural resources both for agriculture and for mining; industry has developed only during recent years; and its economic-geographical position is not favourable for the development of internal communications or for giving it a great share in the transit trade of its hinterland. The result of all this and of the character of many Italians is that the country is far from rich. Therefore earnings are low. This has always been the case in modern times. I have calculated the index numbers of purchasing power of wages paid per hour. In these calculations the increased welfare and insurance activity referred to below has not been taken into account. They are based on the cost of living index numbers of the Central Institute of Statistics (base June 1928 = 100) and on index numbers of wages paid per

[1] It is the author's opinion that these sanctions and their negative result have had an enormous influence on the development of Fascist Italy. They have created a profound patriotic sentiment which has been a factor of great importance in making people believe in the value of the economic and social activity of the Government.

hour in industry, calculated by the Confederation of Industrialists (base year 1928 = 100), and reduced to June 1928 = 100. These index numbers are for June of each of the following years:

Year	*Cost of Living*	*Wages Paid*	*Purchasing Power*
1928	100·0	100·9	100·0
1930	97·5	100·9	102·6
1932	85·0	91·9	107·3
1934	77·4	85·7	114·2
1936	83·8	87·6	103·6
1937	91·0	103·3	112·5

This summary of conditions may be ended with the following data on average wages paid per hour in different branches of economic activity during February 1938: Agriculture, 1·48 lira; sugar factories, 2·88 lire; building of houses, roads, waterworks, 2·33 lire; mechanical industries, 2·71 lire; metallurgical industries, 3·02 lire; clothing industries, 1·63 lira; shoe and other leather industries, 1·83 lira; weaving of silk, 1·63 lira; industries for the production of artificial fibre, 2·02 lire. These are average figures for the whole country, for skilled and unskilled labourers, for men and women.

B. Position of Labour during the Pre-Fascist Period

1. After the War we find Italian labourers mainly organized in Socialist and Catholic trade organizations. Of minor importance were Republican reformist unions. The Fascist movement, founded in 1919, soon started grouping its members in " corporations " which after some time absorbed an ever greater percentage of the working classes.

The Socialist trade organizations were grouped together in the General Confederation of Labour (Confederazione Generale del Lavoro). The workers adhering to it were organized in large national federations, as far as possible separately for each of the main branches of agricultural, industrial and commercial activity. These workers were at the same time members of the " red " chambers of labour, where such existed (these local chambers were composed of branches representing the different economic activities). The member-federations and chambers were based on the principle of class war and their purpose was declared to be " to help the working classes in their movement of resistance."[1]

[1] Section 2 of the Statute of the Confederation.

The Confederation was not an organization of the Socialist party; later on—during the first years of Fascist government —it even insisted strongly on distinguishing itself from the party.

The Catholic Italian Confederation of Workers (Confederazione Italiana dei Lavoratori) had a constitution not very different from the socialist one. It received its main conceptual impulse from the papal encyclical "Rerum novarum" (of Leo XIII) and looked largely to local autonomy and small ownership as factors for social improvement. Like the Confederation of Labour it had a keen interest in co-operation. In practice it also took part in and even organized strikes, with the object of propagating its ideals.

2. Social legislation before 1915 had been very meagre in Italy, but during the War it was felt necessary to satisfy somewhat more the wants of the working class. This legislation was amplified in 1919, 1920 and 1921, in part as a direct result of the action of the trade unions, in part in accordance with general tendencies which ruled everywhere at that time. We thus find the following measures in force before Mussolini came to power.

A number of laws starting with the codified law No. 818 of November 10, 1907,[1] contained stipulations concerning the limitation of work for young persons and women in industry. In most instances the age limit was twelve or thirteen years; for dangerous or unhealthy work it was fifteen years for boys and twenty-one for women. Women could not be employed for a month after childbirth. Law No. 337 of June 16, 1907, which dealt with the specially hard work on rice fields, stipulated that children under fourteen and pregnant women during the last month of pregnancy could not be employed on weeding rice fields. The codified text of the health acts (No. 636 of August 1, 1907) provided further that nursing mothers were to be allowed the time necessary for nursing their children, without deducting the period of absence from the hours of work.

Three sorts of bodies existed for State intervention in collective disputes:

[1] This law was amended by law No. 425 of July 3, 1910; law No. 886 of June 26, 1913; decree-law No. 1136 of August 6, 1916, and Royal decree No. 1180 of July 15, 1920, contained regulations concerning the same subject. The first mentioned law was further amended by decree-law No. 748 of March 14, 1923.

(*a*) Under law No. 295 of June 15, 1893, Conciliation Boards (Collegi dei Probiviri) were set up. They were elected councils composed of equal numbers of employers and workers, which, under decree-law No. 1672 of October 13, 1918, were legally empowered to settle collective disputes and disagreements in all industries, subject to certain guarantees and only for certain specified purposes. If parties did not agree with the probiviral award they could apply to the Permanent Labour Committee, which was the administrative organ of the Supreme Council of Labour (an advisory body attached to the Ministry of Labour).[1]

(*b*) The Permanent Committee for securing uniformity of treatment for workers employed in the public transport services could, under law No. 835 of July 14, 1912, act as an arbitration tribunal for collective disputes on request of the parties.

(*c*) Under decree No. 1726 of September 14, 1919, Provincial Agricultural Committees were set up, the duty of which included dealing with labour matters. Attached to them were Executive Conciliation Committees, which had to settle difficulties and disputes concerning agricultural labour. They were presided over by a member of the provincial tribunal and composed of four members, two nominated by the employers' and two by the workers' organizations, or failing this, by the Agriculture Committees. They could intervene on request of the parties or of the Prefect of the Province or on their own account. In this connection may be mentioned also the district arbitration committees—which had to deal with disputes relating to the leasing of land, including renting of small-holdings and share-tenancy[2] and the Conciliation Committees for disputes relating to the labour contracts of rice workers (law No. 337 of June 16, 1907). Their jurisdiction was limited to disputes of a juridical character; they lost their importance when

[1] After the War many projects were made for changing the Supreme Council of Labour into a technical Parliament (bill of Abbiate and proposals of Socialist and Catholic labour organizations). The Council was re-organized under a decree signed the day before Mussolini came to power and abolished it by decree No. 861 of March 25, 1923. The Conciliation Boards then came under the supervision of the Minister of Justice and appeals against their awards had to be carried to the civil courts.

[2] Small-holders and share-tenants were often members of trade unions and are now, under Fascist legislation, classed in the Confederation of Agricultural Labourers. The district committees were abolished by decree No. 1437 of November 14, 1922, and their powers transferred to the ordinary juridical authorities.

the above-mentioned committees with larger power were set up.

Decree-law No. 212 of February 9, 1919, gave a definition of a *Private labour contract* other than that for manual labour and laid down rules for discharge. A minimum period of notice had to be given (running, according to the position of the employed person, from one to twelve months) and in the case of persons having right to the maximum notification period, a compensation had to be paid amounting to a half month's salary for every year of work passed with the employer. The law also established the right to yearly holidays with normal payment (ten to twenty days per annum).

Accident insurance was already compulsory at the beginning of this century but the legislation was brought up-to-date several times.[1] Practically all persons, other than employers, occupied in industrial work which, in some way or another, may be considered as dangerous were under the obligation of insurance. The allowance, in case of permanent complete inability to work amounted to six times the annual salary, in case of permanent partial inability to a sum in proportion, in case of death to five times the annual salary, in case of temporary inability to a daily payment equal to half the daily salary of which the victim was deprived. Special rules were laid down as to insurance of sailors (including the whole crew and officers of a ship under the Italian flag) and for workers in the Sicilian sulphur mines.

Insurance against accidents in agriculture was made compulsory under decree-law No. 1450 of August 23, 1917, amended by law No. 297 of March 20, 1921. Permanent and temporary workers and, in so far as they habitually perform manual labour, also proprietors, tenants, share-tenants and their families and supervisors were *de iure* insured. The insurance premium was to be paid in proportion to the size of the holding and the amount of the land tax.

Compulsory insurance against involuntary unemployment was established by decree-law No. 2214 of October 19, 1919. Provision was made for (i) a general insurance fund and (ii) insurance funds for certain separate industries (*inter alia* a

[1] Codified law No. 51 of January 31, 1904, amended by decree-law No. 1825 of November 17, 1918, and law No. 296 of March 20, 1921, and the rules promulgated in connection with these laws. Further law No. 312 of March 24, 1921.

fund, which covered the whole country, for the paper and printing industries), and various regional funds for metallurgical, building, hat-making and textile industries.

Motherhood insurance was compulsory under law No. 520 of July 17, 1910, modified by decree-law No. 322 of February 17, 1917. All women between fifteen and fifty years of age, subject to the law on work of children and women, had to be insured. There was a yearly premium to be paid, amounting to seven lire (three lire paid by the woman, four by her employer). On confinement a subvention of 100 lire was given.

Finally we may mention the insurance against invalidity and old age, which was made compulsory under decree-law No. 603 of April 21, 1919, for all persons between fifteen and sixty-five years of age who work for others. Only employees earning at least 350 lire per month and small tenants and share-tenants, who are supposed to make an earning of at least 3,600 lire per year, were excluded. The object of the insurance was to give, besides invalidity and old age pensions, a temporary pension to the widow and the orphans of the insured person and to take preventive measures against incapacity for work. Premiums were paid to an equal amount by the employer and the worker; the State also gave a contribution.

3. Before 1915 collective labour agreements had been mainly concluded in industrial centres; during and immediately after the World War they became of great importance also in other districts. The movement was accelerated by the legislation passed during the War period, the special organization of industry in which this resulted and the setting up, in 1919, of a central organization of industrial employers—the General Confederation of Italian Industry (Confederazione Generale dell'Industria Italiana).

In 1919 and the following years collective agreements in industry contained a number of new principles:

(*a*) The eight-hour working day and the forty-eight-hour working week were already included in all agreements in 1919. Pre-Fascist governments, however, did not succeed in passing complete legislation in this matter.[1]

(*b*) In many industries special internal workers' committees

[1] Two Royal decrees of May 15 and June 15, 1919, instituted it for the staff of private and State railways, tramways and interior lines of navigation for public service.

(Commissioni interne) were set up as a result of special stipulations in the collective agreements. They were elected separately in every factory affected by the agreement. Thanks to the system of voting, minorities were represented. The workers could bring their complaints before their respective committee. It had the right to discuss the matter in question with the employer.

(*c*) In a collective agreement in the metal industry, in September 1920, the terms of discharge were regulated on modern lines, parallel to those contained in the above-mentioned decree-law of February 9, 1919, for non-manual workers. This was followed by a large number of other collective agreements containing analogous stipulations. Workers who had been employed by their firm continuously for at least three years became entitled to compensation in the case of discharge for other than disciplinary reasons. In addition to the customary period of notice (usually a week, sometimes a fortnight) or the equivalent pay, a compensation amounting to two days' wages for every year of employment was to be paid. Under the terms of an arbitration award, pronounced by the Minister of Labour, Labriola, in respect of the electrical industry, even better terms were given. Compensation ranging from a minimum of ten days' pay for each year of service if this period was relatively short, up to a maximum of fifteen days' pay per year when the total service was over thirty years, could be due.

(*d*) Many agreements allowed for some paid holidays (generally between six and fifteen days per year).

(*e*) If the work had to be stopped for reasons other than the action of the workers, the agreements entitled them to some compensation.

(*f*) In many agreements penalties were laid down for various breaches of discipline. The offences were punishable, according to their seriousness, by fine, suspension or dismissal.

(*g*) In many instances payments were regulated by classifying the workers into clearly defined grades, each including workers with specified qualifications. The simplest method was by age and sex alone, another by these criteria plus specifications such as skilled, unskilled and general labourers; but most industries graded the workers on a purely technical and occupational basis.

(*h*) The collective agreements also contained rules for the settlement of collective disputes. These rules enlarged and strengthened those contained in the legislation treated above. For the most part the declaration of a strike or lock-out, for other than purely political reasons, was prohibited until conciliation had been tried by the respective organizations. Offence against this stipulation, in the case of a strike, was punished by the loss of the guarantee deposited with the employers for the observance of the rules of the agreement and, in the case of a lock-out, by the payment of an equal sum by the employers. In some agreements the awards of the arbitration committee were *a priori* declared binding on both parties. Of special interest is the National Joint Committee for the Electrical Industry (Commissione paritetica nazionale per l'Industria elettrica), established as a consequence of Labriola's arbitration award. This award denied the right of strike or lock-out in the public services and applied this principle, rather in the way of an experiment, to the electrical industry.

The agreements did not generally compel the employers to use the intermediation of the special employment exchanges, set up under Royal decree No. 2214 of October 19, 1919.

In agriculture conditions were rather different: labour employment, especially in the North, was very unsatisfactory before the War. Owing to the organization of large modern farms agricultural labourers found occupation only during certain parts of the year.[1] Therefore the workers insisted on adding a special clause to the collective agreement, namely, the obligation on the part of the employers[2] to use a minimum number of workers proportional to the size of the farms. In 1920 and the following years this " minimum ration of labour " was applied in nearly all collective agreements.

The eight-hour working day was also included in the agricultural agreements. Exceptions were admitted in case of urgent work and if there were no unemployed in the neighbourhood; but on such occasions a higher payment was to be given.[3]

[1] In the Middle Po valley they worked from 180 to 220 days; but in the lower part of this plain (especially in the provinces of Ferrara, Ravenna and Rovigo) the average fell to 120 or 130 days.

[2] Here, as in industry, a definite grouping of the employers took place only after the War: the General Confederation of Agriculture was founded in April 1920.

[3] These clauses were agreed upon during a meeting, held in 1919 at the offices of the Permanent Labour Committee in Rome, between representatives of agricultural labourers and employers.

These same exceptions also existed of course in the agreements concerning industry, but there they were relatively of less importance.

Age limits were not legally fixed for ordinary work in agriculture, except in the rice fields. The following terms were therefore included in a number of collective agreements: boys under thirteen and fourteen and girls under thirteen or fifteen (according to provinces) could be employed only in light work. The agreement concluded by the National Federation of Landworkers for the province of Brescia contained further the stipulation "women may be employed on work suited to their capacity and taking into special consideration their state of pregnancy or recent confinement, if any."

C. Position of Labour during the Transition Period

1. When, on October 28, 1922, after the March on Rome, the King nominated Mussolini as his Prime Minister, there was a fairly complete social legislation, but the social and economic organization did not correspond to it. The reasons for this have been explained in the first section. Mussolini, in his desire to raise the status of Italy *inter alia* through more regular working conditions and a greater volume of production (which, he thought, could be arrived at only through class collaboration and never through class war) began by limiting the power of his opponents.

Royal decree No. 1529 of October 29, 1922[1] laid down conditions for the official registration of employers' and workers' organizations. Registration was voluntary and open to all unions of industrial and agricultural workers in privately-owned undertakings which existed for the defence of the trade interests of their members and the improvement of their economic position and which fulfilled certain criteria. A list of the members must be furnished. The scope of the association, the rights and duties of the members and the contributions of the members must be defined. The latter should cover at least three-fifths of the total income of the association and—in the case of workers' associations—should not be lower than 0·50 lira per member per month (the contribution to the General Confederation of Labour was 1 lira per member of the affiliated

[1] Published and entered in force on December 5, 1922.

federations per year). The registered unions received the right of being represented on public advisory bodies and institutions.

A year later another blow was given to the non-fascist trade unions. As has been mentioned above, unemployment insurance was compulsory under a Royal decree of October 19, 1919. The administration of the insurance funds was in the hands of a special body, the National Employment and Unemployment Office (Ufficio nazionale per il collacamento e la dissoccupazione)[1] and of the trade unions. Contributions came from employers and workers with a subsidy from the State. Royal decree No. 3158 of December 30, 1923, abolished the funds under supervision of the trade unions (amounting to thirty-two million lire), and handed them over to the national insurance fund. At the same time contributions by the State were abolished and the whole burden of insurance was laid on employers and workers, to be borne in equal parts. Further, agricultural workers, domestic servants, artists and all other persons employed in a way which does not lend itself to unemployment control, as well as persons on the staff of the State and other administrative or public bodies and institutions in as far as they were subject to the law on "just treatment" (see below) were excluded from insurance. Workers in branches which are seasonally idle had no right to payment during this period. The legislation of 1919 had not excluded the agricultural labourers.

Decree-law No. 64 of January 24, 1924, signified another step in the same direction. It brought all labour organizations which intended to give economic or moral aid to their members under the supervision of the provincial political authority—the Prefect. He acquired the right to annul the actions of the organization, to dissolve its Council and to nominate a commissar in charge of the funds of the organization and even to take over these funds completely. These steps could only be taken under some special circumstances, among which was included a "well based suspicion that the public confidence had been abused."

[1] Under this National Office were established the local Employment Exchanges. The employers were free to apply to them or to engage directly or through their own agents. These Exchanges never came to great development, because they were lacking in both funds and organization. The new decree abolished them.

The Fascist government also founded other new organs for conciliation and arbitration beside the existing Probiviral Courts and Executive Conciliation Committees. Decree-law No. 2311 of October 19, 1923, created Committees of Arbiters who had to take care that "just treatment" was given to the staff of rail and tramways and lines of internal navigation belonging to bodies other than the State. This matter had been regulated already by law No. 272 of June 30, 1906, and law No. 835 of July 14, 1912, which were intended to prevent strikes and lock-outs on these public services. The law of 1923 regulated the matter anew. It fixes rules for admission, time of probation, advancement, etc., for sick-leave, transfer and exemptions and it regulates the insurance system for the staff. All disputes must be brought before the Committee of Arbiters for the service-body in question; against its awards no appeal is possible (except in case of incompetence or abuse of power), and any action for preventing their execution is an offence against the law.

Under decree-law No. 2686 of December 2, 1923, similar committees were set up for the solution of individual disputes concerning rights resulting from labour contracts of private employees.

Disputes arising from the application of the eight-hour working day (see below) could be conciliated, in as far as industry and commerce were concerned, by the chief of the district for labour inspection. If one of the parties did not obey his award he had the right to bring a case against him before the tribunal. For disputes concerning this same matter in agriculture the Executive Conciliation Committees were competent.

One of the first matters studied by Mussolini's Government was the definite application of the eight-hour working day. Decree-law No. 692 of March 15, 1923, was the first general legal regulation of the subject in Italy. It established the eight-hour working day and forty-eight hour working week for all industrial and commercial undertakings. These limitations did not apply to domestic servants, managing staff, commercial travellers or persons working on board ships. As far as agriculture was concerned, the law applied only to casual workers. As from July 16, 1923, all collective agreements containing dispositions less favourable to the workers than the rules and exceptions prescribed in the decree-law became null and void.

Decree-law No. 112 of February 9, 1919, concerning the private labour contract for non-manual workers, was superseded by decree-law No. 1825 of November 13, 1924. The principal lines of the first regulation were maintained. The period of notice for dismissal was shortened (mostly to two-thirds); on the other hand the indemnity for dismissal was prescribed in all cases (it amounted to a half-month's salary for every year of service).

Decree-law No. 2994 of December 30, 1923, and its amendments contain rules concerning labourers in State service. An exact classification of the different types of labourers is made and it is prescribed that the number of permanent labourers on the staff of every administration or service cannot surpass a maximum to be fixed by decree.[1] The law further establishes the way in which the personnel is to be engaged, how it may be transferred from one service to another, how it is to be paid, that wages may be reduced if the cost of living falls, the conditions under which and the way in which piece work is to be operated, the rules for the eight-hour working day, for extraordinary work and work during the night and on Sundays and festivals, for paid holidays (eight, ten or eighteen working days, according to the class and degree of the labourer), and so on.

2. Under this new legislation and still more under the new organization of Fascist and State police power, the Fascist associations flourished to the detriment of the trade unions of Socialist or Catholic tendency.[2] It is not necessary to discuss here at length the organization of Fascist trade organizations,

[1] This measure forms part of a whole scheme, the necessity of which was felt by Mussolini during the first years of his government, to reduce the number of workers in State and other public services.

[2] As an example may be quoted a complaint which was heard in a meeting on January 15 and 16, 1925, of the Executive Committee of the (Catholic) Italian Confederation of Workers. In several provinces—it was said—practically all work of the organization was hindered by means of the refusal to recognize national trade unions which did not belong to the Fascist organizations. In the meantime the (socialistically inclined) General Confederation of Labour continued to suffer from disagreements in its own bosom: after more than two years of government under Mussolini, there were, during the national congress held in Milan from December 10 to 13, 1924, still strongly divergent opinions. Three resolutions were brought forward: that of the reformists got 62 per cent. of the votes, that of the maximalists 22 per cent., and that of the communists 15 per cent.

because it changed not only during but also after this transition period. Before a definite organization was finally established by law, the basis of the whole organization was the union, which grouped together a certain number of manual or intellectual workers of the same category. The unions were grouped according to category and province. The categories, belonging to the same branches of occupation, formed the provincial corporations. The various provincial corporations united to form provincial federations and at the same time the provincial corporations in each branch were grouped together in national corporations. These national corporations linked up to form the National Confederation of Corporations. It is, however, of more importance to illustrate the political background of this trade movement by quoting the objects of the Corporation of Industry and Commerce. These, as established in the beginning of 1923, were:

(*a*) to support the Fascist government in its efforts to develop amongst the general public confidence in the economic and industrial future of Italy;

(*b*) to denounce and oppose all privileges and monopolies in industry and commerce and to encourage private initiative;

(*c*) to develop the system of collective agreements and compulsory arbitration in industrial disputes;

(*d*) to create an industrial organization with a view to preventing undue speculation or profiteering in case of war;

(*e*) to guarantee adequate representation of provincial and municipal authorities on State advisory bodies.

The Fascist trade union Corporations Congress, held in Rome on June 30, 1923, and following days, carried a resolution which declared that labour agreements should not be merely the result of class war but should be based on a careful examination of conditions of production, which can only be secured by means of collaboration between employers and workers. This opinion, however, did not prohibit all strikes, as is shown by a resolution carried by the Grand Council of the Fascist Party (Partito Nazionale Fascista, abbreviated P.N.F.) on April 23, 1925. This happened after the " Fascist strike " of Lombard metallurgical workers in March 1925. In the resolution a strike was declared to be an act of war, to which recourse should be had only when peaceful methods were exhausted (and not at all by workers in the public services). It condemned sympathetic strikes which were part of the socialist system but by long experience had been proved futile. It censured certain Lombard organizations of metallurgical employers on the ground that they were putting their industrial interests before the interests of national production.

A short time later, the Secretary General of the Confederation of Fascist trade union Corporations gave a long account of Fascist trade unionism.[1] During the period when the political struggle was at its height, he said, the Fascist trade unions could not allow themselves to be carried away by economic movements which might have hindered the action of the Government and disturbed the unity of the Party. There was a crisis in national production and therefore the Fascist trade unions thought it desirable to wait for a more favourable moment at which to put forward the claims of the working classes. Later on, when the recovery of national industry made an improvement in the conditions of living of the workers possible, the Fascist unions did their best to obtain advantages for the workers and to consolidate these in labour agreements.

3. During the transition period there was no longer any sharp distinction between legal regulation of labour and the activity developed by the trade unions. Therefore only a few facts, supplementary to legislation, have to be mentioned. When, in 1923, the decree concerning Employment Exchanges was repealed (see above), the matter remained open for some time. Then the Confederation of Fascist trade union Corporations took the initiative in organizing a new system for these exchanges. This work was sanctioned by decree on September 26, 1926. In 1923 and 1924 we find, in the collective agreements concluded between agricultural employers' and Fascist workers' organizations, provision for special conciliation machinery of an entirely private character. Joint arbitration committees, composed of an equal number of representatives of each party, were set up everywhere with a view to facilitating arbitration more than was possible under the existing legislation.

[1] Address by Rossoni (who was Secretary General of the Confederation from its foundation till 1928, when it was split up into six Confederations) given during the fifth Fascist National Congress on June 21, 1925.

At the beginning of 1923 the General Confederation of Industry expressed already the hope that, in accordance with principles of class collaboration, affirmed by the Fascists, a new era of collaboration between employers and workers would begin, and at the end of the same year they were convinced of this possibility of collaboration. This was the origin of the agreement, stipulated on December 21, 1921, at *Palazzo Chigi* between the said confederation and the Confederation of Fascist Corporations. It was declared that trade activity should not be based " on the criterion of the unchangeable conflict between the interests of industrialists and labourers," but on the " sentiment of national syndical co-operation."

The agreement of *Palazzo Vidoni* (October 2, 1925) should also be mentioned. The General Confederation of Industry and the Confederation of Fascist Corporations recognized each other as the only representatives of employers and workers respectively. Consequently all agreements and all further discussion resulting from them had to take place between these two organizations. The Workers' Committees (Commissioni interni) referred to above therefore became superfluous.

D. Position of Labour during the Corporative Period

1. With the famous law No. 563 of April 3, 1926, concerning collective discipline of labour relations, the legislation enters upon a new field, though prepared by preceding laws and activity of the employers' and workers' organizations. In the following paragraphs only the broad outlines of this and successive legislation are given, while all the minor points of organization which eventually were altered are omitted.

The law and the regulations of July 1, 1926 (decree No. 1130) consist of three parts: (*a*) legal recognition of trade associations and of collective agreements; (*b*) jurisdiction in disputes connected with employment; (*c*) prohibition of strikes and lockouts.

For each branch of economic activity (except certain Government offices) one, and only one organization of employers and one of workers can be recognized; this organization obtains legal personality. Membership of this organization is optional, but everyone whose main economic activities are in its field is obliged to pay a certain contribution to it. An organization can only be recognized if, in the case of the workers, at least ten per cent. of the persons employed in the respective branch are voluntary members, and, in the case of employers, if the voluntary members employ not less than 10 per cent. of the workers in the branch. The organizations are further required to include among their purposes the protection of the financial and moral interests of their members and to endeavour to make provision for their relief, instruction, moral and civil training. The persons directing the associations must give guarantees of their capacity, integrity and unwavering loyalty to the nation. The principal effects of legal recognition are:

(i) The association represents in its territorial area all persons of the category for which it is formed;

(ii) It is entitled to levy on all these persons a contribution which, in the case of the workers, may not be more than one day's earnings;

(iii) The collective agreements which it has concluded are binding upon all the persons concerned in its territory;

(iv) It alone has power to bring before the competent authorities actions relating to disputes arising from collective relations.

Individual employment contracts between individual employers and workers who are subject to a collective agreement must conform to the conditions established by the latter, exception being made only when the terms of the individual contract are more favourable to the worker than those of the agreement.

The association which has concluded a collective agreement is responsible for (i) loss or damage arising from non-fulfilment of obligations assumed by the association itself; (ii) non-fulfilment on the part of those to whom the conditions of the agreement apply, in so far as the association may have failed to do everything in its power to secure the fulfilment of the obligations assumed.

The tribunals for labour matters have to settle disputes "concerned with the carrying out of collective agreements or other regulations in existence, or with demands for new conditions of employment." They consist of three magistrates and two citizens, specially appointed on each occasion with the object of giving due importance to the technical and economic consequences of the award, which must have regard to the superior interests of the nation.

Employers who suspend work and workers who strike or work in an irregular manner with a view to obtaining alterations in the employment agreement in force, are liable to a fine. The leaders, instigators or organizers may be dealt with more severely.

2. Another step towards the Corporate State was the Charter of Labour (*Carta del Lavoro*). It was not discussed in Parliament but prepared for and by the Grand Council of the P.N.F. and promulgated by Mussolini during a sitting of this Council (April 21, 1927). It is granted constitutional value by law No. 2834 of December 13, 1928, which, at the same time, authorizes the Government to issue provisions for its complete execution. The Charter contains the most comprehensive definitions available of the corporative system.

In the first sections it is laid down that the Italian nation is an organism of higher quality than individuals or groups of individuals. "It is a moral, political and economic unity, which finds its integral realization in the Fascist State"—and that labour is a social duty and, therefore, protected by the State. Section 3 repeats the principle of the law of April 3, 1926, concerning the representative faculty of one organization for workers and one for employers in every branch of economy. The following sections lay down—on the basis of subordination to the superior interests of production (i.e., of the State)—the principle of solidarity between the various factors occupied in production (Section 4) and the principle that the different groups enjoy legal equality while, above associations of employers and employed, corporations constitute the unifying organization of the forces of production. They will, therefore, be recognized as organs of the State and consequently have the right to issue binding rules for the regulation of the relations between employers and employed (Section 6). This matter was also treated later by laws of 1930 and 1934.

Section 5 mentions the labour tribunals already existing under the law of April 3, 1926, and adds that they will pronounce a verdict not only in relation to matters stipulated in the collective agreements or other existing rules, but also on questions which have not yet been regulated. It may be pointed out that the labour and other courts decide the latter questions on the basis of the mentality inspired by the Labour Charter. The spirit of the latter is also expected to guide the recognized trade associations in making provision for the moral and civic training of their members.

At this point it is convenient to mention law No. 206 of March 20, 1930, which stipulates that before resort is had to labour courts organizations of employers and employed concerned must try to settle disputes themselves. Law No. 163 of February 5, 1934, adds that, if in this way conciliation cannot be arrived at, the corporation under which the respective branch of economic activity is grouped will aim at a solution. This procedure was first rejected by Sections 6 and 10 of the Labour Charter. The law even goes a step further by declaring that if parties do not apply to the court for solution of the unsolved dispute, the magistrate in charge of these labour problems may, if he thinks that the interest of the nation demands this, himself bring the matter before the court. This is an especially creative function in as far as new labour conditions are to be laid down.

The following sections (7, 8 and 9) indicate that private enterprise in the sphere of production is the form which for the Nation as such is most effective and useful, and that, consequently the entrepreneur is responsible to the State, that professional associations of employers are required to promote by all possible means the increase and improvement of production and the reduction of its cost, and that State intervention arises only when private initiative is lacking or insufficient or when political interests are involved.

Sections 11 to 21 are devoted to collective agreements. In part they repeat the legislation already existing, in part they elaborate rules which were at that time not generally applied. They stipulate that wages should correspond to the normal demands of life, to the possibilities of production and to the labour output, that the employed have a right to a weekly day of rest falling on Sunday and, after a year of continued service, to a paid holiday. Further sections deal with Employment Exchanges, welfare and insurance, education and instruction. These subjects will be dealt with below.

3. After this fundamental legislation there followed a period of application and experimentation, finally crowned by law No. 908 of May 12, 1934. As the system of setting up trade associations and regulating their powers has been superseded by the definite rules applied in consequence of the latter law, we may for reasons of brevity omit the intermediate development. The legislation passed in the meantime has much more a political and philosophical character than a direct bearing on labour relations and organization. This legislation may be summarized as follows:

Law No. 1019 of May 17, 1928, modifies the system of political representation in the country. Henceforward national confederations of legally recognized trade associations and institutions of national importance pursuing aims of culture, education, relief or propaganda have the right to propose candidates for the Chamber of Deputies. The Grand Council of Fascism revises and reduces the resulting lists but does not change their character. In this way employers and employed in all trades and professions are represented. Subsequent modifications have introduced the principle of " approval by the people " of lists drawn up by the Grand Council of Fascism.[1] The Chamber so " elected " is to be completely on a " corporative basis." Law No. 2693 of December 9, 1928, recognizes the Grand Council of Fascism as the " supreme organ for co-ordinating and integrating all the activities of the regime."

Law No. 206 of March 20, 1930, concerns the re-organization of the National Council of Corporations. This law represents an intermediate stage, superseded by the law of 1934; in as far as it is still of importance for questions relating to labour organization it will be dealt with together with the latter law. Here it need only be mentioned that the law of 1930 re-organized the Council of Corporations but did not yet create these corporations. A Ministerial decree of December 6, 1930, however, set up a corporation for the entertainment industry and a decree of the Head of the Government of July 27, 1931, assigned to the various sections of the Council certain corporative powers concerning the corresponding economic branch.

The duties of the National Council of Corporations, with the

[1] I.e. the approval by the people of the definite list set up by the Grand Council of Fascism.

participation and under the direct supervision of the State, were to observe, control and harmonize all the economic and social factors of the life of the nation with the object of ultimately creating a new order based on economic efficiency and social justice.

4. Law No. 163 of February 5, 1934, provides, at least for the time being, the colophon to the corporative system. This law, on the constitution and functioning of the corporations, the decrees of the Head of the Government (of May 29 and following days) concerning the institution of corporations, and Royal decree of August 16, 1934, which approves the laws of the confederations in their present form, are all of economic and political importance.

The trade associations, the lowest grade of which covers a single province or commune, are grouped *vertically* in pyramidal form in organizations of gradually increasing scope. The highest but one category of these are national trade confederations. These, once again, are grouped in nine confederations: four pairs, in each of which one represents employers and one employed, for industry, agriculture, commerce, and credit and insurance, and one for artists and *professionisti*.[1] At the same time these trade associations are grouped horizontally, *i.e.* the representatives of the two corresponding associations for the same economic branch are grouped together in equal numbers to form a corporation. The trade associations affiliated to a corporation become independent in the sphere of trade association though they continue to belong to their respective confederation.

Under the legislation of 1926, confederations delegated their power for the conclusion of collective agreements to the minor associations of which they are composed, and these latter were also legally recognized. Under the new law only the confederations and the national trade federations (and the corporations which are State organs) are legally recognized. The only exceptions are found in the Confederation of *Professionisti* and Artists, which owing to the practical requirements of most of its members, retains its former organization of legally

[1] There is no corresponding word in English for this group, which includes, besides professional men like medical doctors and lawyers, also engineers, midwives, chemists, accountants, journalists, private teachers, authors, etc.

recognized national, inter-provincial and provincial associations. The regional associations of the other confederations continue to function. In order to avoid the necessity of resorting to the national federation for the conclusion of a collective agreement of purely local or regional character, it is provided that the central bodies may delegate the power to conclude such agreements to the regional associations.

The duties of the confederations are to exercise, in collaboration with the P.N.F., political supervision over the affiliated associations; to co-ordinate the activities of these associations and organize and operate services of common interest; to supervise the economic and financial management of these associations; to promote the creation of institutions for economic assistance, vocational training, and moral and national education; to appoint their own representatives to all bodies, committees and institutions on which such representation is allowed; to negotiate collective labour agreements and agreements to regulate collective economic relations affecting the general interests of the categories covered by the affiliated associations.

The national federations, in turn, have to promote in the general interests of the nation the technical and economic development of the category they represent; to negotiate collective labour agreements or agreements to regulate collective economic relations affecting their category; to appoint representatives of the category to the corporation and all other bodies and institutions on which such representation is allowed; and to organize assistance for their members.

The National Council of Corporations, at its session of November 13, 1933, defined the corporations as instruments which, under the aegis of the State, exercise complete organic and unitary control over the forces of production with a view to developing the wealth, political power and well-being of the Italian nation. The law of February 5, 1934, gives no definition but refers to the Labour Charter, which deals with them in Section 6. The law provides that the corporation, on the request of the competent Ministers or of one of the affiliated federations, and with the approval of the Head of the Government, shall draw up rules for the collective regulation of economic relations and for the uniform regulation of production. This same power, but subject also to the approval of all the associations concerned, was conferred on the National Council of Corporations by the law of 1930. The corporations may, further, fix scales of earnings, of the prices of economic services and of the prices of consumption articles offered to the public on special terms. They have also advisory functions in economic matters and, lastly, are to act as conciliation authorities of second reference in collective labour disputes, after conciliation by the trade associations concerned has failed and before the dispute is referred for judgment to the labour court.

Three types of corporation have been set up:

(*a*) for cycles of production embracing agriculture, industry and commerce (eight corporations);

(*b*) for cycles of production embracing industry and commerce (eight corporations).

(*c*) for occupations providing for services (six corporations).

For example there are corporations for cereals and for textiles under the first class, for metal working, engineering and for chemical industries in the second, for inland communications and for hotels and restaurants in the third.

5. It has been mentioned already that the Labour Charter contains a special chapter on Employment Exchanges. According to the principles of this document the State considers the arrangement for employment as a public function or a public service which must be under its direct supervision. While the decree of September 26, 1926 (see above) had recognized the organization of Employment Exchanges by the Confederation of workers, another Royal decree of 1928 altered this organization, prescribing that the Exchanges shall be directed by an administrative council composed of a president and an equal number of employers and workers. The Exchanges are organized on the basis of occupation[1]; there exist Exchanges for the whole country, for a group of provinces and for each province separately. The first class is

[1] They have been created, by Ministerial decrees, for workers in rice fields, agricultural workers in general, workers on the olive harvest, industrial workers, workers in commercial enterprises, workers in theatres, cinemas, etc. They do not apply to persons working directly for the State, to dock workers and fishermen (special provisions for these workers have been made in a number of decree-laws of February 1st, 1935) or to sailors (their conditions, including employment regulations, are laid down in a law of December 31st, 1928).

presided over by the Minister of State, Secretary of the P.N.F., the second and third by lower political officials indicated by him. Separate sections of the provincial exchanges exist in every centre of population where they are considered necessary.

It is compulsory for the unemployed to register with the exchanges and for the employers to notify vacancies to them. In giving employment, the length of time during which a person has been waiting for employment, his vocational training and political qualities will be taken into consideration. The employer has no right to choose his workers except when specially skilled labourers are needed.[1]

In this relation should be mentioned also the Internal Migration Committee. It regulates internal migration, encourages movements in the labour supply, and facilitates land settlement.

With a view to facilitating the activity of the exchanges, law No. 112 of January 10, 1935, introduces the workers' labour record (*libretto di lavoro*). Many trade associations had already felt the need of such a record before the law came into force, and had inserted in the collective agreements a clause by which the possession of documents of this order was made compulsory. The record which every worker must now possess contains information as to his vocational training, so that he may be provided with work suitable to his capacity and be encouraged (or obliged as the case may be) to improve his qualifications. It also contains details as to the various posts filled by its holder, his wages, accidents while at work, illnesses and the number of his social insurance card.

6. The last sections of the Labour Charter contain an idealistic conception of the social service to be rendered for welfare and insurance. Fascist literature insists very much on the difference between the system followed in this respect in pre-Fascist times and now. In the first period the insurance was completely private in scope: the payment, on an actuarial basis, of an indemnity to the insured person. Now—it is said—there has been added a conception of a political and social character. In the first place the activity regarding welfare is not limited to the payment in money of indemnities and subsidies, but great care is taken to ensure the prevention of accidents

[1] Decision of the Grand Council of Fascism of February 17, 1935.

and occupational diseases, while everything possible is done for curing completely the suffering worker so that he may take up his work again. Further, the pre-Fascist insurance was based completely on legal prescriptions. Nowadays in their collective agreements the associations of employers and workers often make wider and more generous provisions. On February 1, 1937, there existed for workers in industry more than 2,000 mutual insurance funds, which had legally recognized rules of a standard type and provided for indemnities in case of illness not caused by labour accidents covered by compulsory accident insurance. The premiums are paid in equal parts by the employer and the worker. On the date mentioned nearly 2,120,000 labourers were insured in this way. Some 530,000 labourers were insured in mutual organizations of a somewhat different character and funds for employees in industry, set up under analogous terms, covered some 112,000 persons. Similar insurance funds exist for workers and employees in agriculture and commerce, and in many branches of transport and electricity works. Dock-workers and fishermen have insurance societies in which no employers' contribution is paid.[1]

Another difference from pre-Fascist insurance is the relation between the indemnity and the size of the family. This principle had been adopted (within rather narrow limits) in the invalidity and old-age insurance, the tuberculosis insurance and the unemployment insurance.

A law of 1912 had created an Inspectorate for Industry and Labour which had the functions of inspecting industrial and commercial establishments and surveying the execution of laws concerning labour and insurance. This Inspectorate has been superseded by a corporative body (*Ispettorato Corporativo*), which acts on the lines of decree-law No. 1684 of December 28, 1931. It has also the function of a labour police organization, including the control of the execution of collective agreements. It is at the same time an advisory body, which may be asked to give its opinion on rules laid down in new agreements, but not yet published.

[1] The Confederation of Fascist employers in industry has created a special institute for welfare work in favour of injured workers and for the improvement of hygienic conditions in factories, named *La Vigila*.

As from April 1, 1937, new legislation concerning accident insurance in industry is in force. The insurance which is also in favour of the relatives of the insured worker, is *de jure*, i.e., even if the employer has not paid the premiums, the insurance payment is made to the injured worker or those who may rightfully claim for him. Medical and surgical assistance has to be provided. An indemnity for loss of wages has to be paid in case of temporary disablement. It amounts to two-thirds of the daily pay of which the worker is deprived and is paid during the whole period of disablement. For bachelors without dependants it is reduced to half-pay, as long as the medical or surgical assistance is given. An allowance amounting to half the daily pay is given to a worker who has become permanently and completely unable to work. If the disability is only partial, the allowance is reduced in proportion. In case of death due to the accident, a widow's and orphan's pension is given, amounting to two-thirds of the wages.

The same law also lays down rules for insurance in respect to old age, unemployment, tuberculosis and maternity. This last matter has been further regulated by decree-laws of 1934 and 1937. They refer to women who are not in fixed State service (for these special regulations have been made). The first decree-law established that women shall not work in paid service from one month before the confinement is expected till six weeks after it shall have taken place. The second decree-law prescribes that pregnant and nursing women in State service on private contract shall receive during a maximum of two-and-a-half months a half salary though they are absent. The first decree-law increases the allowance given in case of confinement to 300 lire.

Insurance against tuberculosis was first made compulsory by decree-law in 1927, but it was regulated anew by the decree-law of 1935. Insured persons are to be treated in case of tuberculosis in special sanatoriums and those who have dependants receive an allowance.

It should be added here that the decree-law of October 4, 1935, provides also for the definite organization of the central Institute of Social Insurance (*Instituto nazionale fascista della Previdenza sociale*) which deals with all the different forms of compulsory insurance. This Institute received during the year 1936, as contributions, 891 million lire. It paid out in the form of indemnities and allowances the following sums: for pensions—393 million lire; for prevention and treatment of invalidity—10 million lire; for unemployment, anti-tuberculosis and maternity allowances—130 million, 168 million, and 7 million lire respectively; and for accident compensations—11 million lire.

7. In the preceding paragraphs little has been said of the activity of the trade organizations in relation to the improvement of labour conditions. It should be kept in mind, however, that the greater part of the social progress made by the working classes has been initiated in the form of some special stipulation in the collective agreements. A typical example of this ever-widening power of such initiative taken by trade organizations is the forty-hour week. On October 11, 1934, the two Confederations of Industry signed an agreement which brought a reduction of the working hours to forty per week with a proportionate reduction in wages (to be supplemented by family allowances), and with the object of employing more workers. Overtime had to be abolished as far as possible, employment of women and young persons was to be limited in favour of men, employment of persons in receipt of pensions to be prohibited. The National Federations for the different branches of industry were charged with the application of these limitations within the possibilities of their special field. Within a short time some sixty agreements had been concluded by these Federations. It was proved possible by this means to provide employment for a further 200,000 workers in industry. On February 16, 1935, the Grand Council of Fascism having noticed these results, decided therefore " that with or without international agreement, the forty-hour working week shall be placed on a permanent basis and wherever possible, strictly enforced." In March the Ministry of Corporations invited the employers' and workers' organizations to adopt permanent agreements on this matter. This was done on June 23 following.

These agreements applied to all workers employed in industrial, handicraft, and co-operative undertakings which are covered by the current legislation on hours of work.[1] Finally

[1] The agreements, however, did not apply to certain classes of workers: near relatives of the employer, home-workers, persons employed in domestic work, etc.

the subject was regulated by decree law in May 1937. The latter confirms and consolidates the measures introduced by collective agreements. It provides for a normal maximum working week of forty hours for work of an industrial nature (forty-two hours for operations which are necessarily continuous). For other classes of work the forty-hour week may be introduced by royal decree. The law does not apply to near relatives of the employer, to persons employed in domestic work, to home-workers, to persons employed on board ship, to persons who are merely to attend or watch over premises, to persons employed in industrial work accessory to agricultural holdings, or as far as special regulations for their working times are promulgated to persons employed on public services (even if these are rendered by private individuals). Exceptions may be allowed only when absolutely necessary and the employer is obliged to pay to the special Unemployment Fund (which is under the supervision of the Insurance Institute) a sum equal to 10 per cent. of the salary which his workers earn in overtime, except when the collective agreement stipulates a higher payment for work in overtime. In no case may there be more than fourteen hours overtime per week or more than twelve hours on a weekly average of nine weeks.

In commercial and banking enterprises analogous regulations have been agreed upon. They first entered into force on October 28, 1934; at the end of February 1935 already 25,000 workers had been reabsorbed.

A Royal Decree of June 1935 introduced the principle of the Saturday half-holiday. In public and private undertakings work must stop on Saturday at one p.m. Exceptions within certain limits may be provided for by collective agreements. This " Fascist Saturday " was applied before its legal institution in a number of agreements. In many agreements it is now indicated that—besides the paid annual holiday to which every worker has a right (and which cannot be annulled by any event subsequent to its acquisition)—the normal wage will be paid in respect of the so-called national holidays on which labour (except in quite special conditions) is prohibited.

Under the collective agreement of October 11, 1934, which regulated the application of the forty-hour week, a National Family Allowance Fund was set up. It was supported by equal contributions of employers and workers (1 per cent. of wages per working week of forty hours, 5 per cent. of wages earned in overtime). To heads of families who had children under fourteen years of age at their charge, an allowance was to be paid. By decree-law of August 21, 1936, the system was extended and made compulsory to all industrial workers. It is estimated that this scheme applied to two-and-a-half million workers of whom 800,000 had families with 1,700,000 dependent children. Collective agreements of December 1936 and January 1937 applied the scheme to commercial workers, and to workers in credit and insurance houses and in tax-collectors' offices. Finally the decree-law of June and a Royal decree of July 1937, enlarged the system considerably. It now applies to all workers for whom no special and more favourable regulations have been made (*inter alia* State officials), excepting persons who earn more than 2,000 lire a month, persons in domestic service, near relatives of the employer, individual or collective share-tenants. The employers pay a higher contribution than the workers. In the case of agricultural labourers the worker pays 0·10 lira a day, the employer 0·35 lira. The family allowance is 2·40 lire per week for families with one dependent child, 3·60 lire for families with two or three, and 4·80 lire for families with four or more dependent children. In the case of industrial workers the premiums are 1 per cent. of the wage, to be paid by the worker, and 3·5 per cent. by his employer. The allowances amount to 3·60 lire, 4·80 lire and 6·0 lire according to the number of children.

E. Bargaining Power of the Workers

1. From the preceding sections it will be seen that before the March on Rome, the workers had obtained, thanks to the power of their organizations, an ever-increasing influence on their own economic position. But at the same time it is evident that this power had no firm background: the workers had not sufficient leaders, the majority had no experience of trade union activity and very little education. Mussolini, in re-organizing Italy, limited the power of these unions. Only from 1926 onwards was the influence of the working classes increased again. It has been explained already that this was done on quite a different principle. In this respect part of

Section 6 of the Labour Charter may be repeated. It reads: "Legally recognized professional associations ensure legal equality between employers and workers, control the discipline of production and labour, and promote the improvement of both." This rule is brought into practice by the power given to confederations and national federations of workers and of employers to bargain as equals. This is not only true in theory; the whole apparatus of the State (Fascist Party, Labour Courts, Corporative Inspectorate, Corporations, each from its own point of view) takes care that this fundamental principle is not violated. Its influence during recent years may be shown from the following examples:

(*a*) Collective agreements in agriculture for the year 1935–1936 were renewed without any important change, except for the fact that, in view of the improved economic situation in this branch, the employers took over the payment of the whole of the contributions to the mutual sickness funds, which, before, had been paid in equal shares by employers and workers.

(*b*) Before the official devaluation of the lira, prices had risen already some 10 per cent. The various national federations started to conclude new wage agreements providing for increases in pay. Up to October 15, 1936, there had been concluded 133 such agreements, providing for increases ranging from 5 per cent. to 11 per cent. They affected 3,305,000 workers in industry, 2,107,000 in agriculture, 873,000 in commerce and 62,000 in insurance.

(*c*) The devaluation of the lira made it necessary to intensify price control. This control was entrusted to the P.N.F. which at once asked the trade organizations to co-operate, so that the action of the committee of control might be directed as much as possible towards maintaining the purchasing power of the less well-to-do classes of the population.

The ways by which the forty-hour working week and the family allowance were obtained (as illustrated in the preceding section) are further examples of this considerable bargaining power of the Workers' Organizations.

The statement that in practice workers' trade unions have more influence than in 1920 to 1922 does not, however, mean that every individual labourer has become a more powerful bargainer. He may bring forward his wishes only through the official channels, and his association, before backing his desires, will first see that their fulfilment does not harm production as a whole. This principle has to guide all the decisions of the organizations which represent the workers. At the same time, on the basis of this principle these organizations are powerful in a completely new field. In the corporations (which within certain limits are empowered to secure collective regulation of economic relations and to lay down rules on a uniform basis for the discipline of production) there are, besides representatives of the Government and the P.N.F., an equal number of representatives of employers' and of workers' organizations (and, in as far as is necessary, representatives of the *professionisti* and artists).

The social welfare work is also, at least in part, the result of workers' organizations' activities. Certainly, in practice, this is not everywhere organized as perfectly as official speeches and propaganda pamphlets may suggest, but it should be borne in mind that a large part of this work is completely new, and that financial means are not always adequate and that it has not yet been possible to find in all circumstances the right man for the job.

SCANDINAVIA

BY

HALVARD M. LANGE

SCANDINAVIAN LABOUR 1920–1937

THE term Scandinavia or, as it has of late become customary to say, The Northern Countries, usually covers the five small independent States of North-Western Europe: Denmark, Finland, Iceland, Norway and Sweden. The present paper on Scandinavian Labour does not, however, deal with either Finland or Iceland. It limits itself to the three kingdoms of Denmark, Norway and Sweden.

A few simple facts must be kept in mind as a necessary background for an understanding of the present development and problems of labour organization in these countries. They are all of them small countries as far as population is concerned. Denmark has 3,705,559 inhabitants, Norway 2,895,000, and Sweden 6,249,489. Denmark is a small country also in extent, with an area of 42,931 square kilometres, which gives an average density of 86·3 per square kilometre. Norway and Sweden, on the other hand, cover considerable areas, and are relatively sparsely populated. With an area of 322,599 square kilometres, Norway has no more than 9 inhabitants per square kilometre. Sweden, with 448,953 square kilometres, has a density of 13·9. Both Norway and Sweden, consequently, have to cope with the problem of distance to a greater extent than most European countries.

Neither of the three countries is by far as highly industrialized as either Great Britain or Germany. Agriculture, horticulture and forestry still support a considerable proportion of the population, in Denmark 30·3 per cent., in Norway 29·9 per cent. and in Sweden 34·2 per cent. Mining, industry and handicraft account for 28·6 per cent., 27·6 per cent and 31·7 per cent. respectively. Commerce, shipping and other transport for 17·7 per cent., 19·7 per cent. and 15·5 per cent. The high Norwegian percentage in the latter group is due to the unique importance of shipping. With 1,412 gross tons per 1,000 inhabitants Norway has a higher figure than any other country, while Denmark, with 309 gross tons ranks third and Sweden with 243 sixth. In the structure of Norway's economic life fishing and whaling further play an important part, supporting 7 per cent. of the total population, the corresponding figures for Denmark and Sweden being 1 per cent. and 0·6 per cent. respectively.

Capitalist industry is a comparatively recent growth. Denmark's industrial revolution did not start in earnest till the 1850's, Sweden's not till the 1860's and Norway's not till the 1860's and 1870's. Though the world-wide tendency to concentration in large units did make itself felt, it has not proceeded as far as in the main industrial countries, and during the post-war period a marked counter-tendency has emerged, more especially in Sweden and Norway. Owing to the development of motor transport and the wide distribution of electrical power there has been a large increase in the number of industrial units employing ten workers or less.

Agriculture is mainly carried on by small independent owners of family holdings. The percentages of holdings with less than 10 ha. of cultivated land are: in Denmark 51·7 per cent., in Norway 93 per cent. and in Sweden 77·8 per cent. Denmark has 44·9 per cent. holdings with 10–50 ha., Norway 6·9 per cent. and Sweden 20·4 per cent. Of these two main groups of holdings, only the latter employ wage labour to any appreciable extent.

So far points of likeness in the economic structure of the three countries have been emphasized. There are, however, very important differences which must be noted.

Foremost among them is the dominating importance of agriculture in Denmark as an export industry. In 1935 the value of agricultural exports amounted to 74·7 per cent. of Denmark's total exports. The corresponding figures for Norway and Sweden were 5·8 per cent. (including furs) and 7·7 per cent. respectively. Denmark is very poor in industrial raw materials and in power resources, having neither minerals nor forests of any importance, and no water power. Danish industry, therefore, works mainly on the basis of imported raw materials and sells most of its products in the home market.

In Norway and Sweden, on the other hand, the products of mining and industry make up the bulk of their exports, while agriculture sells practically all its produce in the home market. Both Norway and Sweden have vast resources of water power, which they have developed to a considerable extent. Their extensive forests supply raw materials for important export industries. Sweden is, moreover, very rich in iron ores, which form the basis of a highly developed engineering industry working for the world market, and in addition are an essential element of Swedish exports. Norwegian iron ores are much poorer, and owing to their situation in the far north are exported, while the Norwegian engineering industry relies on imports of half finished products. Norway further exports large quantities of pyrites and molybdenum ores as well as nickel and copper, while Sweden has sulphide ores which contain copper, silver, gold and still other minerals.

To these differences in natural resources, which have largely determined the corresponding differences which we find in the economic structure, and especially in the structure of industry in the three countries, must be added differences in monetary and financial policy and in the structure and traditions of labour organization. Despite the parallelism which exists in many respects, Scandinavian trade unionism is best understood if studied separately in each of the three countries.

I

During the war and post-war boom years Denmark, with gold payments suspended, experienced an inflation which, by 1920, had brought the wholesale price index, based on the statistics of foreign trade to 390 (1913=100). Thanks to drastic measures of price control the cost of living had been kept down to some extent, the index reaching 262 (1913=100) in the summer of 1920. Wages had lagged behind during the war years, but the boom of 1919–1920 enabled the trade unions to secure increases, which brought the level of real wages considerably above the 1913 figure. An index of real yearly earnings for all categories of workers, counting in loss through unemployment, illness and labour disputes, shows 128·7 for 1920 (1914=100). During these years the trade unions also succeeded in securing the eight-hour day for all industrial workers.

The post-war slump made itself felt from the autumn of 1920, the wholesale price index falling to 223 in 1921 and 171 in 1922. The rapid fall in prices produced great disturbance in economic life. The country's largest credit bank failed, and unemployment among trade unionists rose from 2·1 per cent. at the end of July 1920, to 15·1 per cent. at the end of December. The yearly average reached 19·7 per cent. in 1921 and 19·3 per cent. in 1922. The cost of living culminated in January 1921 with an index figure of 264, and then dropped rapidly. The employers' federation demanded drastic wage cuts, which were accepted by the trade unions and the index of real yearly earnings fell to 116·5 in 1921 and 103·2 in 1922.

During 1923 and 1924 prices rose once more, mainly owing to the policy of the Central Bank which, in an attempt to avoid the failure of private banks, expanded credit liberally. The wholesale price index reached 226 in 1924, and unemployment percentages fell to 12·7 per cent. in 1923, and 10·7 per cent. in 1924. Cost of living figures rose from 198 in January 1923 to 221 in January 1925, but wage agreements were prolonged with automatic regulation according to the movement of the cost of living index. Owing to increased employment the index of real yearly earnings showed 109·1 in 1923 and 114·3 in 1924.

Early in 1925 the trade unions, pointing to the continued rise in prices, put forward demands for an increase in wage rates. The Employers' Federation countered by locking out 100,000 workers for two months, the result being a compromise allowing an increase of 3 to 4 per cent. in hourly wage rates.

Although economic activity during this period of renewed inflation had on the whole been developing satisfactorily, the continual depreciation of the Danish krone measured in dollars caused anxiety, and attempts were made to stop the rise in foreign exchanges by restrictions of imports, regulation of the trade in foreign exchange and the establishment of an "equalization fund." In December 1924, an Act was finally passed obliging the Central Bank to reduce the rate of exchange of dollars from kr. 5·80 to kr. 5·32 by January 1, 1927.

As a result of credit restrictions together with the deflationary measures carried out by the Government, which paid off debts by means of extraordinary taxation, the foreign exchanges dropped so that the dollar rate of kr. 5·32 was arrived at as early as May, 1925. This rapid recovery was influenced by a favourable movement of the prices of Danish export commodities, by the labour stoppage which caused the demand for foreign exchange to drop and, last but not least, by the speculation which developed when it became clear that the provisions of the 1924 Bank Act were to be realized. The parity of the Danish krone with the dollar was practically restored at the close of 1925, and in December 1926 the gold standard was re-established at the pre-war gold parity.

The result, as far as the volume of industrial production is concerned, was a drop from 131 in 1924 to 122 in 1927 (1922 = 100) and an increase in unemployment percentages from 10·7 in 1924 to 14·7 in 1925, 20·7 in 1926 and 22·5 in 1927. The reduction in employment was due also to the measures of rationalization adopted in the main industries. The trade unions during this period pursued a moderate policy, contenting themselves with automatic yearly adjustment to the cost of living index figure. The index of real yearly earnings varied as follows: 109·5 in 1925, 111·1 in 1926 and 107·1 in 1927. The drop in money wages during the period, from the beginning of 1925 to the close of 1927, amounted to about 15 per cent., while the cost of living index fell from 221 in January 1925, to 176 in July 1927. By March, 1927, wholesale prices, after a rapid decline from 243 in January, 1925, to 172 in January, 1926, and a slower downward movement during 1926 had reached a new equilibrium at 153, a level which was maintained with few variations until the summer of 1929.

In 1928 an upward movement began to make itself felt, which lasted till the second half of 1930, the index of industrial production (1922 = 100) rising to 132 in 1928 and 140 in 1929, and unemployment percentages dropping to 18·5 in 1928, 15·5 in 1929 and 13·7 in 1930. Money wage rates remained unchanged during 1928 and 1929, while the cost of living index, which had stood at 176 from July 1927 to July 1928, fell slowly to 170 in January 1930.

The trade unions during these years gradually succeeded in removing from wage agreements the provision for automatic adaptation to the cost of living figure. The result of the drop in cost of living and the increased volume of employment was a rise in the index of real yearly earnings to 114·3 in 1928, 120·3 in 1929, and 132·1 in 1930, this latter increase being due to a rise in money wages obtained in the summer of 1930.

The downward movement which began to make itself felt in earnest in October 1930, was not due to home conditions, but to the world depression. The Danish mercantile fleet was first hit, gross freights dropping from 205 mill. kr. in 1929 to 175 mill. kr. in 1930.

From September 1930, agriculture was hit by the rapid decline in the prices of animal products, though the price of imported grain fell still more. The export surplus of agriculture was reduced from 959·3 mill. kr. in 1929 to 930·6 mill. kr. in 1930. Industrial activity kept well up till October 1930, benefiting from the fall in the price of imported coal, iron and timber, and building activities also kept up most of the year. From October, however, unemployment figures started to rise rapidly.

In the spring of 1931 the employers threatened a big lock-out, which was averted when the trade unions agreed to some reduction in money wages in exchange for holidays with pay of six days' duration for certain groups. As the cost of living was falling, the net result was a further slight increase in real yearly earnings to 133 in 1931.

On September 27, 1931, the Danish krone, along with the Swedish and Norwegian, followed sterling off gold, but the drop in prices, specially of animal products, continued. Danish agricultural exports were also hit by import restrictions in Germany and the adoption of a protective tariff in Great Britain, and still more by the quota policy adopted after the Ottawa conference of 1932. Gross figures of agricultural exports dropped from 1,400 mill. kr. in 1929 to 800 mill. kr. in 1932, while industrial exports fell from 300 mill. kr. to 200 mill. kr. and gross freights continued their fall from 175 mill. kr. in 1930 to 100 mill. kr. in 1932.

The result was a disastrous situation for agriculture. Most Danish holdings were saddled with heavy debts which they were no more able to honour. Though prices were eventually raised through trade agreements with Great Britain, the quota restrictions led to severe restrictions of output, resulting in the throwing off of some 40,000 agricultural wage earners. The crisis in agriculture, restricting the purchasing power of the agricultural population and bringing building activities in the countryside nearly to a standstill, reacted on industry. The average unemployment percentage rose to 31·7 in 1931. The groups that were worst hit were the building trades with an average of 44·2 per cent. unemployed and the general workers with a yearly average of 36·8 per cent.

In 1932 the employers made a new effort at forcing down the wage level, but to no avail. Money wage rates were maintained despite a further slight decline in the cost of living. Owing to the high unemployment percentage, however, the index of real yearly earnings fell to 110·1.

In the autumn of 1929 a Social-Democrat-Radical coalition government had taken office, with a clear majority in the popular chamber, while the opposition parties dominated the upper chamber. The government in 1931 submitted an extensive programme of state intervention, the main points of which were increased subsidies to the Trade Union Unemployment funds, extended public works and tax relief and subsidies to agriculture.

In October, 1931, this programme was accepted, with modifications as to the mode of financing the extra expenditure. In January, 1932, followed the establishment of exchange control, which was subsequently developed into an instrument not only for controlling the trade in foreign exchange and securities, but also for restricting imports of finished products and favouring imports of raw materials in order to stimulate home industries.

Under pressure from agricultural producers, the government in the autumn of 1932 further agreed to a lowering of the exchange rate of the krone measured in sterling to kr. 22·50 to the £, while prices of animal products in the home market were raised, partly through restriction of output, partly through subsidies. From January 1933, therefore, the cost of living index started rising slowly. Unemployment declined slightly, the average percentage for 1933 being 28·8. When the employers declared a lock-out to force down wages in January 1933, the government succeeded in securing the support of the farmer-liberal opposition for an act prohibiting strikes and lock-outs for one year. Money wage rates consequently were maintained throughout 1933.

In 1934 the improvement in world trade accentuated the recovery which had begun in Denmark the previous year. The index of industrial production, now based on 1931 = 100, rose to 117, the improvement being more marked in the production of consumers' goods (index 124), than in capital goods (108). In 1935 there was a further rise to 125, a figure which was maintained in 1936 despite a long drawn-out lock-out in the early part of that year. Unemployment percentages were further reduced to 22·1 in 1934, 19·7 in 1935 and 19·3 in 1936. The rise in the price of agricultural exports, supplemented by state-aided debt reductions, improved the purchasing power of the agricultural population, while an extensive programme of state subsidized housing and public works stimulated building and subsidiary industries. Despite an increase in the cost of living from 166 in 1934 to 172 in 1935 the index of real yearly earnings, which had reached 112·1 in 1933 went up to 119 in 1934 and was practically maintained in 1935. Despite the long lock-out struggle in 1936 the trade unions obtained a further advance in money wage rates mainly for the lower paid categories of workers, and this improvement was continued in 1937. A further rise in the price of imports, and the necessity of increasing purchases in Germany and Great Britain to secure the sale of agricultural products in 1936 and 1937 forced the authorities, the Central Bank and the Exchange Control, to restrict credit for imports of other commodities, thereby limiting building activities to some extent. Consequently there was some increase in unemployment during 1937, resulting in a probable fall in real yearly earnings.

Against this background we now turn to the development of Danish trade unionism during the post-war period. By 1920, it had behind it nearly fifty years of growth. National unions, most of them on a craft basis, had been formed in most trades by the middle of the 1890's. In 1898 they united to form a National Trade Union Centre which after one year counted 38 national unions and 25 local unions with a total membership of 61,000. After a serious lock-out in 1899, the Trade Union Centre entered into an agreement with the National Employers' Federation which has since formed the main basis of Danish trade union practice with regard to labour conflicts. By the "September Agreement" the two organizations mutually recognized each other's right to proclaim or approve strikes and lock-outs and to negotiate on behalf of their constituent members. Both parties agreed to recognize and support as lawful only such stoppages as had been agreed to by at least a three-fourths majority of the votes cast by the competent body of the organization involved, and further undertook to give notice a fortnight ahead of intended stoppages. The Trade Union Centre further recognized the employers' right of directing and distributing work and of hiring and firing labour. Both parties agreed to give three months' notice of demands for revision of collective agreements, and to deal with any dispute as to the interpretation of agreements by negotiation, mediation or, if necessary, voluntary arbitration. At the demand of both organizations a Court of Arbitration was set up by an act of April, 1900, its competence being limited to dealing with disputes as to the observance of the September Agreement by the two National organizations.

After a further serious lock-out struggle in 1908 the provisions of 1899 were supplemented by agreed rules concerning procedure, the main point of which was an undertaking always to attempt a settlement by peaceful means wherever possible, and to submit to mediation whenever one of the parties involved so demanded. This agreement formed the basis of two acts of April 1910, one replacing the act of 1900 and instituting a new Permanent Court of Labour Arbitration competent to settle finally any dispute arising out of alleged infringements of collective agreements, the other establishing the office of Public Mediator in Labour Disputes.

The Employers' Federation by this date fully recognized the system of collective agreements, signing a common declaration to the effect that " the main basis for the regulation of conditions of work is no more the individual labour contract . . . but the collective agreement negotiated and accepted by Employers' and Labour organizations."

Such was the state of Danish Labour Law at the beginning of the post-war period. The trade union movement by 1920 had reached a total membership of 362,000 in 74 national unions, of which 55, with a total membership of 279,000 were affiliated to the National Trade Union Centre. Nearly all national unions had well developed unemployment insurance funds, which were entitled to state and municipal grants. Statistics presented by the Trade Union Centre estimated the percentage of workers organized in industry, transport and commerce in 1919 at 84·7, in agriculture, forestry and domestic service at 13·2, giving a general average of 54·4 per cent. organized among all groups of wage-earners.

The deflation period brought the total number of trade unionists down to 303,000 in 73 national unions in 1923, fifty unions with 233,000 members being affiliated to the National Centre. The heaviest losses had been suffered by the agricultural workers whose union, formed in 1915, had declined from 32,000 to 20,000, and by the Union of General Workers. The new inflation of 1924–25 brought some increase in membership. But the great lock-out of 1925, involving 100,000 workers and lasting 62 days, resulted in the breaking away from the National Centre of the Union of General Workers, which was dissatisfied at not receiving sufficient financial support during the struggle. By 1926 the membership of the National Centre consequently dropped to 156,000, while that of non-affiliated unions reached 157,000. During the following two years of deflation there was an insignificant decline in the membership of non-affiliated unions, while the National Centre kept on the 1926 level. No major disputes occurred, but on the initiative of a farmer-liberal government formed in December 1926, public grants to trade union unemployment funds were severely cut, and the Supreme Court, giving judgment in suits brought by farmers against the trade unions, severely limited the use of the "blockade" against unorganized employers and sentenced the Agricultural Workers' and General Workers' Unions and the National Centre to pay heavy damages for losses inflicted through regular strike action.

In 1928, negotiations were conducted between the Trade Union Centre, the General Workers' Union and the Employers' Federation with a view to arriving at a longer duration of collective agreements which, owing to the unstable conditions of the war and post-war period, were generally concluded for one year only. No result was obtained, however, and in 1929 the political offensive against the trade union movement was pursued through the enactment of a new Trade Union Act of March 27, 1929. This Act severely limited the use of the boycott and "any kind of economic or personal persecution aiming at limiting in an unjustifiable way the liberty of the individual to work or to belong to or keep aloof from any organization." Penalties included fines upwards of 100,000 kr. or prison. The Act, commonly known as the " Blacklegs' Charter," was strongly resented by all trade unionists and the Labour-Radical Government, after gaining an independent majority in both houses of Parliament in the autumn of 1936, immediately took steps to repeal it.

By 1929, the upward movement in industry was reflected in growing membership figures, the growth of trade unionism being further stimulated by the advance of Labour in the political field at the general elections of that year and the formation of the Social-Democrat-Radical coalition government headed by Mr. Stauning. After settling their dispute with the Trade Union Centre, the General Workers' Union reaffiliated, bringing the membership of the Centre to 250,000 in 1929, total trade union membership once more nearing the 1920 level with 328,000.

The following period of depression and recovery has been one of steady and increasingly rapid growth for the trade union movement, and of marked progress in the efforts of the Trade Union Centre to secure affiliation from independent national unions. In 1929 there were 55 national unions within and 24 national unions outside the Centre. By 1937, the number of affiliated national unions had reached 62, with a total membership of some 425,000, a mere 36,000 in eight national unions remaining outside. The largest increase in membership during the period was registered by the General Workers' Union which in 1934 absorbed the agricultural workers and by 1937 counted some 170,000 members. The second largest union, that of the engineering workers, had 35,000 members.

This growth and concentration of Trade Unionism has to a considerable extent been determined by the policies pursued by the Labour-Radical coalition administration. From 1931 onwards the adverse influence of the world depression was countered by large scale and ever widening interference by the state in the economic life of the country. The extension of unemployment insurance through increased government subsidies enabled the trade unions, as sole administrators of unemployment benefit, to extend their sphere of influence. On the other hand, the public regulation of foreign trade through the agencies of exchange control and trade agreements made it a paramount interest for the government to avoid as far as possible labour disputes which might upset the balance of trade, endanger exports, or react unfavourably on the efforts to stimulate employment. During the two first years of the depression the trade unions, uniting under the leadership of the National Centre, succeeded, with the assistance of the public mediators, in avoiding any stoppage. In 1931 they accepted some reduction in money wage rates in exchange for an extension of holidays with pay, and in 1932 agreements were renewed without material changes. By the beginning of 1933, however, the Employers' Federation insisted on further wage cuts and threatened a lock-out. It was prevented by an act of parliament, passed with the support of the farmer-liberals, which prohibited strikes and lock-outs for one year, fixing wage rates according to proposals put forward by the public mediator and accepted by the trade unions. Though favourable to the workers, this direct interference in a labour dispute aroused considerable criticism within the trade unions, which were opposed on principle to any further limitation of their freedom of action. Criticism was, however, tempered by the satisfaction felt at the considerable extension of social services enacted in 1933. Health and infirmity-insurance was extended to cover 84 per cent. of the adult population, unemployment benefits considerably increased and the administration of the poor law thoroughly overhauled and humanized.

In January 1934 the temporary Act of 1933 was replaced by a permanent Act on Public Mediation in Labour Disputes. This Act empowered the public mediator to declare that any proposed settlement, though covering a variety of industries, must be accepted or rejected as a whole, thus ensuring that the rejection of mediation proposals by minor groups should not endanger a general peaceful settlement. The Act further laid down definite rules as to the majorities required for rejection of mediation proposals. If voting takes place in a delegate body, a simple majority of votes cast is sufficient. A simple majority also suffices if the proposal concerns only one union or if participation in a general poll exceeds 75 per cent. of members involved in the dispute. If participation is less than 75 per cent., however, the following scale applies: 74 per cent. participation requires a majority of 50·5 per cent. for rejection, 73 per cent. a majority of 51 per cent. and so forth. If participation drops to 25 per cent. the proposal is considered as accepted.

These voting rules were accepted by the trade unions without much criticism. The provision for " linking together " proposals for different crafts and industries, on the other hand, created widespread resentment, especially in the smaller unions, representing as it did a decisive break with the traditional autonomy of individual national unions in all questions relating to the actual terms of employment of their members. When the provisions of the new act were first applied in the spring of 1934, two national unions, not affiliated to the Trade Union Centre, the Sailors and the Ship Firemen, who had rejected the mediator's proposals, refused to submit to the majority and struck for twelve days. This irregular strike received spontaneous support from the rank and file of other unions in some of the shipping centres. In Esbjerg there was a one day general strike. But the striking unions finally had to submit and pay heavy fines imposed by the Permanent Court of Arbitration. About the same time a regular strike of the workers in export butcheries was stopped by act of parliament after ten days. This measure was motivated by the necessity of keeping up deliveries of bacon to Great Britain, in order to avoid a permanent lowering of the Danish quota.

In both instances the coercive power of the State had been used against unions not affiliated to the Trade Union Centre. The effect of this experience was a hastening of the efforts to secure affiliation of all unions.

In March 1936, a major labour dispute was once more settled by legislative action. The employers had locked out 130,000 workers. After five weeks' stoppage the mediator's proposals were accepted by the workers while the employers rejected them. Parliament then passed an act prohibiting the continuance of the stoppage and setting up a Special Court of Arbitration which, in the main, confirmed the mediator's proposals as accepted by the majority of the workers.

The executive of the Trade Union Centre, in its annual report for 1936, commenting on this renewed experience of legislative interference, defined the attitude of the trade union movement in the following terms: " It is no secret, that the trade unions would have preferred a settlement without the intervention of any third party. . . . If, nevertheless, a majority of the executive agreed to support the act establishing compulsory arbitration, they had in view the difficult economic situation of the country as a whole and existing trade agreements with foreign countries. The executive was, however, unanimously of the opinion, that by so acting they did not establish any precedent for the settlement of future conflicts by means of compulsory arbitration, and this opinion was further stressed by the General Council of the Centre at its May 1936 session."

While the actions of the Labour-Radical administration with regard to labour disputes has thus evoked serious misgivings in the trade union world, the legislation of the last few years has given material compensation. Having gained an independent majority in the upper house in the autumn of 1936, the government immediately proposed and parliament voted the repeal of the 1929 "Blackleg's Charter." In 1937 and 1938 acts were passed prohibiting overtime and securing for about half a million wage earners twelve days' holiday with pay.

As mentioned before, the trade union movement in Denmark first developed along craft lines, most national unions admitting only skilled workers, the unskilled and semi-skilled workers in industry and transport being most of them organized either in the General Workers' Union, in a separate Women Workers' Union or in separate unions such as the Municipal Workers' Union, the Sailors' Union, the Agricultural Workers' Union and the Market Gardeners' Union. Of the 67 national unions affiliated to the Trade Union Centre in 1937, some 45 were of the craft type. Of the remainder, a few were "mixed," admitting skilled and semi-skilled workers. Among this group were the Printers' Union, the Shoe Workers' Union, the Wood Industry Workers' Union, the Tailors' Union, the Textile Workers' Union and the Tobacco Workers' Union. Unions of the industrial type exist only in the paper industry which, in Denmark, is not important, and on the State Railways, though the locomotive engineers and firemen have their separate union and the private railway workers have theirs. Among non-manual workers, the prevalent type is the "mixed" union of skilled and semi-skilled. Such is the case of the Shop Assistants and Clerks and the Post Office Workers.

Within most national unions there is one local for each town or city, the larger locals subdividing into " shop clubs " and, in unions of the mixed or industrial type, into " branch clubs " for the purpose of studying the special conditions of particular shops or particular sections of the industry, with a view to formulating demands for inclusion in collective agreements. In many instances these clubs also look to the collection of dues and the recruiting of new members. Wage negotiations and strike pay are in the main centralized in the hands of the national union leadership, negotiating collective agreements on a national or regional basis, the local union acting as intermediary between the national union and individual members. Local unions further carry on educational activities in co-operation with the Workers' Educational Association, and social activities of various kinds.

Though collective affiliation of trade unions to the Social Democratic Party does not exist, there are some 125 local trades councils, comprising as a rule the local Social Democratic Party, Women's and Youth sections. These councils, affiliation to which is on a voluntary basis, deal with matters such as the building or hire of halls, committee rooms and office premises. They play an important part at general and municipal elections, raising funds and organizing local propaganda. They also carry on educational activities, arranging lecture courses, providing reading rooms and arranging concerts and theatrical performances. They finance their regular activities by means of a modest membership fee from affiliated organizations.

Most of the National Unions have regular triennial congresses, congressional periods in some unions running to four or five years. In most national unions all locals are entitled to representation at the congress, an exception being made in the large unions such as that of the General Workers, where representation is on a mixed regional and group basis. Union congresses as a rule elect the Union National Council, consisting of the paid officials and district and group representatives. In some cases these representatives are elected by local unions individually or grouped in districts. National Councils meet annually or more frequently as need arises. Within the Council the paid officials and the council members living in the capital form the Union Executive. As a general rule important decisions are made by a general vote of the membership, taken either at annual meetings of local unions or, in some cases, by ballot papers sent to members individually. In some unions voting is obligatory, with fines for non-voters. The general membership poll is now applied in most unions in any question relating to national collective agreements, this method having been made obligatory for all unions affiliated to the Trade Union Centre in cases of simultaneous voting on national agreements for different unions.

About half the national unions have two categories of members : full due and half-due, the latter category comprising women and, in some cases, the lower paid grades, which, in most cases means young workers. Apart from the matter of dues, half-due members have full membership rights.

Under the Unemployment Insurance Act of 1907, as later amended in 1933, most national unions have unemployment insurance funds. Legally these funds are separate institutions and their accounts must be kept separate from union accounts. In practice, they are under union administration. Under the 1933 Act they are entitled to State grants to the amount of 75 per cent. of members' contributions. Municipalities also may give regular grants. In 1935, seventy Unemployment Funds were in existence, with a total membership of some 390,000.

The National Trade Union Centre, its official name being the Co-operating National Trade Unions, is a federation of national unions and of such local unions as are not in a position to affiliate to any existing national union.

The purpose of the Centre is defined in its statutes in the following terms: " By means of co-operation between national unions . . . to support the efforts of workers to improve their position and to work for industrial democracy and socialization. To achieve this general aim affiliated bodies undertake an obligation to support each other in cases of strikes or lock-outs, and endeavour to achieve a uniform policy in their dealings with employers and their organizations. The Centre further undertakes to support affiliated organizations in suits before the Permanent Court of Arbitration, to settle jurisdictional disputes, to support the consumers' co-operative movement and to co-operate with the Social Democratic Party to secure legislative action in favour of the workers nationally and in the municipalities.

The triennial congress of the Centre is composed of the National Councils of all affiliated unions, of one representative from each directly affiliated local union and one representative of each local trades council. The congress elects the Executive, consisting of the paid officials: president, vice-president, one or more secretaries, treasurer, and ten other members. The Social-Democratic party further delegates two members, while two members of the T.U.C. executive are delegated to the party executive.

The General Council of the Centre, which meets regularly once a year, consists of delegates from all affiliated organizations, one for each 2000 members or part thereof.

Annual membership fees to the Centre amount to 0·72 kr. per full-due and 0·36 kr. per half-due member. In the case of approved strikes or lock-outs the National Centre pays to affiliated organizations 10 kr. a week for full-due and 6 kr. a week for half-due members, though not for the first seven days or the first 2 per cent. of the members of any national union. The T.U.C. executive has the right to levy an extraordinary weekly due from all affiliated organizations in support of an approved stoppage. Affiliated organizations must, on the other hand, have a regular due sufficient to enable them to pay annually 10 kr. for full-due and 5 kr. for half-due members to their own strike funds, such funds to be used only in case of strikes or lock-outs or for contributions to the Centre.

The Statutes of the Trade Union Centre do not give its executive any powers to impose on affiliated unions any common tactics when advancing wage claims or formulating other demands for alterations in conditions of work. The initiative as to when to raise such claims, and the decision with regard to their kind, rests entirely with the individual national unions. Until quite recently all national unions were extremely anxious to safeguard their traditional autonomy in this respect. The Employers' Federation, on the other hand, has a much more centralized structure, its executive being in a position to secure uniform tactics and policy.

From 1926 onwards, after the General Workers' Union had broken away as a result of disagreements over tactics during the great lock-out of 1925, the T.U.C. executive made determined efforts to bring non-affiliated unions within the common fold and to secure closer co-operation with regard to tactics at negotiations. Though the General Workers' Union re-affiliated in 1929, these efforts met with scant success till 1931. From that time onwards, owing to the necessity of common defensive tactics in meeting the employers' drive for lower wages, and under the pressure created by the 1934 Mediation Act, with its provisions for "linking together" decisions for different unions, marked progress has been made. In 1932, 1933 and 1934 the T.U.C. executive succeeded in securing agreement on common tactics and a common plan of action on the part of unions both within and outside the Centre. As the common aim was defence of positions attained rather than any new advance, this unity was comparatively easily achieved. Its success in maintaining wage standards nevertheless was an eye-opener as to the usefulness of co-operation under experienced guidance. The experiences of 1934, when compulsory arbitration was applied to stop the butchers' strike and the sailors' unions were defeated when fighting on after a general settlement had been reached, worked in the same direction. It became more and more evident that, under the 1934 Act, there was no point in any individual union attempting to put forward demands for alterations of general importance unless they could enlist beforehand the support of other unions involved in simultaneous negotiations.

The closer co-operation that developed has enabled the trade union movement as a whole to pursue a definite policy of attempting to raise the wage level of those groups and categories of workers who had so far lagged behind: women, young workers, semi-skilled and unskilled. This policy is in line with that pursued in the political field by the Social-Democratic party and the Labour-Radical administration, aiming at a "levelling up" of the standard of life of the unemployed and of groups outside the ranks of organized labour, the small farmers especially.

II

In Norway as in Denmark, the war and post-war boom years were a period of serious inflation. In the summer of 1920 the index of wholesale prices was 369 as compared with 1913=100. It began to drop in the autumn, while the cost of living index did not culminate till December 1920, when it was 335. Wages of industrial workers, after lagging behind the cost of living figure during the war years, had risen considerably in 1919 and 1920. By November 1920 real daily earnings stood at 126 (1914=100). By then, employment had, however, began to shrink rapidly, the percentage of unemployed members in ten representative National Trade Unions rising to 2·8 in October and 9 in December. It continued to rise throughout the spring of 1921, reaching 20·9 in June. There was a slight improvement till October, followed by a fresh rise during the winter months, culminating with 25·1 in February and March 1922. The yearly average for 1921 was 17·6 per cent. and for 1922 17·1 per cent. as compared with 2·3 for 1920. These figures, covering only part of the industrial workers, do not, however, give a complete picture of the unemployment situation. The statistics of industrial undertakings covered by compulsory accident insurance (craft and industrial undertakings employing at least five workers) indicate an even more serious drop in employment, from 132,000 in 1920 to 91,102 in 1921, with a slight rise to 101,000 in 1922. Forest and land workers, sailors, workers in transport and commerce not covered by these statistics also suffered heavily. The main reason for the depression of 1920–22 no doubt was the slump in world trade. Norwegian shipping, which had made huge profits during the war, was especially badly hit, gross freights dropping in 1923 to between 25 and 20 per cent. of the 1920 figure of 1,200 mill. kr.

The monetary policy of the Central Bank which, from the autumn of 1920 sharply raised its discount rate in an attempt to hasten the return to gold parity, aggravated the situation. The policy of credit restriction was, however, countered by the necessity of attempting to avert threatening bank failures. Despite these attempts, several serious failures occurred in 1923.

Wholesale prices, which had dropped to 232 in 1923 (1913=100) rose once more during 1924 (average 267) and part of 1925, owing in part to rising prices in the U.S.A. but mainly to international speculation in Norwegian kroner. Despite serious efforts on the part of the Central Bank, which raised its discount rate from 5 per cent. at the end of 1922 to 7 per cent. one year later, Norway experienced a new period of inflation, the cost of living index, which had fallen to 230 in September 1923, culminating at 259 in March 1925.

Money wages in industry were drastically reduced from 1920 to 1923, despite stubborn resistance from the trade unions which, in the spring of 1921, launched a great defensive strike. From an average of kr. 18·8 in 1920 daily earnings fell to kr. 13·10 in 1923. Owing to the fall in cost of living, however, real wages were actually higher in 1921 and 1922 than they had been in 1920, and did not drop seriously below the 1920 level till 1924, when the cost of living rose without a corresponding rise in money wages. This loss was, however, compensated in 1925, when daily earnings in industry averaged kr. 15·21.

In agriculture, where trade unions had not succeeded in gaining a lasting hold during the war and post-war boom, the wage level fell constantly throughout this period. Men's real wages, which had stood at 134 in 1920–21 (1915–16=100), dropped to 105 in 1924–25. Women's real wages fell from 133 to 123. A similar reduction occurred in forestry, where the real wage index fell from 140 in 1920–21 to 107 in 1924–25.

In 1925, the movement of prices was once more reversed. British wholesale prices dropped, and Norwegian wholesale prices followed suit. The Central Bank now succeeded in carrying through its deflationary policy. By the early summer of 1927 the krone had attained its old parity of 18 to the £, and in May, 1928, gold payments were resumed at that level. For wholesale prices this meant a drop from 253 in 1925 to 161 in 1928. The cost of living index dropped from 259 in March 1925 to 175 in May 1928.

Industrial employment had improved during the renewed inflation period of 1923–25, the average number of workers covered by accident insurance rising from 101,000 in 1922 to 119,000 in 1925, and trade union unemployment percentages dropping from 17·1 in 1922 to 8·5 in 1924. The 1925 monthly unemployment figures remained below those of the preceding year until April, but from May they were considerably higher and from September rose sharply, attaining 26·1 per cent. in December. The average for 1925 was 13·2 per cent.

Unemployment continued to rise during the 1926–27 deflation period, averaging 24·3 per cent. and 25·4 per cent. for those two years. From October, 1927, there was a slight improvement month by month as compared with the previous year, and this improvement continued during 1928. Nevertheless, the average for that year still attained 19·2 per cent. Employment statistics showed a corresponding drop from 119,000 in 1925 to 102,000 in 1927, with a slight increase to 112,000 in 1928.

The deflation brought a further reduction in daily earnings for industrial workers, from kr. 14·18 in 1926 to kr. 11·69 in 1928. The real wage level, however, declined only slightly, from 138 to 134.

The improvement in trade which had started in the summer of 1928 continued in 1929 and the first half of 1930, despite a continued, but very slow drop in prices. The index of industrial production rose, and so did employment, the percentage of unemployed trade unionists averaging 15·4 in 1929 and 15·7 in the first six months of 1930. Average daily earnings in industry rose slightly, from kr. 11·69 a day in 1928 to kr. 11·80 in 1930, and thanks to the continued fall in the cost of living, from 173 to 161, the real wage index for industrial workers rose from 134 to 143.

In agriculture and forestry, on the other hand, the movement of wages throughout the period from 1925 to 1930 differed from that of industry. Deflation, and the consequent drop in prices of agricultural and forest products, brought about a very serious debt situation, and money wages fell continually and more than the cost of living. The real wage index for men in agriculture which had been 105 in 1924–25 fell to 92 in 1930–31. For women in agriculture the corresponding figures were 123 and 113, for forest workers 107 and 89, all compared with 1915–16=100.

By the middle of 1930, Norwegian industry was beginning to feel in earnest the effects of the world depression. The wholesale price index, which had fallen slowly to 138 in May 1930, dropped to 117 in September 1931, when the Norwegian krone, following sterling, went off gold. Industrial employment shrank from 116,000 in 1930 to 92,000 in 1931, the latter figure being, however, specially low owing to a long drawn out labour stoppage. From 1930 to 1932 employment in iron and engineering fell from 27,000 to 22,000, in mining from 9,300 to 7,250, in quarries from 3,000 to 1,650. In the saw- and planing mills, where for other reasons employment had been dropping for years, it fell further from 5,900 to 4,450.

Unemployment among trade unionists averaged 17·5 per cent. for the last six months of 1930, 22·3 per cent. for 1931, 30·8 per cent. in 1932 and 33·4 per cent. in 1933. From February 1934 there was a slight improvement, but the 1934 average still was 30·7.

After the krone had gone off gold, the wholesale price level rose slightly to 123 in January 1932, and with slight variations remained at that level throughout 1932 and 1933. But this general average covered significant variations. The prices of animal products, of prime importance to Norwegian agriculture, declined steadily from an index of 120 in September 1931 to 99 in July 1933, whereas cereal prices reached their lowest level as early as October 1931, with an index of 106, and from then on remained practically stable, thanks to the efforts of the State Monopoly in Grains, till the beginning of 1934. Prices of industrial products followed a similar course, reaching their lowest level in September 1931, with an index figure of 125, then rising very slowly until the spring of 1934. The cost of living index which had fallen to 150 in September 1931, remained at that level till April 1932, and then dropped slightly, giving an average of 149 for the year 1932 and 147 for 1933.

In the spring of 1931, when prices were falling and employment shrinking, the Employers' Federation had demanded drastic reductions in wages and tried to break the resistance of the trade unions by means of a lock-out in the main industries lasting five months. The net result, however, was a comparatively slight reduction in daily earnings from an average of kr. 11·80 to kr. 11·26, less than the fall in cost of living, and the real wage index rose from 143 in 1930 to 147 in 1931. After a slight increase in daily earnings in 1932, to an average of kr. 11·48, followed by a drop to kr. 11·31 in 1933, the industrial wage level was stabilized at kr. 11·34 for the years 1934 and 1935.

From April, 1934, the index of wholesale prices once more began to rise, but very slowly. Yearly averages were: 122 for

1933, 124 for 1934 and 127 for 1935. The cost of living followed, rising from 147 in 1933 to 151 in 1935. With industrial money wages remaining stable, the result was a slight decline in the real wage index, from 150 in 1933 to 146 in 1935.

In the spring of 1935, collective agreements were renewed with an increase in most wage rates corresponding to the rise in cost of living since 1932, thus restoring the real wage level of that year. The lower paid grades, unskilled, young workers and women, obtained an increase beyond that level. From July 1936 prices rose once more, and this time sharply. The wholesale price index which had stood at 132 on July 1, 1936, passed 140 at the end of that year, and by December 1937 had reached 161. The cost of living index, lagging a little behind, reached 158 in April 1937 and 170 by the end of the year. This movement of prices was mainly determined by international factors, though the policy of raising the prices of agricultural products in the home market adopted by a Labour minority government which took office in March 1935, supported by the farmers' party, also played its part. Industrial wages, bound by two years' agreements concluded in the spring of 1935, this time definitely lagged behind. When agreements were renewed in the spring of 1937 they were raised sufficiently to compensate for the rise in cost of living until April of that year. But no compensation was obtained for the further rise which was expected, except in the form of an extension of holidays with pay from an average of nine to an average of twelve working days a year.

While the industrial real wage level, therefore, has tended to decline slightly, wages in forestry and agriculture, in transport and commerce and in the hotel trade have risen materially, owing to the extension into these fields of trade unionism, and to the improvement in the economic situation of the agricultural population created by the large scale state regulation of prices since 1935.

The history of Norwegian trade unionism from 1920–1937 differs in important respects from that of the Danish and Swedish movements. Fluctuations in membership have been greater, and so have changes in policy and in structure. The main reason for the peculiar Norwegian development must be sought in the historical development of Norwegian industry.

Up till about 1905, Norway lagged behind both Denmark and Sweden as an industrial nation, and trade unions existed mainly among skilled craft workers. The total trade union membership as late as 1905 was only 17,500, of which 15,600 belonged to the Trade Union Centre founded in 1899. Such large scale industry as existed, mainly in paper and in pyrite and copper mining, had not yet been organized. From about 1905, however, new large scale industries developed, based on the exploitation of water power. The number of industrial workers proper grew from 77,000 in 1905 to 132,000 in 1920, and there was a more rapid growth still in mining, in the building trades and railway, road and dam construction. This period of rapid industrial expansion also witnessed the unionization of the mining, paper, saw-mill, and textile industries and of the canning and other foodstuffs industries, as well as the newer electro-chemical and electro-metallurgical industries. A major part of the general workers employed in the construction of railways, dams, power stations and new factories were also organized during this period. The membership of the Trade Union Centre grew to 64,000 in 1913, 79,000 in 1916 and by 1920 had reached 143,000. Among the mass of newly proletarianized workers syndicalist ideas, mainly imported by young Norwegian labour leaders who had spent short periods in the U.S.A. working in the I.W.W., gained a strong hold. From modest beginnings in 1911 a well-organized and skilfully led minority movement, advocating industrial unionism and more aggressive trade union tactics succeeded in gaining a majority within the Trade Union Centre in 1920, just before the collapse of the post-war boom. Till then, the Norwegian trade union movement had on the whole differed little from Danish trade unions in structure and methods, though some of the original craft unions also admitted semi-skilled and unskilled workers. The main body of general workers and of factory workers were organized in a General Workers' Union, certain groups, such as the Saw and Planing Mill Workers, the Paper and Wood-pulp Workers, and the Municipal Workers having broken away to form industrial unions of their own. All existing unions of manual workers belonged to the National Trade Union Centre.

Despite the criticism of the opposition, opposed on principle to written agreements, all national unions had entered into collective agreements with the employers' organizations, whereever possible on a national scale. They accepted the jurisdiction of the Labour Court set up by the Trades Disputes Act of 1915 in all disputes about the interpretation of collective agreements and they also submitted to the provisions of that Act for compulsory mediation in labour disputes by public mediators, and observed the time limits laid down in the Act before striking in cases where mediation failed to bring a settlement.

In 1919 and 1920, the reformist leadership of the trade union movement had skilfully used the revolutionary fervour evoked among Norwegian workers by the Russian and German revolutions to wrest important concessions from the employers, not only in the matter of wages but also with regard to working hours and holidays with pay, obtaining in the 1919 agreements the forty-eight hour week, immediately afterwards enacted by parliament and, in 1920, by a compulsory arbitration award which they accepted under protest, an average of twelve days' holiday with pay for all industrial workers.

At the Trade Union Congress of July 1920 the opposition carried a series of resolutions aiming at a complete re-shaping of the structure of the Norwegian trade union movement. It was laid down in principle that all existing national unions were to be dissolved. Local Trades Councils were to take their place as constituent elements of the National Centre. For certain purposes, the local unions of workers in each industry, whether skilled or unskilled, were to federate into "industrial departments" within the National Centre. As a first step, affiliation to local trades councils was made obligatory for all local unions belonging to the Centre, and the trades councils were granted representation to the triennial congress along with the national unions until the reorganization had been completed.

Before they had time to start in earnest to carry through this ambitious scheme of reorganization, the new leadership of the Trade Union Centre was faced with the problems created by the world depression. By the end of 1920, unemployment had driven thousands of workers from the industrial centres back to the countryside, where they soon lost contact with their unions. Early in 1921 the Employers' Federation launched an offensive to force down wages, starting with a demand for a 30 per cent. cut in shipping. The revolutionary temper still prevailing among the workers left no alternative but to fight back, and on May 26, 1921, all organized workers except railwaymen, civil servants, hospital employees and certain minor groups went on strike. The conservative government then in office mobilized marine conscripts to run the coast steamship services and troops to protect blackleg organizations set up under more or less official auspices. The strike had to be called off after a fortnight. It resulted in a compromise on wages, a serious loss of membership, aggravated through increasing unemployment, and further wage cuts enforced by means of lock-outs in the paper and saw-mill industries in the autumn. At the end of 1921, membership of the National Centre had shrunk from 143,000 to 96,000, and by the end of 1922 to 84,000. All unions were badly hit, but the heaviest losses were those of the young Forest and Land Workers' Union which dwindled from 2,239 to 351 members and soon after dissolved, the Sailors' and Firemen's Union which dropped from 4,626 to 1,083, the General Workers' Union from 31,280 to 13,221, the Iron and Engineering Union from 20,937 to 13,230 and the Railwaymen from 8,604 to 5,271.

As a result of these reverses, the reorganization scheme of the Trade Union Centre was abandoned in its original form, more than half the national unions pronouncing against it, and the 1923 Trade Union Congress adopted a plan for reorganization into ten industrial unions in place of the thirty-two unions then existing within the Centre.

Before entering into the history of the attempts at realizing this scheme, however, we had better study the fluctuations in trade union membership and some of the main labour disputes of the period 1923–1937.

During the period of renewed inflation from 1923 to 1925, the trade unions, despite the reduction of unemployment, recovered only a fraction of the members lost during 1921 and 1922. The Trade Union Centre grew from 84,000 to 96,000 members at the end of 1925.

The main reason for the slowness of recovery was political. The Norwegian Labour Party, to which a large proportion of the local trade unions were affiliated, had joined the Communist International in 1919. In 1921 the majority of the party accepted the twenty-one conditions of admittance formulated by the second congress of the International, the result being that the Social-Democratic minority in 1921 formed a party of its own. From 1921 to 1923 the Labour Party was rent by bitter internal dissensions between a minority which accepted in full the principles and tactics of the Communist International, and a majority which, adhering to the special traditions of Norwegian Labour radicalism, found itself in constant opposition to the Moscow leadership. In November 1923 the majority decided to dissaffiliate from the International. As a consequence, the communist minority in its turn set up as a party. From 1923 to 1927 when the Labour Party and the Social-Democrats reunited, three working-class parties were in existence. In view of the long-standing close association of the Trade Union Centre with the Labour Party the internecine feuds of the political movement deeply affected also the trade union world, and in the long run alienated many workers from labour organization of any kind.

The communists, after setting up their own party, also started a vigorous opposition within the trade unions against the leadership of the larger unions and the Centre, dominated by Labour Party members.

In 1922 the trade unions, weakened as they were, had accepted a temporary Compulsory Arbitration Act. The Arbitration award of 1922 involved further wage reductions, a shortening of holidays and provision for automatic regulation of wages according to the movements of the cost of living index.

On the strength of this clause, the employers in the autumn of 1923 decreed a further reduction of wages. The iron and engineering workers answered with an unofficial strike, in which communists soon assumed leadership. In January, 1924, the dockers and transport workers in the coast towns followed suit. The employers declared a lock-out, and the Trade Union Centre countered with sympathetic strikes. The stoppage, involving the major part of the T.U.C. membership, lasted from the middle of February to the end of May, 1924, the dockers' strike continuing till the end of June. The communists all along opposed all efforts at arriving at a settlement and after the conclusion of the struggle accused the leaders of treason. The result was a strong condemnation on the part of the majority at the 1925 Trade Union Congress of all communist cell building within the trade unions.

In the spring of 1925 collective agreements were renewed without conflict. The deflation which set in in earnest in the summer of that year, however, did, as mentioned before, lead to a new rise in unemployment and to demands for wage reductions. They were enforced through a series of lock-outs in 1926 and 1927. The 1927 conflict was finally settled by compulsory arbitration, enacted by parliament against strong protests from the trade unions and political labour. In 1927 the bourgeois majority in Parliament further amended the Trades Disputes Act, introducing heavy fines for breaches of collective agreements, and passed a "Blackleg's Charter" amendment of the criminal code, restricting the freedom of trade unions to apply pressure against strike-breakers.

Despite unemployment, despite the offensive of employers and the anti-trade union legislation, the trade union movement as a whole kept most of its members. Two national unions, however, the Locomotive Firemen and the Electricians, disaffiliated from the National Centre in 1925 and 1926, as a protest against the decision of the 1925 Congress to proceed with the 1923 reorganization scheme. The loss was partly compensated by the re-affiliation of the Bricklayers' Union which had left for similar reasons in 1923, and the Electricians in 1927. Still, total trade union membership at the end of 1927 was only some 96,000, of which 94,000 belonged to the Centre.

During 1928 the improvement in industry, along with the advance of political labour resulting from the reunion of the Labour and Social-Democratic parties, led to a marked advance in union membership, which continued through the next few years. A new Forest and Land Workers' Union was founded in 1927, affiliated to the Centre, and in 1930 the Telegraph and Telephone Workers' Union, formed that year by three existing separate unions, affiliated. By the end of 1930 the Centre with 140,000 members once more approached its 1920 strength.

These years of comparative prosperity were also years of

industrial peace. The young Forest and Land Workers' Union, however, fought hard local battles to win for the forest workers the right of bargaining and of organization. But no major conflicts occurred till the spring of 1931, when the Employers' Federation once more took the offensive and declared a lock-out in all the main industries, which lasted from the beginning of April till the beginning of September, involving more than half the membership of the Trade Union Centre.

The Employers, through their aggressive tactics, created the impression of wanting to break up the trade union movement. The Danish and Swedish Trade Union Centres, however, rallied to the support of the Norwegian workers and through ample loans enabled them to resist the attack. After repeated vain attempts at mediation, the parties agreed to a settlement based in the main on proposals put forward by the public mediator. The trade unions had met the original demands of the employers for a 15 per cent. cut in time rates and 25 per cent. in piece work rates with counter demands for a reduction of working hours from 48 to 42 a week, limitation of overtime and wage increases ranging from 10 to 20 per cent. The settlement was made on the basis of unchanged hours and a reduction of some 7 per cent. in wage rates. Despite the fact that the Bricklayers' union had disaffiliated during the struggle, the membership of the Trade Union Centre at the end of 1931 had increased to 145,000, mainly owing to the affiliation of the Union of Shop Assistants and Clerks early in the year.

Whereas most collective agreements since 1920 had run for one year only, the settlement of September 1931 was made for three years, with the proviso that either party might demand a revision of wage rates on the basis of alterations in the cost of living index by January 1, 1933. The depression years of 1932 and 1933 were therefore years of industrial peace. On the initiative of the Trade Union Centre a new general agreement was reached in the autumn of 1932, the employers waiving their claim for wage reductions on the basis of the fall in cost of living in exchange for a prolongation of existing agreements until the spring of 1935.

In the political field, however, the bourgeois parties which, at the general election of October 1930, had inflicted a severe defeat on the Labour Party, used their increased strength to amend the Trades Disputes Act so as to further limit the freedom of action of trade unions. By the Act of July, 1933, the use of the boycott in labour disputes was practically prohibited, and strikes in undertakings employing less than ten workers were made illegal. These measures aimed at stemming the advance of trade union organization among forest and agricultural workers, in commerce, transport and the hotel and restaurant trade. They did not, however, achieve their purpose. The demonstration of strength given by the trade unions during the 1931 lock-out had greatly increased their recruiting power. By the end of 1933, the membership of the Trade Union Centre had reached 158,000. The attempts at stopping their advance by legislation only strengthened the determination of trade unionists, in co-operation with the political labour movement, to make a determined bid for political power. Following the example of Danish and Swedish labour, the Norwegian labour forces in 1932 and 1933 drew up an immediate programme for combating the effects of the world depression through credit expansion, public works on a large scale, and state intervention to reduce agricultural debts and organize the agricultural market. On the strength of these proposals the Labour Party greatly strengthened its parliamentary position at the October 1933 elections.

One result of this political advance, and of the improvement in trade occurring in 1934, was a further advance in trade union membership during 1934 from 158,000 to 173,000. By a further amendment of the Trades Disputes Act in 1934, on the model of the Danish Act of that year, the Public Mediator was empowered to decree the " linking together " of mediation proposals. In March 1935 the Labour Party took office as a minority government, with the support of the Farmers' Party, which had turned away from its former allies and voted most of Labour's immediate programme for public works in return for state regulation to increase the price of agricultural products, and direct state grants in aid of agriculture. Since 1935 the Labour Government, which strengthened its parliamentary position at the 1936 elections, has continued this expansionist policy, succeeding at the same time in passing important measures of social reform, relying for this purpose mainly on the support of the Liberals. Workers' protection has been greatly extended so as to cover some 450,000 wage earners and secure for all of them a minimum of nine days' holiday with pay. Pensions for the blind and for cripples and old age contributory pensions have been introduced. Health insurance has been extended to cover fishermen (some 100,000), sailors and whaling workers (some 30,000) and the 1927 " Blackleg's Charter " repealed. In 1938 compulsory unemployment insurance was voted, superseding the hitherto existing system of state grants to trade union employment funds.

These achievements in the political field, though partly financed through increased indirect taxation, and involving, as mentioned before, a serious rise in the cost of living, have greatly strengthened the trade union movement. At the end of 1937 the Trade Union Centre counted 325,000 members.

TABLE I, NORWAY

Name of Union	1920	1937	*increase per cent*
I. Crafts and industry excepting building:			
(*a*) Craft Unions:			
Butchers	630	1,839	
Bakers	2,231	2,680	
Bookbinders ...	1,581	2,443	
Lithographers ...	505	945	
Printers	3,620	4,001	
Moulders	2,055	2,865	
Jewellers	657	654	
Tobacco Workers ...	1,166	1,537	
Shoe operatives ...	3,071	3,806	
	15,516	20,770	5,254 = 33·9
(*b*) Industrial and " mixed " unions:			
General Workers ...	31,280	23,830	
Textile Union ...		7,295	
Chemical industries		19,542	
Food industries ...		13,576	

Name of Union	1920	1937	*increase per cent*
Iron and Engineering	20,937	29,011	
Garment Workers ...	3,329	5,891	
Paper industry ...	11,222	15,000	
Municipal Workers (in 3 unions 1920) ...	6,450	24,278	
Wood and Furniture (in 2 unions 1920) ...	2,100	4,137	
Sawmill and planing	5,676	5,548	
Stone industry ...	690	2,140	
Leather industry ...	616	1,537	
	82,300	151,785	69,485 = 84·4
II. Building Trades:			
Bricklayers	2,159	5,000	approx. figs.
Electricians	2,867	3,000	approx. figs.
Painters	1,793	27,855	Building Industry
Carpenters	8,700		
	15,519	35,855	20·336 = 131
III. Distributive Trades, Transport, shipping, commerce, etc.:			
(*a*) Craft Unions:			
Firemen and Locomotive Engineers ...	1,699	1,636	
Postal Workers ...	1,157	2,120	
	2,856	3,756	
(*b*) Industrial and Mixed Unions:			
Transport Workers	10,085	18,538	
Railwaymen ...	8,604	12,368	
Sailors	4,725	24,172	
Telegraph and Telephone ...		2,360	
Shop Assistants and clerks		15,772	
Hotel and Restaurant		5,870	
	23,414	79,080	

Name of Union	1920	1937	*increase per cent*
IV. Agriculture and Forestry:			
Forest and Land Workers	2,239	29,869	
Sum. of III. A and B and IV...	28,509	112,605	84,096 = 295

Table I shows the membership figures of Norwegian Trade Unions in 1920 and 1937, grouped in four main groups. Owing to the changes which have occurred in trade union structure, to be discussed below, no exact comparison between the groups is possible. But allowing for minor discrepancies, the following facts emerge clearly: Of the total of some 180,000 new members gained during the period, forestry, agriculture, transport and the distributive trades account for nearly one half. While the total number of trade unionists in those two categories in 1920 was only 28,810, it had reached 112,605 in 1937, an increase of 295 per cent. as against a 33·9 per cent. increase in the typical craft unions outside the building trades, 84·4 per cent. in industrial and mixed unions in industry and general construction work and 131 per cent. in building. The advance in trade union membership among industrial workers far exceeds the expansion of employment capacity in undertakings covered by accident insurance. Though available statistics do not permit of exact computation, it may be confidently asserted that the percentage of organization in most industries, in transport, commerce and among general workers has risen considerably during the period. There are, however, still large unorganized reserves in agriculture, transport, and among white collared workers, both in private employment and in the civil service. A very small proportion of civil servants so far have affiliated to the Trade Union Centre. Most categories of civil servants have, however, organized during the period, and have developed their organizations more and more along trade union lines. Most of the civil servants' unions co-operate through a Civil Servants' Federation, and on the initiative of the Trade Union Centre a committee representing the Federation, non-affiliated unions of civil servants and the T.U.C. was set up in December 1937, to explore the possibilities of closer co-operation. A field which has so far hardly been touched by trade union organization is that of domestic service.

The present structure of the Norwegian trade union movement is one of mixed craft and industrial unionism. The total number of national organizations of a definite trade union character is thirty-nine, thirty-four of which are affiliated to the Trade Union Centre. Of the non-affiliated unions one is a craft union of manual workers : the Electricians' Union. Four are civil servants' unions : the Postmen's,[1] the Telegraph Operators', the Railway Station Masters' and the Police unions. Of the thirty-four unions belonging to the T.U.C. thirteen are organized on an industrial basis : the Union of Building Workers, the Iron and Engineering Workers' Union, the Chemical Industries' Union, the Stone Workers' Union, the Paper Workers' Union, the Food Workers' Union, the Textile Workers' Union, the Garment Workers' Union, the Railwaymen's Union, the Telegraph and Telephone Union, the Hotel and Restaurant Workers' Union, the Municipal Worker's Union and the Forest and Land Workers' Union.

Four unions, those of the General Workers, the Transport Workers, the Sailors and the Shop Assistants and Clerks are of an intermediate type. The remaining seventeen unions are on a more or less pronounced craft basis. The Printers', Bookbinders' and Lithographers' unions, co-operate for certain purposes through a Graphic Industries Cartel. The Bakers', Butchers' and Tobacco Workers' Unions have refused to amalgamate with the Food Workers' Union but co-operate with it through the Food Industries' Cartel. The Moulders' and Jewellers' Unions have rejected amalgamation with the Iron and Engineering Union, though accepting a Metal Industries' Cartel. The Planing and Saw-mill Workers' Union are in cartel co-operation with the Paper Workers and the Forest and Land Workers. The Leather Workers' Union and the Shoe Operatives' Union have a cartel between them, the Wood and Furniture Workers' Union act in co-operation with the Building Workers and the Bricklayers, without a formal cartel. The Postal Workers' and the Loco-

[1] The Postal Workers' union affiliated to the Centre counts only a minority of the post office workers.

motive Firemen's Unions act in cartel co-operation with the Railwaymen's and the Telegraph and Telephone Unions. Finally, there are two small unions outside any cartel: the Musicians' Union and the Labour Press Association.

The structure here described is the result so far achieved on the basis of the reorganization scheme adopted by the 1923 Trade Union Congress. In most cases where that scheme advocated complete amalgamation of existing craft unions, the half-way house of the cartel has been resorted to. The only craft unions that have disappeared during the period are: the Painters' and the Carpenters' unions, amalgamated in 1923 to form the Building Workers' Union, the Fire Brigade, the Municipal Clerks' and the Barbers' unions, absorbed by the Municipal Workers' Union, the Saddlers' Union, amalgamated with the Furniture Workers. In addition, the Railwaymen's Union has absorbed two smaller unions previously not affiliated to the Centre: the railway Guards' and the railway Clerks' Associations.

One basic principle laid down by the 1923 Congress was that no more than one union was to represent the workers in any one place of work. Despite the difficulties met with in the efforts to achieve amalgamations, that principle has been carried into effect to a very great extent, the only exceptions deliberately made by the Centre being the admission of the Shop Assistants and Clerks and the toleration of the Locomotive Firemen, the Bricklayers and the Moulderers as separate unions.

The Trade Union Centre of Norway is a more centralized body than either the Danish or the Swedish Centres. Membership dues are much higher, amounting to kr. 0.85 a month for full-due and kr. 0.45 a month for half-due members. The dues of affiliated unions must be sufficient to enable them to pay at least kr. 20 a year per full-due and kr. 10 a year per half-due member into the union strike fund. The Executive of the Centre, called the Secretariat, and elected by the triennial congress, consists of the five paid officials and of ten other members. Its powers are more extensive than those of the Danish national executive. All demands for alterations in collective agreements, all strikes or sympathetic strikes must be authorized by it. Members of the Secretariat regularly take part in negotiations between national unions and the Employers' Federation. Whenever negotiations or conflicts concern more than one union, the Secretariat assumes leadership, and may take any step which it deems necessary to secure a satisfactory solution of such conflicts. The Secretariat may call sympathetic strikes, after hearing the union or unions involved. It may levy extraordinary dues.

The Secretariat controls a People's Hall Fund which grants mortgage loans for the construction or purchase of Meeting Halls. It has a statistical department and a law department which are at the service of affiliated organizations. The auditors' department of the Centre audits the accounts of all affiliated national unions and of District Trades Councils.

Co-operation with the Labour Party is secured by a Committee of Co-operation of four, two from each national executive. Of the regular dues levied by the Centre, kr. 0·10 per month and member go to support the Labour Party newspapers. A special Labour Press Fund grants loans to extend or modernize Labour papers or start new press organs. A Joint Labour Assistance Fund gives financial assistance to trade unionists or party members sentenced or victimized for trade union or political activities, and is the central agency for the relief of political refugees and for international labour relief in Norway.

The General Council of the Trade Union Centre consists of representatives of affiliated national unions and one representative from each district Trades Council. Its functions are similar to those of the Danish and Swedish General Councils.

The triennial Congress is more democratically elected than that of the Danish Centre. The bulk of the National Union delegates are elected by local unions, generally voting on a district basis. Paid union officials form only a small proportion of the delegates. District Trades Councils also send representatives to Congress.

District Trades Councils in Norway are pure trade union bodies, membership of which is obligatory for all locals affiliated. There are eighteen such Councils, each district corresponding, with minor exceptions, to a "Fylke" or county. District Councils carry on general trade union propaganda, assist national unions in local negotiations and in the recruiting of members and carry on educational work in co-operation with the Workers' Educational Association. They finance their activities partly through a modest membership fee from affiliated local unions, relying to a considerable extent on grants from the Centre.

III

In Sweden, inflation during the war years and post-war boom had not gone to such lengths as in Norway. The wholesale price level culminated in June 1920, when it reached 366 (1913=100), and the cost of living index for the year 1920 was 269 (1914=100). Real wages by 1920 were considerably above the pre-war level, the index of daily money wage rates, taking 1913 as a base, being 309 in industry, building etc., 316 in agriculture and 323 in forestry. The eight-hour day had been secured in industry through negotiations, and enacted by Parliament in 1919.

Unlike Denmark and Norway, Sweden was able to retain the position as a creditor nation, gained during the war years, through the storms of the post-war slump. By common agreement among all the main parties, the state-controlled Central Bank from the summer of 1920 pursued a deflationist policy, keeping a discount rate of 7½ per cent. until April 1921, when it was reduced to 7 per cent. It did not reach 4½ per cent. till June 1922. This policy ensured a thorough process of liquidation, accentuating the deflation caused by the cessation of the abnormal war-time demand for Swedish products. The average price of industrial products fell from 356 to 200 between 1920 and 1922, the wholesale price level reaching 172 at the end of 1921 and continuing to decline throughout 1922. By the end of that year it was 155. Cost of living figures did not fall quite so much, dropping to 177 in 1923. Money wages indices dropped to 213 in industry, etc., 168 in forestry and 160 in agriculture by 1923, the tendency being, as in Norway, for wages to fall much more rapidly in agriculture and forestry than in industry. Unemployment was heavy during the deflation years 1921 and 1922, rising from 3 per cent. of trade union membership in the summer of 1920 to 28 per cent. one year later, the average for 1921 reaching 34·1 per cent. in production goods industries and 22·5 per cent. in consumption goods industries. The number of registered unemployed was 163,000 in January 1922. There was no national system of unemployment insurance, but owing mainly to the initiative of Social-Democratic minority governments which were in office from February to October 1920, and from October 1921 to April 1923, about 40 per cent. of the registered unemployed were relieved either through money grants or special public works at rates a little below the wage level for general workers.

Early in 1923 production and employment started to improve, despite a continued, but very slow fall in prices. In 1924 Sweden returned to the gold standard at pre-war parity, and a period of steady expansion followed. From 1924 to 1929 the physical volume of production expanded from 106 to 147 (1915=100). During the same five-year period wholesale prices fell from 162 to 140. Cost of living remained more constant, the index falling slowly to 170 in 1929. Unemployment receded, the average unemployment percentage of trade unions for the five years 1926–1930 falling to 11·4 from 15·6 in the preceding five-year period, Money wages in industry increased slowly, the index of daily earnings rising from 213 in 1923 to 232 in 1929, average yearly earnings from kr. 2,350 in 1925 to kr. 2,538 in 1930.

In agriculture and forestry, on the other hand, money wages continued to fall, the index of daily earnings in agriculture remaining practically stable (160 in 1923; 159 in 1929) and falling from 168 to 162 in forestry, while computed yearly averages for men in agriculture fell from kr. 1,251 for the period 1921–25 to kr. 1,116 for 1926–30, for women from kr. 981 to kr. 891.

In the autumn of 1930 Sweden began to feel the effects of the world depression. Till then, the drastic fall in the world prices of the commodities which constitute a large part of Sweden's imports had made the terms of trade more favourable than usual. From the summer of 1930, however, production was shrinking, and the unemployment percentage increased from 8 per cent. in July to 22·9 per cent. in December, as compared with 6·7 per cent. and 17·3 per cent. for the corresponding months 1929. The wholesale price level fell from 140 in 1929 to 107 in 1933, the cost of living from 170 to 154. Unemployment increased throughout 1931, 1932 and 1933, the trade union percentages (annual averages) being 16·8, 22·4 and 23·3 respectively. In the latter year the annual average of unemployed applying for relief reached the figure of 164,000.

As in Norway, and mainly for the same reasons, agriculture suffered seriously, though the general level of indebtedness was lower in Sweden than in Norway.

On September 27, 1931, Sweden had left the gold standard along with Denmark and Norway. Immediately afterwards the Central Bank, which had raised the discount rate to 8 per cent., joined with the Treasury in an official declaration. They announced that their policy would be to maintain the internal purchasing power of the krona. The measures adopted included, as had been the case in Norway, a mild form of credit discrimination. The Central Bank reached an agreement with the Swedish Bank Association to tighten up the conditions on which credits were granted for the financing of imports. The bank rate was kept at 6 per cent. until February 1932, and then lowered, with a temporary interruption due to the Kreuger Crisis in March. By the end of August 1932 the rate was down to 3½ per cent.

In the autumn of 1932 the Social-Democratic Party assumed office as a minority, after a spectacular victory at the polls, won on the basis of a programme of credit expansion, big public works financed through loans, and farm relief through debt reductions. With the support of the Farmers' Party this programme was put into effect from the summer of 1933, supplemented by measures for the regulation of output and sales, to raise prices of agricultural products. In the budgets of 1933–34 and 1934–35, 300 million kronor were raised through loans and used to extend public works, subsidize housing schemes and export industries and raise the wage level for special public works to that of ordinary general labour. By 1936 these loans were repaid, mainly out of the proceeds of increased death duties and other direct taxation.

This expansionist budget policy was accompanied by efforts on the part of the Central Bank to reduce rates of interest. After negotiations with the savings banks, which agreed to adjust their deposit rates, the Central Bank reduced its discount rate to 3 per cent. in June 1933. In September the commercial banks followed, bringing down their rates ½ per cent. In

December the Central Bank reduced its discount rate once more to 2½ per cent. and kept it at that level throughout 1934. At the same time, the Central Bank, through operations in the security market, succeeded in maintaining a stable rate on sterling.

The joint efforts of the government and the Central Bank were greatly assisted by the improvement in world trade, and especially by the armaments boom, which stimulated exports of Swedish iron ores and iron and steel products. Employment in mining and the metal industries, which had dropped from an average of 134,000 workers in 1926–30 to 118,000 in 1933 rose to 160,000 in 1935. The volume of production in industry generally rose from 87 in 1932 and 90 in 1933 to 118 in 1935 and 119·7 in 1937 (1925-30—100). The trade union unemployment percentage fell from 23·3 in 1933 to 15 in 1935 and 10·8 in 1937.

Average yearly earnings of industrial, commercial and transport workers had declined from kr. 2,538 in 1930 to kr. 2,310 in 1932, and daily earnings from kr. 9·29 to kr. 8·73,[1] while the cost of living index had fallen from 165 to 154. In agriculture and forestry there had been a corresponding drop in money wages. But from 1933 the movement was reversed. By 1936 average yearly earnings in industry, commerce and transport had reached kr. 2,499, with a cost of living index of 158, and from 1936 to 1937 there was a further average increase of 4·2 per cent. to 2,604. Average yearly earnings in these groups in 1937 were, for men kr. 2,970, for women kr. 1,742, and for young workers kr. 1,129. For forest workers, there was a marked improvement, daily earnings rising from kr. 4·77 in 1932–33 to kr. 7·16 in 1936–37. The index of real wages in industry, commerce and transport published by the administration of social affairs, taking 1913 as base, was for 1937: hourly wages 177, daily wages 150, yearly wages 149. The corresponding figures for 1920 were 137, 115 and 110.

These improvements in wages were accompanied by important social reforms. In 1934, national unemployment insurance was enacted, on the system of state grants to trade

[1] The Swedish figures of average daily earnings, covering workers in industry, commerce and transport are not directly comparable to Norwegian figures given above, covering crafts and industry only.

union unemployment funds. Though its immediate importance must not be exaggerated, the registered trade union unemployment funds comprising in 1937 only some 160,000 members out of an aggregate membership of 850,000, the Act no doubt will lead to the extension of trade union unemployment insurance in the next few years. Old age pensions were considerably raised in 1937, and the forty-eight hour week enacted for agriculture. In 1938 a special Holidays' Act covering all wage-earners in public and private employment introduced twelve days' holiday with pay. Other social reforms introduced since 1933 include pensions for the blind, for orphans and children of widows, divorced or unmarried mothers, and housing grants to families with three or more children. Through these reforms and through extensions of existing services total budget expenditure for social services increased from 45 million kr. in the 1932–33 budget to nearly 120·5 million kr. in 1937–38.

Trade unionism in Sweden is somewhat younger than in Denmark. Organization among skilled workers started in earnest in the 1880's, chiefly on a narrow craft basis. By 1899, when the Trade Union Centre was formed, the aggregate membership of trade unions had reached 64,000. Thirty-two national unions were in existence, three of which consisted of unskilled workers: the General Workers' Union, founded in 1891 by unskilled building workers, but admitting also unskilled factory workers irrespective of industry; the Transport Workers' Union, founded in 1897 by dockers originally organized in the General Workers' Union, attempting to organize all categories of workers in transport and commerce; the Railwaymen's Union, founded in 1899 and admitting all grades. Two national unions, the Textile Workers' and the Saw-mill Workers' had been established on an industrial basis.

Of the thirty-two national unions, sixteen, with some 37,500 members between them, joined the Trade Union Centre from the start. Between 1900 and 1910 a further nineteen national unions were formed, most of them on a craft basis. Two, the Telegraph and Telephone Union and the Municipal Workers' Union were of the industrial type, another two, the Agricultural Workers' Union and the Crofters' and Forest Workers' Union set out to organize rural labour.

Until 1907, aggregate membership grew rapidly to 231,000 in forty-five national unions, twenty-eight of which with 186,000 members belonged to the Trade Union Centre. In 1906, at the conclusion of serious stoppages, the Trade Union Centre and the Employers' Federation had agreed to the "December Compromise." The two parties mutually recognized each other's right of organization and of collective bargaining, while the trade unions acknowledged the employers' right of "hiring and firing." This compromise later was incorporated in most collective agreements.

With the depression of 1908 trade union membership figures began to fall. In 1909 the Centre, joined by most non-affiliated unions, launched a defensive general strike against lock-outs in the leading industries. This struggle, proportionally the greatest labour conflict that had till then occurred in any country, ended in defeat for the workers and had the effect of reducing trade union membership by one half. In 1911, when the tide turned, aggregate membership was back at 114,000. The Trade Union Centre had only 80,000 members left, one of the consequences of the great strike being the breaking away of syndicalist elements who, in 1910, formed a national centre of their own based not on national unions, but on local trades councils.

The period 1911–1915 was one of steady growth. Aggregate membership reached 158,000 in 1915, the Centre 111,000. The five years that followed witnessed an expansion without precedent. By 1920 there were 399,000 trade unionists in Sweden and the National Centre had 280,000 members in thirty-one national unions. The Syndicalist Centre had grown to 33,000.

In 1916 the first act on public mediation had been passed, setting up seven district mediators. Unlike the Danish and Norwegian Acts, the Swedish Act of 1916 did not make it obligatory on the parties to accept mediation, though by an amendment passed in 1920, they were obliged to meet at the mediators' call. They did, however, remain free to refuse to enter into real discussions and the Act does not lay down any definite time limits. In the absence of a Chief National Mediator, such as provided by the Danish and Norwegian

Acts, the practice has developed for the Government to appoint ad hoc mediation commissions for disputes of national importance.

Whereas 1919 and 1920 had been years of considerable labour unrest, resulting, as we have seen, in wage increases considerably beyond the rise in prices, the deflation years 1921 and 1922 were comparatively peaceful. As in Denmark, the trade unions in Sweden avoided major conflicts and agreed to reductions in wages. Despite very heavy unemployment, the decline in trade union membership was exceptionally small. At the end of 1922 total trade union membership still stood at 344,000. The Trade Union Centre, after a loss of some ten per cent. in 1921, actually increased its membership in 1922, reaching 293,000 by the end of the year. This increase was mainly due to the affiliation of two important national unions which had so far kept aloof: the Printers' and the Railwaymen's unions.

In the winter of 1923 a series of big conflicts developed, mainly due to demands for further wage cuts and for reductions in holidays with pay and other advantages obtained in 1919–20. The trade unions now resisted. Some 22,000 forest workers struck from November 1922 till the middle of February 1923. In January strikes against alterations of working hours in the iron and steel works were countered by a lock-out which lasted from January 29 till the end of July; 17,000 saw-mill workers were locked out from the beginning of February till the end of March, and another 17,000 workers in the paper pulp mills were locked out from the end of January till the beginning of April, to enforce wage cuts. Syndicalists and communists advocated a general strike, but the Trade Union Centre rejected all such demands and concentrated on securing sufficient financial support for the 80,000 workers involved in the struggle. By April compromise solutions had been arrived at for all groups except iron and steel, the result being in most cases the status quo with regard to wages.

With unemployment receding during the latter half of the year the net result was a 6 per cent. increase in aggregate and nearly 7 per cent. in Centre membership during the year. In 1924 no major conflicts occurred while membership increased rapidly, total membership by 14·3 per cent. to 417,000, the Centre by 15·1 per cent. to 360,000. In March 1925 the Employers' Federation attempted in vain to force down wages by means of a fortnight's lock-out involving 100,000 workers in the engineering, saw-mill, paper-pulp and textile industries. Apart from this, and a renewed textile lock-out of about a week's duration in January 1927, no major conflicts occurred till 1928. Trade unions during these three years grew steadily. By the end of 1927 total membership had reached 494,000, the Centre 438,000.

In January 1928 two major conflicts developed in the main export industries. On January 2nd 17,000 paper pulp workers were locked out to enforce wage cuts. Sympathetic lock-outs were declared in the saw-mills from January 30, and the paper mills from March 5, bringing the total number of workers involved to 45,000. A compromise settlement was arrived at early in April, involving some reductions in wage rates.

The simultaneous mining lock-out and strike, developing out of local conflicts in the iron mines of middle Sweden into a national stoppage from January 23, proved very difficult to settle. It lasted till August 27.

Whereas in most conflicts throughout the period since 1920 the trade unions had been on the defensive, the Miners' Union, in declaring a sympathetic national strike in support of the miners locked out in middle Sweden, had taken the offensive. Without consulting the Trade Union Centre, to which they were affiliated, they established co-operation with the Russian Miners' Union, and in the early days of the struggle issued a joint declaration criticizing the defensive policy pursued by the Swedish trade union movement as a whole.

This manifesto created widespread resentment in the trade union world. Though the miners received much more financial support than that to which they were entitled by the statutes of the Centre, their co-operation with the Russians tended to strain relations with the Centre leadership. It also stiffened resistance on the part of employers who viewed the extension of the stoppage as a result of Russian intrigues.

The net result of the eight months' struggle was a return to work on the old conditions, with minor improvements in the matter of holidays with pay.

The labour conflicts of 1928 had consequences in the field of trade union legislation. The liberal minority government which, in 1926, had succeeded the third Labour government, in May 1928 succeeded in passing a Trades Disputes Act setting up a Permanent Labour Court with powers to settle without appeal all disputes relating to interpretation or breaches of collective agreements. The Act was voted against the unanimous protest of the Labour movement, the Social Democratic Party joining with the Trade Union Centre in arranging a national demonstration, involving a half day's protest strike of 370,000 workers on May 22.

In November 1928 trade union leaders representing the majority of organized workers nevertheless accepted the invitation of the government to attend a national Conference on Peace in Industry. On the recommendation of this Conference, a permanent Committee on Peace in Industry, representing the Employers' Federation, the Trade Union Centre and the Government, was set up in December, to discuss measures for better co-operation. No results were, however, obtained and in 1931 the Trade Union Congress withdrew its representatives as a protest against the use of troops in a local conflict in the saw-mill industry. The protest against the Permanent Labour Court and the 1928 Act, on the other hand, soon died away.

Despite the long drawn out conflicts of 1928, involving a serious reduction in iron ore and iron exports, trade unions had continued their growth. During the following two years of industrial prosperity few conflicts occurred, one exception being a strike of shop assistants in Stockholm in 1930, by which they established the principle of collective agreements. By the end of 1930 total trade union membership had reached 614,000. The Trade Union Centre had 553,000 members in thirty-seven national unions. The Syndicalist Centre which, at its 1929 congress, had rejected a majority proposal from its executive for amalgamation with the National Centre, still had some 28,000 members.

Apart from the bottom year 1933, when there was a small loss in membership, the period of depression and recovery from 1930 to 1937 has been one of steady expansion for the Swedish trade unions, and of progressive concentration within the National Trade Union Centre. At the end of 1937 total membership had reached 850,000. Of this total the Centre counted 840,000 members in forty-one national unions.

During 1931 and 1932 a certain number of lock-outs and of defensive strikes occurred, none of which did, however, develop into major conflicts. But a defensive local strike in the sawmill industry in the Ådalen district in the spring of 1931 was marred by the tragic death of strikers. The importation by the employers of organized gangs of strike breakers had provoked the strikers to assume a threatening attitude. Local police authorities asked for assistance in protecting the strike breakers. When troops arrived they were met with demonstrations and stone throwing, and fired into the unarmed crowd, killing four strikers and, by accident, an onlooker. Great indignation was aroused, and unofficial protest strikes occurred in many places.

In the spring of 1933, while the Labour government which had assumed office in the preceding autumn was preparing its public works programme, the employers in the building industry put forward demands for wage cuts of 15–20 per cent. and for important changes in conditions of work. The workers in the three building unions countered with demands for the forty-two hour week with compensation in wage rates and holidays with pay. By the middle of April, negotiations having failed mainly owing to the attitude of employers who desired to create difficulties for the government, the stoppage in building was general. Mediation was attempted in the usual way, but failed. In September the Prime Minister and the Minister of Social Affairs intervened and put forward a proposal for settlement which was accepted by the workers but rejected by the employers. By December 1933 the Employers' Federation demanded the simultaneous settlement of points at issue in all trades subsidiary to building. A new mediation proposal was put forward on February 2nd, 1934, and accepted by the Employers' Federation, which threatened a sympathetic lock-out of 215,000 workers in the main industries if the building workers rejected the new terms proposed. Under strong pressure from the General Council of the Trade Union Centre and from the government, the workers accepted the terms, which involved important wage reductions. By so doing, they saved the government from the necessity of intervening by means of compulsory arbitration. Such intervention had been strongly urged by the opposition and by the Farmers' Party, whose representatives in parliament were also in favour of further restrictive legislation to protect the interests of " third parties " in labour conflicts.

Under pressure from its allies, the farmers, who were strongly in favour of such measures, the Labour government in 1935 put forward a bill placing severe restrictions on both parties in trade disputes. The trade union representatives in Parliament turned definitely against it, and as the Conservatives, representing employers' interests, also opposed the bill, the government dropped it.

In 1936 and 1937 two important Acts were passed securing the rights of wage earners. The 1936 Act on Right of Organization and Collective Bargaining secures those rights for all wage earners whether in private or public employment except civil servants. The 1937 Act grants to civil servants full rights of organization and of negotiation concerning conditions of employment, of work and of remuneration.

Starting on lines similar to those of the Danish trade union movement, the structure of Swedish trade unionism has undergone important changes, moving slowly but steadily in the direction of industrial unionism. As early as 1912 the Trade Union Centre, on the initiative of the Iron and Engineering Workers' Union, adopted a scheme of reorganization, the three leading principles of which were: national unions should organize all workers employed in one industry. The border lines between national industrial unions should be drawn to correspond with the border lines of collective agreements. The workers in smaller but mutually related industries should be organized in common unions. The 1912 scheme aimed at the gradual amalgamation of the then existing forty-one unions into twenty-two industrial unions. In the following ten year period a certain number of amalgamations were effected in the main industries. But the majority of existing craft unions opposed the change, and by 1923 the total number of national unions had grown to sixty-one, of which thirty-three were affiliated to the National Centre. Despite the multiplication of unions, the relative importance of industrial unions had grown. The nineteen industrial unions in existence counted

64·2 per cent. of aggregate union membership, twenty-seven craft unions only 20·2 per cent., while the remaining 15·6 per cent. belonged to four "mixed" unions. The 1926 Trade Union Congress adopted a modified re-organization scheme aiming primarily at securing that henceforward one union only should be responsible for organization and agreements in any one place of work. Instead of the twenty-two unions of the 1912 scheme, thirty-three national unions were to be allowed according to the 1926 decision. Since that date, some progress has been achieved. Of the twenty-seven craft unions seven have disappeared. Four of them have amalgamated to form one Sailors' Union, two to form a Garment Workers' union while one, the Tile Stove Makers' Union, has been re-organized on an industrial basis.

In most cases, however, the cartel solution has been resorted to in Sweden as in Norway. Such has been the case of the Printers', Bookbinders' and Lithographers' unions who have formed a Graphic Industries' Cartel. In the building trades a cartel has been formed comprising the Tinsmiths', the Carpenters', the Electricians', the Bricklayers', the Painters', the Stonecutters' and the General Workers' Unions. In iron and engineering the Moulders' Union has entered into cartel co-operation with the Metal Industries' Union. The Forest and Flotage Workers', the Saw-mill Workers' and the Paper Industry Workers' unions have formed a cartel, and so have the Commercial Workers' and Food Industry Workers' unions.

Table II shows the membership figures of national trade unions in Sweden in 1923 and 1937, grouped in craft unions, and mixed and industrial unions within four main groups: crafts and industries except building; building and allied trades; commerce, transport, etc.; and agriculture and forestry.

TABLE II, SWEDEN

Name of Union	1923	1937
I. Crafts and Industry, except building:		
(*a*) Craft Unions:		
Printers	6,744	10,735
Moulders	4,572	8,754
Bookbinders	2,720	6,527

Name of Union	1923	1937
Barbers	258	2,665
Lithographers	745	2,237
Chimney Sweepers	306	529
Barrel Makers	333	190
	15,678	31,637
(*b*) Industrial and "mixed" Unions:		
Metal Industries	53,303	146,816
General and Factory Workers	31,977	79,673
Municipal Workers	15,141	37,467
Paper Industries	19,332	36,901
Textile Workers	16,413	34,971
Saw-Mills	27,293	27,244
Garment Workers ... ... (1923 in 2 craft unions)	8,167	24,438
Food Industries	9,359	24,356
Wood Industries	6,609	23,310
Road and Dam Construction...	1,602	21,196
Shoe and Leather	8,843	11,102
United Unions	5,894	11,055
Stone Industry	3,732	9,152
Miners	2,808	8,180
Brewery Workers	3,830	6,630
Arsenal Workers	4,029	5,607
Tobacco Industry	3,039	2,462
Tile Stove Makers	581	542
	221,952	511,102
II. Building and Allied Trades:		
Carpenters	8,846	31,611
Painters	3,638	13,845
Bricklayers	3,173	10,633
Electricians	3,848	8,613
Saddlers and Paperers ...	869	2,757
Tin Smiths	1,284	2,621
	21,658	70,080

Name of Union	1923	1937	
III. Distributive Trades, Transport, etc.:			
(*a*) Craft Unions:			
Postmen	4,121	7,916	
Locomotive Firemen ...	4,892	4,919	(1933)
Telegraph Officials	860	1,115	"
Telegraph Clerks	538	446	"
Customs Officials	1,965	2,115	"
Insurance Clerks	238	1,954	
(*b*) Industrial and Mixed Unions:			
Railwaymen	34,741	37,807	
Transport Workers	12,324	32,078	
Commercial Workers ...	6,012	32,007	
Sailors (in 5 craft unions 1923)	12,620	15,774	
Hotel and Restaurant ...	1,704	14,745	
Telegraph and Telephone ...	2,794	8,614	
Total of III, A and B ...	82,809	159,490	
IV. Agriculture and Forestry:			
Agricultural Workers (in 2 regional unions 1923) ...	9,856	34,147	
Forest and Flotage Workers ...	10,158	39,845	
	20,014	73,992	

In important respects the growth of trade union organization within the main groups differs from what we have seen in Norway. In Sweden there is not such a marked contrast between crafts and industry on the one hand and the distributive trades, agriculture and forestry on the other. The main explanation is that in Sweden organization in the latter groups had started earlier than in Norway. Sweden also has experienced a more marked growth in the number of workers employed in industry and building than has Norway.

The Swedish Trade Union Centre differs from those of Denmark and Norway in one important respect: it is primarily an organization for defensive purposes. Affiliated national unions have no statutory right to financial support from the Centre except in lock-outs and in other conflicts arising out of attempts on the workers' part to defend their right of organization or their wage standards and other conditions of work against attacks.

Affiliated national unions, therefore, are under no obligation to ask the authorization of the Centre for advancing new demands or launching offensive strikes except in cases where such moves are likely to provoke lock-outs on the part of employers. Consequently, the authority of the Centre in Sweden is more limited than in Norway, the national unions having a larger measure of autonomy.

In actual practice, however, the tendency during the period under survey has been for national union executives to consult the Centre before advancing new demands or launching strikes of any importance. On the initiative of the Metal Industries' Union, acting in consultation with the other main industrial unions, the practice has developed of inviting representatives of the Secretariat (the Centre Executive) to participate both in preliminary discussions within the unions and in negotiations with employers. The main purpose of the practice thus established is to develop a common policy in the matter of wages, with a view to concentrating efforts on " levelling up " the wage level of economically weaker categories of workers.

The structure of individual national unions and of the Centre is, on the whole, parallel to that of Danish and Norwegian organizations. The Congress period of the Swedish Centre is, however, five years. The system of representation differs in so far as the total number of congress delegates is fixed at 250. Of this total, each affiliated national union elects a number proportionate to its membership, the mode of election being a matter for the individual unions. Local trades councils, which are recognized, but membership of which is not obligatory, have no right of representation either to Congress or to the General Council. This latter body consists of representatives of affiliated unions, one for each 10,000 members until 20,000, one for each 20,000 members beyond that figure. The Council meets regularly once a year and more frequently if need arises.

The Executive, termed Secretariat, is elected by the congress and consists of four paid officials, President, Vice-president, Treasurer and General Secretary and seven other members.

According to the statutes of the Centre, the Secretariat

participates in negotiations with employers at the invitation of affiliated unions, and without such invitation whenever it deems necessary. It has powers to declare defensive sympathetic strikes and to levy special fees in case of conflicts supported by the Centre. As in Norway, the Secretariat controls a People's Hall Fund, and runs a statistical department, and an auditor's department which audits the accounts of affiliated organizations.

The financial arrangements differ from those obtaining in Denmark and Norway. Affiliated national unions must have a minimum membership due for administration and strike fund purposes of kr. 23·40 a year for full-due and kr. 13 a year for half-due members. The regular due to the centre is kr. 0·40 a month for full due and kr. 0·20 a month for half-due members. No definite amount per head is stipulated for support from the Centre to affiliated unions in case of conflicts recognized as defensive. The maximum obtainable is kr. 6 weekly for full-due and kr. 4 weekly for half-due members, but as a rule not for the first fortnight's stoppage and not for the first 3 per cent. of the membership of the union in question.

Local Trades Councils, consisting of local unions affiliated to national unions belonging to the Centre, have been set up in many towns and industrial centres. They are not, however, an obligatory part of the organization structure, are not represented either in Congress or General Council and receive no regular financial support from the Centre. Their functions are mainly to carry on local trade union propaganda and educational work. There has of late been a tendency on the part of the Centre to encourage the formation of trades councils.

With regard to co-operation between the Trade Union Centre and the Social Democratic Party, the situation in Sweden differs from that in Denmark and Norway in so far as the Swedish Centre is not formally an organization working for the establishment of a socialist economy, nor are there any statutory arrangements for co-operation between the two bodies.

The difference is, however, more formal than real. The Social Democratic Party relies to a very great extent on collective affiliation from local trade unions. The proportion of party members collectively affiliated varies considerably from district to district, from nearly 80 per cent. in the south where Social Democracy is strongest to a mere 1·3 per cent. in the North, where independent socialists and communists are strong. Of the total number of trade unionists some 33 per cent. were collectively affiliated to the party in 1933.

In practice, consultation between the Secretariat of the National Centre and the Social Democratic Party Executive occurs frequently. The two bodies co-operate closely in matters relating to labour legislation and the development of social services. At general elections, trade unions give financial support to the Social Democratic Party, though not to the same extent as in Norway, the main reason being, no doubt, the relatively greater influence among organized workers in some districts of the independent socialist party and the communist party.

A development which may prove of decisive importance for the future of Swedish democracy is the beginning of co-operation between the trade union world and the farmers' economic organizations. In the winter of 1935 to 1936 the crofters of Dalecarlia and surrounding districts in middle Sweden joined with the forest workers in a common strike against the great forest companies. The national organization of farmers "Riksförbundet Landsbygdens Folk" joined with the Forest and Flotage Workers' Union in organizing the strike and in negotiations with the Employers' Federation for a settlement. Though no formal or official relations have been established between the respective central organizations, other instances of developing understanding have occurred, tending to cement the co-operation established in the political field between the Social Democratic and the Farmer parties, who, since 1936, form the government coalition.

A few words must be added on the present position of the Syndicalist Centre, formed in 1910, the Central Organization of Employees, founded in 1931, and the organizations of municipal employees and civil servants.

Throughout the period under review, the total membership of the Syndicalist Central Organization has varied around 30,000. The membership, organized in Local Trades Councils, mainly consists of unskilled and semi-skilled workers in the building and subsidiary industries and in forestry, saw-mills, paper-pulp and paper mills. In sharp contrast to the centralization obtaining in the national unions affiliated to the Trade Union Centre, the syndicalist organization is federalistic, giving a large measure of autonomy to local councils, which alone are represented at its congresses. Mainly for purposes of collecting statistics on wages and production costs, individual unions in allied industries form " industrial syndicates " within local trades councils, and these syndicates are grouped nationally in " federations " for each industry and " industrial departments " for allied industries.

In 1931 a certain number of " white-collar " workers' unions, not all of them of a definite trade union character, united to form the Central Organization of Employees. By the end of 1937, seventeen national unions with an aggregate membership of 45,424 were affiliated. Nearly 35,000 members belonged to the four largest unions: The Industrial Employees with 11,000, the Foremen with 9,700, the Commercial Employees with 7,900 and the Bank Employees with 6,150.

Most of these " middle class " unions concentrate on securing the right of collective bargaining, though as a rule they do not aim at collective agreements, nor do they rely on strike action. Under the 1936 Act on Right of Organization and Collective Bargaining, such organizations which declare their determination not to resort to strike action, may register with the " Socialstyrelsen," the government administration of Social Affairs.

The organizations of municipal employees not affiliated to the Trade Union Centre united in 1937 to form the Central Organization of Municipal Employees, with a membership of of some 40,000 in eight national unions.

Among Civil Servants, no corresponding central organization exists and no membership statistics of the large number of unions in existence are available.

IV

The national trade unions of the three countries, in so far as they belong to their respective Centres, are all of them affiliated to their respective Trade Internationals. The Swedish and Danish Centres have been affiliated to the International Federation of Trade Unions throughout the period under review. Not so the Norwegian Centre. Owing to the predominantly communist orientation of the Norwegian Labour Party from 1919 till the reunion with the Social Democrats in 1927, the Norwegian Centre broke away from the I.F.T.U. in 1922, and, though never joining the Red International of Trade Unions, did not reaffiliate till 1935. This break did not, however, affect the membership of its affiliated national unions in their respective trade internationals. Nor did it interfere with the co-operation existing within those internationals among the Scandinavian national unions. This co-operation, including in most cases the Finnish unions, takes various forms, ranging from mutual insurance against strikes and lock-outs with obligatory mutual support to looser "Cartel" co-operation.

Till 1922, close co-operation obtained between the National Centres of Denmark, Norway and Sweden, their representatives meeting regularly in Scandinavian Labour Congresses at intervals of three to five years. These congresses also included the Labour (Social Democratic) parties of the three countries.

The "Russian" orientation of the Norwegian Labour Party and the Norwegian Trade Union Centre from 1920 onwards led to the liquidation of co-operation in the old form. No Scandinavian Labour Congress has been held during the period under survey. Despite differences of opinion, co-operation did, however, continue between the three trade union Centres. During the big strikes of 1923–24 the Norwegian Centre received extensive financial support from the Swedish and Danish Centres. Conferences of Executive members from the three Centres were held in 1924 and 1926. During the great Norwegian lock-out of 1931 the Norwegian Centre once more received ample financial support from Denmark and Sweden. By 1934 regular consultations, not in the form of Congresses but of Conferences of Trade Union Centre and Party Executive members were resumed. These Scandinavian Conferences now included the Finnish Trade Union Centre, and Social Democratic Party. The Centres and Parties of Denmark, Finland and Sweden in 1934 formed a

Scandinavian Committee of Co-operation, the Norwegian Centre remaining formally outside till it joined the I.F.T.U. in 1935, the Norwegian Labour Party till it affiliated to the Labour and Socialist International in 1938. In reality, however, the Norwegian organizations participated in Scandinavian co-operation from 1934.

THE U.S.S.R.

BY

MAURICE H. DOBB

TRADE UNIONS IN U.S.S.R.

BY

M. H. DOBB[1]

Trade Unionism in Russia had no long-standing tradition prior to the revolution of 1917. In Tsarist times unions were subject to suppression as illegal bodies, with the possible exception of the brief period of the 1905 revolution, after which they were suppressed more ruthlessly than before in the reaction that followed. Such rare associations as appeared in the late nineteenth century were disbanded and their organizers punished. While there were a number of strikes in the 'seventies, and a South Russian Workers' Union was formed in 1875, and a Northern Union of Russian Workers in 1878, these attempts at organization were short-lived, the elected deputies of the workers being quickly arrested by the police. In the period between 1904 and 1908 there had been some modification of the official attitude. In the brief period of what has been termed " police socialism " after 1901, sanction was given to associations of workmen that were " recognized " by the authorities. But these bodies, subsidized as they were and even at times officered by police agents, were far from being trade unions in the usual sense, being little more than clubs and mutual aid societies and not bargaining bodies : they were of the type that in America would be termed " yellow unions " and were clearly designed to offset the tendency to independent organization. But in this intention they were altogether unsuccessful; and on their heels there gathered a mushroom-growth of unofficial trade unions. So fast was this growth in the semi-legality of these years that an all-Russian-conference of trade unions was held in 1905, and repeated in the following year; while in Moscow and other towns Trade Councils, to co-ordinate the activities of the various unions, were set up. By 1907 the number of unions had grown to the surprising figure of 650, with an aggregate

[1] The author is indebted to Mr. Jacob Miller for assistance with much of the Russian material connected with this chapter and for information supplied by him to the author on a number of points.

membership of some 250,000, of which over a third were in the metal and textile trades. Most of these, however, were small local societies; some of them little more than spontaneous strike committees at a particular enterprise: only twenty-two of the 650 had more than 2,000 members, and as many as 350 had less than 100 members. In 1908 came a new wave of repression. Over 100 societies were dissolved by a single decree; others were closed down by the police for aiding and abetting strike-action; funds were confiscated and the organizers and even the active members of unions were arrested and exiled.[1]

Despite some revival of organization and activity in the years immediately preceding the war, it was not until the first revolution of March 1917 that Russian trade unionism, as a legal and continuous organization, can be said to have begun. On the eve of this revolution "the total membership of all trade unions cannot have exceeded a few tens of thousands." Yet three months later there were nearly a thousand separate organizations with a membership of a million and a half: a figure which had grown to more than two million by November.[2] In these months of ferment and class struggle the preoccupation of the trade unions was largely with immediate political issues; and the protagonists of rival political views were battling for supremacy within the trade union structure. In the All-Russian Conference of Trade Unions which met in June there was a fundamental cleavage between those who interpreted the present revolution as no more than a "bourgeois-democratic revolution," with the implication that the immediate tasks of trade unions were confined to securing concessions and reforms on the basis of the *status quo*, and those who followed Lenin in seeing the situation as one in which a "bourgeois revolution was growing into a workers' socialist revolution" and in claiming that in this situation the trade unions must assume a political and a revolutionary rôle. At this Conference the Mensheviks, who upheld the former view, had the majority and occupied most of the executive positions. But the Bolsheviks were strong in number in the large industrial

[1] S. P. Turin, *From Peter the Great to Lenin*, 113 et seq.; Mavor, *Econ. History of Russia*, 413 seq., 451 seq.
[2] S. and B. Webb, *Soviet Communism*, 164–5.

centres and in the metal industry. In the course of the year the Bolshevik influence steadily grew, until at the Conference called in January of the following year, after the Soviet revolution had taken place, the Bolsheviks secured a three-to-one majority, and from thenceforth were dominant in the trade union movement. At the same time with great rapidity there developed factory committees in each enterprise, in large part independently of the trade unions, and even at times in rivalry with them. These played a considerable part in the revolutionary events of these months. It was from them (or, at least, from factory meetings similar to those from which these committees were elected) that delegates to the Workers' Councils or Soviets were appointed; and these factory committees were quicker to reflect the growing dominance of the Bolsheviks than was the trade union structure. In the early months after the November revolution they were given extensive powers, under the Decree on Workers' Control, to interfere in the management of enterprises, virtually as statutory organs of local control over capitalist enterprises. Even these powers were, in fact, in many cases exceeded; and in the first half of 1918 a pronounced syndicalist tendency developed among them in the direction of the conduct of industry by factory committees: a tendency which both the government and the trade unions later took steps to curb.[1]

Soviet trade unionism has sometimes been held to be peculiar, by contrast with the trade unionism of other countries, in that it is dominated by a particular political party. But in this, of course, its position is not unique. The trade unions in pre-Nazi Germany were dominated by the Social-Democratic Party ; and in England the unions are in very close association with the Labour Party, and are controlled by an official element which has the principal voice in forming the policy of the political party itself. What makes the position and the functions of the Soviet trade unions unique is the fact that they

[1] Cf. the writer's *Russian Economic Development since the Revolution*, 38 seq. The trades union congress of January 1919 had laid it down that factory committees must cease to " carry on an existence separate and apart from the trade union" and must become local organs of the trade union. (Cf. Webb, *op. cit.* 166.) But for some months after this factory committees continued to maintain a large measure of autonomy.

exist in a socialist system, and that the party which controls them is at the same time the governing party of the State. Whereas in all other countries trade unions exist as protective associations and bargaining bodies in relation to private capitalists who control industry, in this case they are organizations of the workers which deal, not with private employers, but with the State, and with a State administration the personnel of which is elected by trade unionists in their capacity as electors and which may even contain direct representatives of the trade unions themselves. Moreover, they operate in a social system in which profit and revenue on property no longer exist as a category of income, while wages and salaries constitute the only (or at least the predominant) form of income. Clearly in such circumstances the position and the functions of a trade union must necessarily be very different from what they are in other countries. How different they must be is not a question that yields on first sight any easy answer: and it is hardly surprising that this question has been the subject of prolonged and acute controversy in the Soviet Union itself. Those who are inclined to treat the difference between a capitalist and a socialist system as a difference of degree rather than of kind will tend to belittle the difference in the proper rôle of trade unions in the two cases; and persons who hold this view are generally critical of Soviet trade unions for departing in many respects from what they regard as the traditional character and functions of trade unionism. But at any rate there will probably be general agreement that in a socialist state it must be part of the duty of a trade union to share in the responsibility for the efficient conduct of industry, and to subordinate sectional interests to the general interest, as well as to safeguard the position of its members: in fact, to undertake functions which the more ambitious sponsors of joint control so often advocate, and which socialists generally consider to be impracticable under capitalism.

The Communist view of the position and function of trade unionism in a socialist state first took shape in the famous discussions at the end of 1920 after the period of civil war and "war communism." Already in 1918 there had been some discussion as to whether or not the trade unions should become " organs of the State "; but, apart from reaching a negative answer to this question,[1] the discussion had not proceeded further: the preoccupations of civil war and the urgent requirements of military improvisation had intervened. With the termination of the war, the whole question of economic policy in the reconstruction-period, and with it of the rôle of trade unions, became a pressing one. In fact, the discussion started as a discussion of the trade union question and then raising more fundamental issues, as it inevitably did, broadened out into the discussion on the so-called New Economic Policy. Here two extreme views emerged. On the one hand, Trotsky, who as Commissar of Transport had converted the railway unions into virtual military units, advocated the transformation of the unions into units of a labour army, subordinated directly to the State and organized along semi-military lines. At the other extreme were the proposals of the so-called " workers' opposition," which advocated a syndicalist régime under which the trade unions should be reconstructed as autonomous bodies and the control of industry be placed entirely in their hands. Between the two extremes were a number of intermediate proposals. The policy which was to be adopted as the policy of the Party and of the Government was embodied in the so-called " platform of the ten."[2] It provided for the retention by the trade unions of a considerable measure of independence from the State apparatus: they were to become State organs neither in the sense that their autonomy was lost and their personnel appointed from above nor in the sense that they were to be sovereign bodies in the economic sphere. Trade unions were to regain their position as democratic bodies which they had to a large extent lost during the civil war period; their officials to be subject to election and not to

[1] At the trade union congress of January 1919, at which Lenin spoke against the " nationalization of the trade unions," it was laid down that, while the unions should " co-operate with the Soviet authorities," " perform certain of the functions at present discharged by the Soviets," and " aid in the setting up of various State institutions," they should not at present be transformed into State organs.

[2] This " platform of the ten " was the report of the trade union commission of the Party, presided over by Lenin, on which Trotsky had refused to serve. Among its signatories, in addition to Lenin, were Stalin and Tomsky. Bukharin, after inclining initially towards Trotsky, subsequently produced a " buffer " proposal which was a compromise with the syndicalism of the " workers' opposition." In the application of the new policy at the Fourth T.U. Congress, however, Tomsky also had disagreements with the official view and for a year was removed from the Central Committee of Trade Unions.

appointment. Their principal duty was to represent the interests of their members with regard to wages and working conditions in their dealings with the administrative organs of industry. At the same time they were to participate in the control of industry by appointing representatives to the governing boards of industry, while the factory committees were to exercise certain functions in each enterprise in the control over working conditions.[1]

This definition of trade union function was elaborated at the Fourth Trade Union Congress in 1922, and was implemented in the Labour Code of the same year. Here it was provided that trade unions might " appear before the various authorities in the name of wage-earners as parties to collective agreements and represent them in all matters relating to their work and their conditions of life " (Article 151). A trade union could secure legal recognition by registration with the Central Committee of Trade Unions established under the statutes of the Trade Union Congress; but no body that was not so registered and accepted for affiliation could enjoy the legal status of a trade union (Articles 152 and 153). As such it was a body competent to acquire and manage property and to conclude agreements within the limits of Soviet legislation. The duties of factory committees, as the basic executive unit of union organization, were defined as being to " represent the interests of the wage-earning and salaried employees in relation to the management of the undertaking, institution or enterprise " as well as " before the Government and other public authorities "; to supervise the enforcement of labour legislation and " co-operate with the State authorities concerned in the protection of the workers " ; and to " co-operate in the regular carrying on of production in State undertakings, and participate in the regulation and organization of economic activities " (Article 158). It was further provided that State authorities should render trade unions every facility in the execution of their functions; and the management of undertakings were not only prohibited from hindering the activities of factory committees and dismissing their members, but were obliged to provide the use of a room for such committees, with " free access to all persons on the business of the committee " and to

[1] C.f. the writer's *Russian Economic Development*, 152 seq.

defray their expenses (Articles 160–5). A number of matters were subsequently listed in a supplement to the Code as being subject to the joint control of the trade union and the management. These included the " rules of employment," standards of output for the purpose of wage-payment, and the working of overtime; while notice of the dismissal of workers, whether for technical or disciplinary reasons, had to be given to the factory committee (in the normal case, two weeks' notice being necessary); the latter possessing right of appeal against the management's decision. Among the matters provided for in the " rules of employment " was the imposition of fines; and the arbitrary imposition of fines outside the provision of these rules was expressly prohibited. " Unrestricted right of entry to all workshops, departments, laboratories, etc. " was guaranteed to trade union officials and representatives; and at the special labour sessions of the People's Courts (courts of first instance) it was provided that one of the three members of the bench should be a representative of the trade union.[1]

Strike action remained formally legal under this legislation, although a strike conducted without the sanction of a trade union could be made (on the initiative of the union) the occasion of a prosecution before the People's Court. As a trade union journal stated at the time : " it would be absurd for trade unions to deny the possibility of labour disputes .. . an agreement inevitably implies the possibility of disagreement and dispute."[2] At the same time, it was held that in socialized industry in which the trade unions were no longer engaged in a class struggle over the division of the product, but were co-operating partners in production, neither a strike nor a lock-out could be countenanced save in exceptional circumstances ; and the Central Committee of Trade Unions proceeded to issue instructions to its affiliated bodies that strike action was to be employed only as a last resort after every use had been made of the machinery of conciliation. The resolution of the Eleventh Congress of the Communist Party summed up the matter in these words: " In the case of friction and disagreement between any section of workers and the institutions of

[1] Cf. *The Trade Union Movement in Soviet Russia* (I.L.O. Studies, A.26) 266 seq.; J. Freeman, *The Soviet Worker*, 108 seq.

[2] *Vestnik Truda*, 1922, No. 12.

the workers' State it is incumbent on the trade unions to assist in terminating the dispute as quickly and as effectively as possible by endeavouring to secure for their members such improvements as are compatible with the economic development of the workers' State and are without injury to other sections of workpeople." While, therefore, strikes continued to occur, they were rarely countenanced by the trade unions.[1] In practice, where a dispute has reached an acute stage it is usually dealt with under the powers originally given to the Commissariat of Labour to intervene at its discretion and make arbitration compulsory in the case of a dispute in a State enterprise. To handle disputes, and to secure a settlement without a stoppage of work, a fairly elaborate system of conciliation and arbitration has been instituted. In the first place there are joint disputes committees (R.K.K.) in each enterprise (and sometimes in larger enterprises disputes committees in each workshop). These are representative jointly of the management and of the factory committee, with a chairman and secretary from each side holding office alternately. Secondly, there are the special labour sessions of the local People's Courts, which include a trade union representative. Thirdly, there are local conciliation boards instituted as *ad hoc*, and not as permanent bodies, and originally attached to the local organs of the Commissariat of Labour. These include one representative each of the parties to the dispute with an impartial chairman. Finally, there are arbitration courts, consisting again of representatives of the two parties, with plenary powers, together with an impartial chairman, and empowered to deliver a binding award.[2]

[1] In 1922–3 there were 505 strikes affecting 154,000 workers and involving 322,000 lost working-days. The majority of these were in State enterprises and only eleven of these had the authorization of the trade union. In about a third of the cases the workers were granted their demands *in toto* and in another third their demands were " partially " granted. In 1924 there were only 79 strikes affecting 24,000 workers; in 1925 some 200. (*Trade Union Movement in S.R.*, 179–181). Collective agreements usually stipulate that if there is a disagreement over piece-rates, etc., the worker has " no right to refuse to perform the work assigned to him " pending reference of the matter to the Disputes Committee.

[2] By Article 33 of the decree of TSIK and Sovnarcom dated August 29, 1928, governing conciliation and arbitration procedure, it is provided that, while an arbitration court may be set up at the request of one party alone to adjudicate on any question concerning the interpretation of an existing agreement, it is only competent to take a decision, which involves an actual change of principle or the termination of an existing collective agreement " before the expiration of the period of the agreement," with the consent of *both* parties.

In the early years of their existence, the competence of these various bodies was not clearly defined, with the result that there was overlapping of jurisdiction, considerable overloading of the dispute-machinery and delay in the final settlement of disputes. By a new Order in 1928[1] their powers were more closely defined and the procedure simplified. Three main types of dispute were distinguished. The first involved some modification of a collective agreement, either by explicit amendment or by an interpretation which raised a question of principle. In this type of dispute only a conciliation board or an arbitration board was competent; reference to the former requiring the agreement of both parties (one of the parties being the trade union concerned), but compulsory reference to the latter being possible at the request of either party alone in the case of a State enterprise.[2] The second type of dispute concerned the application of an existing employment-contract or collective agreement to some particular case. Here the worker concerned could choose between a reference to the disputes committee of his own enterprise, or to the labour session of the People's Court, with the latter as final court of appeal (subject to the condition that where technical questions were involved, requiring intimate knowledge of the particular enterprise, the reference must be to the disputes committee). Thirdly, there was the type of dispute that arose from a charge against the management of contravening some existing piece of labour legislation, or some existing collective agreement. Here the People's Court alone was competent; the matter being treated as an ordinary criminal charge for breach of a collective agreement or of the labour law.[3]

The quite considerable powers exercised by the factory committees were facilitated by the fact that trade union organization ran on industrial, and not on craft, lines: or rather, on that particular version of industrial unionism that has been

[1] Order of TSIK and Sovnarcom, August 29, 1928. In the previous year there had been some 5,000 disputes, involving four million workers. Of these over 80 per cent. had been brought before the arbitration courts, and only 15 per cent. had been settled by the conciliation boards.

[2] Cf. however, the footnote to the previous paragraph.

[3] *Conciliation and Arbitration in Industrial Disputes*, I.L.O. Studies, A. 34, 395–409; *International Labour Review*, Vol. XXI, 209 seq.; *Spravochnik Sovetskovo Rabotnika*, 1937.

termed " employment unionism."[1] In general, the trade union follows in its scope the frontiers of some administrative unit, so that all the employees of an enterprise or an institution are members of the same trade union. Thus there is the Agricultural Machinery Workers' Union, to which all employees in an enterprise manufacturing agricultural machinery belong, clerical workers, technical staff, fitters and general labourers alike; there is the union of workers in higher educational institutes and scientific research institutes, to which professors, laboratory assistants, porters and the cleaning staff all belong. Originally, in the 'twenties, there were no more than twenty-three unions, each covering one of the main departments of the national economy. Some of them were very large, like the Metal Workers' Union with over a million members, and covered what was properly a group of kindred industries rather than a single industry. With the intention of breaking up unwieldy bureaucratic structures, and bringing the union machinery in closer touch with the membership, this number was increased to forty-four in 1931 and subsequently to as many as 162 by 1937.[2] The Metal Workers' Union, for example, which formerly had had to deal with twenty-eight industrial *combinats*, was broken up into seven independent unions, to cover such branches as machine-construction, non-ferrous metals, aviation and motor cars, electrical engineering. The Miners' Union was divided into four, one each for coal, iron, other ores and peat. The Agricultural Workers' Union was divided to follow the lines of four specialized sections in the administration of State farms.[3] The basic unit, or " branch," is therefore the meeting of trade union members in a workshop or enterprise; from which the *Fabcom* or *Mestcom* (according as it is a factory or some other institution) is elected (formerly by show of hands, but nowadays by ballot). In the larger enterprises each workshop may have its shop-committee, or even a shift-committee, composed of delegates from each shop or shift, as well as a *Fabcom* for the whole factory. These committees are appointed for one

[1] This basis of organization is not a product of the Soviet revolution: industrial unionism was the declared policy of the Russian trade union movement as early as 1906.

[2] Cf. A. Losovsky, *Handbook on the Soviet Trade Unions* (Moscow, 1937), 19.

[3] Cf. J. Freeman, *op. cit.*, 112–4.

year, although individual members can be recalled or a new election held at an earlier date at the request of one-third of the union members in the enterprise. They are required to meet at least once a week. There is also appointed at the same time an audit and control committee, whose function it is to investigate and to make an independent report on the work of the *Fabcom*.[1] In a particular locality the various factories in a certain industry combine to appoint a district or regional committee and at intervals to hold a regional congress. On an all-Union scale each trade union is headed by a central committee elected at a general delegate conference ; while at the top of the trade union hierarchy is the All-Union Central Committee, which is elected at the general Trade Union Congress of the whole of the Soviet Union.[2] This congress meets as a rule in alternate years and consists of between 1,000 and 2,000 delegates elected, not from the national committees, but from the provincial congresses of the various unions. By virtue of the fact that recognition of a trade union is dependent on registration with the All-Union Central Committee, and on affiliation to it in accordance with its statutes, this latter body, and the general congress to which it is responsible, has extensive powers of controlling both the forms of organization and the policies of the separate unions, with the result that the autonomy of the latter is strictly subject to the general regulations issued by the All-Union Central Committee. For example, the central body has, in fact, powers to define and to change the frontiers between the various unions and so to decide any disagreements over demarcation. As will later be seen, key questions concerning wage-regulation, such as the scale of variation between grades and the total wages-fund allotted to various industries, have in recent years come to be centralized with this body, for agreement between it and the higher economic administration.

According to the Code and supplementary regulations of 1922, membership of a trade union was to be voluntary, and

[1] Such direct information as the writer possesses suggests that this check is important and effective, and that it is a common practice for the audit committee to issue a very full and critical report on the work of the *Fabcom* or *Mestcom* for the year. The quorum for the election is defined as being one-half of the members; and it is generally provided in union rules that three days' notice must be given of the time and agenda of the meeting.

[2] This central council consists of some 170 members from which a small presidium, and in turn a secretariat, is elected.

membership of a union was not made a condition of employment.[1] At the same time membership carried important privileges, such as a higher rate of insurance benefits and pensions and the sponsoring of a complaint before a disputes committee or a labour court; and it was open to a trade union or a *Fabcom* to include a clause in a collective agreement requiring that preference of employment be given to trade unionists —a condition that was fairly widely exacted and which had considerable importance when there existed a large reserve of unemployment prior to 1930. On the other hand, membership of a trade union is now open to all persons without discrimination, provided that they come within the category of persons employed at a wage or salary and subject to a contract of service. This includes the technical staff of a factory, but not any person " personally possessing the right to engage or dismiss "; and it likewise excludes members of co-operative productive units, such as an industrial co-operative or a collective farm. After the introduction of N.E.P. in 1921 the membership of trade unions fell considerably owing to the reversion to voluntary membership and the exclusion of independent handicraftsmen and co-operative producers; and in 1924 it stood at rather less than six million as compared with over eight million in 1921. Since then this figure has increased more than threefold, partly due to an increased proportion of workers enrolled in trade unions, but chiefly due to the great increase in the numbers of the industrial workers during the period of the first and second Five Year Plans. In 1924 the number of wage and salary-earners in the Soviet Union was between eight and nine million, of whom about two-thirds were members of trade unions. By 1928 the total number had grown to 11·5 million, three years later to eighteen million and to-day to over twenty-five million, of whom twenty-two million, or 84 per cent., are members of a trade union. The smallest proportion of trade union members is found in agriculture and in building; to be explained in the former case presumably by the scattered

[1] The statement commonly made, e.g. by a writer in *Foreign Affairs* of New York (April 1938, p. 538; article by M. Gordon) that in U.S.S.R. " trade union membership is compulsory " is incorrect. Similarly certain statements which follow in the same article to the effect that the trade unions " have even less power than our company unions . . . (and) are merely a form of labour exchange or government employment bureau " have no ascertainable basis in fact.

nature of the industry, and in the latter case by the high proportion of migratory and seasonal workers.[1]

The *Koldogovor*, or collective agreement, which is made between a union and the administration of an industry, takes the form of an agreement with the *Fabcom* or *Mestcom* in each individual enterprise. The separate agreements are fairly standardized in their general form; but as regards detailed application they vary considerably according to the circumstances of a particular enterprise. The *Koldogovor* is an impressive and comprehensive document; and nowadays embraces not only the obligations of the management to its employees but also the obligations of employees to the management. In the first place it fixes the time-rates to be paid to different categories of workers, and the appropriate relation to be observed between the normal earnings of piece-workers and time-workers. It defines the classes of workers who are to be employed on piece-work, and any system of bonuses or premiums to be used. It stipulates the conditions under which overtime is permitted; the conditions under which workers can be transferred from a job in a more highly paid to a lower paid category; the method under which new labour is engaged, and the right of a worker to receive adequate notice of dismissal. In a typical agreement of this kind the management undertakes, *inter alia*, to give adequate consideration[2] to any proposals for improvements submitted by production conferences of trade unionists, or by individual workers, and if the proposal is accepted to arrange (through the factory inventions committee) for the award of a premium and the carrying of the proposal into effect; to issue written instructions to piece-workers, indicating the work required and the rate at which it is to be paid; to inform the *Fabcom* of all new engagements, so as to enable them to " lodge a reasoned objection within three days "; to provide adequate facilities for training, not only in the case of learners and apprentices, but also in the form of " improvement " and " refresher-

[1] Cf. *Industrial and Labour Information*, xlv, 199, lx, 249–251; Webb's *op. cit.* 174–5; Losovsky, *op. cit.* 19. Education and the Arts and Public Health, however, show a higher proportion than factory industry.

[2] In the agreement cited by the Webbs (*op. cit.*, 505 seq.) " within ten days " is stipulated; also that the author of each proposal be informed within the same period of the fate of his proposal.

courses " for all workers, and in consultation with the *Fabcom* to pay for the attendance of selected workers at technical classes outside the factory; to provide working clothes and locker-accommodation, drinking-water, washstands with soap and towels, shower-baths and a dining-room; to provide short-term courses of instruction in safety technique and to take specific measures for the improvement of health and the reduction of accidents; to spend a certain specific sum from the building-fund of the enterprise for construction and repair of workers' houses, club and nursery premises, a sports field, etc., and to allocate apartments in such houses in consultation with the *Fabcom.* On its side the *Fabcom* undertakes, *inter alia,* to co-operate loyally in enforcing " labour discipline," in reducing absenteeism and bad time-keeping and in attaining the planned production-quota of the enterprise; to " mobilize the workers for fighting theft and for the protection of socialist property " ; to refer all disputes and individual grievances to the disputes committee and to co-operate in keeping the aggregate wages-bill within the estimates; to provide effective supervision and control over the running of the factory store and dining-room and the factory crêche; to carry on a campaign among the workers concerning safety-measures, and to keep the management continually informed of undesirable conditions of work or inadequate safety measures.

How far is it the case that the general level of wages in an industry is determined by collective bargaining and hence is within the power of the trade union to control? There seems little doubt that during the period of N.E.P. in the 'twenties the process of bargaining between each trade union and the administration of the industry played an important rôle in determining the level of wages in the trade. Wage-rates and earnings differed quite considerably in different industries; and while there was some co-ordination and attempts were made to secure greater uniformity, the decisions affecting wage-policy appear to have been considerably decentralized. At the same time this bargaining was not the process of " trial by strength " of two opposing parties that is familiarly associated with the term: both management and trade unions were limited in the demands that they severally made by the terms of co-operation between them and by the influence over each exerted by the Party. Moreover, it was open to the Central Council of Trade Unions to pass binding resolutions concerning the wage-levels in various trades (as did the general Congress in 1926 with regard to the relative wages in light and heavy industry); and the practice prevailed for the *average* wage-increments for all industry to be decided in the first instance by a process of bargaining between the Central Council of Trade Unions and the Supreme Economic Council, and for this decision to be announced *before* the separate unions entered into contracts with their several industries.[1] Even in the later years of the N.E.P. period the principle adopted both by the authorities and by the trade unions was that changes in the general level of wages should be strictly related to changes in productivity. But a situation of autonomy (or even partial autonomy) of separate industries in the fixation of wages, while it could exist in the special circumstances of this period, could hardly persist without drastic modification in the new circumstances introduced by the first Five Year Plan, with its comprehensive and detailed planning of the output-programme of each industry. In this respect, at any rate, the powers, if not the position, of trade unions, as defined by the decisions of 1921, were bound to be changed as soon as a transition was made to a more centralized system of planning. If the Plan is to stipulate the output-programme for an industry, it must include some estimate of cost in relation to productivity; and such an estimate will be disturbed if the wages-bill of the industry is fixed independently of the planning authorities and is open to subsequent alteration. Moreover, it is now the case that the production-plan is supplemented by a financial plan, which controls the credits to be granted to the various economic units to cover their wages-bill and the purchases of plant and materials required to fulfil their planned output-quotas. Consequently it has become the practice for the wages-bill of an industry to be settled as a constituent element of the annual plan. Prior to the final settlement of this figure, it is of course open to the trade union concerned to advance its own claims in the preliminary discussion. But though its influence may be considerable, this evidently cannot be decisive; and the ultimate decision inevitably becomes a

[1] Cf. Chase, Dunn, Tugwell, *Soviet Russia in the Second Decade*, 202–5.

centralized policy-decision, like those which govern other elements of the Plan. How much influence an individual trade union can exert by making appropriate representations during preliminary discussions of the Plan is a matter of current practice, not of legal rules, and is difficult for an observer who is not a participant in the process to estimate. But it appears to be the case that the practice has come to be for the general wage-allocations and also the main principles of wage-policy, such as the relations between the various grades, to be decided by a general conference of the Central Council of Trade Unions with the leading economic authorities and the Council of People's Commissaries.[1] Any question of broad principle involved in this decision (for example, in what proportions the national income is to be divided between consumption and investment) will in all probability be covered by a prior decision of the Party. In these circumstances, the collective agreement that a trade union makes with an industry, or a *Fabcom* makes with the management of its enterprise,[2] operates, so far as wage-rates and wage-scales are concerned, within the limit set by the general Plan. It can have latitude with regard to the wages of particular workers, or the ratio of earnings between various categories (subject to general principles of grading), and also with regard to the use of certain funds that are in the disposal of the enterprise, such as funds for premiums, or the share of profits allocated to the so-called director's fund for welfare purposes. But it is not competent to decide the total wage-allocation of the enterprise or the industry; and the output-standards that are settled between the union and the management as the basis of piece-work payment have to be related to the pre-determined output-plan of the factory. Only if the stipulated output-quota is exceeded is the aggregate wage-allocation to an industry or factory allowed to be augmented. In a system of centralized planning and financing it is difficult to see that the position could be otherwise.

[1] Cf. Webbs, *op. cit.*, 184. The Webbs state that this discussion takes place "early" in each year, while the collective agreements are usually drawn up in March.

[2] In the early years of the Five Year Plan, the practice of collective agreements between the central committee of a union and an industrial trust was replaced by separate agreements between the *Fabcom* and the management of the particular enterprise. The former practice has now (since 1937) been resumed, so that both types of agreemen now exist.

It was questions of this kind, affecting the functions of the trade unions in the new period of the Five Year Plan, that were the occasion of sharp discussion and disagreement in 1929: disagreements which led to the replacement of Tomsky as chairman of the Central Council of Trade Unions as well as to extensive changes in the leading personnel of the trade union world. Tomsky, and those colleagues who supported him, while accepting in principle the policy of industrialization embodied in the Five Year Plan were inclined to oppose a high, in favour of a low, rate of investment, in the interest of maintaining higher levels of wages in the immediate future. It also seems clear that in his view the rôle of the trade union in bringing pressure on industry as independent bargaining bodies took precedence over their rôle as partners in administration, co-operating to improve production. The tendency which he represented was, at any rate, attacked as being "syndicalist" in character, and as neglecting the rôle that the trade unions must play in the new epoch of planning, particularly of planning in the interests of rapid industrialization of the country. Complaints against the unions for failing to take any steps to check the indiscipline of their members had begun to accumulate in the early months of 1929. It was said that on appeal workers were reinstated who had been dismissed for most serious offences, such as rowdyism in the factory, or assaults on the technical staff; with the result that managers frequently felt that their hands were tied. There was also at this time an extraordinarily high labour-turnover, amounting to as much as 100 per cent. per annum or even more. Such "slackening of labour discipline" was variously attributed to the large number of raw peasant recruits newly drawn into industry, to increased consumption of alcohol and to bad housing conditions. But the complaint made by the critics was that the unions did nothing in the matter.[1]

The slogan of "turn towards production," was accordingly issued, and the duty of trade unions to co-operate with the management in enforcing workshop discipline and improving production was brought to the fore. The old leaders of the

[1] *Econ. Jizn*, 3.3.29; also for estimates of labour-turnover *Narodnoe Khosiaistvo 1932*, 449. Labour turnover still remains high, and was the reason for the decree of Dec. 28th, 1938, which provided for the grading of social insurance benefits according to length of service in the enterprise.

Central Council were declared to be "incapable of appreciating the rôle of the unions during the period of economic construction," and accused of "opposing efforts to reorganize the unions so as to remove mistakes." The organ of State industry declared in the summer of 1929 that "until recently the trade union leaders were inclined to omit from their functions their due part in improving labour discipline, raising the worker's output and fulfilling the Plan. They also treated the collective agreements as an effective means of extorting the maximum concessions from the leaders of industry at the minimum cost to the unions."[1] Trade unions must not only defend workers against bureaucratic tendencies in the administration of industry; they must also resist tendencies among the workers to "regard the Soviet State as a capitalist State and to work as little as possible while obtaining as much as possible from it." The new Central Council proceeded to place emphasis on the encouragement of "socialist competition" between different groups of workers and between the factory committees of different enterprises; on the organization of "shock-brigades" among workers; and on comprehensive schemes of technical training. Ever since the early days of the revolution piece-rate payment had been practised, and considerable differences had prevailed in the rates of pay of different grades. But it had apparently been the recent policy of the trade unions to move in the direction of greater equality of payment between grades. To provide an incentive to improve production, piece-rates and bonus-systems were now extended; and to provide encouragement to workers to acquire technical skill as well as in order to improve the living conditions and efficiency of the more responsible grades, particularly the technical staffs, the tendency towards equalization in wage-scales was reversed and the ratio between the various grades widened. Finally, in 1931 came Stalin's "Six Points," adherence to which was to form the preface to most collective agreements in subsequent years. "We can no longer have the

[1] *Torgovo-Promishlennaia Gazeta*, 4.6.29. The report of the Central Council to the Ninth Trade Union Congress in 1932 stated: "The old leadership gave precedence to the 'defensive' work of the trade union, contrasted with their task of co-operating in socialist construction." In the person of Tomsky the old leadership declared it "impossible simultaneously to manage an enterprise on the basis of commercial accountancy and be the spokesman and champion of the worker's interests."

situation," he declared, "where an iron-founder is paid the same as a cleaner and an engine-driver no more than a copyist." Trade unions and industrial managers alike must fight against "lack of responsibility" with regard to machinery, against "petit-bourgeois" views about equalizing all wages, against the old hostile and suspicious attitude towards "specialists" and the old technical staffs; they must struggle to "master technique," to increase the training of skilled workers and to enforce strict "cost-accounting" methods in industry.[1]

The position with regard to wages to-day is that about sixteen separate wage-grades are distinguished (the number varying with different industries and types of work); the four lowest of these applying to untrained beginners and falling below 100 roubles a month; and the highest grade receiving between 450 and 500.[2] The weighted average amounts to-day to about 250 roubles or rather more a month, ranging from 200 in textiles to 280 to 300 in coal mining and railways. The normal hours of work in 80 per cent. of industry are limited to seven a day, with a maximum of six in specially dangerous or strenuous occupations, such as underground work, puddlers and foundry-workers, telephone-operators, etc. Piece-work is widely in use—more widely than in this country—some 70 per cent. of the workers being paid on a piece-work basis.[3] Piece-rate scales are supposed to be adjusted so that a worker who produces the "normal" or standard output shall earn 25 per cent. more than a worker on a time-rate. Various forms of "progressive piece-rate" payment are now very widely in use, under which all output in excess of the

[1] Cf. Freeman, *op. cit.*, 127 seq.; *International Labour Review*, Vol. XXIX, 212 seq.; Shvernik, *Sadachi Profsoyusov v Reconstructivnii Period.*

[2] Cf. S. Nekrasov, *Pamiatka Sborschiku Chlenskich Vsnosov v Profsoius*, 21. These rates apparently represent the rates payable for a normal output, and do not include special premiums to workers who exceed the standard output. Technical specialists often get paid at special rates outside this scale. The trade union contribution is graduated and amounts to approximately 1 per cent. of the wage. It is to be noted that the *range* of incomes, when expressed in real terms, is less than might at first appear, since the price-structure in U.S.S.R. at present is such as to make necessities relatively cheap and luxuries relatively dear—i.e. the dispersion of prices of these things is much greater than elsewhere.

[3] In coal-mines 80 per cent. of all workers, and 90 per cent. of underground workers were put on piece-work. In building even bricklayers and painters have a form of group payment by results. (*Industrial and Labour Information*, Vol. XL, 113.)

standard is remunerated at a progressively higher rate.[1] In some cases, for example, all output in excess of the standard is paid at a rate 50 per cent. higher than the basic piece-rate; in other cases a 10 per cent. increase on the standard is paid at a 50 per cent. higher rate, a 20 per cent. increase at a double rate, and so on. Workers, on the other hand, who fall below the standard are paid for their output at the standard rate; and if the slowness of their work is due to causes outside the workers' control, their earnings are subject to a guaranteed minimum of two-thirds of the normal earnings.[2] Overtime is paid for at a rate of time-and-a-half for the first two hours and double rates for anything in excess of this ; while night-shifts are generally one hour shorter, with piece- and time-rates raised by one-fifth or one-sixth.

The actual movement of real wages over the last decade is almost impossible to estimate with any approach to precision, in view of the multiplicity of price-levels for different categories of buyers during the rationing period.[3] During the first Five Year Plan there was a stringency in the supply of a whole range of commodities—meat, vegetables, cotton goods, sugar—and the consumption per head of these things undoubtedly fell. At the same time the output of certain other things—boots and shoes, and tinned foodstuffs, for example—increased considerably. What was the immediate effect on real wages

[1] In iron and steel in 1937, 75 per cent. of all workers were on piece-work and "over half" of these were paid on progressive piece-rates. (*Methodika Planirovaniya Chornoi Metallurgii.*)

[2] Cf. L. Weinstein, *Zarobotnaia Plata* (Profisdat 1937), 24 seq. The standard, of course, is calculated as a rate of output per unit of time (e.g. an hour or a shift) It appears to be the case that the fixing of this standard is influenced, if it is not actually determined, by the rate of output of so-called "shock-workers." The two-thirds minimum guaranteed to slow workers amounts to two-thirds of the hourly earnings of a worker producing at this standard rate, i.e. about 15 per cent. below the usual rate of time-workers. *Industria* of February 14, 1938, cites an interesting case of a meeting at the Orjonikidze Metallurgical Works of slow workers who did not attain the standard output. These amounted to 6 per cent. of all piece-workers. The meeting was said to have been an eye-opener for the management; and the reasons given for their low output were: too frequent change of foremen, stoppages of machinery, too much of the workers' time being occupied in preparing the place of work, and insufficient instruction. Special attention to their conditions of work, facilities for training, and a system of individual patronage over slow workers by more experienced workers were advocated as a cure.

[3] The official Retail Index Number was discontinued in 1930. In 1928 Professor Paul Douglas (*Sov. R. in Second Decade*, 244–249) estimated that the working class standard of life at the end of the N.E.P. period was (including social services) 30 per cent. higher than in 1913.

of the abolition of rationing in 1935 is, again, hard to estimate. The new uniform prices were higher than the old rationed-prices, but lower than the old "commercial shop" prices, and still lower than prices on the open market. Since then, however, there have been some price-reductions, and money-wages have been rising. To judge by figures of consumption of basic foodstuffs, there seems to be little doubt that in the concluding years of the second Five Year Plan the average level of real wages has risen considerably.[1] At the same time both the total number of employed workers and the output per head have shown quite a remarkable expansion. The number of wage-earners has more than doubled in the decade; while the output per head in industry is said to have increased by 50 per cent. between 1928 and 1933, and was estimated to increase by 40 per cent. in the boot and shoe industry and as much as 100 per cent. in iron and steel during the second Five Year Plan.[2]

The general policy of subordinating changes in wage-rates to changes in labour-productivity has been adhered to even more strictly in recent years, in view both of the high rate of investment, characteristic of the period of the first and second Five Year Plans, and of the considerable increases of productivity that the installation of new methods and modernized

[1] According to figures given by *Pravda* the urban *per capita* consumption of bread in 1936 was 28% higher than in 1932, of sugar 42%, of meat and fats and dairy produce 80 to 90% higher.

[2] Comparisons between the purchasing-power of the rouble and of the £ are peculiarly difficult owing to the widely different price-structures and actual expenditures in the two countries, and any attempt to express the comparison in a single figure is bound to be meaningless. Suffice to say that a number of estimates which have recently been made and which quote a figure of over 100 to the £ as the true purchasing-power parity of the rouble, are almost certainly too high (i.e. they *under*estimate what the rouble can buy in terms of things bought by the majority of wage-earners). Sir Walter Citrine has suggested a figure of 100. But, in arriving at this estimate, he omits rye bread, which is little more than half the price of wheaten bread and has, in the past, been a staple item of working class consumption (although to-day an increasing proportion of wheaten bread is being consumed), and he omits also the staple meal per day that the vast majority of workers (often also their families) obtain in a factory restaurant or club, and which is relatively cheap. Inquiries based on data collected by Mr. Jacob Miller during more than a year's stay in the country, on a comprehensive price-list published in a Bulletin of the Industrial Conference Board (March 7th, 1938), etc., suggest that for meals in factory and club restaurants a parity of about 40 is appropriate, for bread, milk and potatoes about 55 to 60, for meat and eggs between 80 and 100, for butter 120, and for clothing between 100 and 200. Social services are generally estimated to add the equivalent of slightly more than one-third to the wage.

plant has made possible.[1] Thus in the Plan for 1937 the average increase in labour-productivity was fixed at 19 per cent. and the increase in wage-rates at 10 per cent. Of the difference part is intended to contribute to an increase of investment and construction in the economic system at large, and part to a cheapening of the price of finished output. The most striking result of this new emphasis on labour-productivity in all wage-questions is the famous Stakhanov movement. What distinguishes this from the previous campaigns for "shock-brigades" and "socialist competition" of the early 'thirties seems to be its emphasis on rationalized methods of work organized on the initiative of workers themselves and usually involving specialized team-work, by contrast merely with increased exertion on the part of individual workers. The original innovation at the Irmino mine in the Ukraine which started the movement involved a simple principle of division of labour: a separation of the two processes of coal-cutting and the propping of the workings, which removed the necessity for each hewer to change continually from one operation to another and enabled picks and mechanical drills to be continuously utilized throughout the shift.[2] By this means a team of Stakhanov and two timberers, working with a mechanical drill, attained the remarkable output of 100 tons in a shift of five and three-quarter hours, and later even more. Similarly, Vinogradova introduced a new system of team-work in the minding of ring-spindles; and Smetanin in a Leningrad boot and shoe factory claimed to surpass the records established at the Bata factory in lasting shoes.

There are signs, however, that the increased attention paid by trade unions in these years to co-operating in the campaign for higher productivity was not without an important adverse

[1] There seems to be little doubt that in the early years of the Five Year Plan the maintenance of money-wages at a higher level than the existing ratio of investment to productive capacity warranted was a primary cause of the inflationary symptoms of those years, leading to "goods-scarcity" and to rationing.

[2] This was later supplemented by a new method of working a vertical seam, so as to ease the strain on the hewer and to enable the coal as it was hewn to drop directly on to the conveyor, thereby getting the coal away from the face more quickly. Stalin, addressing the first conference of Stakhanovites in 1935, eulogized them as being "free from the conservatism and stagnation of certain engineers and business administrators; smashing antiquated standards of output; and introducing amendments into the estimated capacity of industry and the economic plans prepared by the leaders of our industry."

effect on other aspects of union activity. Failure to pay sufficient regard to improving the working conditions and housing conditions of their members was a fairly common complaint in the middle 'thirties; and there seem also to have been plenty of cases of arbitrary action by trade union officials in substituting appointment for election within the union, and even overriding elections—" flagrant abuses of trade union rights and a neglect of the needs of union members," as the leading trade union journal described it.[1] Whether these were of recent origin or of long-standing is not clear. Cases were also quoted where workers were illegally deprived of their " rest-day " by the management, under pretext of " voluntary labour," without any protest from the trade union, and *Fabcoms* were accused of giving " passive support to the management in such abuses."[2] To judge by an order of the Soviet Control Commission in 1936, forbidding certain practices, breaches of regulations concerning disciplinary penalties and the hearing of appeals and complaints had been frequent.[3] In 1936 a drastic reduction was made in the paid staffs of trade unions (which had previously amounted to the large total of 76,000 persons, and had swallowed up three-quarters of the members' contributions) presumably with the intention of striking a blow at bureaucratic tendencies. Thenceforth a maximum was set for expenditure on administrative staff, amounting to 40 per cent. of a trade union's income; the declared object of this reform being to make the unpaid voluntary worker, instead of the paid official, the central figure in trade union activity.[4] Criticism came to a head at a meeting of the Central Council of Trade Unions in the spring of 1937. The secretary, Shvernik, in his official report quoted examples of undemocratic practices and criticized the inadequate attention paid to safety measures and to cultural work. The resolution that was adopted and received wide publicity instructed all trade union bodies to

[1] Cf. *Trud*, 26.3.37; also 27.2.33 and 24.4.34 for cases of anti-democratic procedure.

[2] *Trud*, 27.4.35.

[3] *Isvestia*, 30.5.36. This order forbade "communications of a confidential character relating to workers transferred from one establishment to another" and the imposition of disciplinary penalties without the culprit being given a hearing. It further provided for the registration of all complaints and the fixing of a time-limit for their consideration.

[4] Cf. *Trud*, 15.1.37; cit. *Industrial and Labour Information*, Vol. LXII, 34 seq.

terminate the practice of filling vacancies on committees by co-optation, and the practice of voting for office on the basis of "lists" instead of by individual candidature. New elections were called for within three months, to be conducted by secret ballot, on the basis of candidates proposed from the floor and open to public discussion and criticism. Increased attention was to be paid to the work of the labour inspectorate, to ensure an improvement in safety devices and the reduction of accidents, and the appointment of voluntary inspectors from among the rank and file was to be particularly encouraged. To increase the amount of rank and file control over the allotment of social insurance benefits, each *Fabcom* was to institute an insurance council to act as a jury in all applications for disablement benefit, children's aid, or places in sanatoria and rest homes.[1]

There are two functions which have assumed a special importance in the work of Soviet trade unions in the last five years: factory inspection and social insurance. Since the disappearance, in 1933, of the Commissariat of Labour, and the transference of its functions to the Central Council of Trade Unions, the latter has become to this extent what in Britain would be called a statutory body, not only responsible for the enforcement of labour legislation through an inspectorate, but competent to issue decrees on matters concerning labour conditions. It had always been the practice for the Commissar for Labour, both of the Union and of the various Republics, to be nominated by the Central Council of Trade Unions; and the trade unions had also appointed the factory inspectors employed by this Commissariat. Similarly the director of social insurance, under the same Commissariat, was always appointed in consultation with the trade unions, while in the localities the insurance committees that administered the payment of benefits were under trade union control.[2]

The social insurance system, as it stands to-day, is divided into three sections, of which the largest is administered by the

[1] Cf. *Industrial and Labour Information*, Vol. LXII, 449–52; also *Bloknot Agitatora*, No. 14 (176), Moscow 1937.

[2] Cf. Freeman, *op. cit.*, 122; I.L.O., *Trade Unions in S.R.*, 186, 198. The number of inspectors attached to the Labour Commissariat at the time of its dissolution was 3,500, although in the case of some of these it was said "their qualifications were not always of the best." (Cf. Report of Ninth T.U. Congress, cit. *Industrial and Labour Information*, Vol. XLIII, 73.)

unions. The first, health insurance, is administered by the Commissariat of Health and its local organs, and financed by funds contributed from central and local budgets. Up to 1937 its administration was shared by the trade union, and the sums involved actually passed through the budgets of the trade unions (amounting in 1936 to a quarter of their insurance budget); payments being made by the latter to the various medical institutions. The second, a combined insurance, which includes disablement and maternity benefit, funeral allowances and superannuation pensions, children's aid, maintenance of rest-homes, and subsidies to mutual aid funds, is administered entirely by the trade unions, and financed by a tax on all enterprises, amounting to between 4 and 11 per cent. of their wage-bill according to the nature of the occupation. The administration of these benefits is in charge of the insurance committees set up by each *Fabcom*, subject to general regulation by the central trade union authorities. In 1937 the total trade union insurance budget amounted to 5,000 million roubles, of which some 40 per cent. was allotted to disablement benefit, 17 per cent. to the maintenance or construction of rest-homes and sanatoria, 16 per cent. to maternity benefit and 10 per cent. to special aid to children of insured persons.[1] Thirdly, there are old age pensions and pensions to the totally disabled, which come under the control of the Commissariat for Social Assistance, as does also the relief of persons not employed for wages. In addition to this, the trade unions spend certain sums on special kinds of welfare and cultural work. The dividing line between this work and social insurance proper does not appear to be sharply drawn: it seems to be in the nature of a decentralized trade union supplement to statutory insurance benefits, which figures in the trade union budgets and not in the central social insurance budget which has to receive government sanction. Of the total about a quarter is spent on administration, the remainder contributing to such purposes as general education, mutual aid, sport

[1] Karavaiev and Trephilov, *Posobia po Sotsialnomu Strakovaniyu* (Moscow 1935); *Industrial and Labour Information*, Vol. LXIII, 346–7; Vol. LXII, 165–7. The old age pensions which pass through the trade union budget are pensions paid to persons over sixty who continue in employment and continue to earn wages (which they are entitled to do while drawing the pension). Similarly the disablement benefit covers partial or temporary incapacity. Total and permanent disablement is separately dealt with in the third category.

and physical culture, and the upkeep of musical and art clubs and libraries.[1]

The insurance scheme covers all physical risks, and not only those incurred in the course of employment (except in the case of temporary and seasonal workers); and the benefits for illness and accident include both medical treatment and payment for lost working time. Benefit payable for temporary disablement amounts to full wages (at the normal time-work rate) for trade unionists who have been three years in employment, provided that two years of this employment has been in the same undertaking. Those who do not fulfil this condition receive benefit at a lower rate; while non-trade unionists are entitled to half their normal wages. Total disablement pensions are similarly graded both according to the degree of disablement and to the length of employment; amounting to 100 per cent. of the normal wage for those who are so disabled as to require attention, and varying between 40 per cent. and 70 per cent. of the normal wage, according to the period for which they have previously been in employment, for persons who are incapable of work but do not require attention. Old age pensions, originally introduced in 1927 for textile workers and in 1929 extended to certain other basic industries, now cover all wage- and (since 1937) salary-earners. These provide pensions varying between 50 per cent. and 60 per cent. of the wage to all men who reach the age of sixty after having been twenty-five years in some employment and to all women who reach the age of fifty-five after having been twenty years in some employment. There are also pensions for dependent survivors paid to families who have been deprived by death of their breadwinner.[2]

It is clear that the position of trade unions in the U.S.S.R.

[1] Cf. *Industrial and Labour Information*, Vol. LIX, 315; also, e.g., *Otchet Ts. K. Soius Rabotchikh Mukomolnoi Promishlennosti.*

[2] *Industrial and Labour Information*, Vol. LXIII, 348; *International Labour Review*, Vol. XXVIII, 539–546; Karavaiev and Trephilov, *op. cit.* Formerly persons "deprived of electoral rights" were debarred from participation in old age or disablement pensions. By an order of Sovnarcom of July 31, 1937, this restriction was removed except in the case of persons deprived of civil rights under a judicial sentence. By the recent decree of December 28, 1938, sickness benefit was reduced to 50 per cent. of the normal wage for those with less than two years' service in an enterprise, and graded so as to rise to 100 per cent. after six years' service in the same enterprise. The aim was to reduce the very high rate of labour turn-over that still exists. Persons dismissed for offences against discipline were to be disqualified from receipt of benefit until they had worked six months in the same enterprise.

has been to some extent a changing one over the past twenty years; the most important changes being that which emerged from the discussions of 1921 and the subsequent modification in this position (which was a modification of practice, rather than of legal status) at the beginning of the first Five Year Plan. The formal change represented by the abolition of the Commissariat of Labour in 1933, and the transfer of its functions to the Central Council of Trade Unions, is also outstanding. But in view of the relationship which had always prevailed between this Commissariat and the trade unions, the change would appear to have had less substantial importance than it has interest as a constitutional innovation. It can hardly be expected that the present position which the trade unions occupy is final and unchanging. But the direction that any future change is likely to take is not easy to foretell. The whole question, as we have seen, raises issues as interesting as they are crucial concerning the rôle of trade unions in a socialist state. How far is it consistent for trade unions to retain an autonomous position as collective bargainers over wages? It may be that the very nature of a socialist economy, where planned decisions concerning the allocation of national resources have replaced the *laissez-faire* play of barter and bargaining, makes it a mis-statement of the problem even to pose the question in this way. Clearly there can be no question of each industry framing its own wage-policy in isolation, since by affecting the price-policy of the industry it is exerting far-reaching influence on other branches of the national economy and affecting other wage-earners in their capacity as consumers. Moreover, this would involve the danger, so often quoted against the advocates of syndicalism, of a tug-of-war between sectional monopolies, each anxious to exploit the rest. Clearly such sectional decisions must be subject to some degree, at least, of central arbitrament. But there is a further consideration which must be paramount in a system of economic planning : it is that (given the resources and the intensity with which they are being utilized) decisions which govern the rate of investment (i.e. of capital construction) are *ipso facto* decisions as to the current rate of consumption and hence of the level of real wages. It seems to be of the essence of any socialist planned economy that the former should constitute a key policy-decision to be decided by the highest organs in the economic sphere, and not be left to chance or to bargaining and " the free play of economic forces " ; and if this decision is taken centrally, then so also must the decisions which control the general wage-level. While it is possible, indeed essential, for the trade unions to participate in the making of this decision, this participation will have the form, not of a bargain struck between two independent agencies, not even of the independent advocacy of the interests of one social group against others, but of the representation of one functional aspect of the community in the general counsel.

This is what has eventuated in the Soviet Union: financial decisions of a *general* character are centralized, and in deciding them little that resembles the older form of bargaining between autonomous unions and managements has any part. In matters of detailed application of general principles to particular circumstances, in deciding on the concrete ways of employing certain financial allocations, there is clearly nothing inconsistent with a planned economy in an extensive decentralization. Here the Soviet trade unions to-day play a large rôle, and a rôle which we may expect to see increased rather than decreased—questions of working conditions, safety devices, welfare work, industrial training and social insurance. In particular there are signs of the lower units of trade union organization, like the *Fabcom,* having increasing autonomy in certain of these matters, and signs of increasing stress being laid on activity and control by the rank and file member by contrast with the paid official.

However, there can be small doubt that some of the centralization of matters affecting the output of labour in the past decade has been the special product of a transitional period of economic construction: of a period, moreover, of abnormally rapid construction carried out under the lengthening shadows of war. It is, at least, arguable that, even if decisions as to wage-*rates* are matters of social policy which are necessarily centralized in a planned economy, decisions affecting the total amount of work that is performed at a given rate (in so far as this decision is capable of being separated) are properly the sphere of the trade unions in any system of industrial democracy. The discretion given to trade unions in the matter of permitting overtime and (within limits) controlling premiums and bonus systems can, perhaps, be cited as a partial recognition of such a principle; and in " normal " times (if there can still be said to be any such thing in the world as it is to-day) one might expect the autonomy exercised by trade unions in such questions as hours of work and intensity of work to increase.

THE UNITED STATES OF AMERICA

BY

SELIG PERLMAN

LABOUR AND CAPITALISM IN THE U.S.A. 1920–37

TABLE OF CONTENTS

LABOUR AND CAPITALISM IN THE U.S.A.[1] 1920–1937

1. Basic American Institutions and Labour

The seventeen years covered in this survey present for American labour two distinct periods dramatically separated by the arrival of the New Deal. Following the Armistice, labour lost whatever standing as a national institution the war emergency had brought it and faced anew the Sysiphus task of winning an approximate equilibrium with the employing forces. The society which the New Deal and labour have jointly sought to transform was characterized, first, by an extreme entrenchment of the institutions of private property and private initiative and, second, by a governmental system structurally ineffective as an instrument of economic reform.

American capitalism emerged from the war confident of its unquestioned acceptance by an overwhelming majority of the American people. The mass of the American people were at one with President Harding in craving for "normalcy." But normalcy to them meant not just freedom from war-time control over private enterprise but also a repudiation of the reform movements of the decade before the war: Theodore Roosevelt's campaign against the "malefactors of great wealth" and Woodrow Wilson's effort at stemming "monopoly." The only demand bearing any resemblance to the nationalization and socialization programmes then resounding through Europe was the Plumb Plan for the railways—an unconscious gild socialist proposal by the railwaymen's unions bent on perpetuating their favourable war-time job-bargaining situation. Congress paid no attention to this demand and, moreover, in returning the railways to their private owners, instructed the Interstate Commerce Commission to base rates, not upon the "physical value" principle, to which Senator Robert M. La Follette of Wisconsin, the veteran "anti-monopoly" leader, thought he had converted the nation, but upon a vague and elastic "aggregate value."

[1] The author wishes to express his indebtedness for valuable assistance in the preparation of this chapter to the following students who were members of his graduate seminar at the University of Wisconsin: Samuel Berger, Arthur Ballansky, Lorace E. Catterson, Myron Gordon, Lucy Hancock, Ronald W. Haughton, Emily Hornblower, Alberta Lee, Saul Minkoff, Lionel Silverman, and Benjamin Stephansky.

The depression which broke in the summer of 1920 and lasted for two years failed to shake this joyous allegiance to capitalism. It but spurred Secretary of Commerce Herbert C. Hoover to throw himself into making capitalism "depression proof," by the application to the whole capitalist system of the principles of scientific management which Frederick W. Taylor and his school had worked out for individual productive establishments. So confident were the leaders of American capitalism that their structure rested upon solid foundations and was sound in its framework that whereas an earlier generation of American business men had shied at the terms "capitalism" or "capitalist system," both undoubtedly of socialist derivation, and preferred to speak of the American order as "triumphant democracy," the Hoover group virtually emulated the French Jacobins' espousal of the name "sans-culotte."

The brief post-war depression gave way to an industrial expansion of unheard-of proportions: a building and highway construction boom, automobile manufacturing on a gigantic scale, and an extensive railway rehabilitation activity. Capital exports, including three and a half billions to Germany, maintained a broad base for commodity export, and seemed further to justify investment. This mass investment, together with the drastic restricitions of immigration after 1924, counteracted on the labour market the simultaneous mechanization of production. The enormous rise in national income and diffused purchasing power created new job opportunities in other directions than manufacturing: service trades, marketing of goods to the consumer, and like occupations. Only two industries, coal mining and textiles, acknowledged as sick industries, marred the picture of prosperity—in addition to agriculture, which, not yet knowing the depths of the depression awaiting it in the early 'thirties, felt greatly "in the dumps." To the leaders of capitalism these depressed areas within the economic system, while a regrettable phenomenon, merely demonstrated the lot of the laggard in the scientific management procession, and solace was found in pointing out the "temporary" nature or the special causes of their distress: inter-sectional competition in textiles and coal mining and the post-war disarray of Europe affecting the demand for wheat, meat and cotton. Meantime, the fame of the American capitalist miracle was drawing business men and statesmen from abroad to study how America did it. In America, however, the certainty that the formula for eternal prosperity had at last been discovered was not confined to businessmen and engineers: middle-class groups and even leading sections of organized labour shared the same conviction. President Calvin Coolidge, nurtured in the tradition of New England's rural and small town individualism, personified this union of the contented middle groups and big business. So strong indeed was this alliance that the President was able to nullify by his veto power the law enacted in Congress by the pressure of the Mid-Western and Western farmer *bloc* aiming at price parity with prosperous industry, and to gain wide acclaim for doing so.

The chronic crisis in American capitalism since 1929 has at last legitimatized in the eyes of the American community several sorts of violations of the *laissez-faire* principle, but only as a comprehensive course of therapy for capitalism. Different economic groups variously defined the nature and duration of that course of therapy as well as its intensity. "Big business," especially the financiers, desired government to stop with the "sanation" of the banks and with a propping up of the leaning towers of the securities' structure of the leading corporations. The manufacturing interests demanded and, under the National Industrial Recovery Act, were given the authority to control prices. For the farmers a rise from the disastrous price level of 1932 to the much coveted "parity" with industry could only be effected through a government-instituted system of production control. The New Deal leadership well understood how to employ pecuniary and other inducements to instil in the traditionally individualistic farmer a willingness to submit to a production discipline and to achieve it through the efforts of 30,000 unpaid farmer committee men; in other words, to build a farmer social movement as part and parcel of the production control programme. Organized labour, unshackled by the prolonged depression from its traditional distrust of governmental interference in industrial relations, now demanded the creation of jobs by public action, both through a drastic reduction of the working week in all employments and by public works, and a publicly enforced "right to organize" and to bargain collectively. Furthermore, labour rejoiced to find the most important tenet of its own "political economy," that depressions are caused by the inadequate purchasing power of the wage earners, elevated to the status of an official doctrine. Nevertheless, it would be a mistake to assume that all of these demands for a government-imposed "discipline" on the several economic agents—bankers, manufacturers, farmers, employers, and wage earners—actually denoted a revolutionary departure from the traditional individualist ideology of the American people.

In a country in which 43·8 per cent. of the people are domiciled on farms or in communities of 2,500 or less, the position of capitalism is virtually determined by the attitude of the rural and semi-rural population. Two kinds of individualistic ideological patterns are found among American farmers: the one quite identical with the unqualified economic individualism of big business, the other an "anti-monopoly" pattern. In the north, Lake Michigan and the western boundary of Illinois roughly delimit the provinces of these patterns, while the rural south, allowing for the lesser political education of the people of that section, is solidly "anti-monopoly." Like the business man's ideology, "anti-monopoly" begins with the premise of abundance of economic opportunity, but whereas the former arrives at pure *laissez-faire*, the latter insists that individualism can be rendered safe for the small man only when monopoly power has been curbed. The curbing must be effected through the united political action of the "producing classes": the farmers, the honest business men, the labourers. The "people's government" must step in to restore to the producer the full range of economic opportunity which the monopolists—variously identified at various periods of the anti-monopoly movement as the railway companies, the "money trust," the meat trust, the produce exchange speculators—had fenced in with the aid of corrupt government. At bottom, however, anti-monopoly farmers are staunch upholders of private property and prone to find "monopoly" also in the "job control" by trade unions. At best, the "progressive" farmer only tolerates organized labour as a counterpoise to monopolistic business. But let labour become identified in his mind with a frontal attack on private property—through a sit-down strike, violent mass picketing or from a clash of "group customs" as, for instance, when the teamsters' union seeks to impose union job control upon farmers' co-operative creameries—and the farmer's individualism comes to life with lightning-like rapidity.[1]

In brief, eight years of depression, in which the army of the unemployed numbered at no time less than eight millions, appear to have altered the basic economic attitude of the American people only in the sense that numerous groups, in the middle and lower strata, without questioning capitalism as a system, have each come forth with a pragmatic cure so conceived that, beginning with an amelioration of its own position, it would result in a restoration to health of the American capitalist society as a whole. Under these conditions an eventual socialization of large American industry is not precluded, but in all likelihood it would come through the pressure of the immediate interests of wage earners, farmers, and small business men, and in the name of saving capitalism! Even as regards the more limited demand by organized labour for union recognition there is the ever present danger that the great middle classes, to-day seemingly benevolent onlookers, to-morrow will turn without warning into auxiliary troops of the anti-union employers. The change might result either from an accumulated displeasure over wage demands or from a sudden success of the employer propaganda identifying labour with subversive social movements.

If America's historical development has resulted in an environment potentially or at times actually hostile to labour movements, which even in their most restrained variants must function as campaigns against the absolute rights of private property, the structure of American government has made labour's task even harder by blocking the political highway to economic change. For under a system of one national and forty-eight state governments with the term "interstate commerce" until recently so interpreted that industrial relations came largely within the jurisdiction of the several states, the more progressive states were lockstepped with

[1] In December, 1937, the lobbyists of the Farm Bureau Federation, the largest farmer organization, helped defeat in Congress the Rooseveltian Wages and Hours Bill championed at that stage by the reputedly radical Committee for Industrial Organization.—*Christian Science Monitor*, December 28, 1937.

the more backward ones in the scope that they could give to labour legislation, since " driving capital out of the state " loomed as the penalty of too determined a pioneering. An even more serious handicap was the splitting up in each governmental unit of the power to legislate among the two houses of the legislature, the executive (through its veto power and leadership) and the judiciary (through its power of judicial review). Thus after many disappointments labour was forced to keep at a minimum its political action and to concentrate on the economic or industrial front. For on that front, while warfare was rough, with quarter rarely if ever given, fate did not hold in store for labour the discomfiture of possibly winning all the battles but losing the campaign through an adverse dictum of the " nine old men " of the United States Supreme Court.

But in the spring of 1937 this time-hallowed political system underwent a veritable revolution, a revolution which at long last has placed American labour on a near equality with labour in the European democracies as regards the wieldiness of government as a tool in its hands. This came by the United States Supreme Court[1] staging a " counter-reformation " to ward off the Roosevelt " Reformation." The " revolution " endowed the national government with a far-reaching jurisdiction over industrial relations (" manufacturing " having been declared to be " interstate commerce "), covering both the enactment of minimum standards as well as union-promotion activities by national boards. The court simultaneously lifted the heavy restraining hand upon the legislatures, national and state, of the " due process " clause of the constitution, which, as formerly interpreted, virtually embedded in that document the social philosophy of Herbert Spencer. Henceforth, disregarding the possibility of a reversion to type, political action ceased to be a blind alley for labour, so that, even the most " rightist " labour leadership will be bound by its very pragmatism to forsake the narrow " economism " of yore. All in

[1] N. L. R. B. *v.* Jones and Laughlin Steel Corp.; N.L.R.B. *v.* Friedman-Harry Marks Clothing Co., Inc.; N.L.R.B. *v.* Fruehauf Trailer Co.; Washington, Virginia and Maryland Coach Co. *v.* N.L.R.B.; and Associated Press *v.* N.L.R.B.; all decided April 12, 1937, 301 U.S. 1–147. Also Steward Machine Co. *v.* Davis, Helvering *v.* Davis, and Carmichael *v.* Southern Coal and Coke Co., all decided May 24, 1937, 301 U.S. 548, 619 and 495.

all, while matters have not changed for American labour so radically that it henceforth can afford to cease exercising the greatest care in the choice of its targets (for the suspiciousness of the middle classes as to its aims remains a vital factor), yet it is a double barrelled shotgun that it now has at hand.

In the following historical exposition the author's aim has been not so much a comprehensive presentation of the factual material in the usual chronological order as to point out wherein American labour action and the American industrial scene are unique and peculiar and to help the reader, non-American as well as American, to form judgments as to the probable future. With that in mind, the space was so allotted that events which held the contemporaries spell-bound both for their intrinsic drama and lasting effects have been treated briefly in favour of other events which, while less dramatic and with results apparently inconclusive, yet help to bring out the "environment" of the American labour struggle. The author feels free to confess to the absence of any sense of shame for having treated the Harding-Coolidge-Hoover segment as little better than "prehistory."

2. Trend of Strikes, 1919–37

The years with which our period opened and closed were the most outstanding strike years. The year 1919 gave an all time high[1] with 4,160,348 participating in 3,630 strikes; in 1937, according to officially made preliminary estimates a peak was reached in the number of strikes (4,533), with 1,855,864 participating. Next to these as a strike year was 1922 with 1,612,512 striking. An all time low in the numbers striking was 1930 with 102,975. The biggest strike periods were 1919–23 and 1933–37, with 1923–32 an era of quiet. On the basis of man-days idle (reported only since 1927) 1937 led with over 28 million contrasting with 3 million in 1930.[2]

The following industries—textiles, building, mining, foundries, lumber and metal trades[3]—named in the order of importance

[1] This explains why this section begins one year before the beginning of the remainder of the book.

[2] However, there were twenty-six million idle man-days in 1927, due to strikes in coal mining.

[3] The metal trades were usually in the fifth place in the 'twenties.

—were responsible for 50–60 per cent. of all strikes, 1919–33. Since 1934 mining and metal trades contributed considerably fewer strikes, while trade, lumber, food, domestic and personal service have risen in importance. Textiles were far in the lead every year, 1919–33, with 15–39 per cent. of all strikes, except in 1921, when building and printing and paper ranked first and second, and in 1930, when building again took first place. However, building was not among the first five industries in either workers involved or man-days idle during 1934–37.

Four eastern industrial states—New York, Pennsylvania, New Jersey, Massachusetts—accounted for over 50 per cent. of all strikes, 1919–34. New York alone was responsible during 1919–37 for 15–27 per cent. During 1934–37 New York and Pennsylvania together accounted for 30-35 per cent. of the workers involved and for 24–28 per cent. of the total man-days of idleness. Among the cities New York held the first place each year, 1919–37, with 10–19 per cent. of the total of strikes and also led in numbers involved and man-days idle. Philadelphia and Chicago were usually in second and third places; Boston was important in the earlier years, while San Francisco, Cleveland and Akron have recently risen in importance.

Wages and hours were the main issues in about 50 per cent. of all strikes, 1919–33, and union matters in 20–30 per cent. In the strikes since 1934 union matters were the main issues in about 50 per cent. and wages and hours in 32–39 per cent. Except in 1935, when 60 per cent. were engaged in strikes over wages and hours, the same proportions held in the number of workers involved.

Between 1919 and 1934, 25–36 per cent. of the strikes ended in favour of the strikers, except in 1921 when only 17 per cent. ended in their favour. In the same period 26–46 per cent. of the strikes were definitely lost and 14–26 per cent. ended in compromise (except in 1919 when 36 per cent. were compromised and in 1933 when 37 per cent. ended in compromise). In 1934, 62 per cent. of all strikers won partial gains. Since 1935, 44–49 per cent. of all strikes have resulted in substantial gains to the strikers and only 14–17 per cent. were complete failures. Also 41–54 per cent. of all the workers engaged in strikes since 1935 won substantial gains. During 1934–37, 38–50 per cent. of the strikes involving wages and hours resulted in substantial gains and 36–52 per cent. of the strikes fought over union matters were substantially won.

In 72–86 per cent. of all strikes between 1920 and 1932 labour organizations were involved at the time of origin, but only 56 per cent. in the banner strike year 1919, and 57 per cent. in 1933. During 1934–37 labour organizations were initially involved in all but 6–8 per cent. of the strikers. During 1934–36 the American Federation of Labour was involved (not necessarily at the time of origin) in 76–77 per cent. of all strikes and these strikes accounted for 69–88 per cent. of the total number of strikers. In 1936, the C.I.O. was connected with 6 per cent. of all strikes having 15 per cent. of the number involved.

The intense strike activity during 1919–22 paralleled the post-war prosperity with its soaring cost of living, the collapse that followed, and the recovery in 1922. The next and quieter period, 1923–29, coincided with a high level of industrial production and employment and high real wages resulting from a return to the war-time money wages coupled with a lower level in the cost of living. The quietest years, 1930–32, the years of the Great Depression, saw labour's bargaining power shrink to the vanishing point but with the falling cost of living holding up the real wages of those who remained employed. The return to the strike on a mass scale[1] during 1933–37 was the direct consequence of the change of America's political climate with the advent of the New Deal.

3 Post-War Militancy

The outbreak of the European war relieved the depression in American industry and furnished the opportunity to American unionism to resume an advance, which, except for the miners' and garment makers' unions, had been stopped nearly a decade earlier. The conquest of the eight-hour day in the metal trades and its spectacular establishment in the train operating trades in the railway service by congressional enactment in

[1] Mention should be made of the "general strikes" during this period. In addition to the one in San Francisco, of which more below, there were such strikes in Terre Haute, Indiana, and Pekin, Illinois—in sympathy with striking local groups.

1916 to avoid a national railway strike, marked this phase of labour's advance. With America's entry into the war in April 1917, unionism was elevated at a stroke to the position of a recognized national institution, an elevation symbolized by President Wilson's journey to Buffalo in November 1917 to address the convention of the American Federation of Labour. With the aid of the government, unionization spread apace: to the railway shops, office and maintenance services, to the meat-packing industry, to the metal trades, now the munitions industries *par excellence*, to say nothing of the trades in which unionism had already been strong before the war. When the Armistice came, American labour, like labour in Europe, was poised for the attainment of that democracy in industry which the national leadership had solemnly promised it in the course of the " war for democracy " but also was restless from a more prosaic cause, the lag of wages behind the soaring cost of living together with the havoc wrought with established wage " differentials " by the uneven advance of wages in the several industries and grades of service within industries during the hectic war years. The union leadership now discovered that the very extension of the agreement system, which was in its eyes the biggest gain out of the war, had tossed into its lap in consequence of the wage stabilization written into those agreements, the problem of " insurgency " in the ranks. The recently swept-in new membership lacked the training in orderly industrial government possessed by older unionists. But even among the latter devotion to " due process " cooled when the purchasing power of their agreement wages was waning under their very eyes and especially, when they saw other workers unbound by any agreements taking full advantage of the heavy demand for labour begotten by the post-war prosperity spurt. Post-war militancy such as unauthorized or " out-law " strikes against existing agreements and their inevitable defenders, the union leaders, attained dramatic proportion in the printing pressmen's trade and on the railways, where a switchmen strike in April 1920 tied up the Chicago railway yards for two weeks. True to the practice of American unions, forever fearful that an unauthorized strike, unless suppressed, might become the beginning of a " dual " union[1],

[1] See below in section on the " Civil War in American Labour."

the union officials rushed in in both instances with *cadres* of union strikebreakers and, aided by the employers and the government, ended the revolt. To insure against repetition they saw to it that the " ringleaders " were refused employment.

From the standpoint of effect on the public the two most outstanding manifestations of the post-war militant spirit were the Seattle general strike and the Boston police strike, both in 1919. The Seattle strike began as a shipyard strike for higher wages by the Metal Trades Council. The strikers' ire was aroused by the rumour that the employers were willing to yield, but were coerced by the chairman of the Emergency Fleet Corporation, who threatened to cancel their government contracts or deny them the necessary steel. The Seattle Central Labour Council called for a vote by all unions on the matter of a general sympathetic strike. The appeal stressed the dependence of the prosperity of all the Seattle trades on the high wages of the 32,000 shipyard workers. At the outset the Central Labour Council ceded its power to the General Strike Committee whereupon for four days following February 6, 1919, the city knew but one authority, that of the General Strike Committee. For instance, the hospital laundry wagons were allowed to operate, but were compelled to carry the sign, " Hospital Laundry Only. By Order of Strike Committee."

The general strike was brought to an end by the concerted efforts of the international union officials of the trades affected, apprehensive over the breach of contract by their locals out on this sympathetic strike. The strike was not " revolution," as wishful thinkers on the " left " and scheming politicians on the " right " tried to represent it, but a manifestation of a solidarity wider than in the usual strike but not unknown to America before or after. Yet it cannot be gainsaid as evidence of profound social unrest.

The Boston Police Strike, indirectly the cause of the eventual elevation of Calvin Coolidge, then Governor of Massachusetts, to the Presidency of the United States, was a similar non-revolutionary wage conflict, although it is conceivable why to many the spectacle of the streets of a big city deserted by the guardians of the law[1] and therefore for a short time the prey of

[1] The striking policemen thought they had given ample warning to the authorities to call out the state troops to maintain order.

hoodlums and marauders, appeared like the American counterpart of the Bolshevik revolution.

The attempt to unionize the steel industry which culminated in a strike by more than 300,000 in September 1919 was an "authorized" militancy as contrasted with these unauthorized examples. It was begun under a mild wartime political climate but had to stand the crucial test when, with the war ended and the communist scare, a severe glaciation set in. The effort radiated out of the Chicago Federation of Labour, where John Fitzpatrick, its president, and his then intimate friend William Z. Foster, having entrenched unionism in the packing industry with the aid of a government administrator, turned to do the same to steel. Foster, a former syndicalist of the French rather than the American Industrial Workers of the World pattern, appeared to have gone over to the Gompersian variety of a labour movement and, with Gompers' blessing, became secretary and leading genius of the National Committee for the Organizing of the Iron and Steel Industry. The Committee had co-operating with it twenty-four international unions with jurisdictions in the steel industry. The plan was to organize by mass movement methods but later on to group the recruits by crafts and to join them together into local steel councils analogous to building trades councils.

The response was a tribute to Foster's organizing genius as well as an unmistakable register of the degree of unrest in that industry, in which unionism had been completely banned since 1909 and partially so since 1901. But the "co-operating" twenty-four internationals scarcely deserved that designation: if they were not indifferent they were altogether too conscious of their prerogatives, like the Amalgamated Association of Iron, Steel and Tin Workers with a jurisdiction enormous on paper which forever met the Committee's plans by "reserving freedom of action."

Finally the demands were drawn up as follows: The right of collective bargaining; reinstatement of discharged union men; one day's rest in seven; the abolition of the twenty-four hour shift; an American living wage; double pay for overtime; the check-off and seniority; and the abolition of company unions and physical examinations.

It goes without saying that the die-hard steel industrialists refused even to meet the union's Conference Committee. Meantime, the punitive discharges of union members assumed such proportions that even the twenty-four internationals could not withhold their sanction of a strike. The strike began on September 23 and affected every steel producing region. The Committee claimed 343,000 on strike. There was hardly a strategem of strike smashing left untried by the employers, notably the United States Steel Corporation—from a complete withdrawal in Pennsylvania of the right of peaceable assembly and the pitiless riding down of the strike pickets by the state police, whom labour had nicknamed the Cossacks, to a most widespread press and poster propaganda identifying this movement for union recognition and for the establishment of one day's rest in seven with red revolution. The men held out for six weeks at the cost of eighteen lives, and then mass surrenders began. Steel was to remain open-shop until 1937. In 1921 the equally trustified meat packing industry similarly vindicated the open shop by nullifying the war-time gains of the Amalgamated Meat Cutters' Union.

President Wilson from his sickbed had tried to prolong the war-time truce between the employers and labour beyond the war's duration. However, the Industrial Conference he summoned in October 1919 broke up on the issue of collective bargaining, the employers defending the "open shop" which they insisted was negatived by the resolution moved by Gompers stressing the wage earners' right to be represented by "representatives of their own choosing." But the open shop campaign hardly needed a prelude of this sort.

The employers' campaign to liquidate labour's war-time gains, like the open shop campaign of 1902–07, was conducted on the front of ideals and sentiments as well as on the more tangible industrial one. The campaign was designed to display as its objective the return to time-hallowed American principles, the inalienable right of every American to enter any trade or business he chose, to accept employment under conditions satisfactory to himself without interference from the union business agent. An appeal was made to the more conservative farmers' organizations as well as unorganized farmers to battle shoulder to shoulder with the employers for the "American Plan." The American Plan movement, powerfully favoured by an anti-red hysteria which was sweeping the country, purported to abolish the " un-American " closed shop, but as in previous open shop crusades, the destruction of unionism was its real objective. By the autumn of 1920 the country was covered with a network of open shop organizations. The outstanding successes of the open shop campaign were in the building trades in San Francisco and Chicago. In San Francisco the veritable labour barony established by P. H. McCarthy, the boss of the building trades council, seems to have succumbed more to a sudden " crisis of self-confidence " than to assault from without, although it had to face the united strength of that city's financial and business groups. In Chicago, too, the long dominant building trades suffered defeat in conjunction with a unique arbitration procedure before Judge K. M. Landis who certainly went beyond his terms of reference when he made the union working rules, then under widespread assault on the ground of their restrictiveness, a matter to arbitrate in the same dispute. When the unions rebelled, they were faced by a militant " Landis Award Committee." It took these unions five or six years to liquidate the Landis incident. The building trades, so far as the public was concerned, were the heel of the labour Achilles, resulting from exposures by legislative committees, notably of New York, of collusion between corrupt employer association and equally corrupt labour union leadership. Moreover, the public has become most painfully aware of the phenomenon of "racketeering."

For the purpose of exact classification, although not of differentiation of moral judgment, one should distinguish between " hold up " unionism and labour racketeering. When a union leader who has sprung from his group and on the whole represents more or less successfully its interests, is simultaneously engaged in blackmailing some employers under threat of calling a strike, he is a " hold-up " unionist. When a rank outsider, mostly from the criminal class, coerces a group of workers to join his " union " and proceeds to batten on their contributions, without troubling to give them any protection in return, in addition to levying blackmail on the employer, he is a labour racketeer. It is the latter variety that the 'twenties contributed to America's social types and in the actual situation unionism was the victim of the country's "noble experiment" rather than the original breeding ground of that type. When prohibition was decreed in a country which never excelled in law enforcement, a menace was created to every existing type of association. An illicit traffic of staggering proportions soon sprang up with property interests running into hundreds of millions but without any protection to such property from rival "bootleggers" by the established agencies of government.

The inevitable consequence was the creation of private armies of gunmen to protect one's property as well as for conquest of more "territory." However, when one important industry is brought under the law of the gun and the bomb, it rarely stops with that industry. The racketeer in search of new provinces of opportunity invades (the expression is "muscle in") other fields, especially fields in which violence has been endemic. Labour unions and trade associations in the most competitive industries with numerous small productive units, soon become such added provinces. When all is said, the wonder is not that a number of unions have thus been taken over but that relatively so few of them have. It would be nearer to the truth if without condoning the malpractices of union officials—and they have ranged from embezzlement even to murder—one should recognize that, by and large, unions, which have offered strenuous resistance often at the risk of their leaders' life, have been far more frequently American society's self-appointed policemen than they have been racketeers' tools.

On the railways the open shop movement took a more sinuous course than in the other industries, discovering an ally, at the crucial turn, in the Railway Labour Board set up by the Transportation Act of 1920. The railway unions emerged from the era of government administration which lasted until April 1920, well endowed with favourable "working rules" protective of the men's rights and of the unions' status. Since a wage increase was long overdue the first act of the Railway Labour Board was to award a generous raise in July. However, with the speedy collapse of prosperity the Board, believing that a revival could be had only through wage and cost deflation, made an immediate turn about and began to help the railways reduce costs both by wage cuts and revision of the "working rules." The four strong brotherhoods of the train service personnel were treated sparingly, but the weaker and more recently unionized shop craft, office and maintenance unions were given the full brunt. In addition, many of the railways found a way of escaping from such working rules as were effective by "contracting their work out." The Board condemned this practice, but was powerless to stop it. A 10 per cent. wage cut, effective July 1, 1922, coming on top of an equal earlier reduction, forced the hands of the leaders of the unions grouped under the Railway Employees' Department to call a nation-wide strike of 400,000. From the first the leaders knew that they were beaten. The strike continued till the end of August when it ended in the so-called Baltimore Agreement in which a minority group of railway executives, headed by Daniel Willard[1], granted what amounted to an amnesty to the striking unions. The majority of the railways, headed by the Pennsylvania Railway Company, replaced them with company unions.

Simultaneously with the serious weakening of railway unionism came the decision of the United States Supreme Court in the Coronado case holding unions responsible for damages to employees resulting from labour disputes as if they were formally incorporated bodies. It followed a succession of decisions begun in 1921 which interpreted out of existence the alleged immunities from the injunction procedure granted unions by the Clayton Act of 1914. This brought labour hard against the necessity of trying a newer and more effective method of political action.

In early American labour history political action was paramount. It was the accompaniment and logical consequence of the aspiration to escape from the wage system into self-employment—self-employment as an individual as on the open frontier or "collectively" through co-operative workshops—which was believed barred by "monopoly." Hence labour was eager to join with the farmers and other producing

[1] Willard was and is President of the Baltimore and Ohio Railway Company. It was with this generous settlement as a background that the "union-management co-operative plan" developed on this railway after 1923. As it enlisted the union men in a campaign to raise the road's efficiency and to reduce costs, the "Baltimore and Ohio Plan" was famous during the efficiency-minded 'twenties.

classes in a political anti-monopoly crusade, " greenbackism," " populism," free silver, etc. However, with the victory of the American Federation of Labour over the Knights of Labour (the last and most formidable of the " escape the wage system " movements) in the late 'eighties, independent political action by labour came under a cloud : the Gompers leadership was willing to accept the wage system provided it could get " union recognition " and union job control. This meant concentrating on the economic front and holding down to a minimum political action with its danger of sowing disunion in a labour group lacking the cementing influence of class consciousness. Thus arose American labour's characteristic " economism."

Later when the unions came under attack by the courts and the politicians were discovered deaf to their plea for succour, the earlier " economism " was somewhat modified by the addition of a limited " reward your friends and punish your enemies " strategy. It was in effect carrying the collective bargaining method into politics—labour as a collectivity bargaining with the political parties as similar collective entities for anti-court injunction and similar legislation. With the advent of the open primary, under which nominations on party tickets were no longer made by the party " bosses " but each individual candidate was free to appeal directly to the electorate for his nomination, labour as well as other organized groups were given the opportunity to alter the former two-sided collective bargaining into a one-sided one (labour bargaining with individual politicians) or better yet to nominate their own trusted men on the ticket of the party which was most likely to win on election day. This was the basis of the bi-partisan " blocs," labour, farmer or other, which so exasperated regular party men like President Calvin Coolidge, when he found that Representatives and Senators of his own party looked not to him, their party leader, but to " organized minority groups " holding the balance of power in their constituencies, as controlling their political fortunes. However, this method is ineffective as regards nominations for President and the framing of national party platforms, since the nominating conventions notwithstanding that their delegates are chosen by the primary election method, continue under the control of the party leaders, with whom consequently labour is obliged to continue the two-sided collective bargaining arrangement. Furthermore, in a presidential election the interests concerned are so variegated and above all the task of selecting the best available candidate is so delicate that the job is of necessity left to experts, the outstanding politicians of the party. These, however, until liberalism had become endowed by the New Deal with a formidable mass attraction, inclined to conservatism both in platform and candidate.

" Pressure politics " of the above description means maintaining a " lobby " in Washington, a thorough familiarity with the alignments in every Congressman's and Senator's constituency and an adequate block of voters in the several constituencies willing to bestow reward or administer punishment at the order of the national organization. It means, better still, a permanent organization with branches in the localities.

In the situation created by the sharpened need for relief from judicial interference following the Coronado decision, labour's active instrument was the Conference for Progressive Political Action formed in February 1922. The railway unions were in the forefront since their wages and working conditions now depended on governmental decisions. In this the unions within the Railway Employees' Department of the A.F. of L. were at one with the train service brotherhoods. Other international unions of socialist antecedents, like the garment unions, joined primarily for idealistic reasons. The strategy was to establish local " conferences " but to give them perfect freedom to act within the primaries of the old parties or by third ticket nominations.

The socialists, who were admitted into the Conference, came in in the belief that under their prodding it might give birth to a Labour Party. However, the union leaders were content with the result of the 1922 congressional elections in which the method of infiltrating the old party tickets was employed. In the spring of 1924 the independent candidacy for President of Senator Robert M. La Follette, the veteran anti-monopoly fighter, became an issue. The re-nomination of Coolidge was a foregone conclusion. When the Democrats nominated the conservative, John W. Davis, the support of a third ticket by the Conference became inevitable and the endorsement of La Follette only slightly less so.

La Follette invited the progressive groups to follow his leadership. He quickly shook off the communists who, having captured the farmer-labour convention in St. Paul, offered him the doubtful gift of their endorsement.

On July 4 the Progressive convention met at Cleveland, and nominated La Follette, who sent his son with the platform on which he meant to make his run. For Vice-President, again at La Follette's request, the Democratic Senator Burton K. Wheeler of Montana was nominated. Also in compliance with La Follette's wishes the La Follette-Wheeler ticket was not to be a third party ticket but an independent one.

The La Follette candidacy was endorsed by the convention of the Socialist Party. The Executive Council of the American Federation of Labour faced a grave decision. Traditionally unwilling to lend its strength to the building up of third parties and independent candidacies, it yet had no choice in this campaign where both parties had nominated candidates unfriendly to labour. Gompers threw his influence on the side of the La Follette candidacy. On August 2, 1923, the Executive Council denounced both parties: "Both the Republican and Democratic national party conventions flaunted the desires of labour, the Republican convention in an arrogant manner, the Democratic convention by that evasiveness which is the customary mark of insincerity." After announcing that La Follette and Wheeler were endorsed, Gompers reconciled it with his past political policy by stressing that the Federation had neither committed itself to nor identified itself with the doctrines of any other group supporting the La Follette candidacy—meaning the socialists. Nor did it signify that the Federation had committed itself to a third party. The alliance with La Follette and his other supporters was only for the present election.

La Follette received the unqualified support of the railway organizations, both within and outside the Federation, and the socialists. The other unions, on the whole, supported him too. In the Congressional districts the Federation's old policy of supporting old party candidates was continued not only by the Federation but for the most part also by the Conference for Progressive Political Action. The New York Trades and Labour Assembly endorsed La Follette, but the Executive

Council, closely allied with Tammany Hall, arbitrarily rescinded the endorsement on the eve of the election.

The results of the election, in which only slightly less than five million votes were cast for La Follette, were acclaimed by the socialists and the advocates of a third party as a most promising beginning. It was largely a city vote; for instance, La Follette carried Cleveland, Ohio. Only in his own State, Wisconsin, which he carried, and in North Dakota did he draw heavily from the farmers. To the leaders of the railway unions and of the American Federation of Labour, who measured the outcome from the standpoint of its immediate results regarding employment conditions on the railways and the labour injunction, the experiment was a disappointment. Gompers found solace in the thought that the five million votes cast for the independent ticket would teach the old parties a salutary lesson. To the railway unions, desirous above all for a return to free collective bargaining unhampered by the Railroad Labour Board, the path that beckoned now was that of an understanding with the railway managements, equally opposed to the Board, to effect its removal by pooled pressure on Congress and the Executive. This was consummated in the Railway Labour Act of 1926.

The Conference for Progressive Political Action held its meeting in February 1925. The unions, including the railroad brotherhoods, were opposed to a third party movement. The Conference was liquidated.

Just as in Britain in the 'twenties the coal miners' struggle epitomized the whole industrial struggle, so in America the labour history of that decade is most graphically drawn in a picture of the vicissitudes of the coal miners' union. The history of American coal unionism from the Armistice to the New Deal is, as in England, the history of unionism in an industry suffering from excess productive capacity but complicated, in addition, by bitter strife within the union.

At the end of the last century the United Mine Workers had succeeded in establishing an agreement system in the so-called Central Competitive Field whereby through a skilfully adjusted wage rate structure the market and job opportunities were shared by the several producing districts in that field. In reality this stabilization of competition rested upon the shoulders of the union. Subsequently when the southern districts, first West Virginia and then Kentucky, which belonged to the same competitive area, favoured by geological advantages, sprang into prominence as producing districts and showed determination to keep the union out in order not to be brought in under the " communism of opportunity " scheme, the union was compelled by its very obligation to the operators in the unionized districts to lay constant siege to this recalcitrant region. The war was fought, as mining wars have always been fought in America, without the benefit of international law, the union pitting its fighting contingents against private employer armies together with employer-controlled state forces. Except for short intervals the union was held at bay.

The world war benefited both contestants: the southern operators expanded their mines beyond the other operators but the union likewise expanded, although not to any great extent in the southern districts. The world war ending, the mining war was due to be resumed, even with increased ferocity, owing to the chronic depression soon to descend upon the industry.

For a time the basic weakness of the union's position was concealed by the general though short-lived post-war prosperity. It was that which accounted for the union's victory in the autumn of 1919, resulting in a substantial wage increase, although the government itself, abandoning its war-time benevolence and stooping to casuistry, moved for an injunction to declare the strike illegal. The union was likewise successful in the biggest strike in its history, in 1922, when both the anthracite and bituminous branches were simultaneously on strike. The agreement system was preserved as well as the high wages and when, in 1924, the so-called Jacksonville agreement was signed to run for a three-year period, so as to insure a long time stability, hopes ran high and the leadership of John L. Lewis, President since 1919, seemed triumphant.

Lewis' leadership has been from the beginning a high-handed one. He knew how to throw back every " insurgent " attack, including that led by the redoubtable and popular Alex Howat of Kansas, who went to jail in defiance of the Kansas law of compulsory arbitration of 1919. At this period Lewis personified union " bossism " to " leftists " and progressives in and out the labour movement. He was contrasted with Sidney Hillman, President of the Amalgamated Clothing Workers, "progressive" both in the sense of working-class consciousness and in the sense of his "efficiency consciousness", unique in a labour leader, which moved him to initiate technological change in his industry. Lewis' slogan was "No Backward Step," meaning in wages and union job control, and his mind was occupied not with efficiency schemes but with fighting strategy.

Lewis' fighting instinct soon found employment. No sooner had the Jacksonville "long peace" been inaugurated than defections began on the employer side under the duress of southern competition. These assaults from without were followed by assaults upon Lewis' leadership from within the union. District 12, of Illinois, the strongest district and led by ambitious rivals of Lewis, was the hot-bed of insurrection. There is little need to give here the peripeteia of that struggle. Suffice it to say that in its process, the agreement system for the whole Central Competitive Field was lost as well as most of the union's membership strength, and that by 1932 a dual organization, the Progressive Miners of America, arose over a considerable portion of the Illinois coal domain.

The militancy of the 'twenties, both industrial and political, was merely a defensive war against the most self-confident employer group in the world. It was in the employer camp that a spirit of joyous aggressiveness coupled with inventiveness was found. America was to dispense with unionism not only because it is hurtful to the employer and harmful to the public but also because it is unnecessary to labour. America was to remain exceptional among industrial countries by offering in "welfare capitalism" a perfect reconciliation of all interests concerned.

4. "Welfare Capitalism"

The most characteristic employer device to realize an American "exceptionalism" in industrial relations has been the "company union."

In spite of their Protean nature, company unions did retain

fundamental similarities. Recent and more systematic studies of company unionism provide conclusions from which a "substantive" company union type can be derived.[1]

Such a union was established for the purpose of integrating management and labour into one harmonious productive entity. It was therefore particularistic, with its entire force of interest devoted to a given company. It had no outside affiliations, although it might be conjoined with similar unions of the same company, or, very rarely, of other companies.

The organizational discipline of membership requirements, general membership meetings and dues-paying were very informal. Membership stipulations were formulated by the management. Belonging to the union was not a necessary condition of employment, although the management often requires automatic membership of its employees.

Treasury funds were rarely accumulated by the company union. However, where a small dues payment was required, and a treasury fund existed, it was allotted for welfare and recreational purposes. Never was the fund used for the services of an outside agent or representative. In fact a representative had to be an employee in good standing and was reimbursed by the employer for time lost.

Membership meetings, invariably held on company property and in company time, were infrequent and irregular. They were either annual, bi-annual, monthly, or call meetings, rarely convening as often as each week.

There was seldom a written trade agreement outlining the respective rights and duties of the company union and the employer. The items discussed by the representatives of each were subject to final action by the employer. These items, in their order of frequency in discussions were: individual grievances; health and safety; general wage changes; wage rates for specific occupations; changes in hours; general rules; methods of sharing work; discharges; rules of seniority; and types of payment.

[1] The conclusions embodied in the description of the "substantive" company union type are from studies conducted by the Bureau of Labour Statistics of the U.S. Dept. of Labour, published in the *Monthly Labour Review*, October 1935, and December 1935; and from a study conducted by the Twentieth Century Fund, published in *Labour and Government*, ed. by A. L. Bernheim and D. van Dores, 1935, pp. 96-113.

Major controversies might be subject to arbitration, if both parties agreed, but the latter restriction rendered an arbitration clause a " paper concession." The right of hiring and firing was the exclusive prerogative of the employer, who reserved also the right to modify or revise the company union plan. Termination of the plan was provided for if both employees and employer were so agreed.

The type of company union described above was found most frequently in companies employing 500 to 1,000; but a far greater number of employees were included in the smaller number of company unions found in companies employing 5,000 or more. This was true because the company union was more at home in the technologically advanced mass production industries, including chemicals, iron and steel, transportation equipment, machinery and rubber products. In non-manufacturing industries, the company union was most often found in public utilities, and, less frequently, in railroad and motor transportation.

The war period was significant in the development of company unionism for several reasons. In order to insure increased and efficient production and industrial peace, the war economy was mobilized by the War Labour Board and other federal boards established in the fuel and coal, transportation, copper mine and shipbuilding industries. In their labour policy these boards assured the established trade, and company unions their existence, but sponsored " shop committees " where no unions existed. This policy, at first resisted by employers, was later accepted to offset a restive labour movement, when the " shop committees " were seen to be effective substitutes for trade unions. Thus, in widely acclimatising industry to company unionism, and in emphasizing industrial efficiency, the war administration helped create the setting for " Welfare Capitalism "—the post-war decade of mature company unionism.

Post-war capitalism faced an expanding labour movement which doubled its membership between 1917 and 1920. But instead of the forceful ripostes of the earlier " supply and demand " capitalism, " welfare capitalism " resorted to methods of inducement. It offered a planned economy on the principles of " scientific management and long range planning."

Such an economy promised the worker more than those advantages indirectly secured by the trade union's restrictive working rules: the eight-hour day; accurately determined wage rates safe from arbitrary cuts; profit sharing and stock distribution; hygienic and pleasant surroundings; regular employment; personnel management to insure freedom from arbitrary discharge; group insurance, life and disability insurance, and old age pensions.

"Welfare Capitalism" enjoyed a decade of success, for it seemed to fulfil its lofty promises. It was greatly assisted by the material rise in real wages. So great was its success that the American Federation of Labour could not find the prosperity years of the 'twenties favourable to its growth, and yielded to a flourishing company union movement which more than trebled its membership between 1919 and 1927.[1]

"Welfare Capitalism" was continued by a number of the largest corporations into the depression and after the stock market crash of 1929 big business made a genuine effort to fulfil its promise to President Hoover to preserve the purchasing power of the wage earning group by refraining from wage

Period	*Number of employees having wage changes*	
	Increases	*Decreases*
Last third of 1929	20,930	4,102
First third of 1930	23,958	19,489
Second third of 1930	4,607	62,185
Last third of 1930	1,096	39,307
First third of 1931	2,396	127,648
Second third of 1931	1,908	125,999
Last third of 1931	312	401,040
First third of 1932	1,278	390,775

reductions.[2] For instance, the United States Steel Corporation,

[1] *Collective Bargaining Through Employee Representation*, a study made by the National Industrial Conference Board, N.Y., 1933. The growth in company unions in this period was from 196 in 1919 to 869 in 1928; membership in company unions increased from 403,765 in 1919 to 1,547,766 in 1928.

[2] The above table is a summary of the number of employees affected by increases and decreases of wages by four month periods as compiled by Dr. Solomon Ozer, from the *Monthly Labour Review*, from October 1929 to July 1932.

which prior to the New Deal period practised "Welfare Capitalism" without, however, resorting to the company union, did not cut hourly rates until August 1931, and adopted a "share the work" policy which when business was at the lowest ebb gave income of a sort to about 75,000 more workers than would otherwise have been employed. In addition "each employee's situation was continuously but unobtrusively checked by plant committees, visiting nurses, Good Fellowship Clubs and other employee organizations, and whenever hardship appeared, the Corporation gave direct relief or credit or secured it through the Good Fellowship Clubs." Employees were provided with land, fertilizer, seed and tools for gardening. In 1932 the employees worked 80,475 individual home gardens and community plots and raised produce to the value of $1,213,503·92. The Corporation furnished instructors to teach housewives how to can vegetables. Between January 1930 and December 31, 1933, the Corporation spent $219,611,123 for improvements and betterments of its plants.[1]

Nevertheless the depression was *ipso facto* the failure of "Welfare Capitalism," and its symbol, the company union, has persistently been attacked since 1933. The New Deal administration asserted an interest in an independent and self-determined labour movement as essential to recovery and restoration of purchasing power. The New Deal was first heralded in industrial relations in the National Industrial Recovery Act (N.I.R.A.) passed in June 1933 and administered by the National Recovery Administration (N.R.A.).

5. Labour and the New Deal

(1) *N.R.A. and Labour*

The most indisputable gain under the National Industrial Recovery Act was the removal from industry of about 150,000 children under sixteen, including about 50,000 from hazardous employment. But the corner-stone of its labour programme was re-employment as a result of a drastic reduction of the working

[1] Taylor, Myron C., *Ten Years of Steel*, Extension of Remarks at Annual Meeting of Stockholders, Hoboken, N.J., April 4, 1938.

week, and a minimum wage for each industry. The shortening of hours resulted in an increased employment estimated at the most at 1,750,000 or a re-employment of about one-sixth of the unemployed. On the matter of the minimum wage there was the drawback of the background of the depression wage level and the difficult problem of differentials, especially geographic. It is difficult to make any general statement as to the effect of the minimum wage endeavour, because each industry code had its own peculiar problems and incidental diversities. It is nevertheless obvious that the provisions left much to be desired in the way of effective minimum wage policies.

Some measurement of how labour's earnings fared under the N.R.A. may be gathered from the following data. Average hourly earnings in manufacturing as a whole rose from 41·8c in June 1933 to 57·1c in May 1935 when the Act was declared unconstitutional.[1] The index of per capita weekly earnings rose from 96·7 in June 1933 to 103·0 in October of the same year and after a dip during November 1933–January 1934 and a rise during the spring of 1934, followed by another slight dip, it rose to 117·2 in May 1935[2]. Labour's share in the total national income (" Wages and Salaries ") rose from 67·7 per cent. in 1933 to 68·9 per cent. in 1935, or, including "compensation for injuries, pensions and relief," from 71·7 per cent. to 74·0 per cent. In absolute figures wages and salaries rose from $32,432 millions to $38,755 millions and, including the added items, from $34,353 millions to $41,631 millions.[3] Offsetting this rise in the money income of wage earners of 12 to 14 per cent. (estimated very roughly), there was a rise of about 8 per cent. in the cost of living, from an index of 129·8 in June 1933 to 140·2 in July 1935.[4] Output per man-hour in all manufacturing industries rose 15 per cent. between 1932 and 1936 and labour cost per unit of output 6 per cent.[5]

It must be realized, however, that the entire N.I.R.A. programme was operated as a co-partnership between the govern-

[1] " Labour in Depression and Recovery, " in *Monthly Labour Review*, December 1937, pp. 10–11.

[2] *Ibid.*

[3] Simon Kuznets, *National Income and Capital Formation, A Preliminary Report*, National Bureau of Economic Research, 1937, New York, pp. 24–25.

[4] " Cost of Goods Purchased by Wage Earners and Lower Salaried Workers in thirty-two Large Cities," *Handbook of Labour Statistics*, Edition of 1936, p. 81.

[5] *Labour in Depression and Recovery*, p. 22.

ment and the trade associations with labour merely permitted to offer recommendations on the labour provisions of the codes. Even in coal mining, in which the union leadership was quickest to perceive and grasp the New Deal opportunity, the " Code of Fair Competition for the Bituminous Coal Industry " originally set up six divisional code authorities, all of whose members (except one, with no vote, appointed by the President of the United States) were representatives of coal operators and without a single labour representative on the National Bituminous Industrial Board. Only after a formal protest by William Green and John L. Lewis who declared that " the Labour boards are meaningless and unsatisfactory to labour "[1] was the latter placed on the national board, the other fifteen representing the operators.

It was thus an irony of fate that while the New Deal Administration sought to promote independent unionism,[2] its most ambitious enactment, the N.I.R.A., in effect turned into a potent stimulant of " company unionism," which reversed the decline of 1930 to 1932[3] and brought an increase of 180 per cent. in the first six months of the new law.[4]

The United States Bureau of Labour Statistics found in 1935 that of the 14,725 firms reporting, 30·2 per cent. of the total number of workers were in establishments dealing with trade unions, 19·9 per cent. in establishments having company unions, 7·4 per cent. in establishments with both trade and company unions, and the remainder in establishments dealing solely through " individual bargaining." The percentage of workers in establishments dealing through company unions were: in manufacturing as a whole 24·9 where there were only company unions and 8·5 where there were both trade unions and company unions; in public utilities the figures were respectively 15·2 and 6·8; in retail trade 5·8 and 9·7. In the durable goods industries the company union obtained more heavily than in non-durable goods industries: in chemicals

[1] *New York Times*, September 17, 1933.

[2] See below for an account of the first two labour boards which sought to enforce Section 7a of the N.I.R.A.

[3] The number of plans declined 27 per cent. but membership only 7·9 per cent. (National Industrial Conference Board, *Collective Bargaining through Employee Representation*, New York, 1933).

[4] National Industrial Conference Board, *Individual and Collective Bargaining in May* 1934, New York, 1934.

54·9 per cent. of the workers were in plants where there were only company unions and 5·7 per cent. in plants with both trade and company unions; in iron and steel the figures were 49·3 per cent. and 8 per cent., in transportation equipment 39·7 per cent. and 19·7 per cent., in machinery 39·6 per cent. and 10 per cent. and in rubber 13·1 per cent. and 65·6 per cent.[1]

(2) *Unionism and Industrial Government*

(*a.*) *Expansion of Unionism*

The very revival of company unionism in 1933 was an attestation of the new vigour that has come to the union movement.

As regards unionism the initial effect of the New Deal has been similar to the lifting of a previously submerged continental shelf by geological forces: the contour now above the water line was roughly identical with the one below that line during the submerged period. It was only later that new chains of hills and plateaux began to rise from what had previously been flat lowlands. In other words, reunionization preceded unionization anew. The unions that effected a most vigorous " come-back " were the United Mine Workers, the International Ladies' Garment Workers and the Amalgamated Clothing workers. The submergence of the first two antedated the general depression: the miners as a result of chronic depression in the bituminous industry through the 'twenties and the ladies' garment workers following the fight for control between communists and anti-communists in the middle 'twenties. Another instance of reinvigorated unionism was railway unionism, which, early in the New Deal, under the friendly ministrations of Railway Coordinator Joseph B. Eastman, saw the final liquidation of the company unions, the hated symbols of the defeat of the national shopmen's strike of 1922.[2]

[1] " Types of Employer-Employee Dealing," *Monthly Labour Review*, December 1935, pp. 1445–1463.

[2] While the chief problem of the railway unions, of chronic unemployment in a no longer expanding industry, together with other vital issues are scarcely yielding to solution, we feel that we may be permitted to dismiss this branch of unionism from further consideration in this survey. The unemployment issue is most acute in the train operating trades as a conflict between the older men clinging to the

Not much needs to be said here about the almost miraculous revival of the miners' union due to the extraordinary alertness and boldness of stroke of John L. Lewis assisted by an able group of lieutenants. Their rôle in the greatest upheaval in American labour history will be related in its proper place. Here, it suffices to point out that having re-conquered all provinces lost in the disastrous latter 'twenties and having extended the union's domain to embrace even the West Virginia, Alabama, and Kentucky fields, and "captive mines,"[1] they proceeded to stabilize the competition in their industry by law. The "Guffey Act" of 1935 which fixed both wages and prices was declared unconstitutional by the then as yet "unreformed" United States Supreme Court on the ground that coal mining was not interstate commerce and hence wage regulation by federal enactment was *ultra vires*. Whereupon the miners countered by the second Guffey Act, of 1936, which operates solely through price and production regulation enforced through a tonnage tax. Thus Congressional legislation has been introduced to effect the same kind of sharing of market opportunity among the operators in the several fields and the simultaneous sharing of job opportunity among their employees which in the past had been achieved strictly through collective bargaining.

In the clothing industry, both the Amalgamated (in men's clothing) and the International Ladies' Garment Workers, have won from the very first, in part by a clever play on the personal prestige of their respective leaders Sidney Hillman and David Dubinsky[2] springing from their "closeness" to the White House, a commanding position on the code authorities of their several industries. Taking up a relentless pursuit to their farthest lairs of the shops which had "run

seniority principle and the younger men demanding a more equal chance for employment. The other perennial issue, the wage issue, is linked with the "job rules" in the charge levelled at the railway trades of bringing ruin to the industry as well as to the men themselves. Notice should also be taken of the remarkable record of adjusting disputes without strikes under the skilful handling of the specially created National Mediation Board.

[1] These are the mines owned by corporations in other industries, such as steel and power production, and operated as integrated units of those industries. The determined anti-unionism of the steel industry, broken only in 1937, made these mines especially difficult objects of conquest.

[2] Hillman was a member of the Labour Advisory Board of the N.R.A. and later one of the leading members of the National Recovery Board. Dubinsky's ascent to political prestige came in the Presidential campaign of 1936.

away " from the metropolitan centres in search of cheap labour, they have restored their former job control. Furthermore, in the process of expansion these unions have become something like the industrial unions in pre-Hitler Germany, namely unions embracing several distinct industries, " compound-industrial unions " as it were[1]. The merger of the old United Hatters of America (of the Danbury Hatters' Case fame) with the Cloth Hat, Cap and Millinery Workers' International Union under the able leadership of Max Zaritzky is another illustration of the same tendency.

In addition to the phenomenon of re-invigorated unionism[2] and to the expansion of unionism into factory industries previously weakly held, as in textiles, or into industries heretofore altogether barred to it, like the mass production industries (both varieties to be treated at length below), there have emerged under the New Deal some union species[3] new to America, such as white collar unionism outside government employ, or even new to the world, such as the " unionism " of the recipients of public relief and of the holders of work relief jobs. The American Newspaper Guild, organized in 1933, typifies the former and the Workers' Alliance of America the latter. The Alliance grew out of the numerous unemployed leagues established during the depression, and is to some extent a federation of them. The unemployed organizations had been started for the most part by " leftist " political groups, Socialist, Communist, and American Workers' Party (later " Trotzkyist "), but turned before long into agencies for collective bargaining with the relief dispensing authorities, adjusting individual grievances such as the right to, and the amount of, relief as well as general relief standards. With the firm establishment of work-relief under the Works Progress Administration (W.P.A.) in the autumn of 1935, this type of organization, since 1936 principally the Workers' Alliance of America, has functioned as the trade union of the W.P.A. employees, taking up

[1] Thus the Amalgamated has extended into the men's shirt industry and recently also into the laundry industry.

[2] The building industry, which has stayed depressed, saw no revival in its unionism.

[3] Mention should be made of agricultural workers' unions, especially in California fruit growing, in the beet and onion-growing fields in the Middle West and the East, and of the unions of Southern share croppers.

individual job issues as well as bargaining with the government[1] over W.P.A. appropriations.

The growth of the International Brotherhood of Teamsters and Chauffeurs from about 95,000 in 1933 to 210,000 in 1937 is the biggest expansion by any A.F. of L. union and demonstrates also the new importance of highway transportation. It will also be seen how the teamsters[2] have been used, notably on the Pacific Coast, as A.F. of L. shock troops against the C.I.O. The expansion of unionism under the latter will be taken up under the respective industries.

(b) *Textiles*

The Code of Fair Competition for the Cotton Textile Industry, approved July 9, 1933, was the first adopted under the N.I.R.A. and was long considered the "model code." Its provisions were: (1) a basic forty-hour week; (2) machine operations limited to two shifts of forty hours each; (3) general wage minima of $12 in the South, $13 in the North, for forty hours' labour; (4) no child labour; (5) pay of workers receiving more than the code minimum prior to July 17 not to be decreased; (6) no worker to receive less for forty hours than for forty-eight or more prior to July 17; (17) no worker to be required to do more work than as of July 1, unless approved by the Code Authority or the N.R.A.

A month later the Cotton Textile National Industrial Relations Board was created and the code provision which stipulated that there be no further increases of work load was rescinded.

The code contained no express provisions regarding administration. Co-operation with the N.R.A. Administrator was to be had through the code authority, which was constituted by joint action of three employer groups, the Cotton Textile

[1] The leaders of the Alliance have had audiences with President Roosevelt. The Alliance, following its predecessors, specializes in "hunger marches" and has even resorted to temporary "occupations" of state capitols. In a number of cases the organized unemployed have helped employed strikers and have even carried unionism to them, notably in Milwaukee and Racine, Wisconsin.

[2] In Minneapolis, however, the teamsters' local, out of favour with its own international office, has become, since the bloodily fought strike in 1934, in which the Farmer-Labour Governor, Floyd B. Olson, came to its aid by prohibiting heavy traffic, the missionary centre of unionism in that region. It is under "Trotzkyist" influence.

Institute, the American Cotton Manufacturers' Association, and the National Association of Cotton Manufacturers. There was no labour representation. The executive order of approval of the code provided that the N.R.A. should appoint three members without vote.

The code brought about notable improvements in the industry: (1) child labour was out for the first time; (2) hours were reduced from an average of 53 to a maximum of 40; (3) wages were increased from $8–10 to $12 and $13; (4) there was a 70 per cent. increase in hourly earnings during the first months under the code; (5) there was a rapid increase in payrolls and employment.

The business spurt of the first half of 1933 was followed by a recession. The code authority granted a 25 per cent. reduction in operations during December, with no increase in hourly wages rates. There was no public hearing on the order.

The early months of 1934 saw another business spurt. Then again, in May, the code authority asked for a 25 per cent. curtailment. This was granted for June, July and August, with no mention of wage increases and without a public hearing.

Before adoption of the code, the United Textile Workers, the only labour organization in the field national in scope, had claimed no more than 20,000 members in all textiles. An organization campaign followed the code adoption and brought a rapid increase in membership. By May 1934 the United Textile Workers claimed 300,000 in cotton textiles alone.

During 1933 and the organizing campaign, labour disturbances were few and minor in extent. Discontent, however, was growing around the issues of the growing work load or "stretch out," the denial of union rights, and the reduced earnings resulting from curtailments with no rise in rates of pay.

Matters came to a crisis with the announcement of the curtailment in May, at which time a general strike was threatened in the industry. A strike was averted by an agreement in June which, while retaining the 25 per cent. curtailment order, provided for an investigation by the N.R.A. "Division of Planning and Research" into basic conditions and added one member from labour and one from the employers to the Industrial Relations Board.

The code was amended by the N.R.A. to permit the mill conference committees under the Industrial Relations Board to select worker representatives from outside the mill if they so desired. This was made under protest from the Code Authority.

Strike rumblings were heard anew at the United Textile Workers' convention in the middle of August 1934, when many code violations were charged. Southern delegates were especially militant in their demand for action. At the convention there were only ten dissenting votes from the five hundred delegates in favour of a strike. The American Federation of Labour Executive Council voted its support to the strike but the United Textile Workers' treasury held less than $1,000,000. George Sloan, President of the Cotton Textile Institute, reiterated his charge that a strike would be against the code and the government, and described the " stretch out " as nothing more than mechanical improvement calling for no greater effort and strain and often less. Two days later, August 26, the curtailment order then in effect was to end at midnight. The Cotton Code Authority recommended that it be given power to extend the curtailment. This request was denied by the Labour Advisory Board of the N.R.A. on the ground that the spirit of N.R.A. required that a proportionate wage increase must be included. It was the first time a wage increase had been mentioned.

An incident occurred which raised considerable protest and gave an outlet for disapproval of the strike. A Southern American Federation of Labour organizer was reported to have stated on good authority that the Federal Emergency Relief Administration could be depended upon to finance the strike by extending relief to the strikers. Harry L. Hopkins, the F.E.R.A. Administrator, had previously announced that strikers were being fed when in need. The *New York Times* remarked editorially that textile unionists had no faith in government mediation, but in its ability to feed them.

On August 29, Francis J. Gorman, the Secretary-Treasurer of the United Textile Workers, demanded as follows: a 30-hour week with the same pay as for 40 hours and more uniformity of wages in the different sections of the country; a maximum work load in the various divisions of the industry; reinstatement of workers discharged in violation of 7a; recognition of United Textile Workers as bargaining agency of workers, and the signing of trade agreements; and arbitration tribunals binding upon both parties. Gorman also commented at this time that the strike would be called whether government relief was given or not, adding that textile workers were never too well fed even when at work.

The employers' leaders held that the individual mills of the industry had authorized neither the Code Authority nor the Cotton Textile Institute to deal for them with the workers.

The strike was called as scheduled on September 1. There were in the industry approximately 300,000 operatives in 1,280 mills. The strike was extended to the woollen and worsted divisions, with an estimated coverage of 650,000 workers and also to the silk branch, establishing for it the claim of the largest on record. The Associated Press estimated that 199,200 were out.

In the South a meeting of 1,000 delegates attained the fervour of a religious "camp meeting." Bands of motorized pickets, called "flying squadrons," were in action. President Roosevelt had kept informed but silent. On September 5 he appointed a committee of three, headed by Governor John G. Winant of New Hampshire, to investigate and report not later than October 1. Meanwhile, the strike had gained in violence and intensity. When the strike was in its sixth day, the total dead had reached ten as "flying squadrons" fought with police, guards and other workers.

The Winant board began hearings, both Gorman and Sloan testifying. The centre of violence moved to New England and Gorman appealed to President Roosevelt for federal troops to protect the strikers and to start arbitration.

On September 10 came the first evidence of weakening, as mills began to reopen in the South, and to find ready workers. Strike leaders there were finding that the relief problem was breaking the strikers' morale. In New England manufacturers stated that workers were "almost pleading" that mills be reopened.

On September 14 General Hugh S. Johnson, National Recovery Administrator, added fuel in a speech before the N.R.A. Code Authorities, in which he called the strike an "absolute violation" of the June agreement; blamed Thomas

W. McMahon (President of the United Textile Workers) for bad faith, and Norman Thomas, the socialist leader, who had addressed the union convention, for fomenting the strike; and backed up the statements by Sloan, for whom his " heart wept." Gorman retaliated by demanding the resignation of Johnson, whom he held to blame for the strike because he allowed violations of the code. It was recalled that the June agreement was not to have prejudiced the right to strike.

On the 17th, Governor Talmadge of Georgia established by executive order internment camps for strikers arrested by guardsmen. The Department of Labour by this time had begun to send investigators into the strike areas.

On September 20, the Winant Report was transmitted to the President through the Secretary of Labour. As a result of its findings, the Board recommended, in summary: (1) Creation of an impartial board of three to be known as the Textile Labour Relations Board with powers and duties to be similar to those exercised by National Labour Relations Board and the Steel Labour Relations Board, and authority to administer, in addition to 7a, other labour provisions in cotton, silk and wool codes. (2) That the President direct the Department of Labour and the Federal Trade Commission to investigate and report on the ability of cotton, silk and wool textiles to support an equal or greater number of employees at higher wages. (3) That the codes be amended to provide for special committees under the Textile Labour Relations Board, to report to President Roosevelt not later than January 1, 1935, a permanent plan for the regulation of the " stretch out," under which employers shall be required to secure approval of an impartial agency before increasing the work load. (4) That the Department of Labour be directed to study definitions and classifications of occupations and existing wages, and to make information available to labour and management, to guide them in making agreements, and to aid in enforcement of code wages provisions.

In conclusion, the Board said: " We therefore earnestly hope that the United Textile Workers will call off the strike on the basis of these recommendations. At the same time we request the employers in the industry to take back the workers now on strike without discrimination."

In accepting the report, President Roosevelt asked for a return to work on these conditions. The United Textile Workers immediately indicated willingness to accept. The Chairman of the Silk Code Authority recommended rehiring without discrimination in the silk industry, but the cotton and woollen executives avoided the point in their statements.

On September 22 the Executive Council of the United Textile Workers voted unanimously to end the strike, and to accept the Winant report without reservation, interpreting it as a strike victory including union recognition. Yet on the last point the Winant Report had said that: "The Board feels that under the circumstances of this situation an industry wide collective agreement between the employers as a group and the United Textile Workers is not at this time feasible, and that collective dealing between labour and management in this industry can, for the present at least, best be achieved through development on a plant to plant basis." The Cotton Textile Institute continued to preserve silence until the manufacturers had expressed themselves on the discrimination issue.

Trouble immediately began to arise on that issue. Southern labour leaders reported "lock-outs" and the use of the National Guard in North Carolina and Georgia to keep workers away from the mills. There were also reports that a "non-union" pledge was exacted at some mills as a requirement for re-hiring. From New England came similar reports. Paterson's silk workers, however, met with no discrimination, though the manufacturers declared the old contract void.

The President appointed the Textile Labour Relations Board and the Institute formally accepted the Winant Report, claiming that it sustained its contentions on two points: (1) That working conditions had improved under the Code; and (2) that industry-wide collective bargaining with United Textile Workers was not feasible at the time. The Institute took the position that there would be no vengefulness in the rehiring, but that "lawless" strikers would not be rehired.

Reports of discrimination continued and Gorman reported "terrific pressure" to renew the strike. The workers were told, however, to reapply for work, and report grievances to the new textile labour board. The best was made of the situation.

Textile unionism had to await the organization in the

summer of 1936 of the Textile Workers' Organizing Committee (T.W.O.C.) by the C.I.O., with Sidney Hillman as chairman, before resuming as a mass movement.

(c) *Automobiles*[1]

Labour's ineffectiveness in using the N.R.A. to conquer new ground showed even more in the automobile industry than in textiles. Here there was the additional difficulty that this compact and self-confident industry radiated a prestige from which even the highest officials of the New Deal Administration were hardly immune. This in part accounts for the success of the Automobile Chamber of Commerce, the industry's trade association embracing all companies except the super-individualistic Ford Motor Company, in incorporating in its N.R.A. code the so-called merit clause stating that "employers in industry may exercise their right to select, retain, or advance employees on the basis of individual merit, without regard to their membership or non-membership in any organization." This clause, notwithstanding protests from labour, was consistently retained through the several renewals of the code during the lifetime of the N.R.A. The other cause of the employers' complete success, prior to the stirring days of the winter of 1936–7, was the unpreparedness of the officials of the A.F. of L., who acted in behalf of the automobile workers in the absence of an international union organization of their own.

In August 1933, when the original code was passed, automobile unionism was represented by the Mechanics Educational Society, a new and somewhat leftist organization of the skilled tool and die makers successful that summer in winning demands, and three other minor groups, all independent of the A.F. of L.

The A.F. of L. dispatched a small band of organizers to form Federal Labour Unions embracing whole plants.[2] Subsequently these organizers proved incapable, even with the

[1] The best account of the automobile workers' strikes is in Edward Levinson, *Labour on the March*, Harpers, 1937.

[2] In the past, the federal labour union had been a provisional form preparatory to an allotment of the new members among the internationals for which they were eligible. In this novel situation this form was considered as a possible preliminary to an international industrial union.

aid of their superiors in Washington, either of impressing the employers or of holding for more than a short while the confidence of the employees in the industry. Meanwhile, company unions took root.

In March 1934 the first test came. The federal labour unions had been joined by tens of thousands and demands resounded for the reinstatement of local leaders discharged allegedly for union activity, a 20 per cent. wage increase, a thirty-hour week and union recognition. The employers refused to meet with the Federation's spokesmen to say nothing of bargaining over the demands. Finally President Roosevelt intervened personally and made a settlement granting " collective bargaining " of the pluralist variety, that is one in which the labour side may be represented by a plurality of mutually competing unions including company unions. The settlement also created an Automobile Labour Board, under Dr. Leo Wolman, who was also chairman of the Labour Advisory Board of the N.R.A., to implement the " collective bargaining " agreement.

But the Wolman Board refused to heed the demand by the unions to proceed forthwith to the certification of bargaining representatives notwithstanding that it had the union membership lists at its disposal and instead devoted precious time in dealing dilatorily with discrimination cases.

The A.F. of L. leaders could hold back a general automobile strike only with difficulty. In Cleveland the workers in the Chevrolet and several other General Motors plants actually struck and returned only when William F. Knudson, for the General Motors Corporation, agreed to an informal union recognition in several plants " as an experiment." In Toledo, the Electric Auto-Lite Company plant struck in disregard of the A.F. of L. and the Wolman Board and won concessions including the abolition of the company union.

Meantime, as the Wolman Board continued to delay in the matter of bargaining representatives, automobile unionism, at its crest at the time of the Presidential settlement, ebbed away. When the Board finally got around to the main issue, it carried out, again over the protests of the unions and subject to their boycott, a series of plant elections which in a vote of 163,000, gave 88·7 per cent. for representatives unaffiliated with any organization and only 8·6 per cent. for the A.F. of L.

The spring of 1935 witnessed another but lower peak of unrest among automobile workers. Another strike at Toledo, this time at the General Motors Chevrolet plant proved conclusively the ineffectiveness of the Board but ended in an inconclusive settlement ratified only under A.F. of L. threats and oratory. As far as the auto workers were concerned the A.F. of L. and the Wolman Board were equally discredited.

In August 1935 the several automobile locals, which had previously been united under a " National Council " resembling in prerogative the " territorial " form that preceded statehood in American political life, held a " constitutional convention " to receive from President Green their formal charter as an international. The convention was anything but a happy family gathering assembled to set up a young couple in housekeeping on their own, as the " dowry " in terms of " jurisdiction " was held woefully deficient. Under pressure the United Automobile Workers accepted Green's candidate for international president but resolved to protest to the Atlantic City Convention of the A.F. of L. against their treatment. However, at that convention the C.I.O. was born and with it was linked the next, real upswing of automobile unionism as well as the greatest labour upheaval America has ever experienced.

The upheaval began with the rubber workers in Akron, Ohio. The rubber workers had encountered since 1933 the same opposition to union recognition by their employers, the Goodrich, Firestone and Goodyear Companies, as had the auto workers, and the same experience with the A.F. of L. In September 1935 they were given an international charter, but, warned by the example of the auto workers a month earlier, the rubber workers' constitutional convention bluntly rejected Green's candidate for president of their union. In January 1936 the Goodyear Company cut wages, the second cut in three months. Lewis came to Akron and addressed a mass meeting. A month later a number of employees, constituting a whole shift in a department, were dismissed. While a delegation remonstrated with the officials, the other shift " sat-down " at their machines. This was the third sit-down in the Goodyear plant since November and may be said to have inaugurated this method of labour struggle in America. As the management refused redress, a strike began and the plants were completely besieged by more than 10,000 strikers and sympathizers. The C.I.O. came to their aid with money, encouragement and technical advice. After five weeks the company offered a satisfactory settlement although falling short of recognition, and the strike ended. This was the C.I.O.'s debut as the leader and inspirer of the mass production workers.

In May 1936 the auto workers held their second national convention and replaced the nominee of Green by Homer Martin, a former minister who upon the loss of his pulpit due to radicalism had worked in the industry and helped organize the union. In October the union won a material and psychological victory in the Chrysler and Dodge plants in Detroit on the seniority issue as well as reinstatement of discharged employees. The next significant victory came after a fourteen-day sit-down at the Midland Steel plant, also in Detroit. During this strike Chrysler and Dodge locals had informed their managements that they would not work on steel frames coming from Midland's Cleveland plant. With several other smaller victories to its credit, and with the C.I.O. giving its counsel and encouragement, the auto workers' union was preparing for an assault on General Motors in January when the production season would be near its peak.

The strike began with the shutting down of the Fisher Body plant at Cleveland, but the heart of it was at Flint, Michigan. The corporation was vulnerable because of its very specialization of production in its several plants: the shut-down of one strategic plant was tantamount to a general suspension. In Fisher Body Plant No. 1 at Flint were important dies, which if removed to a less strong union centre, might become dangerous to the success of the strike. Therefore on December 30 the plant was occupied and held by its 4,000 employees. Thus began the most dramatic "sit-down" strike in America. Fifteen other General Motors plants, some in Flint, others elsewhere, were also on strike, of the sit-down or ordinary variety. By January 11, 112,800 of the corporation's 150,000 workers were on strike.

The union demanded an immediate conference to discuss the following demands: a national agreement, abolition of piece work, minimum day rates and time and a half for over-time, a thirty-hour week, reinstatement of men discharged for union activities, seniority in lay-offs, joint regulation of the speed of the belt-line, but above all recognition of the union as sole bargaining agency.

Governor Frank Murphy, an ardent New Dealer, energetically intervened as peacemaker. The company refused to meet with the union so long as the illegal seizure of its properties through the sit-down continued. Finally a truce was reached whereby the company agreed to negotiate on all the demands made by the union provided the plants were evacuated; the negotiations were not to be broken off for at least fifteen days and no dies or other equipment were to be removed from the plants in the meantime. Two plants outside Flint were evacuated on January 16 and the all-important Flint plants were to be surrendered on the following day. A few days earlier a pitched battle had occurred at the gates of Fisher Body No. 2 plant which brought 1,500 Michigan National Guardsmen to the city, but now at least peace was in sight.

But the truce was not to be a preliminary to immediate peace. On the morning of the 17th it became known that the corporation had assured George E. Boysen, a former General Motors paymaster and now the head of the " Flint Alliance," a thinly disguised company-union, of its readiness " always to discuss with your group or any group of our employees any question without prejudice to anyone." The union now charged deliberate deception, as the main demand, recognition as sole bargaining agency, was thus denied even before a resumption of negotiations, and the evacuation was indefinitely postponed.

Thereupon ensued a series of ineffectual moves to settle the strike in Washington and a " battle of newspaper headlines " in which figured President Roosevelt, John L. Lewis, George L. Sloan, President of General Motors, and Secretary Perkins. On the actual battlefield the company applied for an injunction from Judge Paul V. Godola, soon discovered to be a large General Motors stockholder, for the evacuation of the plants. While the court proceedings were on, the strikers secured by a clever ruse the possession of the huge Chevrolet works at Flint as a move to heighten *morale* in the strike which was already one month old. On the following day Judge Godola signed the injunction directing the men to vacate the Fisher body plants under pain of imprisonment for contempt and heavy fines. The strikers in a telegram to the Governor refused to obey the court injuction and threatened, unarmed as they were, resistance to the end. A movement of strikers and strike sympathizers from Detroit and elsewhere on Flint in anticipation of the battle was begun. Governor Murphy, to avoid bloodshed, ordered the sheriff to delay enforcement of the court injunction.

The corporation was now willing to listen to President Roosevelt's request for the renewal of negotiations. The conference met with the Governor again as peacemaker. Lewis made a dramatic journey from Washington to act as the strikers' spokesman. A settlement was reached February 11, and included a pledge by the corporation that it would not, without the Governor's consent, for a period of six months recognize or deal with any other employee spokesman than the United Automobile Workers in the seventeen plants closed by the strikes and in all other plants the union was recognized as the agent of its members. Further negotiations on the other original demands were to ensue. The C.I.O. had triumphed over America's most self-confident capitalist corporation.

Soon thereafter the United Automobile Workers obtained a similar agreement from the Chrysler Corporation after what was perhaps an unnecessary " sit-down " of four weeks in that company's nine Detroit plants and all other employers in the industry except Ford likewise signed-up. Yet industrial relations in the industry have hardly become stabilized, the responsibility resting in part with the previous " conditioning " of the executives and foremen and in part with the lack of seasoning on the union side. A contributing factor to the latter has been the incessant factional struggle within the union, a struggle strongly influenced by outside " ideological " groups.

(*d*) *Steel*

Before the N.R.A. the steel industry as a whole had opposed employee representation plans and Eugene Grace, President of the Bethlehem Steel Company, was one of the few steel industrialists who wanted company unions in the iron and steel code. He won in a struggle for power within the Iron and

Steel Institute. The proposed code, as announced on July 15, 1933, declared in Article 4 of Section 2 that the " plants of this country are open to capable workmen without regard to their membership or non-membership in any labour organization " and in Schedule C sketched the procedure whereby " collective bargaining " would be realized as follows: (1) nomination and election of representatives was to be on company premises; (2) representatives were to be chosen from employees only; (3) only the selected representatives could confer with the management; and (4) final decision on wages, hours, and working conditions were to rest with the employer. At the hearing before the Labour Advisory Board of the N.R.A., the American Federation of Labour fought both the open shop declaration and Schedule C and the industry agreed to leave them out. The final code as accepted included 7a of the N.I.R.A. without modification.

The concession, however, was merely verbal. Company unions were set up in a great majority of the iron and steel plants. The Iron and Steel Institute claimed that most of the 430,000 workers were satisfied with company unions, but President Michael F. Tighe, of the Amalgamated Association of Iron and Steel and Tin Workers, branded these plans as mere tools of the employers and in the spring of 1934 threatened a strike.

From 1919 to 1933, the Amalgamated Association had remained dormant. Following the approval of the steel code it started an organizing campaign and within two or three months it had more than 125 new lodges. Membership jumped from 3,000 in the middle of 1933 to anywhere from 60,000 to 100,000 in April 1934. The success of the campaign, however, was due to the spirit of the time rather than to aggressive recruiting on the part of the union officials. These new thousands demanded action. At the national convention in April 1934 the younger, unskilled elements forced a resolution for wage demands and union recognition under threat of a national steel strike and appointed a Committee in Charge of Offensive Action (later called the Rank and File Committee) to co-operate with the national officers. The steel companies duly refused the separate formal demands for recognition and after fruitless offers and counter-offers between the Iron and

Steel Institute and the two factions of the Amalgamated (for the national officers and the Rank and File Committee had promptly split), the Amalgamated convention reconvened to decide upon a strike. Here the younger element was outmanœuvred with the aid of President Green who brought President Roosevelt's promise to appoint a National Steel Labour Relations Board.

The executive order creating this Board set forth the majority rule principle in elections, at the same time guaranteeing minority groups the right to deal with their employers. The Board committed itself to the issuance of election orders in the case of the Duquesne and McDonald (Ohio) plants of the Carnegie Steel Company, when, on December 31, 1934, it ordered the company to produce the pay-rolls so that the Board might decide who should vote. The company refused and fought the case in court.[1] On January 8, 1935, the Board ordered elections in the Youngstown Sheet and Tube Company plants in Chicago and the Gary plant of the Illinois Steel Company, but the orders were fought in the courts, where they stayed until the demise of the N.R.A. A similar fate overtook the order for an election in the Monessen and Allenport plants of the Pittsburgh Steel Company. In the only election under the Board the results were 62·7 per cent. for a trade union, 35·4 per cent. for a company union, and 1·9 per cent. for some other type of dealing.

Under the ministrations of the Board, the union dwindled to almost nothing. President Tighe was busy revoking the charters of the insurgent or "Rank and File Committee" lodges. However, the Committee equally lost prestige. The next and crucial labour awakening was to come from an unexpected source.

As early as the late summer of 1935 company unions had begun to come to life and show an unwonted spirit of independence. In September, 1935, thirty-two delegates from twelve company unions in the American Sheet and Tin Plate Company (a United States Steel Corporation subsidiary) met at New Castle, Pennsylvania, and demanded a 15 per cent. wage

[1] Nominally the company unions fought the case but they were represented by a lawyer paid by the company (John A. Fitch, "Steel, 1936," *Survey Graphic*, August 1936, p. 465).

increase, vacations with pay and a revision of the pension system. The Company financed this meeting and organized a "safe block of delegates to keep discussion away from dangerous matters," but the representatives asserted themselves in spite of this. Following the New Castle meeting, wage demands, all of which were refused, were made upon the Aliquippa and Pittsburgh plants of the Jones and Laughlin Company, the Duquesne and Gary plants of the Carnegie-Illinois Company, the Weirton plants of the Weirton Steel Company, the Cleveland and Warren plants of the Republic Steel Company, and upon the National Tube Works at McKeesport and the Edgar Thompson Steel Works at Braddock. All this added up to a sum of activity remarkable for company unions. But there was a guardian angel watching from the outside over these daring adolescents.

In February, 1936, Lewis wrote to Green offering to support any effective move that might be made in organizing the steel industry along industrial lines in conjunction with the newly formed Committee for Industrial Organization. He offered trained organizers and $500,000 cash, provided the remainder of the unions contributed $1,500,000 and the leadership in the campaign was such as to inspire confidence in its ability and loyalty to the industrial union principle. Green referred the offer to the Executive Council and on April 3 the request was formally refused. Meanwhile Lewis made the offer of $500,000 to Tighe. It was perfectly timed as the convention of the Amalgamated was to meet April 28. At that convention the young rank-and-file progressives were eager to accept the offer, but were defeated. However, they forced through a compromise plan for organizing steel along industrial lines, with no mention of the C.I.O. offer. Tighe and Green had several conferences, but Green refused to give any aid to an industrial plan. Finally early in June 1936 the Amalgamated accepted the C.I.O. offer.

The drive that was subsequently launched was entirely controlled by the Lewis group. Technically the new members joined the Amalgamated but the latter had handed everything over to the Steel Workers' Organizing Committee except the actual issuance of the charters. Only two of the eight original members of the S.W.O.C. were Amalgamated representatives.

The S.W.O.C. retained all dues and had the power, in conjunction with the Amalgamated officers, to deal with the steel companies.

The S.W.O.C. applied a most carefully planned organizing technique. Over 150 salaried organizers were employed. Aware of the impoverished condition of the steel workers, since the steel industry was the latest to show recovery, it at once waived initiation fees and in November 1936 suspended all payment of dues. It entered into a friendly relationship with the fraternal orders of the several foreign-speaking nationalities composing the steel workers (important centres of social life among these groups); it enlisted the aid or at least secured the neutrality of the clergy;[1] and recruited effective legal and research staffs. Yet on the eve of the national election it looked as though the campaign would take years. But on November 4 Roosevelt was re-elected and the smashing victory electrified the men. The organizers had stressed throughout the supposed intimacy between Lewis and Roosevelt. There arose a feeling that the President wanted the men to join the union and they were certain that there was in Washington an administration that was interested in the welfare of the common man.

However, before Roosevelt's re-election the process of fermentation within the company unions had already proceeded apace. In October the Chicago-Pittsburgh Representatives' Council, in which the movement for agglomeration among the company unions in the plants of Carnegie-Illinois Steel Company, the main subsidiary of United States Steel, had found expression, came out for a wage increase of 25 per cent., a $5 a day minimum, a forty-hour week and a National Wage Scale Committee under the aegis of the Steel Workers' Organizing Committee. President Benjamin F. Fairless of the Carnegie-Illinois refused all demands, including the one for an election to determine whether the workers wanted the Council or the several company unions to represent them.

A month after this refusal the company did grant a 10 per

[1] In South Chicago, for instance, the Greek-Orthodox priests counselled the younger men to join the union but the men near to pension or too old to find another job to stay away from union activities. I am indebted to S. Carmel, of Chicago, for data relating to the S.W.O.C. organizing campaign, especially at South Chicago.

cent. wage increase, making it seem as if the company unions had been responsible for the increase and that it was the result of collective bargaining, but stipulated that any wage change in the future would be tied to the cost of living. The S.W.O.C. claimed credit for this concession and simultaneously roused the men's resentment at the effort to freeze their standard of living. Secretary of Labour Perkins, likewise, commented unfavourably.

In December 1936 the C.I.O. brought the Carnegie-Illinois Steel Company before the National Labour Relations Board on the ground that the employee representation plan was not collective bargaining. The employees' representatives[1] hired a law firm to represent them at the hearings (since there were no dues, the source of the funds was a mystery), and in February 1937, upon their return from Washington, the lawyers, after a conference with the representatives, announced the organization of the Steel Employees Independent Labour Organization to include workers in the United States Steel plants in the Calumet (Chicago) district. The S.E.I.L. was fated to be the last move in the company's anti-union campaign.

President Myron C. Taylor, Chairman of the Board of Directors of the United States Steel Corporation, had met John L. Lewis twice in January but in the words of Mr. Taylor, they " did not reach any conclusion that would conform with our policy " (proportional representation in collective bargaining).[2] The negotiations were resumed February 25 and concluded February 28, 1933. The contract, good for one year, granted the eight-hour day, the forty-hour week with time and a half for overtime, vacations with pay and seniority rights. On the union issue the Company did not recede from its statement of principles but the recognition of the S.W.O.C. although not formally as the sole bargaining agency, reversed the policy never to deal with organized labour to which the Company had held steadfastly since 1901. Within a month all of the subsidiaries of United States Steel with 250,000 employees had signed. America's principal citadel of " open shop " for thirty-five years had surrendered.

[1] " Conservatives " temporarily regained control in the Pittsburgh district.

[2] *Ten Years of Steel*, Remarks of Myron C. Taylor, Annual Meeting of Stockholders. p. 4. Hoboken, New Jersey, April 4, 1938.

In the words of Mr. Taylor uttered at the renewal of the contract in February 1938: " The union has scrupulously followed the terms of its agreement and, in so far as I know, has made no unfair effort to bring other employees into its ranks, while the Corporation subsidiaries, during a very difficult period, have been entirely free of labour disturbances of any kind. The cost of a strike—to the Corporation, to the public and to the men—would have been incalculable."[1]

Significantly the " independents " in steel did not follow the " trust's " example of recognizing the S.W.O.C. without a strike. The S.W.O.C. called a strike by the 25,000 employees of the Jones and Laughlin Steel Corporation, which ended with an agreement to have an election under the National Labour Relations Board. As the vote was 17,000 to 7,000 for the union, it won sole bargaining rights. But among the big independents Jones and Laughlin was the only conciliatory employer; the others were determined to battle to the end for rugged individualism.

These were the Bethlehem Steel Corporation, with 85,000 employees; the Republic Steel Corporation, with 52,000; the Youngstown Sheet and Tube Company, with 18,000; and the Inland Steel Company, with 10,000. The sole issue was the companies' refusal to sign a contract with the S.W.O.C. even if it won a majority in a Labour Board election, as the C.I.O. was not a " responsible group." On May 26, about 75,000 in twenty-seven plants in five states operated by the Republic, Youngstown Sheet and Tube and of the Inland were on strike. The first major violence occurred on May 30 (the " Memorial Day Massacre ") when eight pickets were killed and two score injured in a battle with the police outside the gate of the Republic's South Chicago plant. The La Follette Civil Liberties Committee declared that the blame lay with the police which either showed gross inefficiency in the performance of duty or else made a deliberate effort to break the strike.

On the Ohio front the operation of slow siege by the strikers marked the struggle. Here, too, the Republic kept on operating on a limited scale; and, as in Chicago, it kept the remaining workers within the plant. The Company attempted to send food to the besieged strike-breakers through the

[1] *Ten Years of Steel*, p. 43.

mails but reported its parcels refused by the Post Office as "irregular."

The great Midwest steel strike did not involve the Wagner Act. The union, despite its demands, was insignificant in some plants and far short of majority support in others. Plant by plant, at the commencement of the strike, the union would have won some elections and lost many. With both sides playing for the "undecided" steel workers, it was obvious that neither really wanted an election.[1] By June 12 the strike had been extended to two Bethlehem Company plants.

The rôles of the governors of the states affected were significant. The governor of Indiana who sympathized with the strikers refused to supply military protection to the Inland Steel Company and obtained a virtual surrender from it on the one and only demand of a signed agreement, although the settlement was a face-saving triangular arrangement, each side signing with the State Department of Labour. The governor of Illinois deplored the Memorial Day affair but left the local authorities free to act. The governor of Ohio called out the troops and after brief hesitation used them to enforce order against the strikers. Governor Earle of Pennsylvania likewise called out the troops with the purpose, it appeared, of closing the plant, but receded from his pro-strike attitude when the newspapers of the country were plastered with paid advertisements protesting against a free hand to the S.W.O.C. Executives of local political units were generally on the companies' side. By the end of June it became evident that the resistance of the die-hard companies, including a skilful control of public opinion through citizens' committees and other means, had won the day for them.

Thus the C.I.O.'s "March to Victory" which had begun with the sit-downs in the auto industry and culminated in the United States Steel Agreement, came to an abrupt end and with it also the latest "great upheaval" in the American labour movement. Subsequently, the defeat was partially retrieved through favourable decisions by the National Labour Relations Board in every one of the steel cases. However, these "victories" coming as they did in the midst of the new depression

[1] Under the rules of the Labour Board only the S.W.O.C. could have asked for such an election.

scarcely sufficed to efface the effect of the original check to the C.I.O.'s advance.[1]

(*e*) *The Pacific Water Front*

After thirteen years of complete employer domination the maritime workers on the Pacific Coast were awakened by the passage of the N.I.R.A. A majority of the longshoremen immediately joined the International Longshoremen's Association. Late in 1933 wages were raised and a verbal agreement was made for joint control of the hiring halls through which the worker gets assigned to a job. It was over the union control of these hiring halls, the gateway to a job and therefore also to union job control, that the great maritime strike of 1934 was principally fought.

Throughout this strike longshoremen, marine workers and teamsters presented a united front to the ship owners from Seattle, Washington, to San Diego, California. Dave Beck, acknowledged teamster czar of the Pacific Northwest, joined the president of the San Francisco teamsters in promising aid to the longshoremen's and seamen's cause by refusing to haul merchandize on and off the struck docks. A joint strike committee, with Harry Bridges, a longshoreman for chairman, was formed with ten unions participating and all agreeing to return to work only on a joint settlement for all. This agreement caused the longshoremen overwhelmingly to repudiate a settlement negotiated a month later by Joseph Ryan, president of the I.L.A., which made no provision for the 13,000 striking marine workers. By May 16 ocean traffic had been brought to a standstill.

The strike was conducted as a siege operation. The strikers besieged the docks *en masse* and were in turn besieged by massed police with an occasional attempt by the latter to convoy through the strikers' lines a party of strike breakers. Clashes occurred with some fatalities. The solid aid of the teamsters was a strong factor on the strikers' side. On July 5 (" Bloody Thursday ") several hundred police charged two thousand

[1] The agreement renewed with the U.S. Steel in February 1938 contained an " escape clause " providing for ten days' notice to renew negotiations and for a dissolution of the 1937 agreement if within twenty days of such notice no understanding was reached.

union men congregated to stop cargo movement and fired in reply to a hail of missiles, with several dead and many wounded. In response, the teamsters of the San Francisco Bay region voted to come out on a strike and President Vendeleur of the San Francisco Labour Council threatened a general strike of all labour. The employers' side was taken by a Citizens' Emergency Committee with the usual slogan of " Americanism." By July 13 there were thirteen Bay area unions comprising 32,000 members on strike. On July 14 a convention, representing 65,000 workers, voted 315 against fifteen for a general strike on June 16.

The San Francisco general strike was at no time as complete as was its predecessor, the Seattle General Strike of 1919. In an effort to maintain favourable public opinion, milk, bread and ice were delivered through its duration. In addition ferry boatmen, the printing trades, electricians and telephone and telegraph operators were left on the jobs. A force of 5,000 state troops was held in readiness. The usual vigilante raids on " red " headquarters were made with the police only " mopping-up."

The general strike came to an end after three days under pressure from President Green and the heads of the international unions. The outcome of this second general strike in America was much like the outcome of its predecessor in Seattle in 1919. Although no gains were made, West Coast labour had again demonstrated its solidarity.

The longshoremen and maritime unions continued the strike for the control of the hiring halls; all other demands they were willing to leave to arbitration. Their position was greatly weakened when the San Francisco teamsters voted, on June 20, four to one to return to work unconditionally, and also to remove the boycott on the strike docks. A month after the desertion by the teamsters the striking unions agreed to return to work pending arbitration by the President's Mediation Board. The strike lasted eighty-three days and cost at least eight lives and an estimated 200 million dollars. The award, on October 10, gave the longshoremen a virtual control of the hiring halls which, though nominally under joint control, were to be administered by a dispatcher appointed by the union. The seamen were given higher wages and shorter hours.

Out of this strike the two leading personalities in Pacific Coast labour emerged: Harry Bridges of San Francisco and Dave Beck of Seattle. Beck is in the true "labour boss" tradition. He said: "It's old fashioned to organize just the employees; organize the employers." Bridges is a class conscious, "rank and file" longshoreman from Australia and supposedly a one-time member of the Communist party, an allegation which, due to his alien status, may render him subject to deportation. Beck's Council of Teamsters, through its "Promotion League" and also through its control of the Seattle Labour Council, decided in 1936 the election of John F. Dore for mayor of Seattle.

Beck established a veritable labour barony in Seattle. He scarcely needed the encouragement of the official award of the American Federation of Labour of teamster jurisdiction over brewery teamsters to act to annex them to his domain. As a result he became the overlord of the north-west breweries as well as of the brewery jobs and protected the market of his employer-following by a boycott on "California beer." The teamsters further extended their domain to "Produce Row" or the commission houses adjacent to the water front, soon thereafter to become the battleground between Beck and Bridges, as well as over the bakers and a miscellany of others.

While Beck was building his barony, Bridges was marshalling all maritime labour within the Maritime Federation of the Pacific Coast. This Federation, formed in April 1935, was refused a charter by the American Federation of Labour as a "dual" body, was boycotted by the teamsters from its inception and has functioned as a propaganda rather than an executive agency. In the ninety-eight-day-long maritime strike of 1936–37 not the Maritime Federation but the several unions figured.

The shipowners tried to split the united front by offering a renewal of the agreement to the longshoremen but not to the marine unions. Bridges indignantly refused. This time the demand was for an undisguised union control of the hiring halls. The stronger position of the unions in this strike compared with 1934 was attested by the employers making no attempt to move cargoes. The strike was won all along the line, Bridges' longshoremen, although the employers were willing to grant their demands at the beginning, being the only union on strike through the entire duration.

On August 7, 1937, the Committee for Industrial Organization issued a charter to the Pacific Coast District of the International Longshoremen's Association and Bridges was appointed C.I.O. director for the Pacific Coast. Yet with all the " advanced " views of Bridges the union has been careful to protect " vested interests." Few new members are taken into the organization, while among those who are thus fortunate, the sons of members are given preference. No attempt is made to have enough union members to handle all the work at peak periods. Instead the membership is kept down to a number small enough so that steady work is available to members. So-called permit men are called in to work during rush periods. The longshoremen's conflict with the Sailors' Union over loading and unloading steam schooners, a half century old conflict, which Bridges' union has continued, pertains to the same category of issues. Bridges asserts that it is the lower rate charged by the sailors that he is combating; on their side the sailors maintain that if they charged the longshoremen's rate the work would go to the latter. The Sailors' Union of the Pacific is a militant, compact union distrustful of any outside authority (it had disaffiliated itself from the International Seamen's Union even before the longshoremen's breakout began) including a " united front."

Harry Bridges discovered during the 1934 strike that cargoes could be moved by rail if the waterfront was tied up. His next move, therefore, was to try to achieve control of freight movements by enrolling the warehousemen in the longshore organization. This action, termed as Harry Bridges' " march inland," was bitterly opposed by the coast teamsters' union.

Although the longshoremen had been first to organize the warehousemen in Seattle, the teamsters instituted a similar programme in the fall of 1936. In February 1937 they were given a charter by the American Federation of Labour. Striking warehousemen affiliated with the longshoremen were told by their employers that they could return to work only if they changed their affiliation. The delegate of the Longshoremen's and Warehousemen's union was unseated by the teamster-dominated Central Labour Council. The controversy came to a head in San Francisco. Beck demanded unconditional surrender as the price of peace. William Green backed him up by declaring that the American Federation of Labour would not recognize the decision of the National Labour Relations Board in favour of the longshoremen. However, when a flying wedge of seven hundred longshoremen broke through a ten deep line of teamsters to escort their group to their jobs, the blockade was withdrawn and the Beck forces acknowledged defeat. The teamsters explained their retreat by their consideration for the interests of the California growers whose crop was endangered.

On July 24, 1937, 125,000 sawmill and lumber workers of the Northwest withdrew from the affiliation with the International Brotherhood of Carpenters and Joiners and joined the C.I.O. to form the International Woodworkers' Association. A boycott, to be in effect on a coastwise basis, was immediately instituted by the A.F. of L. union concerned. Portland employers under A.F. of L. pressure declared a lock-out in the city's seven largest mills. In October the National Labour Relations Board certified the C.I.O. as bargaining agency for the mills concerned, but with no effect on the situation. Portland became the centre of a violent struggle between the two rival unions. Finally governor Martin, a Democrat but not a "New Dealer," stepped in and ordered the arrest of the captain of the A.F. of L. river pickets surrounding the C.I.O. operated mills and the secretary of the Portland Council of Teamsters, charging the latter with the burning of two sawmills. In the mayoralty election of 1938 both the Beck controlled incumbent and his C.I.O. rival were defeated by a Chamber of Commerce man. In the statewide primary election in May 1938, both labour factions, for once united, defeated governor Martin by a narrow margin. Out of the turmoil on the Pacific Coast there is slowly being evolved an orderly industrial government. Bridges' union, in spite of the radical reputation of his leadership, has outlawed "quickies" or direct action strikes and is turning to joint Labour Relations Committees or the conciliation method.

A revival in Eastern coast unionism came in 1937 with the National Maritime Union (C.I.O.), a product of insurgency against the " boss-ridden " remnant of the old International Seamen's Union.

(3) *Government Clears the Way for Unionism*

In no other country has government gone as far as under the New Deal to enable unionism to survive, while leaving it on the one hand the complete freedom to strike and on the other hand refraining from vesting it with the status of a public institution. This the New Deal Administration endeavours to achieve by shielding unionism's tender shoots from being stamped out by the employer or smothered by rival growths of his deliberate cultivation. Owing to the absolute uniqueness of this system, it appears proper to give in this survey what some might consider a disproportionate amount of space to the operation of the national labour boards, the especially appointed protectors of unions. These boards followed each other in close succession but with a shifting statutory base due at first to the semi-improvised character of the recovery legislation and then to the fate of the principal recovery act at the hands of the Supreme Court.

Section 7 (a) of the National Industrial Recovery Act of June 1933, gave employees the " right to organize and bargain collectively through representatives of their own choosing " and to be " free from the interference, restraint, or coercion of employers of labour " in their organizing and bargaining activities. This, it should be noted, was not as such statute law; it became law only when written into the codes for the several industries promulgated by the administration. Two months later the President appointed a National Labour Board composed of representatives of labour, industry, and the public, with Senator Wagner of New York chairman.

The powers and functions of the National Labour Board were not clearly defined, but the statement of the President in forming the Board implied that its guiding objective was to prevent strikes as a menace to recovery. Accordingly, decisions were rendered only as a last resort, the Board favouring informal, bi-partite agreements as a means of settlement.

Although the National Labour Board was not specifically ordained to interpret the labour clauses of the Recovery Act, it addressed itself to this function and evolved the foundations of a " common law " of collective bargaining. It was first to proclaim the so-called " majority rule " principle, that a bargaining agent favoured by a majority of the employees in a given unit was to be the *exclusive* representative for *all* the employees in that unit. The employer, of course, favoured collective bargaining " pluralism," for it enabled him to play off one labour group against another, thus heading off real bargaining or at least granting it on more desirable terms to himself. But while the Board was consistent in its support of majority rule, it was hampered by the conflicting and vacillating interpretations by other administration officials.

In an executive order in February 1934, the President announced in unmistakable terms his sanction of majority rule. But a few days later the administrators of the Recovery Act, Hugh S. Johnson and Donald Richberg, issued a joint statement " interpreting " the President's statement in which they insisted that minority groups held the same right to bargain as the majority group. A second statement by President Roosevelt only served to thicken the fog, for now he seemed to be turning towards the principle of pluralism. This he clearly indicated in his personal settlement of the automobile dispute in March 1934.[1] This action of the President not only reversed the concept of majority rule, but by the establishment of an independent Automobile Labour Board injured the prestige of the Board as well.

On the then crucial question of the company union[2] the National Labour Board held that if *freely* chosen by a majority of the employees, it was like a trade union entitled to speak for all employees. The N.R.A. administrators favoured a " perfect neutrality " policy. " The N.R.A. is not a promotional agent for trade unions," said Donald Richberg. It is noteworthy that in the 546 elections to determine bargaining representatives conducted by the Board, 75 per cent. were won by trade unions.

Another important contribution to the new " common law " of industry was this Board's formulation of the mutuality of obligation of employer and employees in the collective bargain-

[1] See above, p. 359

[2] Section 7a specified that " no employee and no one seeking employment shall be required as a condition of employment to join any company union."

ing process. Bargaining, it held, involves give and take, and the employer is equally obligated with the union to contribute toward reaching an agreement. He must present counter plans instead of passively ignoring the proposals of the workers. The absence of the will to agree on the part of the employer and his peremptory rejection of employee proposals were held to be " repugnant to the very concept of collective bargaining." The employer is not, however, required to strike a bargain. It goes without saying that the Board rejected the claim that a company did not have to bargain with elected representatives " unless such representatives were employees of the mill." The Board favoured written agreements, but did not require them.

There were several reasons why the National Labour Board failed of its purpose. It most often came out second in its disagreements with other administration officials. Although its members were only on a part-time basis, it attempted too many varied activities: conciliation, mediation and arbitration, a quasi-judicial interpretation of the labour provisions of the National Industrial Recovery Act, and at times even general labour law administration. The primary cause of its downfall, however, was the lack of adequate means for enforcing its decisions. Senator Wagner found the Department of Justice too slow and even unwilling to handle the Board's cases; he therefore had to rely on an ineffective method provided by the Compliance Division of the National Industrial Recovery Act.

A joint resolution by Congress (" Public Resolution No. 44 ") empowering President Roosevelt to establish labour boards[1] was passed on June 19, 1934, and on June 29, 1934, the National Labour Relations Board was established. Instead of the tri-partite composition of the earlier Board, whose members busy elsewhere were all too frequently absent from its sessions, the new Board consisted of three experts on a full-time basis.

The N.L.R.B. decided not to repeat the mistake of its predecessor in serving both as a board of mediation and as a quasi-judicial body and confined itself to the latter function, namely, interpreting Section 7a. It held to the same principles as its predecessor on the crucial issues of " majority rule,"[2]

[1] Other boards dealing with specific industries, such as steel, textiles, etc., were established under the same resolution.

[2] As in the famous *Houde* case.

company unions, duty to bargain collectively, but following more closely the older quasi-judicial administrative bodies, it succeeded in establishing these as firm maxims in the place of the somewhat off-hand formulations by the older Board.

The Board conducted 579 elections to determine agents for bargaining. A standard procedure was adopted in which the petition for an election went to one of seventeen regional offices. An employer was not given the right to initiate such procedure since, by requesting an election before there was an independent union on the ground or in sufficient strength, he might head off genuine collective bargaining. Company unions succeeded in winning 30 per cent. of the Board elections. The mutuality of the obligation to bargain was further advanced as the employer was held to the duty to bargain even after his employees went on strike.

As with its predecessor, enforcement proved the most difficult problem. In cases involving elections of bargaining representatives the Board had the power to subpoena witnesses and to resort directly to federal courts of appeal for enforcement. In cases other than involving elections, the Board had two means of enforcement. The first was through the N.R.A. with its sanction of the removal of the Blue Eagle from a recalcitrant employer. But by the beginning of 1935 employers were losing respect for this punishment, and neither were consumers as interested as two years earlier. The second method was through the Attorney General, who, however, appeared to feel that his office was not made to handle all the cases which the Board found necessary to prosecute. When the National Industrial Recovery Act was declared unconstitutional on May 27, 1935, the life of the Board ended.

On June 27, 1935, Congress passed the National Labour Relations Act, which at long last established the principles of collective bargaining in the form of statutory law.

Section 1, the statement of policy, deals with the evil effects of unfair labour practices and labour disputes upon the flow of interstate commerce. The essence of the Act lies in the affirmation in Section 7 that " Employees shall have the right of self-organization, to bargain collectively through representatives of their own choosing, and to engage in concerted activities, for the purpose of collective bargaining or other mutual aid or protection." (This is a restatement of Section 7a of the N.I.R.A.) To clarify these rights, five specific unfair labour practices are listed and prohibited in Section 8:

1. To interfere with, restrain, or coerce employees in the exercise of the right guaranteed in Section 7.

2. To dominate or interfere with the formation or administration of any labour organization or to contribute financial or other support to it.

3. To encourage or discourage membership in any labour organization by discrimination in regard to hire or tenure of employment or any term or condition of employment.

4. To discharge or otherwise discriminate against an employee because he has filed charges or given testimony under the Act.

5. To refuse to bargain collectively with the duly chosen representatives of employees.

It is added, however, that nothing in the Act shall be construed to make illegal a closed shop agreement between an employer and the representatives of his employees.

Section 9a restates the principle that the representatives of a majority of the employees in an appropriate unit shall be the exclusive representatives of all employees in that unit. Section 9b empowers the Board to determine what the appropriate unit for the purposes of collective bargaining shall be, and 9c authorizes the Board to conduct elections in cases of representation disputes and to certify to employer and workers the names of the chosen representatives.

The Board itself cannot inflict any penalties and can secure compliance with its orders only by petitioning the appropriate circuit court, which may issue a decree enforcing, modifying, or setting aside the Board's order. The defendant, similarly, may appeal to the court to set aside or modify the order. In case of non-compliance, the only penalty is that inflicted by the court for contempt of court decree. In reviewing the Board's cases the courts will refuse to hear any new evidence which had not been presented at the Board hearings.

The sensational validation of the Wagner Act by the Supreme Court on April 12, 1937, surprised a great many who were certain that it would be held invalid, including the American Liberty League lawyers who had issued a public brief "proving" it was unconstitutional. The Supreme Court has also ruled in the Bethlehem Shipbuilding Company Case that the district courts may not issue injunctions to prevent the Board from holding hearings. So far (June 1938) the United States Supreme Court has upheld the Board in every case that has come before it.

The Board re-adopted the rule that only employees and labour organizations but not employers may initiate an action. This rule, not prescribed in the Act itself, is deeply resented by the employers who feel that it emphasizes their inequality before the law.

In presenting the principles established by the Board it seems advisable to deal with the material in terms of the specific sections of the Act under which the cases have arisen.

One of the major methods of employer interference with the right of employee self-organization prohibited under Section 8 (1) is that of industrial espionage, either by outside agencies, by the employers themselves, or by their confidential employees. How widespread this activity is has been shown by the La Follette "Civil Liberties Committee."[1] The Board held that espionage in itself does not necessarily constitute a violation of Section 8 (1) of the Act, but espionage related to union activity does.[2] The most common type of interference under subdivision (1) is the spreading of anti-union propaganda. The so-called Mohawk Valley Formula[3] of Remington-Rand, Inc., openly listed the kinds of propaganda necessary to break a strike or organization drive. It is evidently the policy of the

[1] The General Motors Corporation and its Divisions expended from January 1, 1934, to July 31, 1936, $994,855·68 for detective agency service. The Pinkerton Detective Agency, which specializes in industrial espionage, admitted that it had 304 operatives who were members of unions, of whom almost a third held offices of varying importance, including one national vice-president, fourteen presidents of locals, six treasurers and thirty-four secretaries of their locals which gave them access to the list of members.

(*Violations of Free Speech and Rights of Labour*, "Industrial Espionage," Washington, 1937, pp. 25, 28. This is what every labour leader conversant with his job has long known.)

[2] *First Annual Report*, p. 71–3.

[3] This was an outgrowth of the struggle between the Company and the International Association of Machinists begun as a strike in 1936, continued before the Board and presumably ended when the U.S. Supreme Court upheld in 1938 the Board's order to reinstate the several thousand strikers whose places had in the meantime been filled. The "formula" included, among its several "steps," the dramatic staging of "back to work" movements, and the moulding of public opinion through "citizen's committees."

Board to consider as a violation any activity which is prejudicial to unionism, no matter how obscure the connection appears to be on the surface. In the case of the Clover Fork Coal Co. of Harlan County, Kentucky, the Board ordered the Company to sever its connection with the Harlan County Coal Operators' Association because one of the major functions of that Association is to act against the organization of mine workers.[1]

Under subdivision (2) interdicting employer domination of employees' organizations the Board found that a violation may be committed even if the employer does not actively control the organization. In the matter of the Lion Shoe Co. the employer threatened removal of the plant to another place as a means of replacing the independent union with a company union.[2] A similar instance occurred when an employer threatened to move out of town, and a citizens' committee was formed to father an employees' association in opposition to the union.[3]

In the test cases of the Pennsylvania Greyhound Lines, Inc., and the Pacific Greyhound Lines, Inc., decided February 28, 1938, the Supreme Court ruled that the Board had the authority to order the disestablishment of company unions.[4]

In cases arising under subdivision (3) prohibiting discrimination against union members the Board takes into account whether the employer is known to be anti-union and to what an extent this prejudice might be lurking behind the charge of inefficiency if such was given as the cause. The Board will not permit an employer to discriminate against union members when the plant is reopened after a shut-down.

On the duty to bargain collectively specified in sub-division (5) of Section 8 and Section 9a the Board has distinguished four essential factors: that the employer should go farther than merely meet with the representatives of his employees;[5] that there must be a serious intent to adjust differences;[6] that the employer must approach the negotiations with an open mind;[7]

[1] 4 N.L.R.B., No. 33.
[2] 2 N.L.R.B., 819.
[3] Matter of Ansin Shoe Manufacturing Co., 1 N.L.R.B., 929.
[4] 58 Sp. Ct. 571, 577.
[5] *First Annual Report*, p. 85.
[6] Matter of Canton Enamelling and Stamping Co., 1 N.L.R.B., 402.
[7] Matter of Atlantic Refining Co., 1 N.L.R.B., 359.

and that the employer must act in good faith.[1] Although three of the four are subjective and therefore difficult to determine, the presence or absence of other violations constitutes vital clues. It is not necessary, however, that a collective agreement be reached, for when the differences are of such a nature that every effort to resolve them reached an impasse, the duty to bargain collectively has been fulfilled. Should conditions be altered soon afterwards, the employer must begin negotiations again. In the De Witt Insulator case[2] the rift had been considered insuperable and bargaining stopped, but when the employees later went on strike, the Board held that the company should have recognized it as an " auspicious time to meet " with the employees. Naturally, therefore, the occurrence of a strike does not eliminate the duty of the employer to bargain collectively. The employer must indicate his willingness to negotiate in exactly the same manner as if there were no strike, and must fulfil his collective bargaining duties with the same intent and zeal as in peaceful times.[3] Moreover, the employer may not decline to put in writing an understanding reached with the bargaining representatives.[4]

In regard to majority rule, it was held that not only do employees have the original right to select their representatives, but that they may change them at any time they so desire, an existing agreement with the employer passing to the new bargaining agency. In the Hubinger Company case the Board decided that a contract between the company and a plant union is no bar to an order for a new election, even though the plant union had previously been chosen in a " consent election " certified by the Board.[5]

[1] 1 N.L.R.B., 562.

[2] Matter of Jeffrey-De Witt Insulator Co., 1 N.L.R.B., 618.

[3] Matter of S. L. Allen and Co., 1 N.L.R.B., 714. Matter of Columbian Enamelling and Stamping Co., 1 N.L.R.B. 181.

[4] Matter of the St. Joseph Stockyards Co., 2 N.L.R.B., 39. In the famous Inland Steel Co. case, in which the employers *before* the negotiations had begun announced that they would not conclude an agreement with the Steel Workers' Organizing Committee even though the latter's proposals might appear acceptable, the Board held that the " reduction of collective agreements to writing has become an integral element of the collective bargaining process . . . [and that the respondent] must comply with this requirement to the same extent that it must meet, negotiate in good faith, and accept the other conditions of the collective bargaining procedure." (6 N.L.R.B., No. 66.)

[5] 4 N.L.R.B., No. 31.

The most vexatious problem faced by the Board was that of determining the appropriate unit for collective bargaining. In cases of disputes between two unions affiliated with the same central labour body the Board found an easy solution in consistently refusing to take action, leaving the decision to that central organization.[1] The difficulty has come to a head in disputes where both an A.F. of L. affiliate and a C.I.O. union claimed that their organization corresponds to the appropriate unit. Since in a large number of cases the Board has designated the unit covered by the C.I.O. union, the A.F. of L. has frequently stated that the N.L.R.B. is showing favouritism to the C.I.O. In those cases where an A.F. of L. unit is designated, the C.I.O. has of course countered with criticism of an opposite nature, but their statements have been neither as extreme nor as numerous as those of the A.F. of L. To the unprejudiced observer it would seem evident that the Board is not playing favourites either way, but is simply attempting to arrive at the soundest conclusion based on objective facts. The Board uses various criteria in determining the appropriate unit—weighing these as the data of the particular case indicate. These criteria may be summarized as:[2]

1. The history of labour relations in the industry and between the particular employer and his employees. The Board has found it advisable to adhere to traditional units insofar as possible, unless weighty reasons are found for changing the practice.

2. The desire of the employees themselves. This must of course be a major consideration, and is often the deciding factor. In the case of the Greyhound Bus Lines, for example, the Board found that, other things being equal, the employees' choice is the ultimate criterion.[3]

3. Functional coherence and mutual interest. This may include such factors as the nature of the work, level of skill, wages and geographical and physical considerations; in other words, the attempt is to find what organizational unit will be most harmonious internally and will most greatly facilitate collective bargaining.

[1] Matter of Aluminium Co. of America, 1 N.L.R.B., 530.
[2] *First Annual Report*, pp. 113–120; *Second Annual Report*, pp. 125–140.
[3] 4 N.L.R.B., Nos. 37, 37a and 37b.

In the leading case of the Allis-Chalmers plant of West Allis, Wisconsin, a contract of the United Automobile Workers (C.I.O.) with the company left it to the Board to decide whether that union shall be the bargaining agency for the whole plant or whether the craftsmen shall be excluded. The Board in a two to one decision gave each of the three crafts the opportunity to indicate by a majority vote that it wanted to bargain separately. The dissenting members called this a " pseudo-democratic " step, in that it left " a determination of the greatest consequence for the other employees in the plant in the hands of groups known to be hostile to industrial organization." Recently the Board has been following a consistent policy in choosing employer rather than plant units for large companies having many plants. This principle has been evidenced by the cases of the American Steel and Wire Company, the Postal Telegraph and Cable Company, the American Woollen Company, and Swift and Company.[1]

Under Section 9c providing for investigating and certification of representatives, the Board is given authority to certify representatives with or without election. No election is held if a labour organization can present adequate proof that it represents a majority of employees in an appropriate unit. Such proof may consist of petitions or authorization cards required by employees, membership rolls of a union, admission by the employer that a given organization represents a majority of his employees, or adequate and undisputed testimony from union officers. Under normal conditions, the Board provides when ordering an election that those employed on the date of the direction of the election may vote, or preferably that those should vote who are " on the payroll on the date of payment of wages immediately preceding the date of this direction."[2] When a strike is in progress, as in the case of the Saxon Mills,[3] the order stated that those eligible to vote were those who were on the payroll on the last working day prior to the strike. To prevent sabotage by an instigated boycott of the election, the Board held after August 1936, that the term " by a majority of the employees " in the Act meant a majority of those voting.[4]

[1] N.L.R.B. Release, March 14, 1938.
[2] Matter of Pittsburgh Steel Co., 1 N.L.R.B. 256.
[3] 1 N.L.R.B. 153.
[4] 2 N.L.R.B. 159.

In several cases the question of employer choice of the organization with which he will bargain has been raised. The Board held that the employer has no right to exercise such a choice. In the National Electric Products Corporation Case the Board held that if a contract is made with one of the rival organizations, its numerical strength being in doubt, such contract is void.[1] In the Consolidated Edison Company case charges were filed by C.I.O. locals that a company union had been chartered by the A.F. of L. and hence the agreements made were invalid. In this case the N.L.R.B. found evidence of employer favouritism and declared the contract void.[2]

As a last point, the question of certification of company unions must be touched on. If the Board, after formal action under Section 8 (2) finds that one of the rival unions claiming certification is a company union, that union will not be given a place on the ballot. If, however, the bona fide unions or unions involved fail to file charges concerning the illegality of the company union, the Board directs that such an organization is to be put on the ballot.

Yet with all the Board's close scrutiny of unions for signs of dependence on the employer or of his undue favouritism, company unionism is far from outlived in America. Company unionism has met the mandate for an autonomous labour organization through a self-metamorphosis into " independent " unionism with the employer ostentatiously maintaining a hands-off policy. Often in such cases the organizer is a member of the legal profession or another variety of "disinterested citizen." The phenomenon is more common in smaller towns than in metropolitan areas.

" Independent " unions were involved in about one-third of the total number of elections held by the Board between 1935 and December 1937. Of about 237 elections, forty-nine were of the " consent " type where only an " independent " union appeared on the ballot to be voted " for " or " against." " Independent " unions won forty-one and lost only eight of these elections. In the elections involving an " independent " union competing with a trade union, the former won seventy-seven and lost 101 such elections.[3]

[1] 3 N.L.R.B., No. 47.
[2] 4 N.L.R.B., No. 10.
[3] *Business Week*, No. 436, Jan. 8, 1938.

The employers' main line of attack on the industrial relations set-up wrought by the Board is to demand that the trade unions be made "responsible" through compulsory legal incorporation and that the Wagner Act be amended by the inclusion of a list of "unfair practices" by labour unions such as coercion to join a union, the sit-down strike, etc.

(4) *The Civil War in American Labour.*

The rise of the C.I.O., which created the current internal crisis in the American labour movement, has been acclaimed by the "intelligentsia" as the long overdue self-adjustment by American unionism to its capitalist environment and as paralleling British unionism's behaviour of fifty years ago. But exultation aside, the problem is why British labour was able to absorb its "new unionism" without an internal catastrophe whereas here we have an ever sharpening civil war threatening the effectiveness if not the existence of both the "old" and the "new" unionism. Nor will it do to lay the blame on reactionary or adventurist leadership (depending on factional viewpoint) to say nothing of falling back upon the oft asserted predilection of the English for "constitutional" procedure.

To people on the outside the labour movement is either a potential instrument to enact a new social order along the lines of their own particular blueprint or a truculent business unionism. Neither view is conscious of the labour movement as a "going government," with the foremost problem of how much or how little to govern its constituent organizations. On the whole the degree to which a labour movement in a given country operates as such a "government" is determined by the degree of the existing class consciousness which as a cementing influence of the psychological order acts as an effective substitute for the mechanical process of governing. It is here where the difference in the governments of the labour movements of Britain and America lies. British labour still can afford to permit competing unions in the same craft as well as competition for members between craft unions and industrial unions, since the common class consciousness of the British workers will avert disastrous internecine war and, above all, treasonable alliances with the employers by one union against a rival union. Accordingly, British unionism never made its central organization, the Trades Union Congress, into an agency to keep order at home by allotting definite jurisdictions to each union. Not internal government but external policy—pressure on Parliament—was the *raison d'être* of the Trades Union Congress. Thus British unionism as a whole came to resemble in structure what the zoologists call a colonial organism rather than a differentiated and unified organism. In such an " unorganized " cluster new growth does not raise a problem of a new internal balance or of an official remaking of internal boundaries. In the 'eighties of the past century when pressure came for a reorientation of policy; when the self-imposed political monasticism of the old leadership stood exposed as a blindness to a real opportunity to advance labour's interests, and their neglect of the unskilled as a failure to hear new voices calling for organization, the combat, so far as the Trades Union Congress was concerned, could go on solely on the ideological plane without involving an internal governmental function. Since the Congress never undertook to stand guard over "jurisdictions," the issue of craft versus industrial unionism could not drag it into a crisis of its internal government. For all the furore of the fight, the Congress could remain a peaceful forum in which each faction made propaganda for its cause.

Different was the governmental evolution of American labour. At the time when new unionism began to grip England, in America the labour movement took shape as the American Federation of Labour. The founding fathers, especially Samuel Gompers, since their handiwork had arisen on the ruins of the Knights of Labour, a centralized body constantly given to interfering in the affairs of the trades, naturally emphasized in their utterances the right of the affiliated unions to unhindered self-government. But as a matter of fact it was the menace of " dualism," namely the menace of organizations under the Knights of Labour engaging in cut-throat competition with the craft unions, that had caused the latter to form a defensive alliance in the American Federation of Labour and above all made them endow that organization with the all-overshadowing function of protecting jurisdictions. Thus while Gompers and his associates kept speaking of the Federation as if it were a perfect anarchist commune which any union was free to join or quit at will, from the beginning the Federation has really functioned as a government, the sole source of all jurisdictional grants and their supreme defender. Instead of being, like the British federation, merely an arena for ideological disputes and for formulating labour's demands on the country, the American Federation has acted as a governing entity. Its annual conventions far from being just meetings for comparing experiences and passing on policies were councils of ambassadors in which the officers of each affiliated international union, frequently caring little for the "generalities" discussed, kept an eye on the jurisdictional issue and were quick to demand their rights from the common government. It stands to reason that in an organization thus constituted a demand for structural changes in the union movement of necessity involves the basic governmental function of the Federation and is therefore prone to evoke a constitutional crisis. For here issues of strategy and personalities, explosive materials in themselves, are fatally commingled with that of maintenance of orderly government. To the open-eyed observer the most startling element in the A.F. of L.-C.I.O. war has not been the *élan* of the newer organization but the solidification of the ranks in the older organization and the spirit of resistance to the bitter end among the very groups in the A.F. of L. ideologically sympathetic to industrial unionism. This did not happen at once, but only as the issue became the defence of the established governmental procedure of the Federation. Progressives and socialists began to prefer conservative government to disruption and anarchy.

That the leadership of the American Federation of Labour, with few exceptions, notably Lewis, Hillman, Dubinsky, and Zaritzky, was utterly unprepared to take advantage of the sudden opportunity that opened with the New Deal goes without saying. The militancy of 1919–1923 had failed to push up into the upper tier of leadership a younger and aggressive group. That militant movement, as was seen, was thoroughly defeated in battle and was simultaneously smothered by "welfare capitalism." Also the attack by the communists, whether as "boring from within" or as assailing from without, drove the "progressives" among union leaders to seek shelter behind the ramparts of the A.F. of L. orthodoxy, in whose defenders the "will to resist" the attacks from the "left" had not been weakened by the profession of a progressive ideology at the time or earlier. In the 'twenties, therefore, the leadership by the elder statesmen and their faithful younger lieutenants remained unchallenged. During the "welfare capitalism" epoch these leaders adjusted themselves without too great a mental conflict to a "territory" resembling Poland after the second partition and felt so weak an impulse towards a "transvaluation of values" that it took three years of depression to shake their opposition to compulsory unemployment insurance. It was upon such leadership mentality that the New Deal burst.

It would be unjust, however, to attribute the failure to exploit that opportunity during 1933–5 entirely to the ineptitude of the A.F. of L. leadership. President Roosevelt, who was and is the New Deal, was unable to decide until his campaign for re-election whether he had been called by history to be the great social peacemaker or the greater organizer of the "underdog" groups. Thus, as we saw, on the crucial issue of collective bargaining representation he vacillated between the majority rule principle and "pluralism," indeed settling upon the latter as far as the nation's most dynamic industry, namely the auto industry, was concerned. Nevertheless, the profound lack of faith on the part of the A.F. of L. leadership in the possibility and in all too many cases even the desirability of adding the mass production workers in the big industries to organized labour cannot but be given first place among the causes of failure. In truth many of these leaders saw in the very fillip to joining unions nothing more than a chance to add a few new members to their small but tightly controlled organizations—not too many for that might upset the existing balance within.

At the convention in San Francisco, in 1934, it appeared as if the frozen surface had at last begun to break. The Executive Council, increased to eighteen with Lewis and Dubinsky among the new members, was authorized to issue national charters to the workers in autos, rubber, cement and aluminium along what the progressives at the time believed to be unstinted industrial lines. Although the resolution specified that the rights of the craft unions were not to be impaired, they regarded it as mere verbal face-saving. However, when it came to issuing the first charter, to the auto workers in the summer of 1935, the Executive Council specifically excluded the craftsmen as well as the plants manufacturing auto parts.[1]

At the next convention, which met in November in Atlantic City,[2] the battle between the conservatives and the progressives was fought out to the end in a debate which will remain outstanding in American annals. In the author's view the conservatives, in this debate as well as in what was to follow, committed two cardinal mistakes based on a misreading of the history of their own movement. They sought to identify the demand for industrial unions in the mass production industries with the earlier broader-based organizations, the Knights of Labour, the American Railway Union, the Socialist Trade and Labour Alliance, the Industrial Workers of the World, and the One Big Union. In reality these earlier " C.I.O.'s " lacked pragmatic validity because they insisted that they had a universal organizational blueprint for all labour. By contrast, the " industrialists " of 1935 merely demanded that the A.F. of L. continue to apply its own " experimental " method in the spirit of the grant of an industry-wide jurisdiction to the United Mine Workers by the Scranton convention in 1901. In the actual situation the pursuit of the traditional " trial and error " method would have resulted in the relinquishing by the craft unions of their unexercised or paper jurisdictions in those industries and in clear, unclouded titles to the industrial unions about to be chartered. In its place the leadership chose to view the new proposals with an ill-becoming intellectual superciliousness as though from the height of the only true interpreters of American labour history. The second error was to read the Dartmouth College Case[3] doctrine into the constitution of the American Federation of Labour, thereby converting a union's grant of jurisdiction as laid down in its charter from

[1] See above pp. 358–363.

[2] At this convention John L. Lewis and William L. Hutcheson, president of the carpenters, had a physical encounter.

[3] In this early constitutional law case the United States Supreme Court decided that a charter issued by a state to a private corporation was a contract which could not be modified by one-sided action by the state.

the A.F. of L. into a " legal " contract unalterable except with the consent of that union. Thus " historians " and " lawyers," perhaps not for the first time in history, have unwittingly laboured to produce a " revolution."

The " revolution " came when the progressives, undismayed by their defeat, eighteen to eleven in a card vote, shortly after the convention adjourned, organized the Committee for Industrial Organization with the avowed purpose of carrying out the plan embodied in the minority report. The unions which formed the C.I.O. were the United Mine Workers, the International Ladies' Garment Workers' Union, the Amalgamated Clothing Workers, the United Textile Workers, the Oil Field, Gas Well and Refinery Workers, and the International Union of Mine, Mill and Smelter Workers. In addition, President Charles Howard of the International Typographical Union and President Max Zaritzky of the Cap and Millinery Department of the United Hatters, Cap and Millinery Workers' Union, joined in their personal capacities. Soon the C.I.O. was joined by the Federation of Flat Glass Workers, the Amalgamated Association of Iron, Steel and Tin Workers, the United Automobile Workers and the United Rubber Workers. Subsequently the C.I.O. accepted two industrial unions which were not members of the A.F. of L.—the Industrial Union of Marine and Shipbuilding Workers, a dual organization to every union in the Metal Trades Department of the A.F. of L., and the United Electrical and Radio Workers, a seceded union from the International Brotherhood of Electrical Workers.

The Executive Council of the A.F. of L. disallowed the claim of the C.I.O. that its purpose was solely to organize the workers in the mass production industries and to bring them within the A.F. of L., and invoked against the C.I.O. the sanctions appropriate in combating a " dual " body. After the accused unions had failed to appear at the set hearing, the Executive Council suspended them from the A.F. of L. and thereby denied them the right of being represented at the next convention. To do so the Council was obliged to interpret the constitution which only specified that *expulsion* of an international trade union may take place by a two-thirds majority of the convention and passed over in silence the procedure in *suspensions*, as itself possessing the latter power by implication.

The convention of 1936 at Tampa, Florida, upheld these suspensions. The C.I.O. unions made no effort to force an entry into this convention except for Zaritzky who was there by undisputed right and ably represented his side.

Prior to the Tampa convention, in response to mediation by Zaritzky, supported by Dubinsky, the A.F. of L. had appointed a committee of three to be in readiness to negotiate with the C.I.O. Lewis refused to convene a C.I.O. conference until after the national election and the movement for peace was left hanging in the air. During the year that ensued the C.I.O. was too busy conquering motors and steel and the A.F. of L., too, had awakened to an aggressive organizing activity under the spur of this rivalry. By the time of the A.F. of L. convention in Denver, in October 1937, both camps had grown enormously, each claiming over 3,000,000, and in the A.F. of L., in which a year earlier the war was but a general's war, the war spirit had penetrated to the lower ranks down to sergeant and corporal. In the meantime the renewal of the depression had strengthened the peacemakers' influence and between October and December a series of meetings took place between the committee of three of the A.F. of L. and a committee of ten appointed by Lewis. A proposal to readmit the C.I.O. as an independent department of the A.F. of L. with final authority over jurisdictional matters was properly dimissed by the A.F. of L. as merely transferring the warfare from without to within its bounds; it might have dismissed it on the ground that it was based on an utter, perhaps wilful misunderstanding of the nature of the American labour movement as a "government." The most troublesome issue was that of finding a place in the A.F. of L. for the two dozen new C.I.O. unions, such as the Transport Workers' and Maritime Workers', which were "dual" to A.F. of L. unions. There exist two conflicting versions as to what the A.F. of L. had really offered: one supported by Dubinsky and endorsed by Green, is to the effect that it proposed to grant industrial jurisdictions to a number of unions and to negotiate with regard to the "dual" unions but to have them all re-enter the portals of the A.F. of L. *en bloc*. The other version, given by Phillip Murray, the C.I.O.'s chief negotiator and to which a public statement of Tobin of the Teamsters (A.F. of L.) has lent some support, insists that the offer aimed at breaking up the C.I.O. solidarity since under it the original C.I.O. unions would have been readmitted forthwith but the new and "dual" unions would have been left to negotiate about their admission. The negotiations were broken off.

But whence this resistance power of the defenders of the cause of the American Federation of Labour, which only as late as 1937 many considered a "lost cause," granted that their will to resist can be explained? Are they not doomed to failure in this age of machine technology and mass production demanding a class conscious labour movement and unionism by industry? Or is there nothing in the theory of the survival of the fittest? The answer is that one must not become overwhelmed by the sole importance of the technological factor in determining the fitness or unfitness of a labour movement. Labour is hardly headed for a metamorphosis into an unskilled factory proletariat. The idea that it is so is a survival from early Marxism. Whether the real deep-seated aspirations of those who joined the new C.I.O. unions differ from those of craft unionists is more than open to question. Both movements can well be explained on the basis of a job consciousness without assuming any revolutionary class consciousness. Both are thinking above all in terms of job control and of formal agreements with the employers.

Nor is there any appreciable difference in their respective fighting effectiveness. Where the C.I.O. has the advantage of a more flexible and more inventive strategy, the older organization derives strength from the greater cohesiveness of those who as craftsmen or near-craftsmen feel that their jobs come out of a well-defined common job-reservoir. Also the A.F. of L. is more readily acceptable to the employers and especially to the middle classes, which, so far as labour is concerned, will more easily forgive violence that does not advertise itself as revolutionary than they will overlook a revolutionary label even if pasted on by an enemy.

A prominent place in the rival interpretations and evaluations by students of the A.F. of L.-C.I.O. controversy is occupied by the Knights of Labour.[1] One school viewing the C.I.O.

[1] The "Noble Order of the Knights of Labour" was formed in 1869 and in the middle of the 'eighties it became the beneficiary of the Great Upheaval of Labour at that time. It reached a membership of 750,000 in 1887 but soon declined.

as the re-incarnation of the Knights with their insistence on the solidarity of all labour but without the Knights' "excess baggage" (meaning apparently their middle class, frontier, anti-monopoly beliefs), feels that it must explain the demise of the latter on grounds other than the unfitness of its broad base of organization and discovers it in the inadequate leadership of Grand Master Workman T. V. Powderly, described as a meddling windy orator without a glimmer of realism. Powderly is contrasted with a Mephistophelean Gompers who appealed to the lower nature of the trade unionists, their craftsmen's "job-consciousness" (a more idealistic Gompers, so the theory goes, would have been equally successful had he appealed to their upper nature upholding labour solidarity), imparting to the whole a pseudo-idealistic aspect by tying it together with "voluntarism" and the right of the self determination of each group. The other school, to which the present author belongs, convinced that the foremost problem of American labour has forever been that of organizing and staying organized against the disruptive influences of the predominant individualism, interprets the victory of Gompers and the American Federation of Labour not as a demonstration of an all-time superiority of unionism by craft but as proof that in the American environment unity around the job had always been the sole realizable unity. This principle spelled craft unionism under the circumstances of fifty years ago as it spells industrial unionism in the modern mass production industries. To this the "Wisconsin" theory makes the further emphatic *addendum*: while a widening labour solidarity is inevitable under modern industrial conditions, yet where craft or compound-craft units had already been formed with delimited nation-wide "job-territories," such wider solidarity is easiest secured through the "federal" principle rather than through merger or amalgamation. By contrast, where, as in the mass production industries, the field has remained unplowed (because the employer had kept the union plowman out of bounds), unionism by industry should be the natural form. Here, too, however, it would be a transgression against realism and hardly a service to labour idealism to overlook the "going government" aspect of the American labour movement. In sum, to-day the C.I.O. is cementing new, "stream-lined" units of solidarity, repeating under modern conditions Gompers' service of an earlier day. But with leadership in the rôle of the modern building architect eager to break new paths, cognizance must still be taken of the total situation, the heritage of the past as well as the creation for the future. And since the job is obviously not only that of new construction but also of mutually adjusting the old and the new, with the common enemy forever at the gate, elementary prudence should forbid carrying on blasting operations seemingly for the sheer joy of seeing the older building shake in its foundations.

(5) *Political Action*

By and large the New Deal was a windfall to labour. When labour supported the Democrats in 1932 it hardly expected in case of success more than a sort of a Wilson Administration revised up-to-date, an administration which would not whittle down the improved legal rights of the unions granted by the Norris-La Guardia Act[1] but endeavour to enlarge them, in addition to helping restore union wage standards and to extending aid to the unemployed. Instead the little-looked-for occurred: with all of its vacillation on the issue of majority representation in collective bargaining, labour found the Administration elevating into its official creed many of its own most cherished principles. Accordingly, in the campaign of 1936 this administration deserved at the hands of labour more than the customary endorsement given to friendly administrations in the past. While the Executive Council of the A.F. of L. was held back by Republican influences within from throwing itself into the election on the Roosevelt side, and contented itself with an indirect and a rather restrained endorsement based on a detailed comparison of the " records " of both parties, many individual A.F. of L. unions joined with the unions now in the C.I.O. to take a more active part in the campaign. The device was Labour's Non-Partisan League under the

[1] The Act specifically declared that contracts, which labour with a purposeful disregard of euphemism designates as " yellow dog " contracts, are contrary to public policy and shall not be enforceable in federal courts; minutely circumscribed the power to issue injunctions by stressing the procedural side of the matter; granted jury trials in cases of contempt not committed in the presence of the court; and obligated the judge concerned, upon the request of the defendant, to refrain from sitting in the contempt case.

chairmanship of George P. Berry, President of the International Pressmen's Union (A.F. of L.). Branches of the League were formed in a number of states; international unions subscribed heavily including more than half a million by Lewis' United Mine Workers, and international union officials campaigned personally.

In New York the League operated as a *sui generis* " third party." There the building trades unions and the Central Trades and Labour Council had habitually delivered their votes to Tammany just as the garment unions had habitually given theirs to the radical parties. In this campaign the socialists in the garment unions who were predominantly of the " old guard "[1] variety, did the unusual and endorsed a Democrat for President. The problem now consisted in securing for Roosevelt the radical voters, to whom the Democratic label spelled Tammany, and was solved by creating the American Labour Party having a list of presidential electors identical with the Democratic.[2] Thus the time-hallowed " reward your friends " strategy was skilfully combined with independent political action, leaving either method or a combination of both available for the future.[3] The party polled 250,000 votes.

In the mayoralty election of November 1937 the party joined with the Fusion group (Republicans and anti-Tammany Democrats) to run the incumbent, Fiorello La Guardia, a nominal Republican and joint author of the Norris-La Guardia Act of 1932. The party's own vote increased to 490,000, giving it the balance of power in the pivotal state of New York and in all probability a determining influence in the Democratic nomination for President in 1940.

In other states the League operated within the Democratic party primaries, differing from the time-hallowed method of the A.F. of L. only by its much greater energy and initiative. In Wisconsin and Minnesota, both of which are governed by " third " parties, the state federations of labour (A.F. of L.) have anticipated the League by several years.

[1] The old Socialist Party had split between the " old guard " and a " militant " younger group drawn more heavily from the native-born intelligentsia. The communists, true to the " new line " of the Comintern put up a perfunctory campaign for their candidate, Earl Browder.

[2] The list included eight American Labour Party men.

[3] See above, pp. 336–338, for the evolution of American labour's political strategy.

It is on the political front that labour is threatened with the gravest consequences from the split in its ranks. On the industrial front the warfare in the form of strike-breaking has been prominent, as was seen on the Pacific Coast in addition to a relatively limited number of minor situations. Another and less sharp form of struggle on the same front, through the conclusion of a closed shop contract with an employer for the purpose of shutting out a rival, might have assumed mass character if the National Labour Relations Board had not put an end to it by refusing to recognize such a contract as a valid contract. The war of the rival labour centres has thus been transferred into the now all-important political arena.

That the whole nature of the American labour struggle has been altered since the election of 1936 and the validation of the Wagner Act in April 1937 is clearly demonstrated by the failure of the employers to take advantage of the recession of 1937–8 to gain back lost ground in wages and union recognition. This " anomaly " is clearly due not to labour's economic bargaining strength but to the shielding it is receiving from the Administration and its boards. Of this even the most conservative A.F. of L. leaders are fully aware. To win employer support against the C.I.O. they might criticize "bureaucracy" and even echo the standard business-men's objection to " spending oneself into prosperity " as well as make much of the " partiality " of the National Labour Relations Board for the C.I.O., yet they have significantly failed to join with the employer and the senatorial critics of the Board in demanding its abolition. Instead they have directed their fire at the way in which the Act is being administered by the present personnel of the Board. The Board would give them complete satisfaction if it followed the " Wisconsin idea " which gives the employer the freedom to conclude an " all-union " (closed shop) contract with any *independent* labour organization regardless of whether it represents a majority of the employees[1]—confident that if such were the case the A.F. of L. would be his certain choice. Obviously, the government-enforced rights to organize and to bargain collectively have

[1] The Wisconsin Labour Act, one of the five state enactments of this kind, thus interpreted the clause legalizing an " all union agreement."

proved far too valuable to risk losing them by a real campaign against the Board.

But if the political weapon has become the unions' paramount weapon, the A.F. of L.-C.I.O. war is threatening to strike it from their hands. In the American community, constituted as it is, labour's success in politics is utterly impossible without unity. The political strategists of the C.I.O. had assumed that their nominees could draw enough support from A.F. of L. membership, the injunction of the leaders notwithstanding, and from the middle classes, to win. This assumption has been disproved in the municipal campaigns in Seattle and Detroit[1] and in the Pennsylvania State primary election—all in the spring of 1938—for while the C.I.O. lists polled a heavy vote, they simultaneously precipitated a fatal anti-labour concentration. These failures contrast with the success in New York where the American Labour Party formally embraces both A.F. of L. and C.I.O. unions. Significantly, in each of these situations the defeat while decisive was by a margin not so wide that a shift of the A.F. of L. vote could not have given labour an equally decisive victory. Recently the danger from disunity has become still graver as shown by the Congressional election in November 1938. Truly the future of American labour may be decided by the speed with which the breach in its economic organization will be repaired. Formerly the Gompers-trained leadership insisted, and with justice, that political action if not cautiously conducted, held the threat of disruption of the economic organization of labour, after which, they said, " all would be lost." At present, by a curious reversal, the existing disruption in labour's economic organization threatens catastrophe to its political influence, after which, although it would be a manifest exaggeration to claim that " all would be lost," yet an opportunity, perhaps unequalled in all American labour's history, might thereby be irrevocably missed.

[1] In the Minneapolis mayoralty election in 1937 the teamsters' candidate (under Trotzkyist influence) succumbed in the elimination primary to the communist-endorsed official Farmer-Labour candidate, enabling the conservatives to win the election as a result of the irreparable split in the labour movement.

STATISTICAL TABLES

TABLE I

Average Weekly Earnings in Representative New York Factories.[1]

Year	Earnings	Year	Earnings
1920 ...	$28·15	1928 ...	$29·44
1921 ...	25·72	1929 ...	29·99
1922 ...	25·04	1930 ...	28·81
1923 ...	27·24	1931 ...	26·42
1924 ...	27·68	1932 ...	22·73
1925 ...	28·26	1933 ...	21·83
1926 ...	29·02	1934 ...	23·19
1927 ...	29·30	1935 ...	24·36

TABLE II

Index Number of Wages Per Hour[2] (1913=100).

Year	Index	Year	Index
1920 ...	234	1928 ...	232
1921 ...	218	1929 ...	233
1922 ...	208	1930 ...	229
1923 ...	217	1931 ...	217
1924 ...	223	1932 ...	186
1925 ...	226	1933 ...	178
1926 ...	229	1934 ...	200
1927 ...	231		

TABLE III

Estimated Annual Average Indexes of Cost of Goods Purchased by Wage Earners and Lower-Salaried Workers in 32 Large Cities Combined.[3]

(Average 1923–25=100)

Year	Index	Year	Index
1920 ...	116·2	1929 ...	99·5
1921 ...	103·6	1930 ...	97·0
1922 ...	97·2	1931 ...	88·6
1923 ...	99·0	1932 ...	79·8
1924 ...	99·2	1933 ...	75·8
1925 ...	101·8	1934 ...	75·6
1926 ...	102·6	1935 ...	80·7
1927 ...	100·6	1936 ...	81·6
1928 ...	99·5	1937 ...	84·3

[1] *Handbook of Labour Statistics*, U.S. Bureau of Labour Statistics, 1936, p. 931.
[2] *Ibid.*, p. 1057.
[3] *Monthly Labour Review*, March 1938, p. 734.

TABLE IV

Trend of Employment and Payrolls in Manufacturing Industries[1]

(1923–25=100)

	Employment	*Payroll*
1920	108·2	117·1
1921	82·3	76·2
1922	90·6	81·3
1923	104·1	103·3
1924	96·5	96·1
1925	99·4	100·6
1926	101·2	103·8
1927	98·9	101·8
1928	98·9	102·4
1929	104·8	109·1
1930	91·5	88·7
1931	77·4	67·5
1932	64·1	46·1
1933	69·0	48·5
1934	78·8	61·9
1935	82·2	70·3

[1] *Handbook of Labour Statistics*, 1936, p. 132.

TABLE V

Employment, Hours, Earnings and Production in Manufacturing Industries as a Whole.

Year	*Index of No. of wage earners*	*Average weekly hour*	*Index of weekly pay rolls*	*Index of per capita weekly earnings*	*Average hourly earnings*	*Index of Total man hours*	*Index of Pro-duction*	*Index of Output*		*Index of labour cost per unit of output*
								per wage earner	*per man-hour*	
					Cents					
1929	159·8	[1](1)	235·1	147·1	[1](1)	[1](1)	189	118	[1](1)	124
1932	100·0	37·9	100·0	100·0	46·5	100·0	100·0	100·0	100·0	100·0
1933	109·9	37·9	106·5	96·9	46·0	109·9	119	108	108	89
1934	126·0	34·7	135·6	107·6	54·8	115·4	124	98	107	109
1935	131·3	36·6	153·7	117·1	56·8	126·8	143	109	113	107
1936	140·3	39·1	177·6	126·6	57·5	144·8	167	119	115	106
July 1937	154·8	37·9	216·4	139·8	65·7	154·8	176	114	114	123

[1] Figures not available.

Witt Bowder, "Labour in Depression and Recovery, 1929 to 1937," in *Monthly Labour Review*, November 1937.

TABLE VI

Percentage Distribution of National Income According to Type of Income, 1919–1935[1]

Year	*Employees' Compensation*	*Entrepreneurial Income Payments*	*Property Income Payments*
1919	68·3	21·4	10·2
1920	69·2	21·0	9·8
1921	67·8	20·5	11·7
1922	68·7	19·8	11·5
1923	69·8	18·5	11·7
1924	69·2	18·9	11·9
1925	69·2	18·2	12·6
1926	70·1	17·1	12·8
1927	69·9	16·6	13·5
1928	69·9	16·3	13·9
1929	70·2	15·6	14·2
1930	69·5	15·0	15·5
1931	70·2	13.8	16·0
1932	70·0	13·3	16·7
1933	71·7	13·3	14·9
1934	73·6	12·8	13·7
1935	74·0	13·0	13·0

[1] Simon Kuznets, *National Income and Capital Formation*, 1919–1935—*A Preliminary Report*, National Bureau of Economic Research, 1937, p. 25.

TABLE VII

American Trade Unions, Total Membership[1] 1920–1937

Year	*Average Annual Membership*	*A.F. of L. Membership*	*Ratio of unionized to organizable workers*
1920	5,047,800	4,093,000	19·4%
1921	4,781,300	3,966,000	
1922	4,027,400	3,273,400	
1923	3,622,000	2,918,900	
1924	3,536,100	2,853,000	
1925	3,519,400	2,830,800	
1926	3,502,400	2,714,800	
1927	3,546,500	2,759,200	
1928	3,479,800	2,808,000	
1929	3,442,600	2,769,700	
1930	3,392,800	2,745,300	10·2%
1931	3,358,100	2,743,000	
1932	3,144,300	2,497,000	
1933	2,973,000	2,317,500	
1934	3,608,000	3,030,000	
1935	3,888,600	3,317,100	
1936		3,542,000	
1937		2,994,300	

[1] Figures for 1920–1935 were taken from Leo Wolman, *Ebb and Flow in Trade Unionism*, National Bureau of Economic Research, New York, 1936, pp. 16, 138–9, and 238. In 1930 the Canadian membership, which is included in all the figures, was 203, 300, *Ibid.*, p. 216.

The figures for the A. F. of L. membership for 1936–37 came from the *Report of the Proceedings of the Fifty-seventh Annual Convention of the A. F. of L.*, 1937, p. 76. The figure for 1938 stood at 3,665,600 for the A.F. of L., and, adding the 3,500,000 claimed by the C.I.O. and another half million for unaffiliated unions, the aggregate membership stood in the early autumn of 1937 at about 7,665,000.

CANADA

BY

LEO WARSHAW

CANADA

CANADA, in its economic life and particularly in the field of organized labour, as also, in consequence, of unorganized labour, is commonly regarded as a satellite of the United States, as the 49th State. In large measure this view is well founded. Not that the mother country has no claim of consanguinity to the Canadian foster-child of labour, for in the 1850's it was the Amalgamated Society of Engineers and the Amalgamated Society of Carpenters and Joiners that helped Canadian labour to franchise its localism in organization and outlook by planting closely linked "locals" in Toronto, Montreal, Hamilton, London (Ontario), Stratford and Kingston. Moreover, British unions also invaded the American field and left their stamp on the labour movement in the United States. But in the 1860's the Iron Moulders, the Printers, the Cigarmakers, the Coopers and other American unions had attained nation-wide strength, and they began to seep through the sluices of the stream of American-Canadian economic relations opened by the Reciprocity Treaty of 1854–66. Canadian branches were set up in all important centres to convert the American National Unions into "International" ones. Nor did the revocation of the Customs Convention inhibit the flow of this invisible export. Rather it gained in momentum and crowded the British unions off the Canadian scene, leaving them but an insignificant fraction of the seventy unions in Canada in 1874. The Canadian sections of the Internationals had established their national centre and "legislative mouthpiece," the Trades and Labour Congress of Canada (T.L.C.C.), on a solid and permanent footing by 1886; and by 1902 the Congress had purged itself of all but sections of Internationals affiliated to the American Federation of Labour. The latter continued to regard the T.L.C.C. as a mere State Federation of Labour until 1910, when it was conceded the exclusive right to issue charters to provincial and local centrals, while unions holding a Congress charter were exempted from getting an A.F. of L. charter.

As a concession, this settlement of 1910 would seem to emphasize the nature of the dominant representative of organized labour in Canada as a satellite of the A.F. of L., until recently the unchallenged spokesman of American trade unionism. But as a demand won by the Congress it indicates rather a divergence from the orbit of a satellite. Moreover, it was the recognition of relevant differences in institutions and problems confronting and to be dealt with by the Congress on the one hand and the State Federations of Labour as well as the A.F of L. on the other that led to the demand and the concession in the first instance. Finally, we shall see that the Congress diverged fundamentally from the A.F. of L. lead in policy on a very basic issue, viz., its relation to the C.I.O. (Committee for Industrial Organization) unions. If New York is no longer sure about the pertinence of representing Canada as the 13th Federal Reserve District on its financial map of the "United States," A.F. of L. headquarters at Washington has long since ceased to regard Congress headquarters at Ottawa as the seat of the 49th State Federation of Labour.

Yet the Canadian economy in all important aspects has, during the period under survey, patterned itself after the American economy and has been influenced by its vicissitudes much more intimately than by any other national economy; and it seems to continue in this course. Only a customs and immigration line divides Canada from her southern neighbour and marks an otherwise fairly intangible political boundary. But the customs do not impede the influx of American capital, which, largely by establishing subsidiaries on Canadian soil, has gained an important position in Canada's mass production industries, from a substantial share in mining, pulp and paper, and public utilities, to a virtual monopoly in autos and rubber goods. Again, neither customs nor immigration laws keep out American papers and periodicals, tourists and trade union organizers, nor can American broadcasts be stopped from reaching the ears of Canadians and conditioning them to American thought and culture. Small wonder, then, that the C.I.O. appeared in Canada almost as soon as it came into being in the U.S.A. in November 1935.

But ethnological differences and differences in the force of British traditions are not irrelevant in accounting for differences in adjustment to similar situations in the two countries, while Canada's lower productive capacity and productivity of labour give substance and emphasis to differences in conditions, problems and policies, political, fiscal and labour. This margin in relative productivity is in many ways crucial to an understanding of Canadian labour problems, for it runs through the Canadian economy like a chasm which the latter seeks to fill by means of tariffs, lower wages and lower standards of living.

We see, then, that Canadian labour problems cannot be adequately treated without reference to the American scene. The above introductory sketch liberates us, however, from the need of hereafter making such references explicit and detailed except in instances where they are indispensable, while Professor Perlman's chapter on the United States may be consulted for the basic background and parallel phases in development.

The post-war boom reached its zenith in Canada in 1920 and prices reached a record height. In May the index of wholesale prices attained its peak at 260·5 of the 1913 base. The typical lag in retail prices brought that index to its apex two months later. In July, the cost of living index (for a family of five) stood at 201, with retail food prices at 230 and clothing at 260, while rents, which had only increased by 34 per cent., continued to rise beyond July.

In absolute terms, the weekly budget of the working-class family on a sort of Minimum Health and Decency Standard called for about $42·20 as against $21 in 1913. Professor H. A. Logan found that a similar standard of living would have cost an American family only $40 a week at that time.[1] Yet 73·5 per cent. of the wage earners in Canada's manufacturing industries in 1920 made less than $30 a week. The median wage for adult males, constituting 77 per cent. of the working force, was $25·97. The average annual wage of all workers enumerated in the census of manufactures for that year was $1,104, yielding $21.23 per week. This represented a slight improvement in real wages as compared with 1913. For the index of wage rates had risen to 207·7 whereas the cost of living index for 1920 as a whole averaged somewhat less than 200.

Not all the trades had achieved such gains in terms of real

[1] Cf. Ware, Logan and Innis, *Labour in Canadian-American Relations* (Toronto 1937), pp. 175–6.

wages. The printing trades had bettered their rates over 1913 by only 84 per cent., while the index of the building trades stood at only 180·9. The metal trades, on the other hand, raised their index to 209·4, common factory labourers to 215·3, miscellaneous factory trades (including machine operators, helpers, etc.) to 216·8, and the railway workers to 221·0. In coal mining the wage index was kept approximately on a par with the cost of living index at 197·7, while in logging and sawmilling the wage index was a little above par at 202·7.

Government policy was only incidental in the world-wide post-war inflation culminating, in Canada, in the summer of 1920. The surtax of 5 per cent. *ad valorem* on commodities imported under the British Preferential Tariff, and of 7½ per cent. on those under the Intermediate and the General Tariff, which was imposed in 1915 as a war revenue measure, naturally gave further protective padding to Canadian manufacturers. Another measure passed in that year, " An Act respecting the Issue of Dominion Notes " (6 Geo. V, c. 4), which substantially liberalized the issue of Dominion notes against gold reserves, may be singled out as another contributing factor. The quantity of Dominion notes outstanding in 1919, 1920 and 1921 (representing some 60 per cent. of the notes in circulation) was larger than in any succeeding year down to the founding of the Bank of Canada in 1935; and the gold reserves were among the lowest, those of 1921 being 31 per cent. and of 1920 33 per cent. respectively—second and third only to the 1929 low of 28 per cent.

What is of greatest interest to us, however, is that the usual failure of real wages to keep pace with a rising cost of living index was not experienced in Canada in the post-war years. One general reason is doubtless that those were years of anxious concessions to wage earners by employers. The October Revolution in Russia, the inspired militancy of the workers returned from the battlefields throughout the world of industrial capitalism, not excluding Canada, and the revolutionary events in Hungary, in Italy and in Germany, all caused anxiety among industrialists, American as well as European, and made them somewhat more prone to accede to the demands of labour.

In Canada, the revolutionary ferment came to a head in 1919. In that year 148,915 workers were involved in 336 strikes against 1,967 employers, entailing a loss of 3,400,942 working days. These figures are greater than any recorded before or since. The number of strikers was about twice as large as that for 1918, itself an exceptional year in that respect. In 1919, too, occurred Canada's most momentous strike,[1] the Winnipeg strike which threatened to become a Dominion-wide general strike. The upflare originated with the Metal Trades Council of Winnipeg, an association of the various A.F. of L. metal trades unions. This body called a strike on May 1, following lengthy but fruitless negotiations with the employers (the Vulcan Iron Works, Manitoba Bridge and Iron Works, and the Dominion Bridge Co.) for various wage increases, a forty-four-hour week, and, most important of all, recognition of the principle of collective bargaining. About 1,100 metal workers walked out in Winnipeg that day, to be joined by 1,200 Winnipeg building trades workers, who walked out the same day with their unsatisfied demand for higher wages.

These strikes would probably have run a " normal " course had it not been for certain developments preceding the strike call. At the 1918 meeting of the Trades and Labour Congress held at Quebec City the " western " delegates (i.e., those from Manitoba, Saskatchewan, Alberta and British Columbia) insisted that their resolution for industrial unionism, which they had succeeded in carrying through the Congress at the 1911 convention in Calgary (Alberta), and which was subsequently but grudgingly reaffirmed and pigeon-holed, be implemented. But the " eastern " delegates, with few exceptions, combined to defeat this motion, and the labour contingents from the west in caucus decided to call a " Western Conference," which met in Calgary in March 1919. This was attended by 237 delegates from the four western provinces and two from Port Arthur and Fort William, the two westernmost cities in Ontario. It was

[1] The printers' strike of Toronto in 1872 is another celebrated event in Canada's labour history. Thirteen local unions and sympathizers furnished a contingent of 2,000 demonstrators on April 14, and 10,000 workers and citizens assembled in Queen's Park to voice their support of the typographers and the book-binders' unions in their strike for a nine-hour day. This strike, in consequence of the public outcry against the arrest of the strike leaders on charges of seditious conspiracy, also led to the passage of the Trade Unions Act of Canada (patterned after the British model of 1871) by the Dominion Government in June 1872.

resolved to take a trade union referendum throughout Canada and, should a " sufficient " number favour the move, to build an industrial union to be known as the One Big Union, and to call a general strike on June 1, for a six-hour day. Other resolutions denounced and repudiated parliamentary lobbying, expressed friendship for the young Soviet Republic, and declared for direct revolutionary trade union action. On June 11, 1919, the One Big Union (O.B.U.) was indeed formally set up, but nothing came of the contemplated general strike.

Yet, when the walk-out occurred in Winnipeg on May 1, the Winnipeg Trades and Labour Council, which had taken an active part in the O.B.U. movement, at once threw its full weight behind the strikers, and, following a referendum on the matter, declared a general strike in Winnipeg. The call was answered by 27,000 workers, including municipal and government employees, on May 15. Most of the returned soldiers, too, expressed their solidarity with the Strike Committee. Moreover, sympathetic general strikes broke out in Calgary, Edmonton, Vancouver, Saskatoon, Brandon and other cities in the West, and found echoes in Toronto and even Amherst, Nova Scotia.

The provincial and federal governments stepped in, however, to check the spread of the strike movement and to stamp it out by June 26, with bloodshed on one occasion, when a " silent parade " of returned soldiers was broken up in Winnipeg on June 21, and with criminal proceedings on charges of sedition against the strike leaders. However, the Metal Trades Council and the building trades in the end won concessions on their demands.

Though the strike wave did not develop into a nation-wide revolutionary torrent, trade union membership grew to an all-time peak (prior to 1937) of 378,047 members, and the record number of strikes occurring during the year brought with it records in the number of strikes fully won or partially successful in any one year between 1901 and 1937. Unemployment during 1919 fell to the low figure of 3·4 per cent., and the consequent scarcity of labour assisted in keeping wage rates in step with, and ahead of, retail prices. The course of development since 1919 can best be outlined by means of the following statistical summary :

Year	A Estimates of the Population of Canada (000's omitted)	B Index of Population (1926 = 100)	C Index of Employment, Canada (average Calendar Year 1926 = 100)	D Percentages of Unemployment in Trade Unions, Canada (average for year)
1920	8,556	90·5	—	4·9
1921	8,788	92·9	88·8	12·7
1922	8,919	94·4	78·8	7·1
1923	9,010	95·3	87·3	4·9
1924	9,143	96·5	89·8	7·2
1925	9,294	98·6	84·9	7·0
1926	9,451	100·0	90·7	5·1
1927	9,636	101·9	95·9	4·9
1928	9,835	104·1	100·7	4·5
1929	10,029	106·1	109·1	5·7
1930	10,208	108·0	111·2	11·1
1931	10,376	109·8	101·7	16·8
1932	10,506	111·2	91·6	22·0
1933	10,681	113·0	78·5	22·3
1934	10,824	114·5	88·6	18·2
1935	10,935	115·7	94·4	15·4
1936	11,028	116·7	99·1	13·2
1937	11,200	118·5	103·8	10·7
1938	—	—	113·4	—

Year	E Index Numbers of Changes in Cost of Living (average prices 1913 = 100)	F Index Numbers of Rates of Wages for Various Classes of Labour in Canada (rates in 1913 = 100)	G Trade Union Membership in Canada
1920	190	207·7	373,842
1921	161	189·9	313,320
1922	157	180·2	276,621
1923	159	184·2	278,092
1924	156	186·4	260,643
1925	160	185·1	271,064
1926	157	186·3	274,604
1927	157	190·4	290,282
1928	158	192·2	300,602
1929	160	196·0	319,476
1930	151	197·1	322,449
1931	135	189·1	310,544
1932	125	177·7	283,576
1933	123	168·3	286,220
1934	123	170·5	281,774
1935	127	175·4	280,704
1936	128	178·6	322,473
1937	133	191·7	384,619

Since 1931, as tables B and C make clear, while, in absolute terms, there was a recovery in employment following the severe setback in 1933 and 1934 below the 1926 level, yet, relative to population, the index of employment has, until 1938, been consistently below the 1926 level.

The heaviest setbacks in employment were sustained in the spheres of communication, transportation and construction. In transportation the lag in recovery of employment is explained mainly by certain measures of co-operation adopted by the two national railway systems, the privately owned Canadian Pacific Railway and the government owned Canadian National Railway, in consequence of the 1932 Report of the Duff Commission and the Canadian National-Canadian Pacific Act passed in 1933 to implement its recommendations. Many duplicate services were eliminated and employment capacity was thereby curtailed. This contraction is reflected in reports to the Department of Labour, which show a drop from 65,987 employees on January 1, 1932, to 59,745 on January 1, 1938. Another contributing factor was furnished by the street railways, where the introduction of onc-man cars in many cities since the early 'thirties has caused a further contraction in employment capacity, which has not been offset by automotive cartage, the expanding branch of the industry.

This unexpected good showing of railway wages is explained by the seemingly ready mobility of displaced railway workers to other fields of employment, particularly mining, and, most important of all, by the organized strength of the railway workers. In 1920 the railway employees' unions had a membership of 93,104, representing 24·9 per cent. of organized labour in Canada. In 1926 the 79,827 unionized railwaymen made up 29 per cent. of Canada's organized labour force ; in 1932 their 75,402 members gave them 26·6 per cent. of the total, and in the latest report published (for 1936) the railway unions are credited with 22·4 per cent. of the trade union membership in Canada, representing 72,239 members.

In the last year cited there were reported 132,781 employees on the railways, including office staff, executives, employees in " outside operations," and others apparently not directly a part of the railroad staff. It appears that about 102,500 railway workers can be regarded as eligible for union membership. The industry is, therefore, 70 per cent. unionized, a proportion which is unequalled in any other industry.

In coal mining, which is perhaps second in solidity of unionization, eighty-eight operators reported 26,277 workers on their pay rolls on January 1, 1937, which does not represent an exhaustive figure as in the case of the railway reports, nor yet a normally high level of employment. Yet the United Mine Workers of America, a C.I.O. affiliate, which dominates the field, reported a membership of only 16,000 for 1936, which represents some 60 per cent. of unionization in the industry. In 1920, the United Mine Workers of America attained a peak in membership with 19,802 members, or some 5,000 above the figure for 1919. In 1926, however, its membership was only 14,820, representing about 52 per cent. of the total employees in the industry. There appears thus to be some stagnation if not a pronounced deterioration in the employment capacity of the coal mining industry since 1920, which was paralleled by the course of wage rates and trade union membership. Despite the continued drop in employment since 1926, however, wage rates have returned to the 1926 level; and union membership, which in large measure accounts for this, has surpassed the mark of that year.

The building trades, too, have always furnished a trade union contingent representing a substantial proportion of organized labour in Canada. In 1920 there were 39,712 unionists (or 10·62 per cent. of Canada's total) in the building trades. In 1926 this figure had declined to 26,660; but by 1936 it had risen again to 32,446, representing the same proportion of the total number of trade unionists as in 1920. In number of union members and percentage of the total of organized labour the metal trades were ever on the heels of the building trades, overtaking them in 1919, and taking third place in 1920 with 33,655 members. In 1936 there was a union membership of 26,200 in these trades. But there was considerable difference between these two groups in relative strength of organization. In the building trades, at best, but 25 per cent. of the industry was organized in 1935. In the metal trades, on the other hand, there was a minimum of 31 per cent. unionization.

This difference is to some extent reflected in wage conditions. While the hourly rate of bricklayers and masons, for example, was higher than that of sheet metal workers, the rates standing at about 80 cents to one dollar, and 60 to 75 cents per hour, respectively, for most cities in 1935, yet the yearly average earnings for metal trade workers was $1,050, and only $655 for building trade workers in that year. Assuming the duration of employment per annum to have increased in the building trades as fast as in the metal trades since then, the 10·5 per cent. increase in wage rates in the latter since 1935 would yield an average yearly wage of $1,207 in 1937, against a 4·2 per cent. increase, yielding a yearly wage of some $683, in the building trades in 1937.

Apparently the " shortness " of wages in the building industry is very poorly compensated by their " height." The relative inferiority of wages, both in level and in rate of improvement in the building trades, can be accounted for by the high rate of unemployment and immobility of labour in the industry, and by the existence of dual and multiple unionism in the field. There are, first of all, the Bricklayers, Masons and Plasterers' International Union of America with a membership of 4,540 in Canada, and the United Brotherhood of Carpenters and Joiners with a Canadian membership of 4,458, both affiliated with the Trades and Labour Congress of Canada.[1] Then there is the Amalgamated Building Workers of Canada with 9,000 members, a purely Canadian union, until 1937 affiliated with the All-Canadian Congress of Labour, but since become an affiliate of the Canadian Federation of Labour which split from the former in September 1936. Finally, there are the Catholic Federation of Building Trades Employees and the National Catholic Union of Carpenters and Joiners, operating in competition with the other two in the province of Quebec. These divisions hamper effective unionization of the large percentage of unorganized building trades workers, and reduce bargaining strength.

The metal trades have not experienced any dual unionism since 1920, when the remaining twenty-four locals, with 3,000 members, of the British Amalgamated Society of Engineers were amalgamated with the International Association of Machinists. Nor did the emergence of the Amalgamated Association of Iron, Steel and Tin Workers of America as a

[1] *Twenty-sixth Annual Report on Labour*, p. 174. To this figure must also be added, among others, the more than 1,000 members of the International Painters' Union, which, together with the Carpenters, experienced the worst clashes with the National Unions.

C.I.O. union in 1936 cause a split and competitive unionism in Canada as in the U.S.A. On the contrary, this development made for the consolidation of unionism in the industry and for the very pronounced rise in the index of wage rates from 170·1 in 1936 to 187·4 in 1937.

The substantial gains in wages in the factory trades are at least in some measure due to the upsurge of trade unionism in recent years. In the most important branch, the "needle trades" (clothing), together with boots and shoes, we find in 1936 an increase in membership over even the *annus mirabilis* of Canadian trade unionism. In 1919 this section of industry contained 20,800 organized workers, making up 5·5 per cent. of Canada's total trade union membership. By 1926 union membership had fallen to some 13,500, and by 1932 the figure had dropped still further to 12,291. In 1936, however, membership reached the record height of 23,285, representing 7·2 per cent. of the total union membership in Canada. The Workers' Unity League, to be dealt with below, contributed in no small measure to this growth by organizing some 2,500 garment workers, 400 overall and shirt workers and 1,200 shoe workers in Canada, largely in Ontario, between 1932 and 1935. Though owing to inter-union rivalry and the loss of some strikes, it failed to achieve the permanent unionization of another 4,000 workers in these trades, it prepared the ground for their subsequent entry into the trade union fold after its own amalgamation with the A.F. of L. internationals in 1935–36.

Canada has never been quite free from dual unionism; and though the minor unions have never constituted a serious challenge to the ascendancy of the Trades and Labour Congress and the international unions, they have, nevertheless, from time to time strongly asserted themselves for good or ill, and have, in some industries and in one province, maintained themselves for a number of decades as determined rivals on "ideological" grounds, nationalist and religious.

In 1920 the Canadian sections of American international unions accounted for 2,455 of the total 2,918 Canadian branches or "locals," and 267,247 or 72 per cent. of the 373,842 trade union members in Canada. In that year the purely Canadian unions, such as the Amalgamated Carpenters of Canada, the Amalgamated Civil Servants of Canada, the

Federated Association of Letter Carriers, and others to the number of about a score in all, together claimed a membership of 25,406. Many of them were affiliates or about to become affiliates of the T.L.C.C. (which the Canadian Brotherhood had just become that year), and the Canadian Federation of Labour. The Catholic unions claimed 45,000; but the O.B.U., which had chalked up a membership of 41,150 in 1919, could report a membership of only 5,000 in 1920. This latter decline was due to the defection of the Lumber Workers' Industrial Union, the members of which had joined, some the Industrial Workers of the World, some the Red International of Labour Unions. Finally, there were the "independent units," mostly local mushroom growths (such as the anti-Red "Khaki Labour Union of Vancouver" organized at the end of the War), with a total membership of 31,189.

In 1932 the International unions had 176,087 or 62 per cent. of Canada's 283,576 organized workers in their ranks; the T.L.C.C. embraced sixty-four unions, sixty-one of which were international, with a membership of 127,264; the All-Canadian Congress of Labour had twelve Canadian organizations with 50,356 members; the National Catholic Unions had a following of 25,000, all confined to the French province of Quebec. For the Workers' Unity League incomplete figures showed 12,500 members; other Canadian Central bodies were credited with 19,332 members: the Independent local units now counted merely 15,496 followers; and the unaffiliated International unions, including five railway organizations and the Amalgamated Clothing Workers of America (which, however, joined the A.F. of L. and the T.L.C.C. in 1933) showed a membership of 33,628.

In 1936 the international unions held 174,769 or 54 per cent. of the 322,473 Canadian unionists. But if the relative strength of the international unions declined, the T.L.C.C. increased its weight since 1932 from 44 to 46 per cent. of the total. The All-Canadian Congress of Labour, following the split in September, but before the defection of the Amalgamated Building Workers of Canada to the Canadian Federation of Labour, numbered 31,383, while the latter Federation had 25,081 members. The National Catholic Unions claimed 45,000 members, other Canadian Central bodies 14,675, and Independent local unions 18,863, while the unaffiliated international unions, including the Industrial Workers of the World, were credited with 38,073 members.

In 1936 the sixty-two international unions whose Canadian sections were affiliated to the T.L.C.C. were also affiliates of the A.F. of L. But in August of that year the ten A.F. of L. international unions which had set up the C.I.O. were suspended from the A.F. of L. The T.L.C.C., however, took no such action against the Canadian sections of these internationals, but, at its annual Convention in Ottawa in September 1937, confirmed the affiliation of the suspended internationals and, in addition, seated delegates from the newly created C.I.O. unions, such as the United Automobile Workers of America, accepting them as integral industrial unions.

A number of explanations can be adduced for this stark divergence of the T.L.C.C. from the course of its acknowledged parent body, the A.F. of L., among which the British tradition of readiness to compromise is probably not irrelevant. More positive, perhaps, is the fact that in 1936 unions having a membership of over 41,000, or a third of the total membership of the Congress, were linked with the C.I.O., while in 1937 the number and proportion were probably much higher.[1] The "original eight" in the U.S.A., it is true, also accounted for a third of the A.F. of L. membership, but that still left the A.F. of L. with over two-million members and without another union in the field (outside the C.I.O.) to rival it in numbers. In Canada, however, if the T.L.C.C. were reduced to a third of its membership it would find itself reduced to almost a par with the Catholic Federation, the All-Canadian Federations and the Railway Brotherhoods, not to mention the C.I.O. itself, which, as American experience showed, might readily outdistance the Congress.

[1] Figures for 1937, just released, report 12 C.I.O. unions and two directly chartered C.I.O. locals, with a membership of 61,498, in addition to three unions with 14,437 members co-operating with the C.I.O., thus yielding a total C.I.O. strength in Canada of 75,935 for 1937. One of the actively co-operating unions, however—the International Ladies' Garment Workers' Union—with a Canadian membership of 8,017, withdrew its support of the C.I.O. in 1938. But though the total membership strength of the C.I.O. in Canada had risen from less than a third in 1936 to rather more than a third of the T.L.C.C. affiliated membership by the end of 1937, the C.I.O. unions had only a fraction of their members—and no more than 30,000 as late as the end of 1938—affiliated to the Congress. On the other hand, the fully paid-up membership of the T.L.C.C. as a whole was only 175,966 at the end of 1937.

Then, too, the painful experience of the O.B.U. which, the Congress feels, was provoked by the latter's obduracy on the long-standing issue of industrial unionism, was apt to make for a more conciliatory attitude to the new upsurge of industrial unionism. Nor must we forget the effects on trade unionists of the depression and the rise of fascist dictatorships in European countries on the magic carpet of a split labour movement. With the emergence of the Communists from their sectarian shell, the international unions that had in the 1920's expelled them, in 1935–36 accepted the W.U.L. unions with their 24,000 or more members into their ranks. The internationals which absorbed the W.U.L. unions were naturally, as a rule, favourably predisposed towards the C.I.O. programme both in Canada and the U.S.A.; but in Canada, for reasons already given, the urgency of the need for conciliation in order to avoid a split was greater.

Another favourable factor was the precedent established by the experience of the British Trades Union Congress with the Iron and Steel Trades Confederation, the National Union of Railwaymen, and the General Labour bodies of the "New Unionism." The empirical solution of the problem of industrial unionism adopted by the Trades Union Congress was much more effective as an object lesson to Canadian than to American craft union leaders. And though the C.I.O. insists on the integral entity of its industrial unions, precluding such invasions and "poaching" of the craft unions on various sections of the industrial union as are tolerated by some of the industrial federations in Great Britain, it does not, at least, make a fetish of industrial unionism, trying to impose it on all organizations in the T.L.C.C. as did the O.B.U. and the I.W.W. Rather does it ask for industrial organization only in industries which have time and again defied organization under the traditional craft pattern, namely, the basic mass production industries such as steel, automobiles, radio, rubber, etc., otherwise respecting the craft unions where they have been successful.

Finally the C.I.O. does not differ much from the T.L.C.C. in policy. Like the latter it endorses "business unionism" and eschews direct participation in the revolutionary movement, though its political programme seems to be more comprehensive and long range than the traditional A.F. of L.-T.L.C.C. line.[1] But there is nothing in this that might alienate the T.L.C.C.

However, the C.I.O. issue is not yet a closed one in Canada. In the T.L.C.C.'s resolution on the subject at the 1937 convention, loyalty to the A.F. of L. was reaffirmed and the fear expressed that " to openly defy or disregard the disciplinary policies of the international unions affiliated with the American Federation of Labour would, undoubtedly, result in the withdrawal from the Congress of many of the large international unions affiliated with the A.F. of L. who loyally adhere to its policies and laws." Indeed the sheltering and acceptance of the C.I.O. unions was ostensibly enacted by the T.L.C.C. as a sort of example to the A.F. of L. and the C.I.O. in order to prevent " what is now only a potential danger[2] (from) becoming a reality."

But the A.F. of L. did not avail itself of this offer and at the Miami convention in January, 1938, the Council expelled the United Mine Workers of America, the Mine, Mill and Smelter Workers, and the Federation of Flat Glass Workers, to be followed, three months later, by the expulsion of the Amalgamated Clothing Workers, the Amalgamated Iron, Steel and Tin Workers, the United Textile Workers, the United Rubber Workers, and the Oilfield, Gas Well and Refinery Workers, leaving the International Ladies' Garment Workers' Union as the only link, under suspension, between the C.I.O. and the A.F. of L. Moreover, shortly after the latest expulsions early in May, Mr. William Green, President of the A.F. of L., was reported in the press to have resolved to visit Canada to press the Congress to expel the C.I.O. unions in Canada under threat of withdrawing financial aid, while Mr. P. M. Draper, president of the Congress refused to comment on his C.I.O. stand, declaring himself pleased to receive Mr. Green to " smooth out any difficulties."

But, though the final outcome will not be known until the 1938 convention of the Congress, there are strong indications of decisive support of unity between the T.L.C.C. and the

[1] See Section on the U.S.A.

[2] The C.I.O. unions were at that time merely suspended but not yet expelled from the A.F. of L.

C.I.O. in Canada. The Toronto Trades and Labour Council, which exerts a significant influence in the Congress, as early as May 21, 1936, adopted a resolution favouring industrial unionism in the mass production industries and explicitly endorsing the work of the C.I.O. by a vote of 95 to 8, and has since, by word and deed, further confirmed this stand.

Again, both the C.C.F.[1] and the Communist Party of Canada, which together control about half-a-million votes in the country and count a large section of trade unionists among their members, have from the outset put themselves behind the C.I.O. The test of Canadian labour's attitude towards the C.I.O. came with the automobile workers' strike at Oshawa, Ontario, April 8 to 25, 1937.

After numerous vain attempts by the A.F. of L. to organize the automobile workers, the latest in Canada in 1928 under Messrs. William Varley and James Simpson, Vice-President of the T.L.C.C. at the time, the United Automobile Workers of America, organized under the C.I.O. and scoring success after success in the U.S.A., helped organize the 4,200 Oshawa, workers, who walked out solidly on April 8, demanding wage increases and union recognition. The Liberal Premier of Ontario, Mr. Mitchell Hepburn, took an unaccountably hostile stand against the International union and swore to keep the C.I.O. and its " foreign agitators " out of the province. Incensed leaders of the progressive parties charged Mr. Hepburn with taking this stand against the C.I.O. in order to safeguard the mining magnates against unionization. And, indeed, it is hard to see what rational justification there was for the premier's stand on which, moreover, he was at loggerheads with the federal leader of the Liberal Party, the Prime Minister, William L. McKenzie King. The fear he had expressed of the C.I.O.'s " sit down strikes," had already been put at rest by his suppression of an attempt at such a strike at Sarnia, Ontario, on March 1 to 3, 1937, and the subsequent pronouncement (March 24) of the Hon. E. Lapointe, Federal Minister of Justice, on the illegality of " sit downs " in Canada. As for his objection to " foreign " organizers, it refuses to

[1] " Co-operative Commonwealth Federation," Canada's Socialist Party, which polled 400,000 votes in the 1935 Dominion elections, though only organized three years theretofore.

square with his avowed approval of the A.F. of L. unions operating in Canada. Moreover, as Professor F. R. Scott has remarked, " Mr. Hepburn called the C.I.O. organizers 'foreign agitators,' but he would welcome an American financier with open arms if he had money to invest in Canada."

However, a strong protest movement arose against the premier's stand. The Toronto District Labour Council and other Congress bodies and unions brought moral and material aid to the strikers, who in the end, after many face-saving formalities, were conceded their demands in an agreement finally signed in Mr. Hepburn's own office and which recognized the union in substance if not in form.

The fraternization between the C.I.O. and the T.L.C.C. unions which occurred in this strike was manifested again in the textiles and garment workers' strikes at Peterborough, Ontario (June to August), Cornwall, Ontario, Montreal, Quebec, and in other strikes; it was reaffirmed at the 1937 convention of the Congress, and, with the stepping into the open of the Fascist movement under Adrien Arcand in 1938, it is probable that unity will be maintained in the Congress.

Before turning to a description of the minority trade union movements, let us fill in some missing details in our account of the T.L.C.C.

Sixty-two of the eighty-eight International unions were affiliated to the T.L.C.C. in 1936. In addition there were four of the twenty-six Canadian organizations under Congress charter. Except for the Brotherhood of Railway Carmen of America and a few unions of railway clerks, telegraphers, etc., the " shop crafts," the International brotherhoods of railway men (mainly the " running trades ") are independent of both the A.F. of L. and the T.L.C.C., forming federal bodies of their own. In 1936 there were also fifteen international A.F. of L. unions whose Canadian sections were not affiliated with the Congress. Thirty-five of the fifty-six city centrals in Canada were chartered by the T.L.C.C. and are generally designated " Trades and Labour Councils." Two of the three provincial Federations of Labour (Alberta and New Brunswick) are also affiliated.

The Congress acts as the political spokesman of organized

labour in Canada, for which purpose it publicizes its legislative programme each year, conducts lobbying at Ottawa and, through a provincial Executive Committee in each province without a provincial federation, deals with the provincial governments. It is officially recognized as the mouthpiece of Canadian labour, in token whereof its nominee has always been delegated by the Dominion Government to represent Canadian labour at the International Labour Conference.

Of the minority trade union groups, the National Catholic Unions are almost unique, Canada being the only Anglo-Saxon country to harbour them, though they are confined to the French population of Quebec Province. It was Pope Leo XIII's encyclical "Rerum Novarum" of 1891 that gave birth to the Catholic labour corporations of France in 1894 and to the clerical propaganda in Quebec (whose population is some 80 per cent. French Catholic) since 1900, which culminated in the establishment of the first "pure" Catholic union among the pulp workers of Chicoutimi in 1912. Even before this the constitutions of some independent unions had been changed, mostly during strikes, to conform to the spirit of the encyclical. By 1918 there were forty-one Catholic unions, and plans were laid for the formation of a "Federation of Catholic Workers of Canada" which came into existence in 1921, at which time some 45,000 adherents were claimed, a figure which has not since been surpassed. In 1936 the Federation had 190 local branches, including study circles and city centrals as well as "syndicates," to each of which a chaplain is attached.

The Catholic Syndicates also designate themselves as "national," which, however, connotes French rather than Canadian nationalism, though it also, of course, implies opposition to international unionism. They renounce strikes, except as a most extreme resort and, to quote Professor F. R. Scott of Montreal, "have hitherto been more concerned with carrying on struggles against communism and the international unions than against employers for better wages." During the strike struggles of 1937, however, the Catholic textile syndicates called out 9,000 workers on a strike in Montreal, which lasted throughout the month of August and during which A. C. Charpentier, President of the Catholic Federation, spoke of co-operation with the international unions. Nothing, however, has so far come of this suggestion.

The Canadian Federation of Labour represents " nationalism " in trade unionism in the broader sense of Canadian nationalism. Unable to make much headway with its anti-Americanism since 1902, when it withdrew from the T.L.C.C., it joined with the Canadian Brotherhood of Railway Employees, the O.B.U. and others, to form the All-Canadian Congress of Labour in 1927. " National autonomy " and opposition to the international trade unions was endorsed, yet not so much on principle as in order to be freed from the " reactionary influence of the United States-controlled unions "; and industrial unionism was endorsed as " the basic organization principle " of the A.C.C.L., though in practice little more than lip-service was paid to it. The nationalistic stand of the parent body, however, did not disappear, but came to a head in 1936, complicated by differences between President A. R. Mosher (from the Canadian Brotherhood of Electrical Railway Employees) and Secretary W. T. Burford (Electrical Communication Workers of Canada) on the question of amalgamation of the Canadian Pacific and Canadian National Railways, which Mr. Burford advocated in the face of universal opposition by organized labour in Canada. In the split Mr. Burford carried six of the twelve affiliated organizations with him to resurrect the name of Canadian Federation of Labour. They were shortly followed by a seventh body from the A.C.C.L. Notable among the dissidents was the O.B.U., which had been for long a nominal adherent of the principle of industrial unionism.

The Industrial Workers of the World (nicknamed Wobblies), which invaded Canada shortly after its formation in the U.S.A. in 1905, was more intent on industrial unionism than the more reformist unions. But its syndicalist philosophy made for the subservience of its unionism to revolutionary ends by direct action through the General Strike, and it succeeded in preparing no more than 4,200 workers for that end at any time during its spasmodic career in Canada.

Somewhat more successful in extending the domain of organized labour in Canada by means of industrial unionism was another revolutionary trade union movement, the Workers' Unity League, a fraternal affiliate of the R.I.L.U.

and brought into existence in 1930 by Communists and other dissidents expelled from A.F. of L. unions. While tending, at first, to regard trade unions merely as schools for the social revolution and aiming to "politicize" established trade unions where possible, the W.U.L. soon came to devote itself directly to the job of organizing the unorganized, neglected by the international craft unions. It did creditable pioneering work among the metal miners, rubber workers, dress makers, furniture workers, boot and shoe workers, fur dressers, food workers, fishermen, domestic servants, cleaners and dyers, and the unemployed, attaining a membership of over 24,000 employed workers in 1934. But its resources were too limited for the task it had set itself and, in 1935, it took advantage of the growing sentiment for labour unity, for which it had long now been agitating, to merge its forces with the international unions, under circumstances described above.

The 1931 census revealed 2,570,097 wage earners in Canada,[1] of whom only 310,544, or less than 13 per cent. were organized; and by 1935 Canada's trade union membership had fallen to 280,704. The situation was identical with that in the U.S.A. where, in 1935, out of 36,400,000 organizable workers only 3,186,000 were enrolled in unions affiliated to the A.F. of L. The eight unions which formed the C.I.O. had the resources and the will to organize those millions on an industrial basis, which seemed the only feasible one. The workers in mass production industries had themselves defied or opposed the efforts of organization by the "carving board" technique, to which they had hitherto and with fatal results been subjected in the process of organization by the A.F. of L. and its craft unions, and had even on occasion preferred "company unions" to A.F. of L. charters. By 1938 the C.I.O. had brought three million new industrial workers into the trade union fold in the U.S.A. and probably a similar proportion in Canada.

[1] Canada Year Book, 1937, p. 144. Professor F. R. Scott allows for a possible half million of high salaried executives in this group and estimates at least two million as eligible for unionization. This, however seems too generous a deduction in the first place, while it takes no account of the 604,502 listed as working on "own account," which includes a large number working on commission, and the 345,839 listed as working for "no pay," including many working for mere board and room (93·3 per cent. in this class are in Agriculture), who are eligible for unionization. Perhaps the figure given for the wage-earning group, viz., the two and a half million, may be taken as representing those eligible for organization.

While the C.I.O. has not, any more than the A.F. of L. or the T.L.C.C., set up any trade unions of women, it has added or given new prominence to an institution, the Ladies' Auxiliaries, attached to the various C.I.O. unions. These not only function as "rearguards" of the existing unions, but also, like the National Women's Trade Union League of Washington (endorsed by the A.F. of L. and the T.L.C.C.), assist in making the working women of the U.S.A. and Canada "trade-union-conscious." Only fifteen of the eighty-eight international unions, with a total membership of 4,132,176, submitted information in 1936 as to their female membership (totalling 122,321), while 269 of the 2,886 Canadian local unions reported 11,034 women members. Since the locals reporting are among the largest, the probability is that the total female trade union membership in Canada is no more than twice or, at most, three times the number reported. Females account for 10 per cent. of the total membership, whereas the 547,837 women wage-earners in Canada in 1931 constituted more than 25 per cent. of the total, so that there seems to be a real need for the efforts now exerted to arouse "trade-union-consciousness" in women workers on this continent.

Government and Wages

Beginning with British Columbia and Manitoba in 1918 all the provinces, except Prince Edward Island, between that date and 1930 enacted minimum wage legislation for women workers, but the New Brunswick statute had not yet been brought into force by the end of 1937. The minimum rate established varied in 1936 from $8 to $12·50 for a forty to sixty-hour week for retail store employees (and from $6 to $10 for learners, minors, etc. up to a maximum of 20 per cent. of the staff) in the Province of Quebec, to $15 for a forty-eight-hour week (with $11 to $14 for learners, etc.) for office workers and telephone operators in British Columbia. The ranges in minimum rates were designed to cover urban as well as rural areas, and males, too, were covered by the same minima in specified respects in most provinces.

Inspection, however, was scarcely concerned with the male worker and, if not lax, was not always capable of checking and enforcing the application of the minimum rate provisions to female employees, as was brought to light by the Royal Commission on Price Spreads in 1934–35. At least one case of flagrant violation of the statute in Quebec revealed undesirable practices in the composition of a Minimum Wage Board.

In many occupations the operation of the Female Minimum Wage Acts tended to work to the prejudice of the male workers. Employers also took advantage of those on the relief rolls, of whom there were still 900,851 in June 1937, to hire male relief recipients for a pittance, thus further depressing wage standards for male workers. There was an obvious need for their protection, and in 1935 the Dominion Government passed a Minimum Wages Act applicable to males as well as females, besides a general Limitation of Hours of Work Act, and Employment and Social Insurance Act, and other legislation designed to correct this situation; but all the Acts were ruled *ultra vires* of the Dominion Parliament by the Privy Council in January 1937.

The provincial governments were now left to seek individual solutions to the problem. Already in 1934 British Columbia had passed a Male Minimum Wage Act which provides for a minimum wage of 25–35 cents per hour for men between eighteen and twenty-five, and for minima above 35 cents per hour variously established in various industries. A board of five, one of whom must be a woman, is entrusted with the fixing of rates for the different industries and administering the Act. In the same year Quebec passed a Collective Labour Agreements Extensions Act which was superseded by the Workmen's Wages Act, May 1937, whereby the parties to a collective agreement between an association of employees and an employer or an association of employers may apply to the Lieutenant-Governor through the Minister of Labour to have the agreement made obligatory for the whole industry or occupation within a specified district, possibly province-wide, which he may do at his discretion. Since September 1, 1937, too, the Women's Minimum Wage Act has been superseded by the Fair Wage Act whereby the minima for women also became obligatory for male employees.

In Ontario, the Industrial Standards Act, which came into force in April 1935 and was last amended early in 1937, is similar to the Workmen's Wages Act of Quebec. In Ontario, however, wage and hour standards are set for the various categories in a given industry over a specified district by the representatives of labour and capital in a conference with the Industrial Standards Officer. Such a conference may be called upon application to the Minister of Labour by either party. The Minister, however, is empowered to designate zones, and expand or reduce established zones wherein the standards are in force. An Industry and Labour Board of five, set up by the Department of Labour Act of 1937 is entrusted with the administration and enforcement of the Industrial Standards Act.[1] Ontario, in March 1937, also enacted a Minimum Wage Act which supersedes the old Act applying to women workers only. By it the Industry and Labour Board is empowered on its own initiative to fix minimum rates, maximum hours and conditions of work for all employees, by industry and category, and to define the zone of application. The Act also fixes a forty-eight hour maximum week for municipalities with a population of more than 50,000, a fifty-four-hour week for localities with less than 10,000 people, and a fifty-hour week for localities of intervening size.

Before the end of 1937 other provinces had enacted similar Industrial Standards Acts and general Minimum Wage Acts, leaving only Nova Scotia without a general Minimum Wage Act, and Prince Edward Island, New Brunswick and Manitoba without an Industrial Standards Act.

There is also a federal Fair Wage and Hours of Labour Act, passed in 1935, to supersede a similar Act passed in 1930. It provides for a forty-four-hour week and for fair and reasonable wages and working conditions, at least equal to prevailing standards, for workers under contractors carrying out jobs for or subsidized by the federal government.

Beginning with Nova Scotia in 1915, each province, with the exception of Prince Edward Island, has enacted Workmen's Compensation Acts whereby a fund made up of compulsory contributions by employers is maintained to compensate workers (at the rate of from 50 to 66⅔ per cent. of the normal wages or by means of lump sum payments to widows) for incapacitating or fatal accidents incurred while at work.

[1] By October, 1937, 217 petitions had been received but only sixty-four schedules established, the majority in the barbering trade. (Information and schedules in operation given the writer by the Ontario Department of Labour.)

Industrial Arbitration and Conciliation

In 1907 the Dominion Government passed the Industrial Disputes Investigation Act which forbids strikes or lock-outs in mines and public utility industries until after a board of conciliation and investigation, made up of one representative of each party to the dispute and a third chosen by these two (or, failing agreement, appointed by the Minister of Labour) has made its report. In 1925 the Act was ruled *ultra vires* by the Privy Council, but each of the provinces, except Prince Edward Island, passed enabling legislation which dovetailed into the revised Dominion Act of 1927, thereby restoring the *status quo*. The machinery of the Act may be extended to other industries with the consent of the parties concerned.

Between March 22, 1907, and March 31, 1937, there were applications for 866 boards and all but thirty-nine strikes were averted. Of the applications 246 came from the steam railways and 148 from street and electric railways with but seven strikes resulting in each. In the fiscal year ending March 31, 1937, there were twenty-four applications for Boards, twelve being actually established, but not a single strike was prevented.

The Federal Department of Labour also maintains Conciliation Officers (one each at Ottawa, for the Dominion, at Toronto, for Ontario, at Montreal, for Quebec and the Maritime Provinces, and at Vancouver for the Western Provinces) who seek to help settle disputes without resort to Boards of Conciliation and Investigation.

Early in 1937 Manitoba passed a Strikes and Lock-outs Prevention Act, which provides for similar conditions and provincial machinery for all industries in the province which are not covered by the Industrial Disputes Investigation Act. Later in the year British Columbia followed with a similar Act.

The clothing industry is the only one in Canada with self-maintained arbitration machinery. The initiation of the plan is credited to Mr. Schaffner of the clothing firm of Hart Schaffner and Marx, of Chicago, Sidney Hillman, then an employee of the firm, now President of the Amalgamated Clothing Workers of America, and Professor Earl Dean Howard. As a result of a strike in 1910 they negotiated in 1911 an agreement setting up an Arbitration Board, consisting of equal representatives of labour and employers and an impartial chairman, elected by both parties. All disputes which cannot be settled within the plant between management and " trade board " or shop council must be brought before the Board where, if conciliation fails, the chairman hands down a judgment which is binding on both parties.

In Canada[1] the Amalgamated Clothing Workers strove to introduce the Chicago plan immediately after its inception there. Between 1913 and 1919 the arbitration clause was embodied in every strike settlement in Toronto clothing shops, and in the latter year the Toronto Clothing Manufacturers' Association was formed to deal collectively with the Amalgamated for the whole Toronto market. The agreements in each shop are fairly co-ordinated through the operation of the Arbitration Board. Each shop has its shop committee with a shop chairman, who strive to settle difficulties on the spot. Disputes which cannot thus be settled are taken before the Arbitration Board for conciliation or judgment by the " impartial chairman " who is appointed jointly by the Union and the Manufacturers' Association. Two *ad hoc* representatives of the employees and the employers constitute the other four members of the Board. The present chairman, Professor J. Finkelman, succeeded Professor H. R. Kemp, both of the University of Toronto, in 1937, and the arbitration judgments have been accepted in the industry in such a manner that no strike has occurred in the men's clothing industry under the Amalgamated in Toronto since 1919. Nor has there been a strike in Montreal since the recent adoption of the plan there, or in any shop elsewhere under the plan. Through this arrangement, which now has the approval of both employers and employees affected, it is claimed the industry has, in but a decade or two, been raised from the worst " sweat shop " conditions to a position in which the 7,500 Canadian members of the Amalgamated enjoy one of the highest standards of wages and conditions in the country. Recently the International Ladies' Garment Workers' Union and the United Hatters, Cap and Millinery Workers' International Union have adopted similar plans in Toronto.

[1] For information on the history and operation of the Plan in Canada, the writer is indebted to Mr. S. Spivak, Toronto Manager and Canadian representative of the Amalgamated Clothing Workers' Union since 1921.

Trade Unions and the Law

The only significant federal legislation on the subject is the Trade Unions Act and the Criminal Law Amendment Act of 1872, which freed trade unions from liability under the common law of conspiracy in the restraint of trade. The former Act also provided for the registration of trade unions to acquire legal personality. But organized labour eschewed this privilege and by the end of 1936 only seventeen, and those national, company and Catholic unions were registered under the Act.

The other relevant acts are provincial in scope, the most significant of which are very recent and are patterned somewhat after the Wagner Act in the U.S.A. Early in 1937, Alberta and Nova Scotia passed the Freedom of Trade Union Association Act and the Trade Union Act, respectively, which declare trade unions and collective bargaining lawful and provide fines for attempts by employers to restrain their workers in the exercise of this right. Both outlaw the " yellow dog " contract while the latter makes collective bargaining obligatory for an employer. A similar Act was introduced in Saskatchewan early in 1938. The Manitoba and British Columbia conciliation and arbitration acts referred to above, contain similar freedom-of-association clauses. So also does the above referred to Fair Wage Act of Quebec. But this and other acts passed in the latter province also seriously curtail the freedom of autonomous unions.[1]

An Act respecting Communistic Propaganda, which became notorious throughout Canada as the " Padlock Law," was passed in Quebec in 1937, whereby the Attorney-General is empowered to close for one year any premises wherein " Communistic propaganda " has been permitted to be voiced. In addition the Act forbids the printing, publishing and distribution of any Communistic literature in no matter what form. The danger of the Act resides in the fact that it does not define what it means by " Communism " but leaves it to the judgment

[1] The Professional Syndicates Act passed in 1924 is still in operation in the province. Its terms are rather suggestive. It provides for provincial registration of trade unions with the Provincial Secretary, much like the Dominion Act; but unlike it, it provides that all the officers and at least two-thirds of the registered syndicate must be British subjects. Practically none but Catholic unions have to date registered under this Act.

of the Attorney-General. As the holder of that office in 1938, M. Maurice Duplessis, also happened to be the Premier of the Province and the leader of the French nationalist party—the " Union Nationale "—organized labour viewed the measure as quasi-Fascist. The fact that M. Arcand, the leader of Canada's Fascist party, was the editor of M. Duplessis' periodical *L'Illustration nouvelle*, and an intimate associate of the Premier, gave emphasis to this view. The unions complained that the statute was aimed at autonomous labour organizations, and protests demanding federal disallowance of the Act poured into Ottawa from coast to coast.

The Collective Labour Agreements Act and the above cited Fair Wage Act of the same Province, passed late in 1937 and popularly referred to as " Bills 19 and 20," affect trade union activity in an important respect. By them absolute authority is vested in the Lieutenant-Governor-in-Council to fix zones and minimum rates without previous consultations. Labour contends that this militates against collective negotiations and weakens its bargaining power. It regards as even more objectionable the clause guaranteeing the worker's " freedom of association " which also guarantees his " freedom from association " and from compulsion to join any particular association. This, it is maintained, throws the gates wide open to company unionism and virtually renders illegal strikes to secure a " closed shop " or enforce union membership. Already, the Dominion Textile Company and a pulp and paper company at Port Arthur have set up company unions to the exclusion of not only the international but also the Catholic unions. Certain firms in the clothing industry are attempting to follow this example. The Montreal Trades and Labour Council has described the measures as " a sword of Damocles suspended over the head of the unions, threatening their very existence." But many of the Catholic unions, too, have protested against these measures and seem to have moved closer to the internationals on this issue.

The dangers which organized labour in Canada feels to inhere in the enactments of M. Duplessis' government and in the latter's entente with Premier Hepburn of Ontario (the " Hepburn-Duplessis Axis ") appear to be not at all imaginary. The widespread appreciation by the autonomous trade unions of this " threat " to their existence will doubtless cause strenuous efforts to be made at the forthcoming convention of the T.L.C.C. to prevent any weakening of that body by expulsion of the C.I.O. unions or defections by A.F. of L. unions.[1]

[1] Since this was written (spring of 1938), events have largely substantiated this anticipation. At the 54th Convention of the Congress held at Niagara Falls, Ontario, the week of September 12, 1938, the 544 delegates, despite the relentless pressure which the American A.F. of L. executive had brought to bear on the Canadian A.F. of L. unions, and to the surprise of the whole country, almost unanimously and amid scenes of tumultuous enthusiasm adopted on September 15 the resolution for the preservation and further consolidation of unity.

Following this manifestation at the Congress, however, the A.F. of L. executive still further intensified its pressure and threats against the T.L.C.C. executive. Strengthened further by the fact that the C.I.O. had in November 1938 converted itself from a " Committee " to the " Congress for Industrial Organization," the A.F. of L. leaders finally succeeded in bringing the T.L.C.C. executive to its knees by demonstrating that the continued affiliation of the C.I.O. unions with the T.L.C.C. would violate Articles III and V of the latter's constitution. As a result, the executive, on January 18, 1939, by a vote of three to one, suspended the C.I.O. unions from the Congress. In his letter of notification to the unions affected, however, Mr. R. J. Tallon, Secretary and acting President, expressed a hope that a way would be found to restore complete unity. The C.I.O. unions in return, in a joint statement, pledged themselves to continued co-operation with the Congress.

MEXICO

BY

WILLIAM E. ZEUCH

MEXICO

THE population of Mexico as of July 1, 1938, estimated from its rate of growth indicated by the official censuses of 1921 and 1930 was close to 20,000,000.[1] As there has never been a complete occupational census covering the whole republic no one knows exactly just what proportion of the people is agricultural, industrial or professional. Most students of the distribution of population in Mexico estimate roughly that 70 per cent. is agricultural, 20 per cent. industrial, and the balance, or 10 per cent., professional and other minor groups. This means that at present approximately 14,000,000 persons get their living from the land, 4,000,000 from industry, and 2,000,000 from all other occupations. Of the 4,000,000 people who depend on industry for a living not more that 750,000 at most are employed workers.[2]

The labour movement in Mexico, however, is not confined to this industrial population. While groups of industrial workers such as miners, railwaymen, textile workers, electricians, and oil workers have been and are the backbone of the labour movement, it includes non-industrial groups also. The most recent report of the Department of Labour[3] lists a total of 4,723 local unions with a total of 612,187 members as of June 1, 1937. This total membership is about equally divided between groups under federal jurisdiction—309,829 members—and groups under state jurisdiction—302,358 members. An examination of the list discloses that nearly 100,000 of this membership comes from associations of agricultural workers. There are also groups of rural teachers, doctors and surgeons, and clubs of socialist women. As the Department of Labour never thoroughly checked the original membership reported by the local unions and as it merely adds without investigation all increases reported later by the local union, the tabulations are far too high. All figures on membership of labour organizations in Mexico are untrustworthy. On the very same day,

[1] The official census showed 14,172,462 in 1921 and 16,584,243 in 1930.

[2] The second national industrial census of April 10, 1935, gave a total of 283,772 workers in all the extractive and manufacturing industries.

[3] Memoria del Departmento de Trabajo; Dapp, Mexico City, 1937.

June 10, 1938, the Department of Labour reported 87,000 unionized railway workers, the Secretary General of the railway union reported 58,000, and the office of the Secretary General of the Confederación de Trabajadores de Mexico, the C.T.M., the national federation with which the railway union is affiliated, reported 45,000 members of the railway union.[1] Just a few contrasts in figures on membership of unions as given out by the Department of Labour and the C.T.M. will point the problem of reliable statistics. These figures are for June 1, 1938.[2]

Union	*C.T.M. estimate*	*Dept. of Labour estimate*
Railway Union	45,000	87,000
Oil Workers Union	16,000	22,000
Electricians Unions	10,000	8,000
Sugar Workers Union	60,000	30,000
Graphic Arts Union	10,000	6,000

It is obvious when government officials and labour officials provide such glaringly contradictory figures on union membership that all estimates are doubtful.

From a study of the Mexican labour movement extending over two years, the writer believes that membership of the various organized groups does not exceed the following:

Professional Workers:	
Government Employees	120,000
Teachers	80,000
Agricultural Labourers	100,000
Industrial Workers:	
Confederación General de Trabajadores	15,000
Confederación Regional de Obreros Mexicanos	35,000
Confederación de Trabajadores de Mexico ...	200,000[3]
Independent Unions	50,000
Total	600,000

[1] These estimates were given to the writer personally by responsible officials.

[2] Figures given to the writer personally by responsible officials.

[3] It should be kept in mind that the C.T.M. includes the Teachers Union from among the professional workers and some groups of agricultural workers. It is doubtful whether the government employees will be permitted to join the C.T.M.

This estimated total of 600,000 is an outside figure for enrolled membership. It contrasts strongly with the claims of the C.T.M. that it alone in 1937 had 945,913 members.[1] It must be emphasized that this estimated total is enrolled membership rather than dues paying membership. It is notorious in Mexico that union members enroll, but neglect to pay dues. If paid up dues were taken as a criterion of membership, this total of 600,000 would shrink greatly.[2]

Labour Beginnings

It has become the custom to date everything in the new Mexico from that October day in 1910 when Madero began the revolution against Diaz. In a certain sense we could begin the history of organized labour in Mexico as from that date. During the second half of the nineteenth century, when new ideas were sweeping and shaking the western labour world, Mexican labour remained almost completely ignorant of them. There was little industry in the country in the modern sense. The masses were illiterate and in actual serfdom. The hacendados ruled the land from their haciendas. The Catholic Church, leagued with political despotism and economic serfdom, insulated the masses from any and all ideas that might lead them to question or challenge the justice of their deplorable status. Slavery for debt was the common practice. These debts, enslaving artisans as well as peons, were inherited from father to son. Workers were bought and sold into this debt slavery like common chattels in many sections of the country down to the Revolution of 1910.

But in a strict sense organized labour had its beginnings somewhat earlier than 1910. There were mutualist societies among some of the debt free workers of the larger cities—ostensibly for educational, social, and burial purposes—during the last quarter of the nineteenth century. Diaz had granted concessions for the building of railroads on an extensive scale. He also encouraged foreign capital in the establishment of commercial and industrial enterprises. It is not surprising, therefore, that small associations of railway workers were

[1] Report of the National Committee of the C.T.M. for 1936–1937. Published by the C.T.M., Mexico City.

[2] Large round numbers have been used in this personal estimate to avoid any impression of exact accuracy that detailed figures would give.

organized in the 'seventies and 'eighties, followed by associations of textile and other workers in the 'nineties. They were weak and isolated groups, constantly under suspicion and surveillance, which broke up and reformed repeatedly. They were more mutualistic than trade union in character although the associations of railway workers tended more and more toward the trade union pattern as the century closed.

By the beginning of the twentieth century anarchist and socialist ideas had begun to seep into the country. A growing section of people of all classes were increasingly weary of Diaz and his Dictatorship. Mutualism was proving to be not enough for the workers. In 1900 the brothers Flores Magôn issued the first number of their newspaper *Regeneración* in Mexico City and the fight against the Dictator and the Catholic hierarchy—linked together in the mind of the rising labour movement—was brought temporarily into the open. Although the printing establishment of the brothers Flores Magôn was soon smashed up and they were forced to flee to avoid imprisonment and probable death, others continued the nascent labour struggle.

Labour groups of various kinds continued to form in mining, textile, and railroad centres despite employer and governmental opposition. Many of them were underground and anarchist or syndicalist in character. Two outstanding strikes occurred during the final decade of the Diaz régime, the first in 1906 in the mines of Cananea in the state of Sonora close to the border of the United States, and the second in 1907 in the textile mills around Orizaba in the state of Veracruz, particularly at Rio Blanco. Both strikes ended in violence, bloodshed and deaths. Diaz attempted to dictate and impose terms of settlement inimical to the workers and sent in federal troops to enforce his will. At Cananea the strike was crushed with troops, and scabs imported from neighbouring mining centres in the United States. At Rio Blanco on January 1, 1907, a bloody battle took place around the mills between troops and workers in which an indefinite number, variously estimated at from twenty-five to three hundred, were reported killed. The failure of these strikes ended unionizing efforts for the time being. The crushing of the workers at Rio Blanco destroyed the Grand Circle of Free Workers, the union that had organized them and directed the strike. January 7, however, became a living symbol of martyrdom to Mexican Labour.

From the Revolution of 1910 *to the Constitution of* 1917

When the political revolution led by Francisco Madero overthrew Diaz and his dictatorship the industrial workers, as indicated, were already somewhat experienced with organization and were thinking in economic and social terms. Madero, primarily a political revolutionist, seems never to have given much thought to the need of social and economic changes in Mexico. When he came to the Presidency in 1911 he found himself surrounded in part, but at a distance, by three groups, the Zapata agrarians, the Flores Magôn anarchists, and the trade unionists, all of whom were thinking of economic and social changes rather than of political reforms. In December 1911 Madero gave a rather doubtful and half-hearted recognition to the existence of a labour problem by the creation of a Department of Labour with strictly limited functions. During 1911 and 1912 strike after strike of textile workers led to armed strife and many deaths. January 7 was not being forgotten. Madero called a convention of the textile employers and employees in Mexico City to reach an understanding. The attitude of Madero is well shown in the fact that the labour delegates were not permitted to sit in the convention but were notified of the decisions of the employers after they were made. But out of this textile convention of 1912 came the first labour contract and the first semblance of collective bargaining in the history of labour of Mexico.

From the general national disorder and disorganization of the Madero period arose the *Casa del Obrero Mundial* the House of the Workers of the World, the first group to give any semblance of coherence to the labour movement in Mexico. The *Casa*, founded in July 1912, was the outgrowth of discussions of a little group of intellectuals and workers, partly foreign refugees, who were convinced that economic and social revolution was of far more importance to the masses of Mexico than political revolution. Branches of the *Casa* were set up in several states. Madero feared the radicalism of the *Casa*. Its newspaper was suppressed, a number of its native leaders were arrested and imprisoned, and its foreign leaders were expelled from the country. This action of Madero shocked all the labour groups and lost him their support when the conservatives turned against him.

Huerta, who instigated the murder of Madero and then succeeded him in the Presidency in February 1913, was a reactionary in every sense of the word. Labour suffered many reverses and suppressions of activities during his year and a half in office. During the war of the Constitutionalists under Carranza, first against Huerta and later against Villa 1913–1915, the labour movement and labour interests were furthered and bettered. At first Carranza, who was no social or economic liberal, ignored the industrial workers. His associates, especially General Obregon, less intransigent and more realistic, pointed out to him the necessity of formulating a programme of economic and social reforms; but he refused to consider the question or to make any bid for the help of labour until he had been driven out of the national capital by the combined forces of Villa and Zapata. Finally, on December 12, 1914, with his back to the wall, from Veracruz Carranza issued his famous decree declaring that,

"The First Chief of the Revolution . . . will expedite and put in force . . . all the laws, dispositions, and measures necessary to give satisfaction to the economic, social, and political needs of the nation . . . ; agrarian laws which favour the formation of small landholdings, the dissolution of the landed estates, and restoration to the villages of the lands of which they have been unjustly despoiled . . . ;and legislation to better the condition of the peasant, of the worker, of the miner, and, in general, of the working classes. . . ."

Carranza followed this decree with another on January 6, 1915, less than four weeks later, providing for the method of division of lands among the peasants. This brought the agricultural labourers to his standard in large numbers. General Obregon pointed out to the leaders of the industrial workers the advantage of joining the revolution under the guarantees Carranza had made in the December 12, 1914, decree. The labour leaders presented demands. Carranza, hard pressed by adverse publicity at home and abroad as well as in a military way, signed an agreement with the labour chiefs. The *Casa* moved its headquarters from Mexico City to Orizaba in March 1915, and set about the organization of

Red Battalions to aid Carranza, battalions that finally numbered 10,000. These were the first labour battalions organized by industrial workers in any country for social revolutionary purposes.

In all there were six of these Red Battalions. Special trains carried them and their families from place to place during the campaign. The workers enlisted in these battalions by unions and selected their officers from among their own members. In strict truth it must be stated that these labour battalions had a much greater propaganda value for unionism than military value for Carranza. Wherever territory was conquered these armed workers established branches of the *Casa del Obrero Mundial*. This done, strikes for an eight-hour day, higher wages, and recognition of the union were invariably called. Since the strikers had the support of the accompanying military they were always successful. Under such conditions labour organization proceeded rapidly. A "fever of unionism" swept the regions conquered by Carranza.

Labour in the Constitution of 1917

The success of the Constitutionalists under Carranza led, as promised, to the calling of a constitutional convention at Queretero and the adoption of the Constitution of 1917. This constitution is popularly supposed to embody what the workers, both agricultural and industrial, had gained from the revolution. But in reality the famous Article 27 covering the land question and the equally famous Article 123, the so-called magna carta of Mexican labour, were and are aspiration rather than realization. They were merely declarations of principles or avowals of intention left to the separate states to implement by legislation. So far as the industrial workers were concerned the aspirations, or principles, or avowals in Article 123 are significant and of great importance as they furnished a guide to what labour might ask for and get if they had the economic power or political power, or both, to back up their requests.

Among many other things Article 123 declares for an eight-hour day; a seven-hour night; one day's rest in seven; equal pay for equal work; legal strikes; legal lock-outs; no labour for children under twelve ; double wage rates for overtime and limitation on hours of overtime; wages to be paid in currency; uncollectability of worker's debts from his children; limitation of rents to 6 per cent. annually of the value of the house; employer liability for accidents and occupational diseases; minimum wages; profit sharing; and vacations with full pay for pregnant women in industry, both before and after the birth of the child.

With the end of the political revolution of 1910 and the promulgation of the Constitution of 1917 the real fight of labour began.

Attempts at National Labour Unity

The present Mexican labour movement in all its veerings and despite all its betrayals has been at base an attempt on the part of the rank and file of the workers to realize the promises in the Decree of December 12, 1914, and in Article 123 of the Constitution of 1917. This is the key to an understanding of Mexican labour.

As soon as Carranza was seemingly firmly established in the Presidency efforts were made to bring about labour unity throughout the country. Three national conventions of Mexican labour, at Veracruz in March 1916, at Tampico in October 1917, and at Saltillo in March 1918, were devoted to trying to find a basis for united action. The first convention brought out sharp theoretical divisions, deep personal hatreds, and the beginning of the struggle of Luis N. Morones for trade union control of the Mexican labour movement. The second convention continued the fights of the first between Anarchists, Syndicalists, and Trade Unionists, with the Syndicalists carrying the convention. Out of this Tampico meeting came the Confederación General de Trabajadores, the C.G.T., a labour federation theoretically committed to economic action and opposed to political action, which has persisted as a minority organization with little strength down to the present. At the third convention, known at the time to be sponsored and financed by the Carranza government, the Trade Unionists triumphed, as they were expected and paid to do, and established the Confederación Regional de Obreros Mexicanos, the C.R.O.M., with Luis N. Morones as Secretary General. The C.R.O.M. was organized as a loose federation of national, state and local unions much on the pattern of the American Federation of Labour, with which Morones and other leaders were closely associated, a type of organization that greatly favoured the power and the permanence in power of the national central committee which was the executive of the whole federation.

Prior to these conventions there had originated in the *Casa del Obrero Mundial* the *Grupo Acción* one of the most unusual groups in any labour movement. It was a body of men, mostly young, never more than twenty in number, which met in Mexico City frequently to discuss ways and means to get " action " in the labour movement. They had diverse philosophies and represented various unions but, strange as it may seem, appear to have preserved internal harmony and an external united front as long as the C.R.O.M. remained dominant in Mexican labour, a record remarkable in a country and a movement shot through with shifting loyalties and outright betrayals. Luis N. Morones was the commanding figure among the fairly independent personalities of *Grupo Acción*.

The Rise of the C.R.O.M.

With their very origins the labour unions of Mexico were enmeshed in politics. Despite the pretence of being non-political they all, either openly or covertly, mixed in political affairs. From the convention at Saltillo, financed by the Carranza administration, down to the present, every labour organization that has played a strong or a prominent part in public affairs has been financed in large part, directly or indirectly, by political personages or the administration in power. This would have been all to the good if political connections had furthered the economic and political aims of labour. Unfortunately the Mexican labour movement most often has been merely a tool of party politics and sometimes merely an instrument of personal politics.

The C.R.O.M. from its inception was opportunistic in a very narrow sense. It accepted the American Federation of Labour programme of shorter hours, higher wages and better working conditions. It had no basic philosophy, no theories, although it did lip service to the idea of ultimate socialization of the means of production and distribution because of the wide-spread collectivist sentiment among the more literate and intelligent peasants and workers. When the occasion demanded, the speeches of the leaders and the literature of C.R.O.M. could reveal a pure Marxism.

As already stated, Mexican labour in the form of the *Casa del Obrero Mundial*, largely through the efforts of General Obregon, had backed Carranza in 1915 in his fight to regain power and retain the Presidency. In 1919 the C.R.O.M. organized the Mexican Labour Party as its political instrument. In 1920 the C.R.O.M. and the Mexican Labour Party, under Morones leadership and on the basis of a written agreement, supported Obregon against Carranza in the "Revindicating Revolution." When Obregon became President the same year C.R.O.M.-supported persons were put into various government positions. Morones was made head of the federal military factories, a position just below cabinet rank.

Almost immediately the C.R.O.M. began to use its government backing to foment strikes in unorganized plants and to harass independent unions and opposition labour federations. Morones was ruthlessly bent on unifying all labour inside the C.R.O.M. President Obregon, not wishing to be dependent on labour alone and fearing the political consequences of a united labour movement under Morones, secretly supported the independent unions and opposition federations and played them against the C.R.O.M., and publicly adopted an attitude of impartiality and fair play as between the various labour factions.[1] Morones must have known of President Obregon's attitude and actions but, evidently, thought loyalty to Obregon the best policy. When the de la Huerta revolution broke out in 1923, it was the loyalty of Morones and the C.R.O.M. with the support they were able to get through the American Federation of Labour that saved Obregon.

As President Obregon tended to turn away from labour support to the support of the peasants, Plutarco Calles the rising political personage and the logical successor to Obregon in the Presidency was growing closer to the C.R.O.M. and the Mexican Labour Party. In 1924 Calles ran for president as a

[1] Many persons familiar with this period of Mexican history, notably Diego Rivera and Bertram Wolfe, maintain that Obregon's whole policy was based on pitting a divided labour movement against the foreign interests in Mexico so that he might continue to rule with the support of the peasants and the army. They call this "The Obregon System."

labour candidate on a labour ticket and was elected as a labour president. In recognition of the services of the C.R.O.M. Morones was appointed to the cabinet as Secretary of Commerce, Industry and Labour, and became the most conspicuous person in the administration next to Calles himself. Morones brought a host of C.R.O.M. members into the administration with him and placed them in strategic and well-salaried positions. By levying toll on the salaries of these office holders, as well as by other grafts well known to the higher Mexican government officials, Morones was able to finance the C.R.O.M., amass a private fortune, give lavish entertainments, corrupt officials of the independent unions, and otherwise exploit his power. The power of Morones and the C.R.O.M. during the early years of the Calles administration enabled them to censor the press, arbitrarily decide labour issues, and terrorize labour opposition.[1] Not that Morones bore down on employers. It is significant that the number of strikes, which measure labour militancy, declined from 310 in 1921, the second year Morones was in a government position and before he had achieved great prestige and power, to seven in 1928 when he was at his strongest as Secretary of Commerce, Industry and Labour as well as head of the C.R.O.M. Despite worsening labour conditions labour militancy was ruthlessly suppressed by Morones.

Decline of the C.R.O.M.

During the ten years of his rise and ascendency in the labour unions and in labour politics, Morones did little or nothing either to develop permanent economic power in the unions or to protect labour by legislation. He looked upon himself as the " patron " of the labour movement, the strong man the movement could look to and depend upon for both economic and political protection. If the movement developed strong independent economic power or achieved legislative protection it would not need him. He wanted to make himself indispensable to labour by making labour dependent on him. There is little doubt but that he hoped to reach the Presidency in this way.

[1] Read the section on Labour in *Mexican Heritage*, by Ernest Gruening, for a detailed description of labour ruthlessness during this period.

When General Obregon was assassinated in June 1928, after his re-election to succeed Calles and prior to his second inauguration, suspicion fell on Morones as "Intellectual author" of the crime. Obregon had frustrated the political ambitions of Morones and great bitterness had grown up between them. There was never any convincing proof offered to support the charge of complicity against Morones. Feeling, nevertheless, ran high. Morones resigned and went into temporary retirement. It was the end of his political power and prestige.

Despite his strength Morones had never been able to subdue completely the independent federations and unions, though some of the latter had been forced into the C.R.O.M. Within the C.R.O.M. itself militant elements had been long restive under the domination of Morones. These militant elements took the occasion of Morones' fall from political power to withdraw their unions from the C.R.O.M. But the economic strength of the unions was so weak that they entered into a period of low prestige and little power. Morones still retained his control in a greatly reduced and weakened C.R.O.M. but the C.R.O.M. was no longer a force that even the politicians respected.[1] From 1928 to 1933 labour in Mexico was in the doldrums. It was a period of marking time and of a struggle for survival.

A Federal Labour Code

But the years in the doldrums were not completely lost years for labour in Mexico. For over a decade there had been a growing sentiment throughout the country that labour legislation by the various states, along the lines indicated by the Constitution of 1917, was a failure. Few of the states had inaugurated such legislation. Neither employers, employees, nor government were satisfied with the resultant situation. As early as 1915 President Carranza had wanted federal labour legislation but his wishes had been denied. Labour thought it could get more from the legislatures of the industrial states where it was most strongly organized. By 1930 almost everybody was willing to admit that Article 123 must be implemented by federal laws if any of its provisions were to achieve full realization.

[1] It is amusing to note that in 1927 the C.R.O.M. claimed 2,500,000 members.

Calles, on the death of Obregon and the discrediting of Morones, had become the dominant political personage in Mexico. He had been a labour man and retained labour sympathies. Portes Gil, with the backing of Calles, had succeeded him for a two-year term as Provisional President. He worked energetically, with the full approval of Calles, to further the movement for a federal labour code. Gil was followed in the Presidency in 1930 by Ortiz Rubio, another Calles puppet. The work on the code continued. It was the strong man's will. Finally, on August 28, 1931, all the labour legislation that had been enacted by the various states was rescinded by the promulgation of the federal labour law, a national code of labour. This code did not enact all the aspirations of Article 123. It made a good start, however, and it did set up federal bodies with broad powers to act in labour disputes. There were teeth in the law for labour as well as for capital. Nonetheless, it marked a great forward step for the workers of the country. It made it possible ultimately to implement all of Article 123 on a national scale whenever labour has the economic and political power to get the enabling legislation. This meant, of course, that labour must organize more strongly than ever and devote itself more and more to political action.[1]

The Rise of the C.T.M.

The era of labour union stagnation is reflected in the number of strikes. In 1928 in all Mexico there were seven strikes, in 1929 fourteen, in 1930 fifteen, in 1931 eleven, in 1932 fifty-six, and in 1933 thirteen. The era of stagnation came to a close and militancy revived in 1933 with the creation, under the leadership of Dr. Vincente Lombardo Toledano, of the *Confederación General de Obreros y Campesinos de Mexico*, the C.G.O.C.M., which brought together some of the unions formerly belonging to the C.R.O.M. Other federations and independent unions were labouring at the same time for unification of the workers. The C.G.O.C.M. and other labour groups expressed themselves courageously and firmly on public issues. There was greater activity on the economic field. In

[1] For details of this federal code consult "The History of Trade Unionism in Mexicó," by Margaret Clark, Univ. of North Carolina Press, Chapel Hill, N.C., 1933.

1934 the number of strikes rose to 202, a great increase from the thirteen of the year previous. Faith in unionism and union leadership was gradually returning to the working masses. A fighting unionism was in rebirth.

In 1933, Calles, still political boss of Mexico, selected General Lazaro Cárdenas for President as the candidate of the National Revolutionary Party organized by Calles in 1929. Morones with the remnants of the C.R.O.M. had allied himself with Calles. Despite the fact that everybody knew that he was as good as elected, Cárdenas made it his business to visit every section of the country so that he could see and be seen, talk with and be talked to by the people. In 1934 he assumed the Presidency. It appears that Calles did not know his man Cárdenas as well as he thought. Scarcely was he in office before he began to act independently. Trouble was soon brewing between Boss Calles and President Cárdenas. The C.G.O.C.M. and other independent unions and federations veered to Cárdenas. They wanted none of the Calles-Morones political control. The showdown came in June 1935 when Calles published threats that he would drive Cárdenas from office (as he had actually done in the case of Ortiz Rubio) if he did not alter his attitude and actions. On the very same day a National Committee of Proletarian Defence was formed, made up of trade union federations and independent unions, including the C.G.O.C.M. The National Committee branded Calles and Morones as enemies of the Mexican working class and issued a call for a National Unification Congress of labour to be held February 26 to 29, 1936. More than 2,000 delegates representing industrial workers, intellectuals, federal employees, and peasants attended this congress, which created the *Confederación de Trabajadores de Mexico*, the C.T.M. Dr. Vincente Lombardo Toledano was elected Secretary General of the new organization.[1]

The two years since the organization of the C.T.M. have been unusually full years for Mexican labour. There have been

[1] Dr. Lombardo is an interesting contrast to Morones. Morones is a worker risen from the ranks. Lombardo is an intellectual from the universities. Morones is an opportunist. Lombardo calls himself a simon-pure Marxian. Lombardo puts primary emphasis on building labour unions as economic weapons. Morones thought political action more important. Both, quite legitimately, are men of personal ambition.

bitter struggles within the labour ranks as well as hard fought struggles with employers. The C.T.M. is a federation of industrial, factory and professional unions. It includes national, state and local organizations. In such a broad and loose organization there is much chance for disruptive elements to foment divisions. In 1937 the Communist Party of Mexico through its members in various unions tried to impose its opinions and tactics on the C.T.M. Failing in this it managed to secure the withdrawal of unions in which it had strong groups. The National Council of the C.T.M. gave the withdrawing unions a time limit in which to recognize their error and return or else suffer permanent suspension. The Communist Party recanted and assured the National Council that it would accept the discipline and tactics of the C.T.M. In the year since this threat to unity the C.T.M. has greatly augmented its membership and has achieved a more unified discipline.

The years 1936 and 1937 were marked by great strikes conducted by the C.T.M. Among these the most important were the one against the Mexican Light and Power Company, a British owned company, the strike of the agricultural workers of the Laguna, the cotton growing centre, and the strike against the oil companies which ended in expropriation and the nationalization of the oil industry. The number of strikes throughout the country increased from 202 in 1934 to 659 in 1936. The balance sheet for strikes, while showing defeats here and there, on the whole reveals a steady advance of labour. Perhaps the saddest thing to record is the bloody struggle, ending in scores of deaths, between the dying C.R.O.M. and the rising C.T.M. for jurisdiction in the textile mill strikes of the state of Vera Cruz.

It should be noted that the labour movement in Mexico has never taken up consumers' co-operation to any extent as a help to the workers' movement. This is in sharp contrast to the peasant organizations. The labour unions have many social clubs in the large cities owned by their membership. The railway union owns and operates in Mexico City the largest and most modern hospital in all Mexico. In February 1936 the C.T.M. organized a Workers' University and in June 1938 established a daily paper, *El Popular*, in Mexico city. These seem to be the preferred type of labour activity. It is probable that labour has not taken to co-operation because it looks forward to national operation of industries. The National Railways of Mexico are already being operated by the Railway Union. In the recently nationalized oil industry the oil workers' union participates in management. Where nationalization is an imminent prospect co-operative activities do not appeal strongly.

Labour Outlook in Mexico

The future of labour in Mexico, for the present at least, is in the hands of the C.T.M. Despite the continued existence of the C.G.T., the C.R.O.M. and some independent unions, they count for little in the national scene. The numbers, the prestige and the power are with the C.T.M. In its ideology the C.T.M. is a class struggle organization. Its guiding intellectuals are Marxists though not necessarily Communists. It should be kept in mind that the national ideological core of Mexico is collectivist. The indigenous population has been collectivist, despite all attempts to make it individualist, since the pre-Columbian era. This ancient agrarian collectivism does not find the industrial collectivism of Marxism objectionable. The industrial workers, recruited largely from the agrarian masses, accept a programme of ultimate socialized nationalism without misgivings. The workers of Mexico look upon the fulfilment of Articles 27 and 123 of the Constitution of 1917 as a step toward that ultimate goal.

At present there appears to be a working understanding and co-operation between the Cárdenas administration and the labour movement. Cárdenas is committed to the fulfilment of the Constitution of 1917, as implemented by the Six Year Plan adopted by the National Revolutionary Party in 1934. The C.T.M. is supporting Cárdenas in every way. When he expressed the wish that the agricultural labourers be organized in a separate national body the C.T.M. agreed. When he proposed the reorganization of the National Revolutionary Party on a broader basis so as to include more groups, the C.T.M. went along. It took a prominent part in the congress of re-organization in April, 1928, that set up the Mexican Revolutionary Party. On his part Cárdenas seems to be taking the wishes of the C.T.M. into consideration on all matters affecting labour. The government grants the money on which the Workers' University operates. There is but little doubt that the C.T.M. furnishes a disproportionate share of the brains and ability of the new Mexican Revolutionary Party.

With all its faults, and it has many measured by any standard, the C.T.M. is the most hopeful organized group in Mexico. Its rank and file have been nourished on and inspired by revolutionary ideals. Its effective leadership is dynamic and driving. There are grafters in the C.T.M., to be sure, men to whom it is just a living, and a good living by Mexican standards. One has the feeling, however, that the historic collectivist ideology of the peasants and the revolutionary ideals of the rank and file of the industrial workers will finally purge the labour movement, no matter what the extent of present corruption.

AUSTRALIA

BY

LLOYD ROSS

AUSTRALIA

I

Out of every hundred Australian male adults, forty-eight are members of a trade union—possibly the highest percentage in the capitalist world. Labour parties have been in control of the Treasury in every State in the Commonwealth and of the Commonwealth itself. A scheme of social legislation influences every aspect of the Australian citizen's life, from birth to death—widows' pensions and child endowment in New South Wales, unemployment insurance in Queensland, maternity allowances, social insurance, and old age pensions in the Commonwealth. Social services in Australia cost £48,000,000 in 1934–5 or about 10 per cent. of the National Income.

The inevitable institutions of modern industry find their counterpart in Australia—organizations of workers and of employers; political and industrial organizations of workers; propagandists with numerous alternatives to the existing institutions. The Labour Movement is strong. But to the problems associated with the growth of a Labour Movement in every country, Labour adds special problems of its own, due to its strength, its history, and to the Australian environment itself. Australian Labour forced on non-Labour parties the establishment of systems of compulsory wage regulation, but is now wondering whether it is imprisoned within its own creation. It developed powerful political organizations, but soon found difficulty in influencing the actions and policy of these organizations. It squeezed concessions from Australian capitalism, but was confronted early and abruptly with the problems arising from saturation. It found its task of winning social reforms so easy that it was unable to adapt itself quickly enough to the changed economic conditions arising from the great depression. It found isolation so satisfying in a world of international complexities and dangers, that it has failed to work out a united policy in foreign affairs which would harmonize international obligations and safeguards with Australia's geographical position and national outlook. The Labour Movement tended more and more to develop along the narrow canal of political victories so that it has failed to win the all-embracing Labour unity of creed and organization necessary for the solution of the problems that confront Australian Labour to-day.

Readers of this book will be able to judge in what directions Australian Labour has failed more than has Labour elsewhere, and where it has succeeded. In any such comparison full appreciation must be given to the strength of trade unionism. With a few unimportant exceptions, dual unionism based on religious or political differences has been avoided.

In every main industrial centre is a Labour Council, composed of affiliated trade unions. Australian unity of policy is obtained—not very successfully—through the Australian Council of Trade Unions. Some interstate unions are bound together under such a system of unified control that the Central body is supreme, as in the instance of the Amalgamated Engineering Union; others are united mainly for arbitration purposes, so that the State units are practically independent and self-governing, as in the example of the Australian Railways Union. Although many skilled unions started as branches of the English unions, the Amalgamated Engineering Union is the only important union which has kept up the English connection.

TRADE UNIONISM IN AUSTRALIA, 1932–6

	1921	1928	1932	1933	1934	1935	1936
No. of separate Unions	382	379	361	356	355	354	356
No. of branches ...	2,555	2,079	2,155	2,168	2,177	2,177	2,157
No. of members ...	703,009	911,541	740,831	739,398	762,567	790,830	814,809
Percentage increase in Membership on preceding year ...	—	—	−3·7	−0·2	+3·1	+3·7	+3·0

The above table shows the latest stage in a development that began when a Cabinet Makers' Society was established in Sydney in 1833, and a Typographers' Society was formed in 1836. Leaving aside the fitful experiences of General Unions formed under the influence of Chartism and Owenism, we find that the first permanent unions were composed of skilled men—engineers, stonemasons, builders and typographical operators. Wages being high, their first interest was in obtaining a shorter working week. Gained first by the Operative Masons' Society in

New South Wales after a short strike in 1855, and by the same Union in Victoria in 1856, the winning of the eight-hour day marks the first permanent victory of Australian trade unionism. From the annual celebrations and the desire to extend the reform arose Trades and Labour Councils, Trades Halls, and Labour Representative Committees.

Anticipating the English development, Sydney trade unionists elected the secretary of the Labour Council to Parliament in 1875; but no independent political party was formed until the 'nineties, when in 1891 New South Wales Labour at the first attempt returned thirty-five members to the State Parliament. State Labour Parties operate in every State, working under their own officers, constitutions and policies. Linking, without co-ordinating, the activities of these is the Federal Executive, carrying out its Federal constitution and laying down policy on Commonwealth issues. The Parliamentary Labour Parties have a large degree of autonomy, generally electing their own leader and deciding their own policies within the vague limits of the decisions of the Parties proper. As a guide to party policy is the Platform, crowned by the Objective. The Federal Objective at present is "The Socialization of Industry, Production, Distribution and Exchange." The platform is composed of hundreds of demands, immediate and distant, fundamental and trivial, general and detailed.

A Labour Party was successful in gaining the Treasury Benches first in Queensland in 1899, but no major successes were obtained until 1910, when a Labour Government was successful in New South Wales, and 1912, when the Commonwealth Labour Government entered upon an intense period of social reformism.

Prominent among the methods followed by such Labour Parties for defending standards were high tariff barriers, restriction of white immigration, prohibition of coloured immigration, factory legislation, and wage regulation by State machinery. The State monopolized such undertakings as railways, tramways, post office, telephones and hydro-electric development; the State competed with private enterprise in banking, house-building, insurance and canneries. A combination of geographical, economic and political factors produced State intervention, irrespective of any political philosophy or Party success. Labour extended a tendency; rationalized a Fabian theory from governmental activities that owed little to Party or political philosophy, and discovered that the more widely was the policy practised the more difficult became the solution of the problems of industrial relations, and of efficient and honest management.

At the head of the system of wage regulation and industrial arbitration is the Commonwealth Court of Conciliation and Arbitration. Established in 1904 mainly for the purpose of promoting goodwill in industry by conciliation and arbitration, and so preventing and settling industrial disputes, the Court extended its powers and influence until to-day it determines the working conditions of the overwhelming majority of wage workers. Since 1907 the Court has declared a "basic wage" for unskilled labour, determined according to Mr. Justice Higgins, its originator, by the "normal needs of an average employee regarded as a human being living in a civilized community." No longer concerned mainly with the settlement of strikes, the Court aims at avoiding trouble by regulating working conditions. Unwilling to wait for disputes to break out, the Court accepts in fact a legal application from one of the parties as justifying its intervention. Because of constitutional difficulties, State Tribunals of varying forms cover part of the industrial field.

Such is a somewhat static description of Labour institutions. The driving forces that turn this description into a talking-picture are impacts with external ideas and people, the influence of changing prices for Australian products overseas, and the changing economy of Australia itself.

II

Australia in 1920–1

Taking 1920–1 as the most appropriate years with which to begin a survey of Australian trade, we are able to use the material of the first census taken after the war, that of 1921. Although the area under crop land expanded considerably since 1900, there had also been a decrease in the numbers employed in agriculture. Increasing use was made of machinery, but of the remaining industries only mining and quarrying showed a decline in numbers employed. Groups that showed an increase were: manufacturing, roads and railways, gas, water and electricity, commerce and finance, public administration and entertainment. The increases of factory employment during 1919–21 were especially marked. The average annual increases during 1917–1921 were 421 factories and 13,977 employees.

The number of unionists had steadily increased. During the nine years before 1921 the annual increase in membership was greatest in the year 1912, when it amounted to no less than 68,492, and least in 1915, when it was only 4,760. Between 1920 and 1921 it was 18,564. Industrial Labour had suffered less than had political Labour from the problems of the war period. Political Labour had lost public support because of its association with groups apathetic to or opposed to war, and had become hopelessly divided on its attitude to war conscription. Industrial Labour remained united and gained relatively in strength with declining unemployment. Never since the great strikes and economic crisis of the 'nineties had there been any possibility of trade unionism being so weakened that it could be ignored in the development of the Australian economy.

Between 1906 and 1921 the number of unions was trebled, but membership increased fourfold. There were more members in fewer unions; the trend was in the right direction. The most notable improvement, in reduction of number of unions and increase of membership, was shown in the woodworking, engineering and food trades. The only groups which showed the reverse process were: other manufacturing; railways and tramways; shipping, etc.; and miscellaneous.

State barriers had been broken down. There were 101 interstate unions, with 568,350 members, embracing 80·8 per cent. of the total membership of all unions. Twenty-four Labour Councils were formed from 644 affiliated unions or branches of unions. Few new unions were coming into existence. Old unions were embracing more members; a few amalgamations were taking place, mainly in mining and clothing; but the number of unions remained a source of weakness. The total union membership in all groups in 1921 reached 703,000, organized in 796 unions with average membership of 883 per union.

Much must be said for the organizing skill of the leaders and the inspiring example of oversea teachers that the most closely knit organization is centred among the pastoral and migratory workers. The Shearers' Union was started in Victoria in June 1886, and grew into the Australian Shearers' Union in January 1887. From it grew the Australian Workers' Union —formed from amalgamations with shearing, unskilled general labouring, construction, mining and cane-cutting unions. Although it dominated politics in different States at different times, it is the only large union which has fluctuated considerably in membership and influence.

Recovering from the adjustments of the reconstruction period after the war, Australian economic conditions moved irregularly until the crisis of 1920–1. The 1919–20 harvest was a poor one. Imports outweighted exports. Exchange and credit difficulties were acute. The recession was due to drought conditions, and to falling world prices for wool and wheat, and was accompanied by a sharp fall in the national income. The only unemployment figures available for these years are those provided by trade unions. These show that the highest percentage of unemployed—12·5—was reached in the second quarter of the year. Tested by Trade Union figures of unemployment, the groups suffering most were: wood, engineering, food and mining. Those in the best position were clothing and books. No major effect on union membership can be traced—a factor which must again be stressed as significant in Australian Trade Union development. Some unions gain in strength; others lose; but not merely does trade unionism as a whole resist any large decline, but the fortunes of particular unions depend more on leadership than on economic conditions. Despite the long-range decline in the mining industry, the unions covering this calling keep at the head of the working-class movement, mainly because of their industrial power. Leaders of small unions have become powerful in the Political Labour Party—only in the instances of the A.W.U. in Western Australia and Queensland has one union played a decisive rôle. The main influence of changing economic conditions is in the realm of ideas and politics. The major effect of the crises of 1920–1 and 1929–31 was to bring to a climax the militant tendencies inside the Labour Movement.

In 1919 a most serious dislocation of industry occurred, loss of wages being £3,951,936, representing 6,308,226 working days. In 1920, 554 disputes were recorded, but there was a decline in the days lost (1,872,065) and in wages lost (£1,223,716). The important disputes were among marine stewards on interstate vessels, factory engine drivers and firemen, gas workers in Melbourne, brown coal miners in Victoria, ironstone quarrymen at Whyalla, and State Civil Servants in Western Australia. In 1921 85 per cent. of the disputes occurred in New South Wales—this dominant position being due mainly to the prevalence of disputes in connection with coalmining and being characteristic of every period since Federation.

The large number of disputes in this period is an index of the general restlessness of the period—the first reaction of the workers to attempts to reduce their wages is to resist by strikes. These failing, the number of strikes falls off with the continuance of the depression. Changes of ideas are accelerated. The Russian Revolution, bursting upon a world weary of war, presented socialists with a working alternative to the Fabianism of Australian Labour. The industrialists were in the ascendant. "We found that in every country, workers' councils and tribunals of industry are being established," said Mr. Holloway, the Secretary of the Melbourne Trades Hall Council, summarizing the results of an international inquiry. "We found that at every conference that has been held, the socialization of industry has been demanded." The ideal of a new social order, let loose as much by the armistice as by the Russian Revolution, became linked with the ideal of "guild socialism" or "self-government in industry," which Mr. G. D. H. Cole and others were attempting to create from the bones of dead Fabianism. These were the years of the English Labour Party Programme—"Labour and the New Social Order"—years too, of strikes following upon the Government's failure to fulfil the promises of setting up a new world for Labour.

The knowledge that workers were attempting to win this world for themselves spread to Australia, where there was waiting a Labour Movement that had suddenly become aware of its own slow progress, in contrast with the speed of the Russian Revolution. Australians were tired of nationalization. They believed that capitalism had reached its limits. The theorists, who always exerted some influence on Labour thought, were in the ascendant in these years. Instead of accepting the complete Russian thesis, the Australians, having experienced the successes of Labour in winning political power, and believing that their political and industrial strength would enable them to achieve socialism without a revolution, wanted to hammer out a policy that would bring Australia, in its own way, into line with European developments. To quote Holloway again: " It is thought that it (the programme of the Australian Labour Party) should be brought up to date, and brought into line with modern thought to fit in with the new psychology and the mental revolution which has taken place among the workers throughout the world." The new Australian objective was to be " Australian Labour's creative contribution to the world's working class." It was a local synthesis—an effort by Australian theorists to create a new State without the appeal to force, or the resulting chaos and bloodshed that seemed necessary in the old world—one further expression of the dominant Australian belief that nothing was impossible in a new country.

To retain unity amid the clash of theories, to keep the militant unions and leaders in the Labour Movement, to consolidate the Party so that the electorate might be won for socialism, to adapt Australian methods to the movements overseas, to use the momentum of the period for political purposes—such were some of the conflicting objectives that produced the All-Australian Trade Union Congress of 1921.

Conference adopted, with minor amendments, the preamble of the Industrial Workers of the World, whose influence had been considerable among the unions and quite out of proportion to their numbers:

> " We hold that there is a class struggle in society, and that the struggle is caused by the capitalist class owning the means of production to which the working class must have access in order to live. The working class produce all value. The greater the share which the capitalist class appropriates, the less remains for the working class; therefore, the interests of these two classes are in constant conflict."

The organization of Australian trade unionism was to be

completely altered; craft unionism was to be abolished; all unions were to be given their place in a new structure built on the principle of industrial unionism. There were to be six departments, with six sub-divisions, the departments representing industrial organizations with their local and district sections.

A Council of Action was established to guide the new organization. A plan for the establishment of a chain of Labour daily newspapers was accepted. Conference not merely altered the objective of the movement from nationalization of industry to socialization, but laid down methods that were to be followed to win socialism in our time. The Labour platform, as adopted and amended by a Conference of the political Labour Party, was as follows:

(*a*) The constitutional utilization of industrial and Parliamentary machinery.

(*b*) The organization of workers along the lines of industry.

(*c*) The nationalization of banking and all principal industries.

(*d*) The municipalization of such services as can best be operated in limited areas.

(*e*) The government of nationalized industries by boards, upon which the workers in the industries and the community shall have representation.

(*f*) The establishment of an elective Supreme Economic Council by all nationalized industries.

The Miners' organization was prepared to fit into the proposed scheme, and turned itself into the " Mining Department of the Workers' Industrial Union of Australia," but this was the only step that was taken. The Council of Action died, because its members generally were more interested in their own unions than in the scheme itself. The stream of militancy, which similar economic conditions released in all countries in these years, was soon lost in the Australian search for immediate political results.

In the years before the crisis there were experiments in every possible field of social reform. Improving social services, made possible by rising prices and high expenditure of loan money, seemed to make unnecessary any radical change in the social system. It was significant, however, that in Queensland, where Labour held office for the longest period in any State, not merely were the relations with State employees unhealthy and hostile, but an end to the expansion of social services was definitely reached. The Australian Workers' Union was so closely identified with the Labour Government, which held office for fourteen years, that there was a danger both that the Government would discriminate against other unions, and that it would use the A.W.U. to stifle necessary criticism from Labour Leagues and Unions.

III

Following the excitement of the radical years of 1920–1, Australia both economically and politically entered a period of comparatively easy improvement. The National Income increased; prices rose; and employment increased.

Looking back, we find that during the period 1912 to 1920 while wages increased steadily, prices increased at a greater rate. The purchasing power of wages was less in each of these years than in 1911. The lowest point was reached in 1915, when the full time index number was 14·6 per cent. less, or, allowing for unemployment, 18·7 per cent. less than for the base year. The year 1921 was the first occasion on which the effective wage was higher than in 1911. Wages increased considerably, while prices declined. The increase in effective wages was 7·6 per cent., but only 0·2 per cent. allowing for unemployment, which reached its peak during 1921. Effective wages for full work were highest in 1922. Allowing for unemployment, the effective wages index number for 1927 was 1,075, the highest recorded during the period under review. There was a rise in the effective wage index number for full work during the year 1928. However, unemployment increased and the effective wage index number declined to 1,044. In 1929 the rise in prices was greater than the increase in the nominal wages. So the effective wage index number declined from 1,115 to 1,082. Unemployment also increased during the year; the index number allowing for unemployment declined sharply from 1,044 to 1,009, the lowest point recorded since 1921. Comparison with 1911 shows that the effective wage for full time work was 1·2 per cent. and, allowing for unemployment, 0·9 per cent. higher during 1929 than in the former year.

At December 31, 1929, the weighted average nominal weekly wage was highest in New South Wales, followed in the order named by Queensland, Victoria, Western Australia, South Australia and Tasmania. This was a year of transition. Little movement occurred in the first quarter as compared with the previous quarter; but the average rates of wages increased in all States during the second quarter. Further small increases in Victoria, South Australia and Western Australia during the third quarter brought the weighted average rate of wage to 101s. 5d., the highest average so far recorded. But slight decreases in the wage rates in New South Wales, Queensland, South Australia and Western Australia during the fourth quarter caused the average nominal rate of wage for Australia to decline to 101s. 2d.

WEEKLY AND HOURLY WAGES AND HOURS

	1925	1926	1927	1928	1929
			Males		
Weekly Wage ...	96s. 9d.	99s. 4d.	100s. 2d.	100s. 5d.	101s. 2d.
Working Hours ...	46·44	45·57	45·46	45·27	45·34
Hourly Wage ...	2s. 1½d.	2s. 1½d.	2s. 2¾d.	2s. 3d.	2s. 3d.
			Females		
Weekly Wage ...	50s. 7d.	51s. 8d.	52s. 10d.	53s. 10d.	45s. 1d.
Working Hours ...	45·78	44·94	44·94	44·79	44·79
Hourly Wage ...	1s. 1¼d.	1s. 1¾d.	1s. 2d.	1s. 2½d.	1s. 2½d.

The tendency between 1924–8 was towards a slight reduction in hours of labour, particularly in Queensland and New South Wales, where a 44-hour week became operative on July 1, 1925, and on January 4, 1926, respectively. Further decreases were recorded in the hours of work per week for male employees during 1927 in all States, excepting Queensland, where hours remained stationary. The decline in the other States was due mainly to the reduction of the standard hours of labour in the engineering industry from 48 to 44 hours per week, as awarded by the Commonwealth Court of Conciliation and Arbitration. In 1928 the decline in the weekly hours in New South Wales, Victoria, South Australia and Tasmania was due mainly to the reduction of the standard hours of labour in the books and printing industry.

By 1928–9, contrasted with 1920–1, there had been a fall in

numbers employed in bricks, wood, clothing and textiles, and an increase in metal, paper and books, and leather, while employment in food and drink, furniture, heat and light was stationary. Agricultural numbers were falling. Again we note that for a number of years the value of machinery employed in agriculture had increased on the average by approximately £2,000,000 per annum.

The record trade union figures were reached in 1928 prior to the peak of production. There were in that year 911,541 trade unionists, organized in 379 unions with 2,079 branches. Organized workers comprised 60·9 per cent. of males gainfully employed and 41·5 per cent. of females. The percentage of males was slightly below that of the record of the previous year (62·6) but was showing a regular increase, while the female percentage was the highest on record.

The chief union groups in 1928 are shown in the following table:

Group	*No. of Unions*	*Members*	*Average per Union*
Wood	18	35,740	1,985
Engineering	60	87,417	1,456
Food	65	71,994	1,107
Clothing	25	56,874	1,475
Books	14	19,771	1,333
Other Manufacturing ...	78	46,779	599
Building	51	60,416	1,184
Mining	17	43,044	2,532
Railway and Tramway	51	116,061	2,276
Other Land	12	20,632	1,784
Shipping	58	38,361	661
Pastoral	8	35,547	4,443
Domestic	24	30,488	1,269
Miscellaneous	287	228,417	
Total	768	911,541	1,185

A relative decline in the strength of unionism in the pastoral industry and in agriculture was not important enough to influence the power of the A.W.U., though a political faction fight in New South Wales brought about the defeat of the A.W.U. leadership on political and personal issues that need not be enumerated here.

The trade union tendency was towards closer organization. Though membership of trade unions increased between 1912 and 1928 by 110 per cent., the number of unions having less than 2,000 members decreased from 360 to 299. Over half of the trade unionists were in unions with a membership of 10,000 and over. This percentage had grown from 52·0 in 1924 to 62·0 in 1928. A further indication of closer organization was the growth of interstate unions between 1921 and 1928 from 101 to 107. Members of such unions (742,271) covered 81 per cent. of the total membership. Since 1912 the number of interstate unions had risen from 72 to 107; and the proportion of the total membership thus covered from 65 per cent. to 81 per cent. The size and membership of the unions in each group had increased in all groups except clothing; but further attempts at obtaining closer unity among all unions by planned-appeals to theoretical necessity had little success.

The 1927 Trades Union Congress discussed the problem of closer unity, and, if it took no further practical steps in the direction of joining all unions into one body, it did approve of a method of slowly bringing about industrial unionism. In 1925 there had been formed in Adelaide a specially convened Commonwealth Disputes Committee, which replaced the defunct Council of Action but which, in its turn, collapsed. A Commonwealth Council of Trade Unions had also been formed for the purpose of discussing the problems that were common to those unions whose awards were decided by the Commonwealth Arbitration Court. Both these bodies were merged in the Australian Council of Trades Unions, although some of the arbitration functions still remained with another body. Formed for the purpose of resisting immigration, finding a common action in strikes, preventing overlapping and assisting in the attainment of the Socialization of Industry, it had some success, both in being recognized for its work and in the number of unions that joined. Unions were represented by direct affiliation, and through the Central Labour Councils in each State.

Proposals for common action in disputes were approved. The following motion was passed:

" The machinery for handling disputes—all unions engaged in a given group representing every phase of the industry. No union can enter into a dispute with the employers with reference to working conditions without first notifying the group of the nature of the complaint. The group will then take up the matter with the employer; failing a settlement, the line of action to be pursued must be decided by the group and put into practice on an industry basis. Whenever a dispute involves unions outside the industry in which the dispute commences, it at once comes within the jurisdiction of the Labour Council of each State, in conjunction with the representatives of the group affected. In the event of a dispute extending, or likely to extend, to another State, the dispute becomes one of national character; therefore the Chief Executive Officers of the A.C.T.U. shall convene immediately a conference of the group which covers the unions involved in the dispute."

When an interstate dispute extended beyond the limits of one group, it came under the jurisdiction of the full Council of the A.C.T.U., in consultation with the bodies affected. "The unions must abide by the actions and decisions of the group affected, Labour Councils or A.C.T.U., in all matters relating to disputes." The Conference thus attempted to hand over to the A.C.T.U. a much wider power of interference and control than is exercised by the General Council of the British Trades Union Congress, while it failed to set up a permanent secretariat, which has been at the basis of the successes of the British body.

Every metropolitan Trades and Labour Council elects two representatives to act on the Executive of the Council; metropolitan Trades and Labour Councils are the State branches of the Australasian Council. The objective of the Council was outlined as the socialization of industry. The methods adopted were (1) The closer organization of the workers by the transformation of the Australasian trade union movement from the craft to an industrial basis by the establishment of one union in each industry; (b) the consolidation of the Australasian labour movement with the object of unified control, administration and action; (*c*) the centralized control of industrial disputes; and (*d*) educational propaganda among unions. The A.C.T.U., however, exercised no influence on the industrial disputes of the period immediately following these resolutions.

III

The world depression of 1929–1933 was felt with peculiar severity in Australia. The fall in prices of Australian exports and the cessation of oversea borrowing were the immediate causes of the fall in the Australian income. Wool constituted 42·2 per cent. of the total value of exports—and wool prices fell by 50 per cent. in 1929–31. Wheat and flour amounted to 19·1 per cent. of the total, and wheat fell by 60 per cent. between 1929 and 1931. The Australian export-price index fell from a base of 1,000 in 1928, to 836 in 1920, 628 in 1930, and 567 in 1931. In four years loan expenditure on public works fell by nearly 75 per cent.; and thereby another element in Australia's prosperity collapsed. The total value of imports fell from £148 million in 1927–8, to £44 million in 1931–2. At the same time, with the fall in prices, the relative importance of the oversea interest-charges in the balance of payments had risen to £35 million in 1927–8, compared with the total exports for the same year of £143 million. While different estimates of the decline may disagree, there can be no doubt that the fall in national income was grave enough, ranging from 15 to 20 per cent.

A decrease in factory employment followed—the first decline of this kind recorded since the war years, when there was a decrease of 6 per cent. spread over three years. In 1929–30 the decrease amounted to 31,288 or 7 per cent.; in 1930–31 to 80,351 or 19 per cent.; and in 1931–32 to 2,185 or 0·6 per cent. Factory employment fell from 1928–29 until the number employed in 1931–32 was 336,658, a decline of 25 per cent. on the average for 1926–29.

The decline in employment was also severe in the industries connected with building (bricks, woodworking, furniture). Employment in those industries declined by approximately 54 per cent. Those least affected were connected with food, drink, chemicals, dyes, skins and leather. Textiles and textile goods even showed a considerable improvement, the increase in employment in 1931–32 over 1927–28 being 4,000 or 15 per cent.

Confronted with this general economic depression, the Australian economists led the attack on Australian standards. The economists adopted in argument the basic principle: "The starting point in economic discussion must be the national income. . . . The ultimate source of private incomes is the amount of the national income." The national income had fallen. Therefore the only question to be discussed immediately was the incidence of this fall: " How best could this be spread over the community so as to promote a rapid recovery? " Leaving aside the question of whether the pre-depression division of reward was the best economically and ethically, they were content to demand, in April 1930, that the loss of real income, so far borne chiefly by the unemployed and the agricultural community, should be distributed more evenly: " Some fall in profits and real salaries and wages is inevitable."

While opposing all forms of currency inflation, the economists at last supported a high exchange-rate to provide the exporter with a bonus, and check the fall in prices. While frequently declaring that budgets must be balanced, they were later prepared to extend the time within which this was to take place. While arguing that the difference between the fall in the price which the primary producer obtained and the costs which he incurred was a grave source of disequilibrium, they could not push their cure further than a 10 per cent. reduction in the real wage, a reduction frequently argued from grounds of justice rather than from economic necessity. Finding it impossible, politically and socially, to deflate so as to balance budgets or considerably to reduce unemployment, they were content to demand some reductions of the standard of living while placing more and more emphasis on a policy of preventing the drift in the public finances, and of regaining, by propaganda, financial confidence.

The reduction in wages began in 1930 in accordance with the fall in the cost of living. Towards the end of the year the Federal Arbitration Court reduced by 10 per cent. practically all wages over which it had any control. Wages declined in all States during 1931 to 1933, the average rates at December 31 (1933) being approximately 17 per cent. less than those ruling at the end of 1930. In 1932 wage rates for a full week's work were highest in books and printing, building, and engineering, and were lowest in agriculture, domestic service, clothing, general land transport, and shipping.

An increase in hours of work began in 1929. In that year the hours of timber workers were increased by the Commonwealth Court, with the result that the weighted average hours for Australia were slightly increased. During the year 1930 Acts of the Legislatures in New South Wales and Queensland providing for a 44-hour week tended to increase the average number of hours of labour per week in those States.

Reductions of wages were resisted by the Unions. Trade unionism saw neither the justice of, nor the need for, a reduction of the standards of living. Was not the total production in Australia greater than ever? Should not the standard of living be rising when everywhere there was abundance? Ignoring the fall in Australia's national income, and the part which supply and demand played under capitalism, the trade unionists argued in terms of a socialist state. Believing that purchasing power had been restricted by banks, they called on governments to increase the note-issue. While the Report of the Unemployment and Immigration Committee of the Central Trade Union body (the Australasian Council of Trades Unions) declared that unemployment was inherent in the capitalist system, it also believed that "the nature and the degree of unemployment are determinable to a considerable extent by factors within the present economic system that are controllable." So the Committee proposed the introduction of a Federal scheme of unemployment insurance, protection to the point of prohibition against goods coming into Australia, provision against the export of goods that could be treated in Australia, nationalization of banking, public works on the day-labour principle with preference to unionists, and settlements of unemployed workers organized on community lines with application of the pooling principle.

Trade union policy was simple enough: to oppose all reductions in standards, to keep wages up, and to lower working hours. The unions, however, were powerless against the combination of Governments, Arbitration Courts and controlled public opinion.

Attention must here be directed towards an institution which, in a survey ending in 1929, would scarcely have been mentioned, but which from 1929 onwards dominated the Australian scene. The Loan Council was the instrument used to enforce reductions in Australian standards of living. Leaving aside the account of the preliminary negotiations and the slow, relentless pressure of the Commonwealth on the States, due to the increased taxing area belonging to the Commonwealth, we reach an amendment of the Constitution. The Constitution, as it has been amended, empowers the Commonwealth to make agreements with the States with respect to the public debts of the States, including: (*a*) the taking-over of such debts by the Commonwealth; (*b*) their management; (*c*) the payment of interest and the provision and management of sinking funds in respect of them; (*d*) borrowing by governments. The Constitution further authorizes the Commonwealth parliament to make laws for the carrying out of any such agreement, and makes such an agreement binding on the Commonwealth and the States which are parties to it, notwithstanding anything in the Commonwealth Constitution, or any State Constitution or in any law of the Commonwealth or any State. Under a Financial Agreement there was set up a Loan Council, consisting of one representative of each State, together with a Commonwealth representative having two votes and a casting vote. Each State representative had one vote. This Council controlled, in fact, practically all public borrowing by the Australian governments whether internal or external, and whether in the form of long-term loans or of temporary bank overdrafts.

We have already noted the dependence of the Australian financial structure on government finance. At the beginning of the depression all the governments were depending heavily upon the banks for overdraft accommodation to meet revenue deficits. Although under the Agreement borrowing solely for temporary purposes was excluded from the control of the Loan Council, the banks, afraid of the influence of huge deficits on the financial structure, insisted that, as from the end of 1930, all governmental borrowing should be made from the Commonwealth Bank and secured by Treasury bills. Not merely, therefore, did the Loan Council obtain the power of regulating the pace and direction of the capital development of the whole country, but events proved that it could enforce its own policy against governments and people, and in ways involving the details of internal administration.

Trade Unionism reached its lowest figure of membership (739,398) in 1933, while 1932 had seen the highest unemployment figures, the trade union percentage in that year having risen to 29. The percentage of unionists to the numbers gainfully employed fell also, and was lowest in 1934 after the tide of unemployment had already turned. From the peak period of 1927–29 the number of strikes declined rapidly, falling as low as 90 in 1933, whereas it had reached 259 in 1929.

Returns of days lost and wages lost show the same tendency, falling to 111,956 days and £95,048 wages lost in 1933. The decline continued longer than the fall in prices, indicating that the unions were still weak from the losses of the depression.

On the whole unionists were fighting desperately against reductions in standards of living. Strikes for higher wages, for shorter hours and to defend trade union rights practically ended in the period of depressed conditions. Two desperate attempts had been made to stop a lowering of conditions—that of the Northern Miners of New South Wales in March 1929, and of the Timber Workers in January 1929, against an increase in hours. The former lasted from March 1929 to June 1930—the latter, ten months. Both were enthusiastically supported by the trade union movement; but both were defeated. The miners found that the owners preferred to keep the mines closed rather than pay the wages, especially as coal could be obtained from other States and from unorganized small mines. The timber workers were fed by the Labour Movement, but found that more and more of their jobs were being filled by non-unionists.

Labour in the Commonwealth came to power in 1929, only to find that it could not withstand the general experience of all depression Governments—namely, that those in power when the depression broke were defeated because the people placed on such governments the responsibilities of failing to solve the crisis without lowering standards. Labour in New South Wales under Lang fought desperately, but was overwhelmingly defeated. Labour in Queensland waited until the end of the crisis to be returned to office, and so reaped the advantages of recovery.

IV

Recovery began earlier just as the depression had begun earlier in Australia than in European countries. The forty-four hour legislation was restored in 1931 in New South Wales and in 1933 in Queensland. A further slight reduction in Queensland was brought about by the introduction in April, 1935, of a forty-hour week for employees on building construction. Unemployment began to fall after 1932, but the level remains higher than in pre-war times.

1932–6 UNEMPLOYMENT

Year	Unions	Membership	Unemployed No.	Unemployed Per cent.
1932	395	415,434	120,454	29·0
1933	394	415,305	104,035	25·1
1934	394	424,035	86,865	20·5
1935	396	435,938	71,823	16·5
1936	392	441,311	53,992	12·2
1937	387	449,588	41,823	9·3

Wages have also improved, but the index figure for real wages, allowing for unemployment, was only 957 in 1934, as compared with 1,044 in 1928 and 1,000 in 1911. Increases began in 1934 and have continued. The weighted average nominal rate for Australia increased by 4s. 4d. per week in the period 1933–6. At December 31, 1936, rates were highest in Queensland, followed in the order named by Western Australia, New South Wales, Tasmania, Victoria and South Australia. During 1936 rates of wages increased in all groups, the greatest increases occurring in books and printing, " miscellaneous," agriculture, domestic service, " other manufacturing " occupations and in food and drink. The increase during the year in the average weighted rate for all groups was two shillings per week. Compared with the average rates at December 31, 1929, the highest point recorded for that date in any year, wages at the end of 1936 showed a decrease of 16s. 4d. a week.

Improvement in factory employment continued from 1932–3 to 1935–6, when a new high level of 492,771 was reached. Although, however, there was a slight relative decline in textile employment in 1935–6, the textile group is the only major class which has consistently grown since 1928–9. With the exception of a decline in 1930–1, textiles progressed each year, rising from 28,117 employees in 1928–9 to 42,031 in 1935–6 or by nearly 50 per cent. during the period. All the other important classes, as was to be expected, lost heavily during the depression. The gains in recent years represent in most cases only the re-engagement of those temporarily displaced. However, in the largest class, industrial metals and machines, employment reached a new high level in 1935–6, the number recorded being nearly 14,000 in excess of the previous peak in 1926–7.

The general position of trade unionism during 1936, near the peak of the period of recovery, is illustrated in the following table:

1936

State	*No. Unions*	*Branches*	*Members*
New South Wales	184	559	315,638
Victoria	147	396	201,616
Queensland	111	314	158,953
South Australia	114	177	59,000
Western Australia	132	211	60,762
Tasmania	76	71	15,839
Northern Territory	5	—	992
Federal Capital	15	1	1,230
Total	784	1,729	814,809

Slowly but inevitably the number of unions decline, not by means of spectacular and planned amalgamations, but mainly through the disappearance of small unions. The total membership of trade unions has not yet reached pre-depression figures, but the average number in a union is higher than in 1928. The position of trade unions relative to the total of gainfully employed was also improving but had not reached the high proportion of 1928.

Industrial unrest increased until in 1937 the number of strikes (342) was the greatest since 1927, while the days lost (557,111) and wages lost (£506,745) were greatest since the year of the coal strike (1929–30). Analysing the causes of disputes in the period of recovery, we find the workers again ready to demand higher standards and to defend trade union rights. The metal unions have had the most success in striking for improved conditions—a development which might be expected since the engineering industry is gaining in importance in the Australian economy. However, the miners have held together, though the industry is declining, and are constantly planning to strike for better conditions.

In general it may be said—on the basis of estimates of the national income and of returns of estates liable to taxation—that between 1927 and 1934 the workers' share of the total product of industry has tended to diminish.

V

At the opening of the year 1938 Labour was in office in Queensland, Tasmania and Western Australia. A Country Progressive Party in Victoria retained power with the assistance of the Labour Party. In the Commonwealth and in New South Wales a Labour victory awaits on Labour unity. In New South Wales, Labour is engaged in a faction fight, partly because members are resisting the dictatorial control and narrow bureaucratic methods that grew up during the depression years, and partly because the trade unions are supporting policies of collective security in international affairs as against the policy of isolation, expounded by the politicians.

New South Wales trade unionism has regained its traditional position as the leader of militant labour in Australia. Although the Communist Party is numerically weak, it is exerting an increasing and in some cases a decisive influence on the attitudes of trade unionism. An All Australian Trade Union Congress refused to support the application of sanctions during the attack of Italy on Abyssinia, but a later Congress decided for collective security and support for Spain. Communist influence on international policy is important, but just as important was the growing determination of industrial Labour to decide its own policies on all important subjects. The improving economic conditions have made this independent stand possible; the fears of war, Fascism and depression have made it necessary. Industrial Labour has learnt rapidly the need for working-class unity; political victories for Labour will more and more be followed by the attempts of industrial Labour to control policies in the interests of Labour unity and Labour militancy.

JAPAN

BY

IWAO F. AYUSAWA

JAPAN

INTRODUCTION

One of the striking events of history in the post-war period is the advance of Japanese trade on the world's markets. So unexpected was the expansion of quantities of miscellaneous goods of Japanese origin in all markets that alarm began to be felt everywhere. Indeed, prices of Japanese goods were often so low as to defy any competition, and even in the years of depression after 1929, Japanese trade alone seemed "exempted", as it were, from the world-wide slump.

Various theories were advanced then to explain the "mystery" of Japan's success. "Social dumping", or the assumption that inferior labour standards were deliberately maintained by Japan in order to keep the price level of Japanese goods low and to push her foreign trade, was one of those theories. "Exchange dumping", or the assertion that Japan expressly devalued the yen in order to derive therefrom advantages in her export trade, was another. The supposition that the Japanese Government was "secretly subsidizing" foreign trade was still another. In any case, the general suspicion prevailing among the critics was that unfair practice or "trickery" of some sort or other must account for the success of this new, formidable competitor.

Barriers have been raised at a large number of markets in the form of preferential or prohibitive tariffs, quotas and other restrictive measures in order to check the further advance of Japanese goods. Of course, tariff walls are not directed against Japanese trade alone, *autarchy* or economic self-sufficiency being the dominant policy of all countries to-day. But Japan suffers none the less sorely from its effects; and rightly or wrongly, on account of the heavy handicaps already piled on her, such as limited area, dense population, scarcity of resources, closed outlets, etc., she feels it more acutely perhaps than other economically more favoured countries when her normal and peaceful economic activities are hampered abroad by artificial means. Peace depends on correct mutual understanding. It is important, therefore, for the world to know the real causes and to grasp the true significance of the industrial progress of Japan.

In order to gain a fair idea of the industrial development of Japan, one must look at it in the perspective of history.

Awakening of Japan

It was more than three centuries ago that the government of the *Shogun*, frightened by the discovery of the "politico-religious" designs of the early missionaries from the West, adopted a policy of rigid seclusion and non-intercourse with foreigners, and it was not until a little over three-quarters of a century ago that Japan opened her doors and resumed relationship with the Western powers.

During the three hundred years that Japan remained peacefully isolated a great change had taken place in the world, and she found then a world vastly different from the one she had left before. Those virile and enterprising peoples, relatively few in number but strong, inhabiting a small area called Europe (which represents hardly one-thirteenth of the dry surface of the globe) had gone out to the ends of the earth, and divided the lands, subjugated the races and turned the continents into their colonies and dependencies. India with her fabulous wealth and three hundred million inhabitants lay prostrate before the advancing troops of the West. China, her great neighbour, with a splendid civilization of six thousand years, was on the verge of being "partitioned," first "leasing out" her richest mines, next "ceding" her best harbours and then losing islands or peninsulas of strategic importance one after another. It was not a safe world that Japan rediscovered.

On awakening, Japan saw dangers all around. Obviously, she did not wish to share the same fate of subjugation and ignominy as the natives of other continents. The statesmen of the Meiji Restoration were determined that Japan must resist aggression and assert not only her existence but equality with the world's powers. That was the policy adopted then—and it was faithfully carried out by the succeeding Cabinets as Nippon's immutable and cardinal policy.

The statesmen of the early Meiji Government saw that in order to carry out this national policy the country must not be either weak or poor. Hence, the slogan of the Meiji era, which permeated all thinking minds and inspired the New Japan, was *Fu-koku Kyo-hei*, or "Rich nation, strong army." In order to achieve a strong army (and navy), Japan learned the western methods of warfare, adopting western rifles, cannon, battleships and their tactics and strategies. Her victory over Russia, in a war in which Japan staked her very life, resulted partly, though not wholly, from this. From the defeat of that huge Western empire by a little nation of the East dates the awakening of the Orientals to the new ideals of Freedom, Equality and Power.

Then, in order to achieve a rich nation, Japan adopted not a short-cut but a surer method—which was to develop industries. The Government and the people began to devote their energies to the carrying out of another watchword, *Sangyo Rikkoku*, or "Founding the Nation on Industries." The result has been the steady industrialization of the country all through these years. This, very briefly, was what happened in the "awakening of Japan."

The "Secrets" of Japan's Industrial Expansion

As explained above, industrialization of this country was a State policy already adopted early in the Meiji era. Thus, the "mystery" of Japan's industrial advance must necessarily disappear. However, if there are any "secrets" about it, they may be summarized under: education, mechanization, rationalization, control and "gumption" and the will to advance. For lack of space here, these items can be dealt with only roughly.

The importance of the compulsory education system enforced rigorously since 1872 cannot be too highly estimated. Over ninety-nine per cent. of the children of school age being in school, illiteracy is practically *nil* in Japan. No one can doubt that this was helpful, or indeed, indispensable, in the effort to raise the nation to the level of other powers, either for intercourse or for rivalry. Besides the eight Imperial Universities, there are forty-one universities with graduate schools in engineering and industry. There are 243 colleges giving courses of from three to five years' duration, of which 35 are for training in industry, agriculture, fishing, forestry, trade, etc. Technical education extends down to the secondary or " middle school " grade. Technical schools of the secondary grade, preparing their graduates for industrial and other occupations are well over a thousand, and in some 15,500 continuation schools, a million and a half students are enrolled. After all, it is not sweated coolie labour, but high grade engineers, trained mechanics and skilled labour who form the backbone of Japanese industry.

Very primitive methods are still employed in Japanese agriculture partly because of the poverty of the peasants, but more particularly because the extremely narrow farm lands do not lend themselves to mechanized processes of cultivation. Greatly different, however, is the situation of industry. The Government, recognizing the advantages of modern machinery in the early Meiji era, spared no pains to adopt the most advanced machinery of the West. It would purchase always the latest machines for the " model factories " it had installed in different parts of the country, and even private manufacturers of small means vie with one another in scrapping the old whenever new models with a higher efficiency have been introduced.

If poor in other respects, Japan has been abundantly favoured with cascades and waterfalls, which her people learned in due course to harness to industrial use. Her deficiency in iron, coal and oil has been compensated largely by this hydro-electric energy. More than 40 per cent. of her factories are run with electric power, and with a total horse-power of 14,270,000, of which Japan is using only a third, she has ninety-nine horse-power to the square mile. Even in remote parts, one finds no house, not a hamlet, which is not lit with electricity. Steam, hydro-electric and other motive powers are rapidly replacing man power, and out of 90,602 factories in 1936, as many as 78,670, or 86·8 per cent. were using motive power, amounting in all to 11,815,000 horse-power.

Another feature of Japanese industry is rationalization, which began early, but was intensified during and after the Great War. A special board was created in 1921 to investigate the *standardization* of equipment, machinery, tools, implements, etc., and in 1930 the Bureau of Rationalization was set up. Since then, rationalizing processes have progressed along the lines of manufacture, distribution of materials, sales, management, etc. The absence of "hedging" among Japanese spinners when there are big, powerful concerns in juxtaposition with small and financially feeble mills—a fact which has often impressed foreign observers—is one instance of "rationalization" in a wide sense. The ingenious method adopted by Japanese spinners of mixing raw cotton of various staples in order to produce yarns or tissues of different grades may also be regarded, not merely as "ingenuity," but as another evidence of rationalization. The insistence of Japanese manufacturers on the use of equipments which are "down-to-the-minute" is still another evidence. The economical arrangement of the staff, enabling the employers to reduce overhead expenses to the minimum, and the adroit management of the hard-working and moderately paid personnel, somehow maintaining reasonable productivity in spite of a continued strain, may not be strictly "scientific" but are highly "efficient," and they constitute "rationalization" of Japanese industry none the less. One may also mention the improvements, now world famous, in the process of overhauling of locomotives; the chain system of organization of small shops which has grown during nine or ten years past in the manufacture of bicycles; the division as well as pooling of certain processes of work adopted in small workshops of knitted goods or for the manufacture of electric bulbs; and the high draught effected in spinning and weaving mills with improvements in blowing, roving and warping sections.

Foreigners visiting weaving mills in Japan are usually struck by the "lonesome" impression, because there are so few workers tending the looms. In England, a worker tends four looms usually and six looms at most. In India, a worker, or sometimes two workers, tend one loom only, whereas in Japan a girl of sixteen years tends 35 to 40 looms. This is because of the automatic "Toyoda loom," a Japanese improvement. Factories in Japan have for years been effecting economy by using the "Takuma boilers" of a high efficiency, which is another Japanese improvement. Above all, the Japan Cotton Spinners'

Association is, perhaps, the most striking illustration of the "rationalized organization," embracing in one body more than seventy companies, or over ninety per cent. of the spinners of Japan.

Rationalization in the broad sense has spread so widely that it would require a whole volume by itself to describe adequately all these phases of rationalization in Japanese industry.

"Planned economy," a post-war development in Europe and America, is nothing new in Japan, for it dates from the Meiji era. When Japan awoke and saw the dangers of the world into which she had been ushered, she realized that she could not do otherwise but become strong and rich. Economic planning began then, and State control ensued forthwith. Therefore, strictly speaking, Japanese capitalists never enjoyed a period of complete *laissez-faire*, having jumped from the agrarian, feudal economy directly into a State-controlled, national economy.

Differing from the practice in other countries, it was the Government, in this country, which took the initiative in starting important industries. Shipbuilding, textile and steel manufacture and many other industries of basic importance which are thriving in Japan to-day owe their origin to the Government's initiative or guidance. The Government, as mentioned already, would start a "model factory" to begin with, installing machines of the latest western type and engaging foreign engineers as experts. After some years of experiment, it would hand over the enterprise to private companies when the experiment had proven satisfactory. Besides elaborating a complete system of education in the country, the Government has been spending considerable sums of money year after year for sending abroad promising young men, University professors, Government officials and engineers to learn the techniques of modern industry in Europe or America.

In addition to these measures, the Government has been pursuing an ever widening programme of industrialization, aiding the small and medium-sized industrial enterprises, giving them financial or other necessary assistance, giving proper guidance to foreign trade and shipping, helping the accumulation of capital within the country by prohibiting the flight of capital to foreign countries and commencing gradually to control the relation between import and export through the control of foreign exchange. After the outbreak of the China Incident, the pace of control has been greatly accelerated, and control is now spreading to the whole field of both industry and trade.

The fallacy of the charge that Japan devalued her yen in order to derive unfair advantages in export trade need not be argued. For devalued currency is a two-edged sword which cuts both ways, giving advantage to exports but disadvantage to the import of the raw matrials which Japan needs badly. Japan is a country of constant import-excess. Though the fall in the exchange value of the yen was doubtlessly helpful in promoting her export trade at one time, the devaluation was not the fundamental cause of Japan's advance.

Nor do we need to refute here the charge of " social dumping," the fallacy of which has been already exposed. It is true that Japan has her slums in Tokyo, Kobe and Osaka just as Britain and the U.S.A. have theirs in London, Chicago and New York. It is unfortunately true also that Japanese workers work long hours at relatively low wages. But, as Mr. Harold Butler, Director of the International Labour Office, pointed out recently, " the assumption that the labour (in countries which produce goods cheaper than the European) is manifestly underpaid, overworked, and otherwise exploited, is made in ignorance of the facts of the situation."[1]

It would be only fair to recognize that there were other factors which accounted for Japan's industrial advance. The factor which the present writer ventures to mention lastly, without discussing it, is what an Englishman would colloquially call " gumption," and in addition, or underlying it, the " will to advance " permeating all Japanese minds.

Origin of the Labour Movement

The modern trade union movement in Japan originated from the *Yūai Kai* (literally "Friendly-love Society ") founded in 1912

[1] Harold Butler: "Report of the Director, Twenty-fourth Session, 1938, International Labour Office, Geneva," p. 76.

in Tokyo by Mr. Bunji Suzuki with fourteen labourers as original members. Shortly after, a printers' union called the *Shin-yū Kai* (literally "Faithful-friend Society") was organized. Precautions wisely taken in the early stage of the rise of trade unionism by Mr. Suzuki not to arouse the suspicion or antipathy of the authorities favoured the growth of his and other unions.

During the War in Europe, capitalism made great strides in Japan. As the wave of the industrial revolution spread over the Empire, labour unrest became increasingly manifest. The Bolshevik revolution in Russia in 1917 and the series of revolutions or upheavals of a radical nature which burst out in Germany, Italy, Austria-Hungary, etc., in succession, supplied stimuli to the proletarian movements in this country. Thus, the later years of the War witnessed the growth of social movements. As a result, 11 new trade unions were formed in 1918, and as many as 71 more unions came into being in 1919; but their total membership did not amount to much in those years.

Along with the growth of trade unions, labour disputes multiplied during those years. Official statistics show that in 1916 there arose 108 cases of labour disputes. The number kept increasing to 398 cases in 1917, to 417 in 1918 and 497 in 1919. The tactics and terminology used by the labour leaders in the disputes were borrowed from European or American labour movements. "Strike," "sabotage," etc., became Japanese words of common use. The influence of Occidental thought and of the practices of European countries copied in these years have left deep imprints on Japanese labour.

Difficulties of Trade Unions

Japanese industry, which expanded during the War in Europe, kept growing in the post-war years, and in the same period the number of workers belonging to trade unions increased gradually. As compared with the total number of industrial workers, the percentage of organized workers, as the following figures show, has always been strikingly small. This is a characteristic feature of the labour situation in Japan.

TRADE UNION MEMBERSHIP 1921–1937

Year	*Total Industrial Workers*	*Organized Workers*	*Percentage*
1921		103,412	
1923	3,958,877	125,551	3·2
1925	4,348,711	254,262	5·9
1926	4,641,681	284,739	6·1
1927	4,703,757	309,493	6·5
1928	4,824,780	308,900	5·5
1929	4,873,081	330,985	6·8
1930	4,713,002	354,312	7·5
1931	4,729,436	368,975	7·9
1932	4,860,276	377,625	7·8
1933	5,126,719	384,613	7·5
1934	5,764,277	387,964	6·4
1935	5,906,589	408,662	6·9
1936	6,090,116	420,589	6·9
1937	6,422,320	395,290	6·2

Figures published by the former Bureau of Social Affairs of the Department of Home Affairs and by the Department of Welfare.

Whereas the total membership of trade unions kept growing steadily till 1936, that is, the year before the China Incident broke out, the proportion of workers organized in trade unions has always remained small. The highest mark of 7·9 per cent. was registered in 1931, and thereafter the percentage of organized workers receded yearly till it dropped to 6·2 per cent. in 1937. Trade unionism has not made great headway in Japan. What accounts for this?

There are five or six reasons why trade unions in Japan are so feeble. To explain those reasons is to relate the characteristics of Japanese trade unions. They are:

(1) *Lack of experience.* Unlike the unions in Europe or America, trade unions in Japan have not grown up by degrees, with sound and constructive economic functions, struggling for generations. On the contrary, they spread rather suddenly under the influence of radical ideas coming from Europe during the turbulent years of the War. Being of only recent origin, they lack experience.

(2) *Frequent dissensions.* On account of the radical, combative social doctrines that dominated the unions in the early years,

dissensions occurred frequently in the unions of leading importance like the General Federation of Labour (*Rōdō Sōdōmei* which grew out of the *Yūai Kai*), weakening the strength and damaging the prestige of the more important unions at each schism.

(3) *No trade union law.* Capitalism has developed to a high degree in Japan without having gone through a period of liberalism as it has in European countries. Consequently, in spite of the great achievements in industry, no legislation expressly guaranteeing the workers' right of association has been enacted. The absence of a specific trade union law is considered disadvantageous for the growth of unionism, though certain provisions of the Public Peace Police Act (Article 17) handicapping the unions in time of strike were repealed in 1926.

(4) *Employers' welfare work.* Employers, particularly in the case of big concerns, are solidly organized,[1] greatly developing welfare provisions in and around their factories and mines or in the dormitories attached to them to such an extent as to make it practically impossible for trade unions to penetrate. Existing unions have their membership mostly distributed in small or medium-sized establishments which are run with small capital outlay and where conditions of labour are, as a rule, inferior.

(5) *Preponderance of young women.* The Industrial Revolution in Japan may be said to have begun with the textile industry. At any rate, hitherto, the textile industry, in which female labour[2] predominates, has been the biggest and most important branch of Japanese industry. A big majority of these female workers are young, unmarried women who work only for a few years until they marry and are naturally uninterested in trade unions. In the middle of 1937, the total number of female workers belonging to trade unions was 23,962, or 1·3 per cent. of the entire female workers, while 1,775,690 workers, or 29·9 per cent. of the total industrial population, were female.

A great deal of the energy of Japanese trade unions has been devoted to, if not wasted in, ideological strife and movements centring around the so-called "proletarian political parties."

[1] E.g. *Zenkoku Sangyo Dantai Rengō Kai* (National Confederation of Industrial Associations).

[2] Of 1,027,917 workers in the textile industry at the end of 1936, 824,248 workers, or 80·2 per cent., were female.

In other words, much emphasis has been laid on the theoretical rather than the practical aspects of trade unionism, though the latter have not been entirely neglected. The activities of Japanese trade unions can be summarized as follows:

Past Activities and Present Strength

(a) Influence of "democracy" and "syndicalism."

A wave of democratic ideas swept over Japan during the later years of the European War. The *Rei-mei Kai* (literally "Dawn-light Society") under the leadership of the late Professor Sakuzo Yoshino of the Tokyo Imperial University, Professor Ikuo Oyama of the Waseda University, etc., headed the campaign to spread democratic ideas and practices. Trade unions joined in the movement and fought vigorously in the years 1919–20 to hasten the enactment of a universal suffrage law. The failure of the campaign for universal suffrage, coinciding with the frequent outbreak of "rice riots"[1] and the spread of strikes during the post-war years of depression, resulted in aggravating general social unrest, which was taken advantage of by radical agitators, like the late Sakae Osugi, an outstanding anarchist. They preached "anarcho-syndicalism" and taught the doctrine of "direct action" which spread among the printers' union first and began to penetrate other unions gradually. It was not long before these radicals commenced to clash with the moderate elements of the General Federation of Labour. Their friction culminated in the split of the trade unions into two hostile camps in 1922 when the National Confederation of Trade Unions (*Zenkoku Rōdō Kumiai Sōrengō*) was founded in Osaka.

(b) Conflict between the moderate and radical elements.

After the great earthquake of September 1923, following the assassination of Osugi, syndicalism in Japan declined. As the Bolshevik régime in Russia began to wield more power, syndicalism was superseded in a short time by communism among the rank and file. Finally, in May 1925, the General Federation of Labour was split by the communists who withdrew from it and formed a rival organization called the

[1] "Rice riot" is a form of protest against the profiteering of the rice dealers, practised sporadically by the mob who break into the rice dealers' shops and take away the rice.

Japanese Council of Labour Unions (*Nihon Rōdō Kumiai Hyogi Kai*). Thereafter a protracted struggle ensued between the unions upholding communism, on the one hand, and those adhering to moderate trade union principles in opposition to communism on the other. The former were organized by the Japanese Council of Labour Unions, the latter by the General Federation of Labour, the Japanese Seamen's Union and other older unions.

(c) Around the " Proletarian Political Parties "

The announcement made by the Yamamoto Cabinet after the 1923 earthquake of its policy in favour of universal suffrage was enthusiastically acclaimed by the nation. Thereupon, the General Federation of Labour issued an important declaration called *Hōkō Tenkan* (literally " Shifting the Direction "), meaning thereby that it would thenceforth positively support parliamentary methods and make use of political means to attain the objectives of trade unions. Other unions of lesser importance followed suit, and meanwhile, the Government's Bill for universal suffrage passed both Houses of the Diet in the spring of 1925. Consequently, in December of the same year, sponsored by the Japanese Farmers' Union (*Nihon Nōmin Kumiai*) and supported by the General Federation of Labour and numerous other unions, the first political party of proletarians in Japanese history, called the Farmer-Labour Party (*Nomin Rōdō Tō*), was organized. But, on the ground that it was tinged strongly with communism, the authorities, within a few hours, ordered its immediate dissolution. Thereafter, under the sponsorship of the Japanese Farmers' Union again but mainly with the support of the unions of the left wing, the Labour-Farmer Party (*Rōdō Nōmin Tō*), only with a reversed title and slightly amended statutes, came into being in March 1926. As against this, in December of the same year, the moderate unions of the right wing, including the General Federation of Labour, the Japan Seamen's Union, the Federation of Workers in State Enterprises, etc., formed the Social People's Party (*Shakai Minshū Tō*). On the other hand, men like Hisashi Asoo, who were not satisfied with the moderate policies of the Social Mass Party, went out and formed the Japanese Labour-Farmer Party (*Nihon Rō-nō Tō*).

The trade unions supporting this Party and disapproving of the moderateness of the General Federation of Labour withdrew from the latter and organized in December of the same year the Japanese Alliance of Trade Unions (*Nihon Rōdō Kumiai Dōmei*). Thereupon, Japanese trade unions were divided for a period of some years into the following three rival camps, fighting one against another:

1. Left Wing unions supporting the Labour-Farmer Party;
2. Right wing unions supporting the Social People's Party;
3. Centre unions belonging to the Japanese Labour Farmer Party.

(*d*) *Towards a united front.*

The trade unions were not slow in recognizing the disadvantages of the incessant strife and internecine rivalry. They saw the truth of the dictum: "United we stand, divided we fall." In disunity they had everything to lose and little to gain, especially in the years of economic depression; hence the movement for a united front from about 1930.

Unity was effected along two lines, one by means of the re-alignment of the proletarian political parties and the other by reorganizing the trade unions. Among the proletarian political parties, to begin with, an important change came about after 1928 as the result of a wholesale arrest of the Japanese Communist Party (which had been secretly organized) and the suppression of the Labour-Farmer Party by the authorities. The remnants of the left wing unions went ahead to reorganize the Labour-Farmer Party, but in view of the imminent danger of suppression, the Party declared its own dissolution. Early in 1937, what remained of the left wing succeeded in forming a Front Populaire in the reconstituted Japanese Proletarian Party; but towards the end of the year, at the same time as the "general round-up" of the Front Populaire, the said Party was ordered to dissolve; and with this final *coup*, any left wing political elements that had survived the series of arrests were completely swept away. On the other hand, the centre party named above, i.e. the Japanese Labour-Farmer Party, succeeded in annexing the odds and ends of the numerous local proletarian parties, and finally organized a party called the National Labour-Farmer Masses

Party (*Zenkoku Rō-nō Taishu Tō*), which, however, was not quite so important as its long title suggests. Meanwhile, the more moderate Social People's Party had made a steady development, and at its suggestion, the two parties were amalgamated into a single and more powerful body, the Social Mass Party (*Shakai Taishū Tō*) in 1932. The President of this Party is Isoo Abe, a veteran leader of the socialist movement, and the General Secretary is Hisashi Asoo. The Party holds at present 38 seats in the House of Representatives.[1]

On the side of the trade unions, a more or less harmonious relationship always existed among the leading unions which supported, and sent their representatives to, the International Labour Conference at Geneva; but there was no organic unity among them. A momentous change in their relationship occurred in 1928 on the occasion of the visit to Japan of the late M. Albert Thomas, Director of the International Labour Office. There was then formed among them a body called the Commission for Promoting Social Legislation (*Shakai Rippō Sokushin Iin Kai*). In the course of about three years thereafter, this modest grouping developed gradually into the Japanese Labour Club (*Nihon Rōdō Kurabu*), embracing in time the more important unions not only of the right wing but also of the centre. This so-called "Club" was formally re-constituted in 1932 into a more substantial organ called the Japanese Trade Union Congress (*Nihon Rōdō Kumiai Kaigi*) modelled after the British. The Congress as a body supports the Social Mass Party and constitutes the mainstay of Japanese trade unions.

After the outbreak of the Manchurian Incident in 1931, nationalism, more commonly known in this country by the term *Nihon Shugi* or "Japan-ism," became more pronounced. The Confederation of Japanese Trade Unions (*Nihon Rōdō Kumiai Sōrengō*), already mentioned elsewhere, assumed the leadership in forming a loose federation of the unions upholding Japanism called the "Friendly Conversation Society of Patriotic Trade Unions" (*Aikoku Rōdō Kumiai Konwa Kai*). On friendly terms with though not affiliated to this Society, are the

[1] Besides this Party, there is the Japan Reform Party (*Nihon Kakushin Tō*), which is "loudly patriotic," standing for "Japan-ism." It has the support of some labour unions, but it can hardly be regarded as a labour or proletarian political party in the strict sense.

Japanese Industrial Labour Club (*Nihon Sangyo Rōdō Kurabu*) and the Federation of Naval Arsenal Unions (*Kaigun Rōdō Kumiai Renmei*), both pronouncedly patriotic.

On the left side, after the suppression by the authorities of the Japanese Council of Trade Unions in 1928, the extremists ventured to resuscitate it by organizing another body under the slightly altered name of "National Council of Japanese Labour Unions" (*Nihon Rōdō Kumiai Zenkoku Hyogi Kai*). Together with several other left wing trade unions such as the Japanese Federation of Traffic Workers (*Nihon Kōtsū Rōdō Sōrenmei*) and the Tokyo Municipal Employees' Union (*Tokyo-shi Jūgyoin Kumiai*), the National Council promoted the formation of a common front. After the arrest of the leaders of the Front Populaire in 1937, however, the National Council shared the same fate of suppression by the authorities as all its predecessors.

Present strength

Classified according to their political tendency, the present distribution of the numerical strength of Japanese trade unions is as follows:[1]

(1) Japanese Trade Union Congress (*Nihon Rōdō Kumiai Kaigi*). It constitutes the main stream of Japanese trade unions, embracing more than two-thirds of the organized workers of the country. It is opposed to three "isms"—capitalism, communism and fascism—stands for industrial co-operation and supports the I.L.O.

Aggregate memberships 269,492

Officers: Komakichi Matsuoka (President);
Mitsusuke Yonekubo (Vice-President);
Alichi Kamijo (General Secretary).

Affiliated organizations:

All-Japan Trade Union Federation[2] ... ... (*Zen Nihon Rōdō Sōdōmei*)	94,926
Japan Seamen's Union ... ... (*Nihon Kaiin Kumiai*)	106,834
Japanese Union of Harbour Workers ... (*Nihon Kōwan Jugyoin Kumiai*)	15,485
Japanese Union of Iron Workers ... ... (*Nihon Seitetsu Jūgyoin Kumiai*)	13,000

[1] Figures are for April 30, 1938.
[2] Formerly, General Federation of Labour.

Mercantile Marine Officers' Association ... 16,553
(*Kaiin Kyokai*)
General Federation of Workers in State Enterprises ... ... (7,091?)
(*Kangyo Rōdō Sōdōmei*)
Japanese Federation of Labour 6,300
(*Nihon Rōdō Sōrenmei*)
Japanese Alliance of Porcelain Workers' Unions 3,500
(*Nihon Seitō Rōdō Kumiai Dōmei*)
Tokyo Gas Workers' Union 3,350
(*Tokyo Gasu-kō Kumiai*)
Tokyo Electric Workers' Union 2,540
(*Tō-den Jūgyoin Kumiai*)

(2) Left wing unions. The following two unions of the left wing have amended their constitutions and effected the "Shifting of the Direction." They now stand for industrial co-operation in much the same way as does the Japanese Trade Union Congress:
Japanese Federation of Traffic Workers ... 22,420
(*Nihon Kotsū Rōdō Sōrenmei*)
Tokyo Municipal Employees' Union 1,300
(*Tokyo-shi Jūgyoin Kumiai*)

(3) Right wing unions:
National Friendly Conversation Society of Patriotic Trade Unions 34,000
(*Aikoku Rōdō Kumiai Zenkoku Konwa Kai*)

Among the unions belonging to this "Society," there is a movement urging the withdrawal of Japan from the International Labour Organization, but the movement has not gained popular support.
Japanese Industrial Labour Club 18,300
(*Nihon Sangyo Rōdō Kurabu*)
This "Club" and the "Society" mentioned above both stand for Japanism and uphold totalitarian principles.

Federation of Naval Arsenal Workers' Unions . . . 41,000.
This is a federation of "company unions" in the naval arsenals, first organized in 1924. It has sent its leaders in the

past to Geneva to participate in the International Labour Conference.

Classifications of Trade Unions[1]

Industrial. According to the statistics of the Department of Welfare, at the end of 1937 there were 837 unions with an aggregate membership of 395,290. As compared with the figures of the preceding year, the numerical strength of Japanese trade unions has declined. This is due no doubt to the pressure of the emergency period. Old unions struggling on uncertain bases are rapidly dying out, while any channel for organizing new unions is being closed on all sides. Classified according to industries, the largest number belongs to the unions in transport, followed by those in machine and tools manufacture, chemical, " miscellaneous " and gas and electric industries. For further details, see the table below:

Numerical Strength of Trade Unions in 1937

Industries	*No. of unions*	*No. of members* *Male*	*Female*	*Total*
Machine and tool	76	96,985	1,844	98,829
Chemical	94	17,983	3,764	21,747
Textile	31	5,036	5,039	10,075
Food and drink	29	4,024	502	4,526
Miscellaneous	115	16,846	2,721	19,567
Mining	14	5,068	—	5,068
Gas and electricity	13	10,425	45	10,470
Transport	117	166,183	5,262	171,445
Communication	41	8,657	91	8,748
Civil engineering	31	6,672	4	6,676
Others	276	35,697	2,442	38,139
Total	837	373,576	21,714	395,290

Structural

When classified by differences in the nature and formation of the unions, there are many more " industrial " than " craft "

[1] From *Rōdō Jihō*, extra number, issued July 28th, 1938, by the Department of Welfare.

unions, on the one hand, and more " single " than " federated " unions, on the other. For further details, see below:

(*a*) *Classified by nature*

Kind	*No. of Unions*	*No. of Members*
Craft unions	207	28,296
Industrial unions	407	335,414
Mixed unions	223	31,580
Total	837	395,290

(*b*) *Classified by formation*

Kind	*No. of Unions*	*No. of Members*
Single unions	451	225,829
Federated unions	386	169,461
Total	837	395,290

Labour Disputes

During the war-time boom, as already stated, in order to cope with the rising prices, the worker assumed an aggressive attitude and strikes spread rapidly and widely. When the War ended, however, Japan was not spared from the world-wide slump of the post-war period. The workers changed from their aggressive to a defensive and more reserved attitude than hitherto, with the result that the number of labour disputes diminished appreciably. Disputes, if any, arose from the workers' fear of unemployment, wage-cuts or other menaces to their livelihood, so that the strikes of the post-war period were mostly for the maintenance of the existing standards in wages, hours and other conditions of employment, the raising of " discharge allowances," recognition of the workers' right to bargain collectively, setting up of works councils, etc.

The economic depression that set in almost as soon as the Armistice was signed began to play more and more havoc as the years advanced. The disaster which happened and aggravated the situation at this juncture was the great earthquake of 1923. In the urban prefectures of Tokyo and Kanagawa more than 11,600 factories were burnt down, causing the unemployment of over 104,000 workers. Incidentally, at about this time, in conformity with the decisions of the Washington Naval Conference, the programme of naval armament was greatly reduced, throwing a large number of workers out of employment. Nevertheless, on account of the self restraint of the trade unions, labour troubles did not grow as serious then as in previous years.

The situation of unemployment was made worse as the employers, in order to cope with the continued depression, began to adopt during 1926 a policy of retrenchment in their works and to "rationalize" the organization of industry. This meant the application of more scientific methods than hitherto in the processes of production, installation of more advanced machines with a higher degree of efficiency, than the older ones, etc.; but it involved also a reduction in the number of workers employed. As the economic depression continued, the employers resorted to repressive measures against the demands of the workers, who were being led by the agitators of the left wing unions. The result was that in 1926, labour disputes assumed grave aspects. The strikes at the Hamamatsu Musical Instrument Factory and the Besshi Copper Mine, which happened during the year, have already become historic for their seriousness.

After 1926, which was a "record year," labour disputes seemed for a time to subside. At any rate, the disputes were not so numerous in 1927 as in the previous year, in spite of the financial panics which had led to the failure of many small and medium-sized industrial concerns during 1927. But a brief review of the past ten years after 1927 shows that the disputes have become bigger and more frequent year by year, and more particularly after the slump which began in 1929. The strikes which occurred at the Soya Sauce Factory of Noda in 1928 and at the Kanegafuchi Spinning Mill in 1930 are of historic importance, the former on account of its long duration,[1] and the latter because it broke out at the biggest textile firm in Japan, the President of which had always boasted of the tradition of "family system" so effective in all his works as to render an attempt to strike in the works "futile and impossible." In 1931 strikes spread further among several coal mines.

[1] The strike lasted a little over seven months beginning in September 1928, costing 140,000 yen to the striking union and causing a damage of well over a million yen to the company.

As the struggle grew more bitter, the workers commenced to demonstrate some ingenuity to arouse public attention and attain their objectives. The "hunger march" is a form of demonstration of the unemployed workers, known in other countries; but the "chimney man" is a unique Japanese invention. One of the strikers climbs up to the top of the tallest chimney of the factory where the strike is on. The man stays at the top of the chimney through night and day exposed to the wind, sun and rain, and refuses to come down until the employer concedes the workers' demands, and the strike is over. This is an improvement on the "hunger strike" in that it is more spectacular and, therefore, more effective. It has become so popular that whenever a strike breaks out, the police immediately guard the chimney so as to prevent any man from climbing it.

Strikes decreased appreciably from about 1931 onward, partly because the left wing unions have been suppressed, and partly because most of the labour unions have lost their former virility owing to the depression, but largely because of the awakening of patriotic spirit after the outbreak of the Manchurian Incident in 1931. In a time of national crisis, everything must be sacrificed for the State. In this spirit, the workers have begun to exercise self control.

From about 1931 onwards, great activities commenced in Japanese industry along two lines, namely, the manufacture of munitions and the manufacture of export goods. Though Japanese industry was hit hard by the slump of 1929 and the following years, it did not suffer to the same extent as the industry of the countries of Europe and America. The mechanization and rationalization carried out by Japanese industry during the preceding years of economic difficulties proved most timely in facing the slump. The fall in the exchange rate of the yen, which happened about this time, spurred the export of the cheap goods manufactured in Japan to the colonial markets where the natives in their penury could not afford to buy European goods.

These manufacturing activities were by no means general. In fact the apparent prosperity resulting from them was unevenly distributed among the working population; and yet, conscious of the gravity of the situation resulting from the

Manchurian Incident, workers' trade unions continued their policy of self restraint. Moreover, the ascendancy of the unions proclaiming Japanism had a " sobering " effect on the working population. Collective agreements spread and labour disputes seemed to diminish considerably in the years after the Manchurian Incident.

The boom was uneven, however, and the rise of commodity prices began to " pinch " the workers, so that their attitude gradually shifted from that of reticence to one of agressiveness. They began to demand wage increases here and there, until in the first six months of 1937 the disputes centring around the wage question assumed alarming proportions. Indeed, the figures of labour disputes in the early months of 1937 were the highest in Japanese history.

Patriotism, however, again altered the situation. Suddenly, after July 1937, the curve of strikes fell so sharply that by the end of the year strikes seemed almost to die out completely. This was all due to the outbreak in July 1937 of the China Incident, which the whole nation regards as a national crisis. The All-Japan Trade Union Federation took the lead in adopting a policy of " refraining from engaging in labour disputes during the duration of the Incident," by adopting a formal resolution to that effect at its annual convention in October. Other unions of lesser importance followed suit, and consequently, labour disputes have greatly decreased in factories where the workers' trade unions exist. This is one of the characteristics of Japanese labour; and therein, no doubt, lies the strength of this country. Only at places where no union exists, does trouble seem to persist regarding wage adjustment under the rising commodity prices. The authorities are taking the necessary measures to ease the situation.

For details of labour disputes, see the following table:

LABOUR DISPUTES 1921–1937[1]

Year	*No. of cases*	*No. of workers involved*
1921	896	170,889
1923	647	68,814

[1] Prior to 1926, the statistics of labour disputes were taken by the Police Bureau of the Department of Home Affairs, and they did not include lock-outs. From 1926, the Bureau of Social Affairs of the Department of Home Affairs began to compile the statistics, including lock-outs. Thus, the statistics given above are imperfect in that respect.

Year	*No. of cases*	*No. of workers involved*
1925	816	89,387
1926	1,260	127,267
1927	1,202	103,350
1928	1,021	101,893
1929	1,420	172,144
1930	2,290	191,838
1931	2,456	154,528
1932	2,217	123,313
1933	1,897	116,733
1934	1,915	120,307
1935	1,872	103,962
1936	1,975	92,724
1937	2,126	213,622

STRIKES DURING 1937

Month	*No. of cases*
January–June ...	481
July	56
August	38
September ...	19
October	14
November ...	15
December ...	5

LABOUR LEGISLATION

Before 1919 when Japan participated in the First Session of the International Labour Conference at Washington, D.C., Japan had but little by way of labour legislation. All she had were the Seamen's Law of 1899, the Factory Law of 1911 and the Regulations for the Employment and Relief of Miners of 1916. The adhesion of Japan to the I.L.O. (International Labour Organization) resulted in promoting the workers' welfare along the lines of (1) Guaranteeing the worker's right of association, and (2) Stimulating protective labour laws.

According to the Constitution of the I.L.O., the States-Members belonging to the I.L.O. must, as a rule, send Government, employers' and workers' delegates to the General Conference, and they must nominate the employers' and workers' delegates "in agreement with the industrial organizations, if such organizations exist, which are most representative of employers or workers, as the case may be, in their respective countries."[1] In spite of this provision, however, the Government of Japan, in view of the imperfect development of trade unions, nominated the workers' delegates for the sessions of 1919 and for some years thereafter, not solely or totally in agreement with the most representative workers' organizations. The arbitrary methods adopted by the Government for nominating the workers' delegate were furiously objected to by the workers' unions, and protests were sent year after year to the Conference of the I.L.O., until the Government felt obliged to alter the methods and to adopt a method favourable to trade unions. From 1924 onward, the Government began to nominate as the workers' delegate the person who received the highest vote in election by allowing one vote per thousand members of any *bona fide* workers' trade union. This served as a powerful encouragement for trade unions, and its effect was almost as great as if a law had been enacted specifically guaranteeing the right of association. It was tantamount to a legal recognition of trade unionism. During a period of a little over a year, as the Government adopted this new policy, the trade union membership nearly doubled, rising suddenly from a membership in 1923 of 125,000—a maximum reached after thirty years of struggle—to 254,000 in 1925. Since the Japanese Trade Union Congress came into being, the Government has appointed the workers' delegates and advisers from among the nominees of this body.

Labour legislation has also been stimulated by the I.L.O. Among the legal provisions now in force in Japan, the following are the more important ones enacted, either directly in conformity with certain provisions of a Draft Convention or Recommendation adopted by the International Labour Conference, or indirectly as a result of their influence.

Prohibition of night work of women and young persons (Amendments to the Factory Act and the Regulations for the Employment and Relief of Miners[2]);

Prohibition of employment of women for underground work in mines (Amendment to the Miners' Regulations);

Minimum age raised for industrial workers (Repeal of a

[1] Treaty of Versailles, Article 389.
[2] Hereafter abbreviated as "Miners' Regulations."

section of the Factory Act and promulgation of a separate Act);

Hours of work reduced for women and young persons (Amendment to the Factory Act and the Miners' Regulations);

Maternity protection, or prohibition of employment of women before and after child birth (Amendment to the Factory Ordinance);

Minimum age raised for seamen (Promulgation of a new Act);

Free employment exchanges (Promulgation of a new Act);

Free employment exchanges for seamen (Promulgation of a new Act);

Workmen's compensation (Amendments to the Factory Act and also promulgation of new Acts).

Besides the laws and regulations referred to above, the more important labour laws which are now in force are: the Health Insurance Act 1926; the Labour Disputes Conciliation Act 1926; the Retirement Reserve and Retirement Allowance Fund Act 1936; the Commercial Shops Act 1938; and the National Health Insurance Act 1938.

As yet Japan has no law providing for unemployment insurance[1] or for fixing minimum wages. Mention has already been made of the non-existence of a trade union law. Nor has this country as yet a law regulating collective bargaining. Actually, however, collective bargaining is carried out on a big scale in some cases. Seamen and mercantile marine officers have established with the shipowners a permanent Joint Maritime Board,[2] which is functioning successfully. Among the workers on land, the All-Japan Trade Union Federation had concluded, at the end of 1937, collective agreements at as many as 117 factories and also established an organ called the " San-kyo Club " for collective bargaining.

[1] It is contended by some people that unemployment insurance is unnecessary in Japan on the grounds that there is not much unemployment in this country; that if such exists, it is amply taken care of by the traditional " family system "; and that in any case, unemployment insurance does not work, having failed in other countries. The Retirement Reserve and Retirement Allowance Fund Act partly supplements the lack of unemployment insurance.

[2] *Kaiji Kyodo Kai.*

Indices of Industrial Progress

During the period under review, that is, since the Great War until last year, Japanese industry continued to expand steadily with but a slight shrinkage during the depression after 1929. If we take the amounts of capital invested in industrial concerns, their increasing figures show that the depression did not disturb investors greatly. As compared with 1921, the total amount of invested capital increased by 79·5 per cent. by the end of 1936. But, during the same period of fifteen years, industrial production more than doubled in value, the net increase in yen amounting to 122·3 per cent. Meanwhile the number of factories increased by 83·4 per cent. and the workers by 58·5 per cent.

The fact that production multiplied more than twofold, while the number of workers increased by 58·5 per cent. and the capital by 79·5 per cent., may be taken to mean that a proper use is being made of the capital outlay, and also that the workers' efficiency is improving. Of course, due account must be taken of the change in commodity prices when comparison of the products is being made in money value instead of in quantity. But, in that case, the prices have not risen. Thus, one may conclude from these statistics that not only has production multiplied but equipments have been improved and the workers' efficiency has risen greatly in the post-war period, though there remains a problem of rising cost of living.[1]

The following tables, on which the above statement is largely

[1] The following three sets of figures show that if the depression year of 1931 is taken as the basis of comparison, the workers' wages have risen only slightly, while a sharp rise is witnessed in the index of prices, resulting in a rise in the cost of living in those years. However, if comparison is made for the whole post-war period, taking the average for the three years 1921–23 as the basis, prices have fallen definitely, though unfortunately wages have fallen even more, causing an acute rise in the cost of living. The index numbers of wholesale prices and of wages are taken from the reports of the Department of Commerce and Industry; those for cost of living are from the *Osaka Asahi* with July 1914 as the basis but available only after 1931.

Index numbers of wholesale prices, wages and cost of living.

	Prices	*Wages*		*Prices*	*Wages*	*Cost of Living*
1921	102·4	96·3	1931	59·1	85·9	158·6
1923	99·4	101·8	1933	76·1	82·3	168·3
1925	103·7	102·9	1935	77·7	83·5	180·5
1927	88·1	101·5	1936	80·5	83·5	184·9
1929	85·5	101·4	1937	98·7	88·5	192·8

based, are taken from the statistical reports annually published by the Department of Commerce and Industry. They cover only factories employing five or more workers. Capital investment figures, moreover, refer only to establishments which are incorporated. Since Japan has an enormous number of exceedingly small workshops, employing less than five people, run by private individuals and not incorporated, the tables must be said to be incomplete. For our present purposes, however, they suffice to show the steady progress of Japanese industry.

INDUSTRIAL PROGRESS 1921–1936

Year	*Capital invested*	*Value of production*	*No. of workers*	*No. of factories*
	(Y 1,000)	(Y 1,000)		
1921	5,962,564	5,513,141	1,635,811	49,380
1925	6,173,953	6,924,911	1,808,381	49,161
1929	7,497,121	7,716,798	1,825,022	59,887
1930	7,543,682	5,962,810	1,683,563	62,234
1931	7,673,519	5,174,579	1,661,502	64,436
1932	7,571,153	5,982,469	1,733,511	67,318
1933	8,008,172	7,871,364	1,901,091	71,940
1934	8,825,336	9,390,060	2,163,453	80,311
1935	9,456,416	10,836,894	2,369,277	85,174
1936	10,701,376	12,257,588	2,592,687	90,602

Index Numbers

Year	Capital invested	Value of production	No. of workers	No. of factories
1921	100·0	100·0	100·0	100·0
1925	113·5	125·6	110·5	99·6
1929	125·7	140·0	111·6	121·3
1930	126·5	108·2	102·9	126·5
1931	128·7	93·9	101·6	130·5
1932	127·0	108·5	106·0	136·3
1933	134·3	142·8	116·2	145·7
1934	148·0	170·3	132·2	162·6
1935	158·6	196·6	144·8	172·5
1936	179·5	222·3	158·5	183·4

Sources: Department of Commerce and Industry. *Kōjō Tōkei Hyo* (Factory Statistics) and *Kaisha Tōkei Hyo* (Corporation Statistics).

Structural Changes of Japanese Industry

After ascertaining the fact of general industrial progress, it is necessary to know along what lines the progress is being made; and there, one finds that some striking changes are taking place, forecasting the future of Japanese industry with unmistakable signs.

Like the rest of the world, Japan did feel the depression, somewhat, after 1929; and the year 1931 was for Japan the worst year of the slump. Let us, therefore, take that year as the basis of comparison. Since that year, production has increased considerably, and after five years, in 1936, textile production had increased by 87 per cent., lumber and wood work by 90·6 per cent., ceramics by 120 per cent., etc. But, even bigger and more spectacular increases happened in the output of the metallic works which multiplied more than threefold, i.e. by 320·95 per cent.; in the manufacture of machines and tools (262·98 per cent.) and in chemical products (166·78 per cent.). In other words, Japanese industry has made big strides in the " heavy " industries and in the industries which require scientific proficiency or mechanical precision. This statement is borne out by Tables A and B below.

That Japanese industry is rapidly shifting in the direction mentioned above, leaving behind the " light " industries and the industries for the manufacture of coarser or less delicate products is clearly shown by Table C below. In it, the relative importance of various industries is shown by percentage of the value of the products for each year. According to this Table C, the textile industry, which used to produce 45·5 per cent. of the entire output, accounted in 1936 for only 28·6 per cent., whereas the metallic products, which were only 6·5 per cent. in 1923, accounted for 18 per cent. Similar changes are taking place in the manufacture of machines and tools, chemical products, etc. Obviously these high grade industries cannot progress by depending on sweated labour, because they all require a high degree of intelligence, proficiency and precision. Japan's progress in these industries bespeaks her scientific attainments as well as the rising standard of her workers.

Indices of Industrial Production, 1923–36

A. *Value of production*
(Y1,000)

Industries	1923	1929	1931	1934	1936
Textile	2,586,778	2,979,827	1,802,997	2,917,633	3,371,684
Metal	370,677	805,204	506,170	1,463,618	2,130,720
Machine and tool	392,066	686,162	443,341	1,082,073	1,609,254
Ceramic	181,022	219,801	142,316	250,859	313,796
Chemical	673,255	1,077,609	825,520	1,514,886	2,202,362
Lumber and woodwork	195,020	194,389	142,823	218,724	272,214
Printing and book-binding	109,446	186,304	167,310	192,742	225,706
Food and drink	958,346	1,124,227	834,687	1,040,682	1,245,961
Others	231,662	246,740	187,515	337,283	436,763
Total[1]	5,698,272	7,532,263	5,052,679	9,018,500	11,808,460

B. *Index of production*
(1931—100)

Industries	1923	1929	1931	1934	1936
Textile	143·47	166·27	100·00	161·82	187·00
Metal	72·23	158·68	100·00	286·16	420·95
Machine and tool	88·43	153·87	100·00	244.07	362·98
Ceramic	127·20	154·45	100·00	176·27	220·49
Chemical	81·56	130·54	100·00	183.51	266·78
Lumber and woodwork	136·55	136·10	100·00	153·14	190·60
Printing and bookbindng	65·42	111·35	100·00	115·20	134·90
Food and drink	114·82	134·67	100·00	124·68	149·28
Others	123·54	131·58	100·00	179·87	233·92

C. *Annual percentages of production*

Industries	1923	1929	1931	1934	1936
Textile	45·5	39·8	35·7	32·4	28·6
Metal	6·5	10·7	10·0	16·2	18·0
Machine and tool	6·9	9·1	8·8	12·0	13·6
Ceramic	3·2	2·9	2·8	2·8	2·7
Chemical	11·8	14·3	16·3	16·8	18·7
Lumber and woodwork	3·4	2·6	2·8	2·4	2·3
Printing and bookbinding	1·9	2·5	3·3	2·1	1·9
Food and drink	16·8	14·9	16·5	11·5	10·6
Others	4·0	3·2	3·8	3·7	3·7
Total	100·0	100·0	100·0	100·0	100·0

Source: Department of Commerce and Industry, *Kōjō Tōkei Hyo* (Factory Statistics)

Outlook

The year 1937, with which the period of the present inquiry closes, was incidentally a year quite appropriate for terminating

[1] Omission of production of gas and electric undertakings renders totals different from those of Table of Industrial Progress.

it, because with the outbreak of the China Incident in July of that year, the period of steady and undisturbed expansion in industry and trade came abruptly to an end. A new chapter in the history of Japan, and presumably of the Far East, must begin in 1938.

The year 1937 was one of momentous changes in the economic and industrial spheres of Japan. The national budget increased almost twofold in the course of the year. Important laws involving radical reforms in the economic life of the nation were promulgated one after another. Industrial production multiplied, foreign trade flourished, commodity prices rose, and meanwhile official control was intensified strongly.

If these events were all, there was nothing " momentous " about them, except that the rate of industrial expansion had seemed accelerated. But a sudden transition took place with the outbreak of the Incident, involving China and Japan in what is a great war in every sense but name. The transition which it occasioned was from the former " quasi-wartime " economy (which had begun with the Manchurian Incident in 1931, but was intensified since the so-called " February 26th Incident " of 1936) to a genuine wartime economic structure. The transition is bound to have far-reaching effects on this country—and on the whole area of Eastern Asia. Nothing would be more difficult than to predict now what the political, economic or industrial situation of this vast area will be like in 1940, or even a year hence.

However, no matter what emerges from the present Sino-Japanese conflict, one thing is certain in the light of the past developments. It is that Japan will have to improve her position in world trade, even if she cease to be an " Island Empire "—which she no longer is in fact, either politically on account of Korea, or economically on account of the " quasi-bloc " economy embracing Manchoukuo. Japan will have to manufacture more goods than ever and sell them widely on the world markets in order to support her population and continue to thrive. The world, under the impression that Japanese goods are " flooding " all markets, is apt to overlook the fact that Japan's foreign trade at the highest point it ever reached (in 1936) did not amount to more than 3·7 per cent. of the world's total. It is, in any case, a vital necessity for

Japan to pursue her traditional policy of industrialization and to carry on her foreign trade.

All thinking Japanese should be aware of this necessity and of its implications. Japan's outlook must be " international " in the full sense of the word. The statesmen at the helm of the Japanese Government recognize this and are prepared to be bound by treaty obligations for adjusting international difficulties in industrial or labour questions. That, no doubt, is one reason why Japan has remained a faithful Member State in the International Labour Organization even after withdrawing from the League of Nations. She is still continuing her collaboration with that international body for world peace. The significance of this fact must not be minimised.

The world, on the other hand, would be well advised to remember that " shutting all doors against the trade of Eastern countries can only . . . . favour the elements which are apt to produce explosions." As Mr. Butler, Director of the International Labour Office, goes on to point out. " The problems of the East are world problems in which every country is interested in finding a just solution, which can only be done in an atmosphere of tolerance and goodwill."[1] Without such an atmosphere, world peace will remain a mere phrase with no content.[2]

[1] Harold Butler, *op. cit.*, p. 77.

[2] Editor's Note : On November 2nd, 1938 (after the above was written) Japan notified the I.L.O. of her decision to retire from the Organization. It was intimated that this decision was taken for reasons independent of her relations with the Organization.

INDEX

O

P

R

S